Thomas Cook

EUROPEAN
TRAVEL
PHRASEBOOK

PASSPORT BOOKS
a division of NTC *Publishing Group*

Thomas
Cook

Published by Passport Books,
a division of NTC Publishing Group,
4255 West Touhy Avenue,
Lincolnwood (Chicago),
Illinois 60646-1975 U.S.A.

ISBN 0-8442-9004-1
Library of Congress Catalog Card Number: 95-69376

Published by Passport Books in conjunction with
the Thomas Cook Group Ltd.

*While every care has been taken in compiling this publication, using the
most up-to-date information available at the time of going to press, the
publishers cannot accept any liability whatsoever arising from errors or
omissions, however caused.*

Translations by UPS Translations, London and Transtec, Stamford,
Lincs
Typeset by Thomas Cook Publishing using Advent 3B2
Printed in Great Britain by Bell & Bain Ltd, Glasgow

Contents

Editor's Introduction

This phrasebook contains a selection of vocabulary essential to English-speaking tourists travelling across Europe through countries where English is not widely spoken.

Languages of countries where English *is* widely spoken or understood (such as the northern European destinations of the Netherlands, Norway, Sweden, Denmark and Finland) are not included; however, any attempts to speak a few words in the native tongue of these countries would no doubt be greatly appreciated. French, Italian and German, which are spoken in more than one European country, are included and between them they cover a large area of central Europe. The Eastern European languages that have been selected for this phrasebook are those spoken in countries with the greatest tourist appeal.

Comment utiliser ce recueil d'expressions

Les expressions contenues dans chaque section de langue sont numérotées pour que les personnes ne parlant pas l'anglais puissent les retrouver facilement dans d'autres langues. Par exemple, une personne parlant le français et recherchant une traduction en polonais de l'expression 57 de la section Français (Où est la boutique hors-taxe?), la trouvera au numéro 57 de la section Polonais (Gdzie jest sklep wolno-cłowy?).

Benutzung dieses Sprachführers

Die Redewendungen sind in den einzelnen Sprachen jeweils numeriert, sodaß man auch ohne Kenntnis der englischen Sprache leicht die entsprechende Übersetzung finden kann.

Zum Beispiel: Jemand mit deutscher Muttersprache schlägt im deutschen Teil die Redewendung Nummer 57 nach (Wo ist der zollfreie Laden?), und weiß dann, daß die Redewendung mit der Nummer 57 im polnischen Teil die genaue Übersetzung wiedergibt (Gdzie jest sklep wolno-cłowy?).

Empleo del libro de frases

La sección correspondiente a cada idioma comprende frases numeradas que remiten al usuario a otros idiomas y facilitan el manejo del libro por parte de quienes no sepan inglés. Por ejemplo, los hispanohablantes que quieran saber el equivalente polaco de la frase numero 57 (¿Dónde está el duty free?) no tienen más que ver la frase del mismo número en la sección de ese idioma (Gdzie jest sklep wolno-cłowy?), que denota lo mismo exactamente.

Como Usar este Livro de Frases

As frases em cada secção de idioma numeradas de modo a que leitores de língua não-inglesa possam encontrar facilmente referências cruzadas. Por exemplo, um leitor de língua Portuguesa pode procurar a frase 57 na secção portuguesa (Onde é a loja duty-free?) e sabe que a frase 57 na secção polaca (Gdzie jest wolno-clowy?) é uma tradução exacta da mesma.

Come utilizzare questo frasario

Le frasi contenute nella sezione di ciascuna lingua sono numerate in modo che chi non parla inglese possa consultarle facilmente. Ad esempio una persona di lingua italiana può cercare la frase 57 nella sezione italiana (Dov'è il duty free?) e sapere che la frase 57 nella sezione polacca (Gdzie jest sklep wolno-cłowy?) ne è l'esatta traduzione.

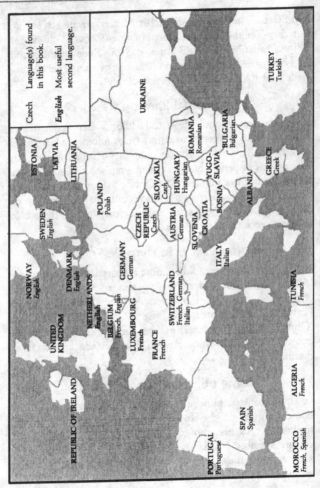

Introduction

Bulgarian is a Slavic language, and like Russian, to which it is distantly related, it uses Cyrillic script, which is a development of the Greek alphabet. Russian itself is widely understood in Bulgaria — English and German are the other two languages which may be spoken to a degree by some people in larger cities, especially in establishments catering to tourists. As with Greek, body language can be confusing if you are unaware that Bulgarians traditionally nod their heads up and down to signify no and shake them from side to side to mean yes. As Western influences increase, you can expect younger and westernised Bulgarians to begin adopting the opposite conventions, which will increase confusion.

Addresses for travel and tourist information

UK: *Balkan Holidays (National Tourist Office)*, Sofia House, 19 Conduit St, London W1R 9TD; tel: (0171) 491 4499.
USA: *Balkan Holidays (National Tourist Office)*, 161 East 86th St, New York, NY 10028; tel: (212) 573-5530 or 722-1110.

ESSENTIALS

Alphabet

А *ah*	Б *bah*
В *vah*	Г *gah*
Д *dah*	Е *eh*
Ж *zhe*	З *ze*
И *ee*	Й *iy*
К *kah*	Л *lah*
М *meh*	Н *neh*
О *o*	П *pe*
Р *re*	С *ce*
Т *te*	У *ou*
Ф *fa*	Х *ha*
Ц *tsa*	Ч *ch*
Ш *sh*	Щ *shch*
Ъ *eu*	ь *y*
Ю *yu*	Я *ya*

Basic Words and Phrases

1. **Yes**
Да
Da
No
Не
Ne

2. **Please**
Моля
Molya
Thank you
Благодаря Ви
Blagodarya vi

3. **That's O.K.**
Няма проблеми
Nyama problemi
Perhaps
Може би
Mozhe bi

4. **To**
До
Do
From
От
Ot

5. **Here**
Тук
Took
There
Там
Tam

6. **None**
Нищо
Nishto
Also
Също
Sushto

7. **How**
Как
Kak
When
Кога
Koga

8. **What**
какво
kakvo
Why
Защо
Zashto

9. **I don't understand.**
Не разбирам.
Ne razbiram.

10. **I don't speak Bulgarian.**
Не говоря български.
Ne govorya bulgarski.

11. **Do you speak English?**
Говорите ли английски?
Govorite li angliyski?

8

12 **Can you please write it down?**
Може ли да го напишете, моля?
Mozhe li da go napishete, molya?

13 **Can you please speak more slowly?**
Може ли да говорите по-бавно, моля?
Mozhe li da govorite po-bavno, molya?

14 **How much does it/this cost?**
Колко струва това?
Kolko stroova tova?

Days

15 **Monday**
Понеделник
Ponedelnik

Tuesday
Вторник
Ftornik

16 **Wednesday**
Сряда
Sryada

Thursday
Четвъртък
Chetvurtuk

17 **Friday**
Петък
Petuk

Saturday
Събота
Subota

18 **Sunday**
Неделя
Nedelya

Morning
Сутрин
Sootrin

19 **Afternoon**
Следобед
Sletobet

Evening
Вечер
Vecher

20 **Night**
Нощ
Nosht

Week
Седмица
Sedmitsa

21 **Yesterday**
Вчера
Fchera

Tomorrow
Утре
Ootre

Numbers

22 **Zero**
Нула
Noola

One
Едно
Edno

23 **Two**
Две
Dve

Three
Три
Tri

24 **Four**
Четири
Chetiri

Five
Пет
Pet

25 **Six**
Шест
Shest

Seven
Седем
Sedem

26 **Eight**
Осем
Osem

Nine
Девет
Devet

27 **Ten**
Десет
Deset

Eleven
Единадесет
Edinadeset

28 **Twelve**
Дванадесет
Dvanadeset

Thirteen
Тринадесет
Trinadeset

29 **Fourteen**
Четиринадесет
Chetirinadeset

Fifteen
Петнадесет
Petnadeset

30 **Sixteen**
Шестнадесет
Shestnadeset

Seventeen
Седемнадесет
Sedemnadeset

31 **Eighteen**
Осемнадесет
Osemnadeset

Nineteen
Деветнадесет
Devetnadeset

ESSENTIALS

32 Twenty
Двадесет
Dvadeset

Twenty-one
Двадесет и едно
Dvadeset i edno

33 Twenty-two
Двадесет и две
Dvadeset i dve

Thirty
Тридесет
Trideset

34 Forty
Четиридесет
Chetirideset

Fifty
Петдесет
Petdeset

35 Sixty
Шестдесет
Shestdeset

Seventy
Седемдесет
Sedemdeset

36 Eighty
Осемдесет
Osemdeset

Ninety
Деветдесет
Devetdeset

37 One hundred
Сто
Sto

Five hundred
Пет стотин
Petstotin

38 One thousand
Хиляда
Hilyada

One million
Един милион
Edin milion

Time

39 9.00
Точно девет часа
Tochno devet chasa

40 9.05
Девет часа и пет минути
Devet chasa i pet minooti

41 9.10
Девет часа и десет минути
Devet chasa i deset minooti

42 9.15
Девет часа и петнадесет
минути

43 9.20
Девет часа и двадесет
минути
Devet chasa i dvadeset minooti

44 9.25
Девет часа и двадесет и
пет минути
Devet chasa dvadeset i pet minooti

45 9.30
Девет часа и тридесет
минути
Devet chasa i trideset minooti

46 9.35
Девет часа и тридесет и
пет минути
Devet chasa i trideset i pet minooti

47 9.40
Девет часа и четиридесет
минути
Devet chasa i chetirideset minooti

48 9.45
Девет часа и четиридесет и
пет минути
*Devet chasa i chetirideset i pet
minooti*

49 9.50
Девет часа и петдесет
минути
Devet chasa i petdeset minooti

50 9.55
Девет часа и петдесет и пет
минути
Devet chasa i petdeset i pet minooti

51 12.00/Midday/Midnight

10

Точно дванадесет часа/
обед/полунощ
*Tochno dvanadeset chasa/Obet/
Poloonosht.*

52 **What time is it?**
Колко е часът?
Kolko e chasa?

53 **It is . . .**
Часът е . . .
Chasa e . . .

ARRIVING AND DEPARTING

Airport

54 **Excuse me, where is the
check-in desk for . . . airline?**
Извинявайте, къде е
гишето за авиолиния . . ?
*Izvinyavayte, kude e gisheto za
avioliniya . . ?*

55 **What is the boarding gate/
time for my flight?**
Къде е изходът за (В колко
часа е) моят полет?
*Kude e izhodut za (F kolko chasa e)
moyat polet?*

56 **How long is the delay likely
to be?**
Колко може да продължи
закъснението?
*Kolko mozhe da produlzhi
zakusnenieto?*

57 **Where is the duty-free shop?**
Къде е безмитният
магазин?
Kude e bezmitniyat magazin?

58 **Which way is the baggage
reclaim?**
Къде се получава багажът?
Kude se poloochava bagazhut?

59 **Where can I get the bus to
the city centre?**
Къде мога да взема
автобус до центъра на
града?
*Kude moga da vzema aftoboos do
tsentura na grada?*

Train Station

60 **Where is the ticket office/
information desk?**
Къде е касата/
информацията?
Kude e kasata/informatsiyata?

61 **Which platform does the
train to . . . depart from?**
От кой перон тръгва
влакът за . . ?
Ot koy peron trugva vlaka za . . ?

62 **Where is platform . . ?**
Къде е . . . перон?
Kude e . . . peron?

63 **When is the next train to . . ?**
Кога е следващият
влак за . . ?
Koga e sledvashtiya vlak za . . ?

64 **Is there a later train to . . ?**
Има ли по-късен влак
за . . ?
Ima li po-kusen vlak za . . ?

Port

65 How do I get to the port?
Как да стигна до пристанището?
Kak da stigna do pristanishteto?

66 When is the next sailing to . . ?
Кога е следващият рейс за . . ?
Koga e sledvashtiya reys za . . ?

67 Can I catch an earlier ferry with this ticket?
Мога ли да се кача на по-ранен ферибот с този билет?
Moga li da se kacha na po-ranen feribot s tozi bilet?

Notices and Signs

68 Вагон-ресторант
Vagon-restorant
Buffet (Dining) Car

69 Автобус
Aftoboos
Bus

70 Питейна/непитейна вода
Piteyna/Nepiteyna voda
Drinking/Non-drinking water

71 Вход
Vhot
Entrance

72 Изход
Ishot
Exit

73 Информация
Informatsiya
Information

74 Гардероб за багаж
Garderop za bagash
Left Luggage (Baggage Claim)

75 Сейфове за багаж
Seyfove za bagash
Luggage Lockers

76 Поща
Poshta
Post Office

77 Перон
Peron
Platform

78 Железопътна гара
Zhelezoputna gara
Railway (Railroad) Station

79 Аерогара/Летище
Aerogara/Letishte
Airport

80 Пристанище
Pristanishte
Port

81 Ресторант
Restorant
Restaurant

82 Пушачи/непушачи
Pooshachi/Nepooshachi
Smoking/Non-smoking

83 Телефон
Telefon
Telephone

84 Билетна каса
Biletna kasa
Ticket Office

85 Гише за регистриране за
полета/Чек-ин
Gishe za registrirane za poleta/
Check-in
Check-in Desk

86 Разписание
Raspisanie
Timetable (Schedule)

87 Тоалетна
Toaletna
Toilets (Restrooms)

88 Мъже
Muzhe
Gentlemen

89 Жени
Zheni
Ladies'

90 Трамвай
Tramvay
Tram (Streetcar)

91 Метро
Metro
Underground (Subway)

92 Чакалня
Chakalnya
Waiting Room

Buying a ticket

93 I would like a first-class/
second-class single (one-
way)/return (round-trip)
ticket to . . .
Искам билет първа/втора
класа/ведна посока за
отиване и връщане ндо . . .
Iskam bilet purva/ftora clasa/
fedna posoka za otivane i
vrushtane ndo . . .

94 Is my rail pass valid on this
train/ferry/bus?
Картата ми за пътуване с
влак важи ли за този влак/
феробот/автобус?
Kartata mi za putoovane s vlak
vazhi li za tozi vlak/feribot/
aftoboos?

95 I would like an aisle/window
seat.
Искам място от
вътрешната страна/до
прозореца.
Iskam myasto ot vutreshnata
strana/do prozoretsa.

96 No smoking/smoking, please.
Не пушете/пушете, моля.
Ne pooshete/pooshete, molya.

97 We would like to sit together.
Искаме да седим заедно.
Iskame da sedim zaedno.

98 I would like to make a seat
reservation.
Искам да запазя място.
Iskam zapazeno myasto.

99 I would like to reserve a
couchette/sleeper for one
person/two people/my family.
Искам място в кушет/
спален вагон за един/
двама/за семейството ми.
Iskam myasto f kooshet/spalen
vagon za edin/dvama/za
semeystvoto mi.

100 I would like to reserve a cabin.
Искам да ре ервирам кабина/каюта.
Iskam da rezerviram kabina/ kayoota.

Timetables (Schedules)

101 Пристига
Pristiga
Arrive

102 Спира На
Spira na
Calls (Stops) at

103 Хранене
Hranene
Catering Service

104 Прехвърляне
Prehvurlyane na
Change at

105 Връзка
Vruska
Connection

106 Дневно
Dnevno
Daily

107 На всеки четиридесет минути
Na vseki chetirideset minooti
Every 40 Minutes

108 Първа класа
Purva clasa
First-class

109 Всеки час
Vseki chas
Hourly

110 Препоръчват се запазени места
Preporuchvat se zapazeni mesta
Seat reservations are recommended

111 Втора класа
Ftora clasa
Second-class

112 Допълнително заплащане
Dopulnitelno zaplashtane
Supplement Payable

113 През
Pres
Via

Luggage

114 How much will it cost to send (ship) my luggage in advance?
Колко струва да изпратя багажа си предварително?
Kolko stroova da ispratya bagazha si predvaritelno?

115 Where is the left luggage (baggage claim) office?
Къде е гардеробът за багаж?
Kude e garderoba za bagash?

116 What time do you open/close?
Кога отваряте/затваряте?
Koga otvaryate/zatvaryate?

117 Where are the luggage trolleys (carts)?
Къде са количките за багаж?
Kude sa kolichkite za bagash?

118 **Where are the lockers?**
Къде са сейфовете за
багаж?
Kude sa seyfovete za bagash?

119 **I have lost my locker key.**
Загубих ключа за сейфа.
Zagoobih klyoocha za seyfa.

On Board

120 **Is this seat free?**
Свободно ли е това място?
Svobodno li e tova myasto?

121 **Excuse me, you are sitting in
my reserved seat.**
Извинете, седите на моето
запазено място.
*Izinete, sedite na moeto zapazeno
myasto.*

122 **Which station is this?**
Коя е тази гара?
Koya e tazi gara?

123 **What time is this train/bus/
ferry/flight due to arrive/
depart?**
Кога трябва да пристигне/
замине този влак/автобус/
ферибот/полет?
*Koga tryabva da pristigne/zamine
tozi vlak/aftoboos/feribot/polet?*

124 **Will you wake me just before
we arrive?**
Можете ли да ме събудите
малко преди да
пристигнем?
*Mozhete li da me suboodite malko
predi da pristignem?*

Customs and Passports

125 **Passports, please!**
Паспортите, моля!
Pasportite, molya.

126 **I have nothing/wine/spirits
(alcohol)/tobacco to declare.**
Нямам нищо/вино/
концентрати/цигари да
декларирам.
*Nyamam nishto/vino/
kontsentrati/tsigari da deklariram.*

127 **I shall be staying for . . .
days/weeks/months.**
Ще пребивавам . . .дни/
седмици/месеци.
*Shte prebivavam . . . dni/sedmitsi/
mesetsi.*

AT THE TOURIST OFFICE

128 **Do you have a map of the
town/area?**
Имате ли карта на града/
областта?
Imate li karta na grada/oblasta?

129 **Can I reserve accommodation
here?**
Мога ли да резервирам
стая тук?
Moga li da rezerviram staya took?

130 **Do you have a list of
accommodation?**
Имате ли списък на
местата за нощуване?
*Imate li spisuk na mestata za
noshtoovane?*

ACCOMMODATION

Hotels

131 I have a reservation in the name of . . .

Имам резервация на името на . . .

Imam rezervatsiya na imeto na . . .

132 I wrote to/faxed/telephoned you last month/last week in . . .

Аз ви писах/телефонирах/изпратих факс миналия месец/миналата седмица в . . .

Az vi pissah/telefonirah/izpratih faks minaliya mesets/minalata sedmitsa f . . .

133 Do you have any rooms free?

Имате ли свободни стаи?

Imate li svobodni stayi?

134 I would like to reserve a single/double room with/without bath/shower.

Искам да резервирам единична/двойна стая с/без баня/душ.

Iskam da rezerviram edinichna/dvoyna staya s/bes banya/doosh.

135 I would like bed and breakfast/(room and) half board/(room and) full board.

Искам стая със закуска/половин пансион/пълен пасион.

Iskam staya sus zakooska/polovin pansion/pulen pansion.

136 How much is it per night?

Колко е за една нощ?

Kolko e za edna nosht?

137 Is breakfast included?

Включва ли се закуска?

Vklyoochva li se zakooska?

138 May I see the room?

Може ли да видя стаята?

Mozhe li da vidya stayata?

139 Do you have any cheaper rooms?

Имате ли по-евтини стаи?

Imate li po-eftini stai?

140 I would like to take the room.

Искам да наема стаята.

Iskam da naema stayata.

141 I would like to stay for . . . nights.

Искам да пребивавам . . . дни.

Iskam da prebivavam . . . dni.

142 The shower/light/tap doesn't work.

Душът/осветлението/кранът не работи.

Dooshut/osvetlenieto/kranut ne raboti.

143 At what time/where is breakfast served?

Кога/къде сервирате закуска?

Koga/kude servirate zakooska?

144 What time do I have to check-out?

Кога трябва да се отпиша?

Koga tryabva da se otpisha?

145 Can I have the key to room no . . ?

Може ли да ми дадете ключа за стая номер . . ?

Mozhe li da mi dadete klyucha za staya nomer . . ?

146 My room number is . . .

Номерът на стаята ми е . . .

Nomera na stayata mi e . . .

147 Do you accept travellers' cheques/Eurocheques/credit cards?

Приемате ли туристически чекове/еврочекове/кредитни карти?

Priemate li tooristicheski chekove/evrochekove/kreditni karti?

148 May I have the bill, please?

Може ли сметката, моля?

Mozhe li smetkata, molya?

149 Excuse me, I think there is a mistake in this bill.

Извинявайте, мисля, че в сметката ми има грешка.

Izvinyavaite, mislya, che f smetkata mi ima greshka.

Youth Hostels

150 How much is a dormitory bed per night?

Колко е легло в обща стая?

Kolko e leglo f opshta staya?

151 I am/am not an HI member.

Аз съм/не съм IУHA член.

As cum/ne sum IYHA chlen.

152 May I use my own sleeping bag?

Мога ли да ползвам спалния си чувал?

Moga li da polzvam spalniya si chooval?

153 What time do you lock the doors at night?

Кога заключвате през ноща?

Koga zaklyoochvate pres noshta?

Camping

154 May I camp here for the night/two nights?

Мога ли да прекарам ноща/две нощи?

Moga li da prekaram noshta/dve noshti?

155 Where can I pitch my tent?

Къде да сложа палатката си?

Kude da slozha palatkata si?

156 How much does it cost for one night/one week?

Колко струва за една нощ/една седмица?

Kolko srtoova za edna nosht/edna sedmitsa?

157 Where can we park our caravan?
Къде може да паркираме караваната си?
Kude mozhe da parkirame karavanata si?

158 Where are the washing facilities?
Къде е умивалнята?
Kude e oomivalnyata?

159 Is there a restaurant/supermarket/swimming pool on site/nearby?
Има ли ресторант/супермаркет/басейн тук/наоколо?
Ima li restorant/supermarket/baseyn took/naokolo?

160 Do you have a safety deposit box?
Имате ли сейф?
Imate li seyf?

EATING AND DRINKING

Cafés and Bars

161 I would like a cup of/two cups of/another coffee/tea.
Искам чаша/две чаши/още едно кафе/чай.
Iskam chaha/dve chashi/oshte edno kafe/chay.

162 With/without milk/sugar.
С/без мляко/захар.
S/bes mlyako/zahar.

163 I would like a bottle/glass/two glasses of mineral water/red wine/white wine, please
Искам бутилка/чаша/две чаши минерална вода/червено вино/бяло вино, моля.
Iskam bootilka/chasha/dve chashi mineralna voda/cherveno vino/byalo vino, molya.

164 I would like a beer/two beers, please.
Искам една бира/две бири, моля.
Iskam edna bira/dve biri, molya.

165 May I have some ice?
Ли малко лед?
Li malko led?

166 Do you have any matches/cigarettes/cigars?
Имате ли кибрит/цигари/пури?
Imate li kibrit/tsigari/poori?

Restaurants

167 Can you recommend a good/inexpensive restaurant in this area?
Препоръчайте ми добър/евтин ресторант наоколо?
Preporuchayte mi dobur/eftin restorant naokolo?

168 I would like a table for . . . people.
Искам маса за . . . човека.
Iskam masa za . . . choveka.

169 **Do you have a non-smoking area?**
Имате ли място за непушачи?
Imate li myasto za nepooshachi?

170 **Waiter/Waitress!**
Келнер!
Kelner!

171 **Do you have a set menu/children's menu/wine list?**
Имате ли меню за деня/детско меню/листа за вината?
Imate li menyoo za denya/detsko menyoo/lista za vinata?

172 **Do you have any vegetarian dishes, please?**
Имате ли нещо вегетарианско, моля?
Imate li neshto vegetariyansko, molya?

173 **Are there any local specialities?**
Има ли някакви местни специалитети?
Ima li nyakakvi mestni spetsialiteti?

174 **Are vegetables included?**
Това включва ли гарнитура/зеленчуци?
Tova fklyuchva li garnitoora/zelenchootsi?

175 **Could I have it well-cooked/medium/rare please?**
Искам го добре сготвено/средно/ал англе, моля

Iskam go dobre sgotveno/sredno/al angle, molya.

176 **What does this dish consist of?**
Какво има в яденето?
Kakvo ima f yadeneto?

177 **I would like the set menu, please.**
Искам менюто за деня, моля.
Iskam menyooto za denya, molya.

178 **We have not been served yet.**
Още не са ни сервирали.
Oshte ne sa ni servirali.

179 **Excuse me, this is not what I ordered.**
Извинявайте, аз не поръчах това.
Izvinyavayte, az ne poruchah tova.

180 **May I have some/some more bread/water/coffe/tea?**
Може ли да ми дадете/още хляб/вода/кафе/чай?
Mozhe li da mi dadete/oshte hlyap/voda/kafe/chay?

181 **May I have the bill, please?**
Може ли сметката, моля?
Mozhe li smetkata, molya?

182 **Does this bill include service?**
Обслужването включва ли се в сметката?
Opsloozhvaneto fklyoochva li se f smetkata?

183 Do you accept travellers' cheques (travelers' checks)/ Eurocheques/MasterCard/US dollars?
Приемате ли туристически чекове/еврочекове/мастер кард/долари?
Priemate li tooristicheski chekove/ Evrochekove/MasterCard/dolari?

184 Can I have a receipt, please?
Може ли да ми дадете разписка/фактура, моля?
Mozhe li da mi dadete razpiska/ faktoora, molya?

185 Where is the toilet (restroom), please?
Извинете, къде е тоалетната?
Izvinete, kude e toaletnata?

On the Menu

186 First courses
Предястия
Predyastiya

187 Soups
Супи
Soopi

188 Main courses
Главни/втори ястия
Glavni/ftori yastiya

189 Fish dishes
Рибни ястия
Ribni yastiya

190 Meat dishes
Месни ястия
Mesni yastiya

191 Vegetarian dishes
Вегетариански ястия
Vegetarianski yastiya

192 Cheese
Сирене
Sirene

193 Desserts
Десерти
Deserti

194 Specialities
Специалитети
Spetsialiteti

GETTING AROUND

Public Transport

195 Where is the bus stop/coach station/nearest metro (subway) station?
Къде е автобусната спирка/автогарата/най-близката гара на метрото?
Kude e aftoboosnata spirka/ aftogarata/nay-bliskata gara na metroto?

196 When is the next/last bus to . . ?
Кога е следващият/ последният автобус за . . ?
Koga e sledvashtiya/posledniya aftoboos za . . ?

197 How much is the fare to the city centre (downtown)/ railway (railroad) station/ airport?

Колко е билетът до центъра/гарата/летището?
Kolko e bileta do tsentura/garata/letishteto?

198 Will you tell me when to get off?
Бихте ли ми казали кога да сляза?
Bihte li mi kazali koga da slyaza?

199 Does this bus go to . . ?
Този автобус отива ли до . . ?
Tozi aftoboos otiva li do . . ?

200 Which number bus goes to . . ?
Кой номер автобус отива до?
Koy nomer aftoboos otiva do . . ?

201 May I have a single (one way)/return (round trip)/day ticket/book of tickets?
Искам билет в един посока/билет за отиване и връщане/дневна карта/кочан билети.
Iskam bilet f edna posoka/bilet za otivane i vrushtane/dnevna karta/kochan bileti?

Taxis

202 I would like to go to . . . How much will it cost?
Искам да отида до . . . Колко ще струва?
Iskam da otida do . . . Kolko shte stroova?

203 Please stop here.
Спрете тук, моля.
Sprete took, molya.

204 I would like to order a taxi today/tomorrow at 2pm to go from . . . to . . .
Искам да поръчам такси за днес/утре в 14 часа от . . . до . . .
Iskam da porucham taksi za dnes/ootre f 14 chasa ot . . . do . . .

Asking the Way

205 Excuse me, do you speak English?
Извинете, говорите ли английски?
Izvinete, govorite li angliyski?

206 Excuse me, is this the right way to . . ?
Извинявайте, това ли е пътят за . . ?
Izvinyavayte, tova li e putyat za . . .

207 . . . the cathedral/the tourist information office/the castle/the old town
. . . катедралата/туристическата информация/замъкът/старият град?
. . . katedralata/tooristicheskata informatsiya/zamukut/stariyat grat?

208 Can you tell me the way to the railway (railroad) station/ bus station/taxi rank (stand)/ city centre (downtown)/ beach?
Можете ли да ми кажете къде е гарата/автогарата/ колонката за таксита/ центъра/плажа?
Mozhete li da mi kazhete kude e garata/aftogarata/kolonkata za taksita/tsentura/plazha?

209 First/second/left/right/ straight ahead.
Първата/втората/наляво/ надясно/направо.
Purvata/ftorata/nalyavo/ nadyasno/napravo.

210 Where is the nearest police station/post office?
Къде е най-близкият полицейски участък/най- близката поща?
Kude e nay-bliskiya politseyski oochustuk/nay-bliskata poshta?

211 Is it far?
Далече ли е?
Dalache li e?

212 Do I need to take a taxi/catch a bus?
Трябва ли да взема такси/ автобус?
Tryabva li da vzema taksi/ aftobus?

213 Can you point to it on my map?
Покажете ми го на картата, моля?
Pokazhete mi go na kartata, molya?

214 Thank you for your help.
Благодаря Ви за помощта.
Blagodarya vi za pomoshta.

SIGHTSEEING

215 Where is the Tourist Information Office?
Къде е туристическата информация?
Kude e tooristicheskata informatsiya?

216 Where is the cathedral/ church/museum?
Къде е катедралата/ църквата/музеят?
Kude e katedralata/tsurkvata/ moozeya?

217 How much is the entrance (admission) charge?
Колко е входът?
Kolko e fhoda?

218 Is there a discount for children/students/senior citizens?
Има ли намаление за деца/студенти/ пенсионери?
Ima li namalenie za detsa/ stoodenti/pensioneri?

219 What time does the next guided tour start?
Кога е следващата обиколка с екскурзовод?
Koga e sledvashtata obikolka s ekskoorzovod?

220 One/two adults/children, please.
Един/двама възрастни/деца, моля.
Edin/dvama vuztrastni/detsa, molya.

221 May I take photographs here?
Мога ли да правя снимки тук?
Moga li da pravya snimki took?

ENTERTAINMENT

222 Can you recommend a good bar/nightclub?
Препоръчайте ми добър бар/нощен клуб?
Preporuchayte mi dubur bar/noshten cloop?

223 Do you know what is on at the cinema (playing at the movies)/theatre at the moment?
Знаете ли какво дават в киното/театъра в момента?
Znaete li kakvo davat f kinoto/teatura f momenta?

224 I would like to book (purchase) . . . tickets for the matinée/evening performance on Monday.
Искам да запазя (купя). . . билети за сутрешното/вечерното представление в понеделник.
Iskam da zapazya koopya . . . bileti za sootreshnoto/vechernoto predstavlenie f ponedelnik.

225 What time does the film/performance start?
Кога започва филмът/представлението?
Koga zapochva filma/predstavlenieto?

MEETING PEOPLE

226 Hello/Goodbye.
Здравейте/Довиждане.
Zdraveyte/Dovizhdane.

227 Good morning/good afternoon/good evening/goodnight.
Добро утро/добър ден/добър вечер/лека нощ.
Dobro ootro/dubur den/dubur vecher/leka nosht.

228 Pleased to meet you.
Радвам се да се запозная с вас.
Radvam se da se zapoznaya s vas.

229 How are you?
Как сте?
Kak ste?

BULGARIAN

230 Fine, thank you. And you?
Благодаря, добре. А Вие?
Blagodarya, dobre. A Vie?

231 My name is . . .
Аз се казвам . . .
Az se kazvam . . .

232 This is my friend/boyfriend/
girlfriend/husband/wife/
brother/sister.
Това е приятелят ми/
приятелката ми/съпругът
ми/съпругата ми/брат ми/
сестра ми.
*Tova e priyatelya mi/priyatelkata
mi/suprooga mi/suproogata mi/
brat mi/sestra mi.*

233 Where are you travelling to?
За къде пътувате?
Za kude putoovate?

234 I am/we are going to . . .
Аз/ние отивам/е до . . .
As/nie otivam/e do . . .

235 How long are you travelling
for?
За колко дълго пътувате?
Za kolko dulgo putoovate?

236 Where do you come from?
От къде сте?
Ot kude ste?

237 I am/we are from . . .
Аз/ ние съм/сме от . . .
As/nie sum/sme ot . . .

238 We're on holiday.
Ние сме на почивка.
Nie sme na pochifka.

239 This is our first visit here.
За първи път сме тук.
Za purvi put sme took.

240 Would you like/May I have a
cigarette?
Искате ли/може ли
цигара?
Iskate li/Mozhe li tsigara?

241 I am sorry, but I do not
understand.
Извинете, не разбирам.
Izvinete, ne razbiram.

242 Please speak slowly.
Моля, говорете бавно.
Molya, govorete bavno.

243 Do you mind if I smoke?
Мога ли да пуша?
Moga li da poosha?

244 Do you have a light?
Имате ли огънче?
Imate li ogunche?

245 I am waiting for my husband/
wife/boyfriend/girlfriend.
Чакам мъжа/жена/
приятеля/приятелката си.
*Chakam muzhu/zhena/
priyatelya/priyatelkata si.*

TRAVELLING WITH CHILDREN

246 Do you have a high chair/
baby-sitting service/cot?
Имате ли детски стол/
детски гледачки/детско
легло?
*Imate li detski stol/detski
gledachki/detsko leglo?*

247 Where is the nursery/
playroom?

Къде е занималнята/
детската стая?

*Kude e zanimalnyata/detskata
staya?*

248 Where can I warm the baby's
bottle?

Къде мога да стопля
бебешката бутилка?

*Kude moga da stoplya bebeshkata
bootilka?*

COMMUNICATIONS

Post

249 How much will it cost to send
a letter/postcard/this
package to Britain/Ireland/
America/Canada/Australia/
New Zealand?

Колко струва да изпратя
писмо/картичка/този
колет до Англия/
Ирландия/Америка/
Канада/Австралия/Нова
Зеландия?

*Kolko stroova da ispratya pismo/
kartichka/tozi kolet do Angliya/
Irlandiya/Amerika/Kanada/
Afstraliya/Nova Zelandiya?*

250 I would like one stamp/two
stamps.

Искам една марка/две
марки.

Iskam edna marka/dve marki.

251 I'd like . . . stamps for
postcards to send abroad,
please.

Искам . . . марки за
изпращане на картички в
чужбина, моля.

*Iskam . . . marki za izprashtane na
kartichki f choozhbina, molya.*

Phones

252 I would like to make a
telephone call/reverse the
charges to (make a collect call
to) . . .

Искам да се обадя/за
тяхна сметка до . . .

*Iskam da se obadya/za tyahna
smetka do . . .*

253 Which coins do I need for the
telephone?

Какви монети ми трябват
за телефон?

*Kakvi moneti mi tryabvat za
telefon?*

254 The line is engaged (busy).

Линията е заета.

Liniyata e zaeta.

255 The number is . . .

Номерът е . . .

Nomera e . . .

256 Hello, this is . . .

Ало, обажда се . . .

Allo, obazhda se . . .

257 May I speak to . . ?

Мога ли да говоря с . . ?

Moga li da govorya s . . ?

25

258 He/She is not in at the moment. Can you call back?

Той/тя не е тук в момента. Може ли да се обадите пак?

Toy/tya ne e took f momenta. Mozhe li da se obadite pak?

MONEY

259 I would like to change these travellers' cheques (travelers' checks)/this currency/this Eurocheque.

Искам да обменя тези туристически чекове/тази валута/този Еврочек.

Iskam da obmenya tezi tooristicheski chekove/tazi valuta/tozi Evrochek.

260 How much commission do you charge? (What is the service charge?)

Колко е комисионната?

Kolko e komisionnata?

261 Can I obtain money with my MasterCard?

Мога ли да използвам мастер кард?

Moga li da ispolzvam MasterCard?

SHOPPING

Names of Shops and Departments

262 Книжарница/Книжарски стоки

Knizharnitsa/Knizharski stoki

Bookshop/Stationery

263 Бижутерия/Подаръци

Bizhooteriya/Podarutsi

Jeweller's/Gifts

264 Обувки

Oboofki

Shoes

265 Железария

Zhelezariya

Hardware

266 Антики

Antiki

Antiques

267 Фризьорски/бръснарски салон

Frizyorski/Brusnarski salon

Hairdressers (men's)/(women's

268 Будка/щанд за цигари

Bootka/Shtant za tsigari

Tobacconist

269 Хлебарница

Hlebarnitsa

Baker's

270 Супермаркет

Soopermarket

Supermarket

271 Фотомагазин

Fotomagazin

Photoshop

272 Играчки

Igrachki

Toys

273 Туристическа агенция

Tooristicheska agentsiya

Travel Agent

274 Парфюмерия/Тоалетни
принадлежности
*Parfyumeriya/Toaletni
prinadlezhnosti*
Toiletries

275 Грамофонни плочи
Gramofonni plochi
Records

In the Shop

276 What time do the shops
open/close?
Кога отварят/затварят
магазините?
*Koga otvaryat/zatvaryat
magazinite?*

277 Where is the nearest market?
Къде е най-близкият
пазар?
Kude e nay-bliskiyat pazar?

278 Can you show me the one in
the window/this one?
Може ли да ми покажете
онова от витрината/това.
*Mozhe li da mi pokazhete onova
ot vitrinata/tova?*

279 Can I try this on?
Може ли да пробвам това?
Mozhe li da probvam tova?

280 What size is this?
Какъв размер е това?
Kakuf razmer e tova?

281 This is too large/too small/
too expensive.
Това е твърде голямо/
малко/скъпо.

*Tova e tvurde golyamo/malko/
skupo.*

282 Do you have any others?
Имате ли и други?
Imate li i droogi?

283 My size is . . .
Моят размер е . . .
Moyat razmer e . . .

284 Where is the changing room/
childrens'/cosmetic/
ladieswear/menswear/food
department?
Къде е пробната/детският
щанд/козметиката/
дамското облекло/
мъжкото облекло/щандът
за храна?
*Kude e probnata/detskiya shtand/
kozmetikata/damskoto obleklo/
muzhkoto obleklo/shtanda za
hrana?*

285 I would like . . .
Искам . . .
Iskam . . .

286 I would like a quarter of a
kilo/half a kilo/a kilo of
bread/butter/cheese/ham/
tomatoes.
Искам четвърт/половин/
един килограм хляб/
масло/сирене/шунка/
домати.
*Iskam chetvurt/polovin/edin
kilogram hlyap/maslo/sirene/
shoonka/domati.*

27

B U L G A R I A N

287 How much is this?
Колко струва Това?
Kolko stroova Tova?

288 I'll take this one, thank you.
Ще взема това, благодаря.
Shte vzema tova, blagodarya.

289 Do you have a carrier (shopping) bag?
Имате ли торба?
Imate li torba?

290 Do you have anything cheaper/larger/smaller/of better quality?
Имате ли нещо по-евтино/по-голямо/по-малко/по-качествено?
Imate li neshto po-eftino/po-golyamo/po-malko/po-kachestveno?

291 I would like a film for this camera.
Искам филм за този фотоапарат.
Iskam film za tozi fotoaparat.

292 I would like some batteries, the same size as this old one.
Искам батерии, същият размер като тази старата.
Isakm baterii, sushtiya razmer kato tazi starata.

293 Would you mind wrapping this for me, please?
Може ли да ми опаковате това, моля?

Mozhe li da mi opakovate tova, molya?

294 Sorry, but you seem to have given me the wrong change.
Извинете, но ми връщате неточно ресто.
Izvinete, no mi vrushtate netochno resto.

MOTORING

Car Hire (Rental)

295 I have ordered (rented) a car in the name of . . .
Поръчах наех кола на името на . . .
Poru hah naeh kola na imeto na . . .

296 How much does it cost to hire (rent) a car for one day/two days/one week?
Колко струва да наема кола за един ден/два дни/седмица?
Kolko stroova da naema kola za edin den/dva dni/sedmitsa?

297 Is the tank already full of petrol (gas)?
Пълен ли е резервоарът с бензин?
Pulen li e rezervoara s benzin?

298 Is insurance and tax included? How much is the deposit?
Включени ли са застраховката и данък? Колко е депозитът?

F klyoocheni li sa zastrahofkata i danuk? Kolko e depozita?

299 By what time must I return the car?

Кога трябва да върна колата?

Koga tryabva da vurna kolata?

300 I would like a small/family car with a radio/cassette player.

Искам малка/голяма кола с радио/касетофон.

Iskam malka/golyama kola s radio/kasetofon.

Asking the Way

301 Excuse me, can you help me please?

Извинявайте, може ли да ми помогнете, моля?

Izvinyavayte, mozhe li da mi pomognete, molya?

302 How do I reach the motorway/main road?

Как да стигна до автомагистралата/главния път?

Kak da stigna do aftomagistralata/glavniya put?

303 I think I have taken the wrong turning.

Мисля, че завих неправилно.

Mislya, che zavih nepravilno.

304 I am looking for this address.

Търся този адрес.

Tursya tozi adres.

305 I am looking for the . . . hotel.

Търся хотел . . .

Tursya hotel . . .

306 How far is it to . . . from here?

Колко е от тук до . . .

Kolko e ot took do . . .

307 Carry straight on for . . . kilometres.

Продължете направо около . . . километра.

Produlzhete napravo okolo . . . kilometra.

308 Take the next turning on the right/left.

Завийте на следващата пресечка на дясно/ляво.

Zaviyte na sledvashtata presechka na dyasno/lyavo.

309 Turn right/left at the next crossroads/traffic lights.

Завийте надясно/наляво на следващото кръстовище/следващия светофар.

Zaviyte nadyasno/nalyavo na sledvashtoto krustovishte/ sledvashtiya svetofar.

310 You are going in the wrong direction.

Вие се движите в грешната посока.

Vie se dvizhite f greshnata posoka.

Parking

311 **How long can I park here?**
За колко време мога да
паркирам тук?
Za kolko vreme moga da parkiram took?

312 **Is there a car park near here?**
Има ли паркинг наблизо?
Ima li parking nablizo?

313 **At what time does this car park close?**
Кога затварят този
паркинг?
Koga zatvaryat tozi parking?

Signs and Notices

314 Еднопосочна улица
Ednoposochna oolitsa
One way

315 Влизането забранено
Vlizaneto zabraneno
No entry

316 Паркирането забранено
Parkiraneto zabraneno
No parking

317 Отклонение.
Otklonenie
Detour (diversion

318 Спри/Стоп
Spri/Stop
Stop

319 Дай път
Dai put
Give way (yield)

320 Хлъзгав път
Hluzgaf put
Slippery road.

321 Изпреварването
забранено
Isprevarvaneto zabraneno
No overtaking

At the Filling Station

322 **Unleaded (lead-free)/ Standard/Premium**
Бензин без олово/
обикновен/супер
Benzin bes olovo/obiknoven/ sooper.

323 **Fill the tank please.**
Напълнете резервоара,
моля
Napulnete rezervoara, molya

324 **Do you have a road map of this area?**
Имате ли пътна карта на
този район?
Imate li putna karta na tozi rayon?

325 **How much is the car-wash?**
Колко струва измиването
на кола?
Kolko stroova izmivaneto na kola?

Breakdowns

326 **I've had a breakdown at . . .**
Колата ми се повреди в . . .
Kolata mi se povredi f . . .

327 **I am on the road from . . . to . . .**

Аз съм на пътя от . . .
за . . .
Az sum na putya ot . . .
za . . .

328 I can't move the car. Can you send a tow-truck?

Не мога да подкарам колата. Може ли да изпратите камион за теглене?
Ne moga da potkaram kolata.
Mozhe li da ispratite kamiyon za teglene?

329 I have a flat tyre.

Спуках гума.
Spookah gooma.

330 The windscreen (windshield) has smashed/cracked.

Предното стъкло е счупено/спукано.
Prednoto stuklo e schupeno/spookano.

331 There is something wrong with the engine/brakes/lights/steering/gearbox/clutch/exhaust.

Двигателят/спирачките/светлините/кормилото/скоростната кутия/амбреажът/ауспухът ми не е/са в ред.
Dvigatelyat/spirachkite/svetlinite/kormiloto/skorostnata kootiya/ambreazhut/aspoohut mi ne e/sa f ret.

332 It's overheating.

Прегрява.
Pregryava.

333 It won't start.

Не иска да пали.
Ne iska da pali.

334 Where can I get it repaired?

Къде могат да я поправят?
Kude mogat da ya popravyat?

335 Can you take me there?

Може ли да ме заведете там?
Mozhe li da me zavedete tam?

336 Will it take long to fix?

Много ли време трябва, за да се поправи?
Mnogo li vreme tryabva, za da se popravi?

337 How much will it cost?

Колко ще струва?
Kolko shte stroova?

Accidents

338 Can you help me? There has been an accident.

Може ли да ми помогнете? Стана катастрофа.
Mozhe li da mi pomognete? Stana katastrofa.

339 Please call the police/an ambulance.

Моля, повикайте полиция/линейка.
Molya, povikayte politsiya/lineyka.

340 Is anyone hurt?
Има ли ранени?
Ima li raneni?

Traffic Offences

341 I'm sorry, I didn't see the sign.
Съжалявам. Не видях знака.
Suzhalyavam, ne vidiyah znaka.

342 Must I pay a fine? How much?
Трябва ли да платя глоба? Колко?
Tryabva li da platya globa? Kolko?

343 Show me your documents.
Покажете ми документите си.
Pokazhete mi dokoomentite si.

HEALTH

Pharmacy

344 Do you have anything for a stomachache/headache/sore throat/toothache?
Имате ли нещо за стомах/глава/гърло/зъби?
Imate li neshto za stomah/glava/gurlo/zubi?

345 I need something for diarrhoea (diarrhea)/constipation/a cold/a cough/insect bites/sunburn/travel (motion) sickness.

Трябва ми нещо за разстройство/запек/настинка/кашлица / ухапване от насекоми/слънчево изгаряне/гадене при пътуване.
Tryabva mi neshto za rastroystvo/zapek/nastinka/kashlitsa/oohapvane ot nasekomi/slunchevo izgaryane/gadene pri putoovane.

346 How much/how many do I take?
Колко се взема?
Kolko se vzema?

347 How often do I take it/them?
Колко често се взема?
Kolko chesto se vzema?

348 How much does it cost?
Колко струва?
Kolko stroova?

349 Can you recommend a good doctor/dentist?
Можете ли да ми препоръчате добър доктор/зъболекар?
Mozhete li da mi preporuchate dobur doktor/zubolekar?

350 Is it suitable for children?
Подходящо ли е за деца?
Pothodyashto li e za detsa?

Doctor

351 I have a pain here/in my arm/leg/chest/stomach.
Боли ме тук/ръката/крака/гърдите/стомахът.

Boli me took/rukata/kraka/ gurdite/stomaha.

352 **Please call a doctor, this is an emergency.**
Извикайте лекар, това е спешен случай.
Izvikayte lekar, tova e speshen sloochay.

353 **I would like to make an appointment to see a doctor.**
Искам час за преглед.
Iskam chas za pregled.

354 **I am diabetic/pregnant.**
Аз съм диабетик/ бременна.
As sum diabetik/bremenna.

355 **I need a prescription for . . .**
Искам рецепта за . . .
Iskam retsepta za . . .

356 **Can you give me something to ease the pain?**
Можете ли да ми дадете болкоуспокояващо?
Mozhete li da mi dadete bolkooospokoyavashto?

357 **I am/he is/she is allergic to penicillin.**
Имам/има алергия към пеницилин
Imam/ima alergiya kum penitsilin.

358 **Does this hurt?**
Боли ли?
Boli li?

359 **You must/he must/she must go to hospital.**

Вие/той/тя трябва да отиде/те в болница.
Vie/toy/tya tryabva da otide/te f bolnitsa.

360 **Take these once/twice /three times a day.**
Вземайте от тези веднъж/ два/три пъти на ден.
Vzemayte ot tezi vednuzh/dva/tri/ puti na den.

361 **I am/he is/she is taking this medication.**
Аз вземам / той/тя взема това лекарство.
Az vzemam/ toy/tya vzema tova lekarstvo.

362 **I have medical insurance.**
Имам медицинска/ здравна застра овка.
Imam meditsinska/zdravna zastrahovka.

Dentist

363 **I have toothache.**
Боли ме зъб.
Boli me zup.

364 **My filling has come out.**
Падна ми пломба.
Padna mi plomba.

365 **I do/do not want to have an injection first.**
Искам/не искам първо инжекция.
Iskam/ne iskam purvo inzhektsya.

EMERGENCIES

B U L G A R I A N

366
↕
372

EMERGENCIES

366 Help!
Помощ!
Pomosht!

367 Call an ambulance/a doctor/
the police!
Извикайте линейка/
доктор/полицията!
*Izvikayte lineyka/doktor/
politsiyata!*

368 I have had my travellers'
cheques (travelers' checks)/
credit cards/purse/handbag/
rucksack (knapsack)/
luggage/wallet stolen.
Откраднаха ми
туристическите чекове/
кредит картите/
портмонето/чантата/
раницата/багажа
портфейла.
*Orkradnaha mi tooristicheskite
chekove/kredit kartite/
portmoneto/chantata/ranitsata/
bagazha portfeyla.*

369 Can you help me, I have lost
my daughter/son?

Може ли да ми помогнете,
загубих дъщеря/сина си?
*Mozhe li da mi pomognete,
zagoobih dushterya si/sina si?*

370 Please, go away/leave me
alone.
Оставете ме на мира.
Ostavete me na mira.

371 Fire!
Пожар!
Pozhar!

372 I want to contact the British/
American/Canadian/Irish/
Australian/New Zealand/
South African consulate.
Искам да се свържа с
британското/
американското/
канадското/ирландското/
австралийското/
новозеландското/
южноафриканското
консулство.
*Iskam da se svurzha s britanskoto/
amerikanskoto/kanatskoto/
irlandskoto/afstraliyskoto/
novozelandskoto/
yuzhnoafrikanskoto konsulstvo.*

34

Introduction

Czech is the official language of the Czech Republic. The language spoken in neighbouring Slovakia is Slovak, but the two are so closely related that speakers of one can easily understand the other. Both belong to the Slavic family of languages that includes Russian and Polish. In larger cities, particularly in the Czech Republic, English is spoken, and German is often a second language for many Czechs. Russian is also widely understood, but not popular.

CZECH

Addresses for travel and tourist information

The following addresses are the tourist authorities for both the Czech Republic and for Slovakia.

UK: *Cedok*, 49 Southwark St, London SE1 1RU; tel: (0171) 378 6009.

USA: *Cedok*, 10 East 40th St, New York, NY 10016; tel: (212) 689-9720.

ESSENTIALS

ESSENTIALS

Alphabet

A	B
ah	*bey*
C	D
tsey	*dey*
E	F
ey	*ef*
G	H
gey	*hah*
CH	I
khah	*ee*
J	K
yeh	*kah*
L	M
el	*em*
N	O
en	*oh*
P	Q
pey	*koo*
R	S
yer	*es*
T	U
tey	*oo*
V	W
veh	*dvoyiteh veh*
X	Y
iks	*oopsi-lon*
Z	
tset	

Basic Words and Phrases

1. **Yes** — **No**
   Ano — Ne
   Unnoh — *neh*

2. **Please** — **Thank you**
   Prosím — Děkuji
   Prosseem — *Dyekoo-yi*

3. **That's o.k.** — **Perhaps**
   Prima — Možná
   Preemmah — *Mozhnah*

4. **To** — **From**
   Do — Od
   Doh — *odd*

5. **Here** — **There**
   Zde — Tam
   Zdhe — *Tahm*

6. **None** — **Also**
   Žádný — Také
   Zhadnee — *Tukeh*

7. **How** — **When**
   Jak — Kdy
   Yuck — *Gdy*

8. **What** — **Why**
   Co — Proč
   Tsoh — *Prroch*

9. **I don't understand.**
   Nerozumím.
   Nerohzuhmeem.

10. **I don't speak Czech.**
    Nemluvím česky.
    Nemluhveem chesky.

11. **Do you speak English?**
    Mluvíte anglicky?
    Mluhveete ahnglitsky?

**C
Z
E
C
H**

12. **Can you please write it down?**
Můžete to, prosím, napsat?
Moozheteh toh, prohseem, nahpsaht?

13. **Can you please speak more slowly?**
Můžete, prosím, mluvit pomaleji?
Moozheteh, prohseem, mluhvit pohmahlayi?

14. **How much does it/this cost?**
Kolik to/tohle stojí?
Kollick toh/toh-hleh stoyee?

Days

15. **Monday** **Tuesday**
pondělí úterý
Pondyellee *Ooteree*

16. **Wednesday** **Thursday**
středa čtvrtek
Stzheddah *Shtvertek*

17. **Friday** **Saturday**
pátek sobota
Pahtek *Sobbottah*

18. **Sunday** **Morning**
neděle ráno
Neddyelleh *Rahnoh*

19. **Afternoon** **Evening**
odpoledne večer
Odpoledneh *Vesherr*

20. **Night** **Week**
noc týden
Nots *Teeden*

21. **Yesterday** **Tomorrow**
včera zítra
Fcherah *Zeetrah*

Numbers

22. **Zero** **One**
nula jedna
Noola *Yednah*

23. **Two** **Three**
dvě tři
Dvyeh *Tzhee*

24. **Four** **Five**
čtyři pět
Shteezhee *Pyet*

25. **Six** **Seven**
šest sedm
Shest *Seddoom*

26. **Eight** **Nine**
osm devět
Ossoom *Devyet*

27. **Ten** **Eleven**
deset jedenáct
Desset *Yeddenahtst*

28. **Twelve** **Thirteen**
dvanáct třináct
Dvunnahtst *Tzheenahtst*

29. **Fourteen** **Fifteen**
čtrnáct patnáct
Shternahtst *Puttnahtst*

30. **Sixteen** **Seventeen**
šestnáct sedmnáct
Shestnahtst *Seddoomnahtst*

31. **Eighteen** **Nineteen**
osmnáct devatenáct
Ossoomnahtst *Devvuttehnahtst*

**12
↑
31**

32 **Twenty**
dvacet
Dvutset

Twenty-one
dvacet jeden
Dvutset yedden

33 **Twenty-two**
dvacet dva
Dvutset dvah

Thirty
třicet
Tzhitset

34 **Forty**
čtyřicet
Shteezhitset

Fifty
padesát
Puddessaht

35 **Sixty**
šedesát
Sheddessaht

Seventy
sedmdesát
Seddoomdessaht

36 **Eighty**
osmdesát
Ossoodessaht

Ninety
devadesát
Devvuddessaht

37. **One hundred**
sto
Stoh

Five hundred
pět set
Pyet set

38 **One thousand**
tisíc
Tyisseets

One million
milión
Meeleeon

Time

39 **9.00**
devět hodin
Devvyet hoddyinn

40 **9.05**
devět pět
Devvyet pyet

41 **9.10**
devět deset
Devvyet desset

42 **9.15**
čtvrt na desset
Shtvert naa desset

43 **9.20**
devět dvacet
Devvyet dvutset

44 **9.25**
devět dvacet pět
Devvyet dvutset pyet

45 **9.30**
půl desáté
Pool dessahte

46 **9.35**
devět třicet pět
Devvyet tzhitset pyet

47 **9.40**
devět čtyřicet
Devvyet shteezhitset

48 **9.45**
třičtvrtě na deset
Tzheeshtvertye naa desset

49 **9.50**
za deset minut deset
Zaa desset minnoot desset

50 **9.55**
za pět minut deset
Zaa pyet minnoot desset

51 **12.00/Midday/Midnight**
dvanáct/poledne/půlnoc
Dvunnahtst/poledne/poolnots

52 **What time is it?**
Kolik je hodin
Kollick yeh hoddin

53 **It is . . .**
Je . . .
Yeh . . .

ARRIVING AND DEPARTING

Airport

54 Excuse me, where is the check-in desk for . . . airline?
Promiňte, kde se odbavuje letecká společnost . . ?
Prohminyete, gde sse ohdbahvuhyeh letetskar spohletchnost . . ?

55 What is the boarding gate/ time for my flight?
Kterou branou/V kolik hodin se nastupuje na můj let?
Kteroe brahnoe/Fkollick hodyin sse nahstuhpuhyeh nah mooy let?

56 How long is the delay likely to be?
Jak velké asi bude to zpoždění?
Yuck velkeh ahssee buhdeh toh zpohzhdyenyee?

57 Where is the duty-free shop?
Kde je bezcelní obchod?
Gdeh yeh beztselnyee ophod?

58 Which way is the baggage reclaim?
Kde je výdej zavazadel?
Gdeh yeh veedey zahvahzahdel?

59 Where can I get the bus to the city centre?
Odkud jede autobus do centra města?

Otkuhd yede aootobuhs dotsentrah mnyesta?

Train Station

60 Where is the ticket office/ information desk?
Kde je výdejna jízdenek/Kde jsou informace?
Gdeh yeh veedeynah yeezdenek/ gdeh sow informatse?

61 Which platform does the train to . . . depart from?
Z kterého nástupiště odjíždí vlak do . . ?
Z ktehraihoh nahstoopishtyeh odyeezhdee vluck doh . . ?

62 Where is platform . . ?
Kde je . . . nástupiště?
Gdeh yeh . . . nahstoopishtyeh?

63 When is the next train to . . ?
Kdy jede další vlak do . . ?
Gdy yeddeh daalshee vluck do . . ?

64 Is there a later train to . . ?
Jede později vlak do . . ?
Yeddeh pozdyeyee vluck doh . . ?

Port

65 How do I get to the port?
Jak se dostanu do přístavu . . ?
Yuck seh dostahnoo doh pzheestavoo . . ?

66 When is the next sailing to . . ?
Kdy jede příští loď?
Gdy yedeh pzheeshtee lodye?

CZECH

67 ↕ 88

⁶⁷ **Can I catch an earlier ferry with this ticket?**
Mohu jet na tenhle lístek dřívější lodí?
Mohuh yet nah tenhleh leestek drzheevyeyshee lodyee?

Notices and Signs

⁶⁸ **Bufetový vůz**
Boofetovee vooz
Buffet (Dining) Car

⁶⁹ **Autobus**
Aootohbooss
Bus

⁷⁰ **Pitná voda/nepitná voda**
Peetnah voddah
Drinking/Non-drinking water

⁷¹ **Vchod**
Vkhod
Entrance

⁷² **Východ**
Veekhod
Exit

⁷³ **Informace**
Informatseh
Information

⁷⁴ **Úschovna zavazadel**
Ooskhovnah zuvvahzuddel
Left Luggage (Baggage Claim)

⁷⁵ **Skříňky na zavazadla**
Skzheenkee nah zuvvahzuddlah
Luggage Lockers

⁷⁶ **Pošta**
Poshtah
Post Office

⁷⁷ **Nástupiště**
Nahstoopishtyeh
Platform

⁷⁸ **Železniční nádraží**
Zheleznechnee nahdrahzhee
Railway (Railroad) Station

⁷⁹ **Letiště**
Letyishtye
Airport

⁸⁰ **Přístav**
Przheestahf
Port

⁸¹ **Restaurace**
Restauratse
Restaurant

⁸² **Kuřáci/nekuřáci**
Koozhahtsi/nehkoozhatsi
Smoking/Non-smoking

⁸³ **Telefon**
Tellefohn
Telephone

⁸⁴ **Pokladna**
Pokludnah
Ticket Office

⁸⁵ **Odbavovací přepážka**
Ohdbahvohvahtsee przhepashka
Check-in Desk

⁸⁶ **Jízdní řád**
Yeezdnyee zhaht
Timetable (Schedule)

⁸⁷ **Záchod**
Zahkhot
Toilets (Restrooms)

⁸⁸ **Páni**

Pahni
Gentlemen

89 Dámy
Dahmy
Ladies'

90 Tramvaj
Trumvahay
Tram (Streetcar)

91 Podzemní dráha
Podzemnee draahah
Underground (Subway)

92 Čekárna
Chekaarnah
Waiting Room

Buying a Ticket

**93 I would like a first-class/
second-class single (one-
way)/return (round-trip)
ticket to . . .**
Prosím jízdenku první/druhé
třídy/zpáteční do . . .
*Prosseem yeezdenkooh pervnee
tzheedy/droohe tzheedy/
zpaatechnee doh . . .*

**94 Is my rail pass valid on this
train/ferry/bus?**
Platí moje sí ťová železniční
jízdenka na tento vlak/na tuto
loď/na tento autobus?
*Plahtyee moye seełyovar
zhelezniychnee yeezdenkah nah
tentoh vluck/nah tuhtoh lodye/
nah tentoh aootohbuhs?*

**95 I would like an aisle/
window seat.**

Přeji si místo u chodbičky/u
okna.
*Pzheye ssi meestoh oo
khodbichky/oo ocknah.*

**96 No smoking/smoking,
please.**
Nekuřáci/kuřáci, prosím.
*Nehckuzhaatsi/kuzhaatsi,
prosseem.*

**97 We would like to sit
together.**
Chceme sedět spolu.
Khtsemeh ssedyet spohloo.

**98 I would like to make a seat
reservation.**
Rád(a) bych si rezervoval(a)
místenku.
*Rahd(ah) bikh sih
rezerrvoval(ah) meestenkuh.*

**99 I would like to reserve a
couchette/sleeper for one
person/two people/for my
family.**
Rád bych rezervoval lehátko/
lůžko pro jednu osobu/dvě
osoby/pro rodinu.
*Rahd bykh rezervohvahl
lehhahtkoh/loozhkoh proh
yednoo osohboo/dvyeh osohby/
proh rodyeenoo.*

**100 I would like to reserve a
cabin.**
Rád(a) bych si rezervoval(a)
kabinu.
*Rahd(ah) bikh sih
rezerrvoval(ah) kahbinuh.*

Timetables (Schedules)

101 Přijede
Pzhiyeddeh
Arrive

102 Zastavuje . . .
Zustahvooye . . .
Calls (Stops) at . . .

103 Dodávky jídla
Dohdaafkee yeedlah
Catering Service

104 Přestupte . . .
Pzhestoopteh . . .
Change at . . .

105 Spojení
Spoyenee
Connection

106 Denně
Denye
Daily

107 Každých čtyřicet minut
Kazhdeekh shteezhitset minnoot
Every 40 minutes

108 První třída
Pervnee tzheedah
First-class

109 Každou hodinu
Kahzhdoow hoddyinoo
Hourly

110 Doporučují se místenky
Dohporuchoyee seh meestenky
Seat reservations are recommended

111 Druhá třída
Droohah tzheedah
Second-class

112 Platí se příplatek
Plahtee seh pzheeplahtek
Supplement Payable

113 Přes
Pzhez
Via

Luggage

114 How much will it cost to send (ship) my luggage in advance?
Kolik stojí poslat zavazadlo dopředu?
Kohlick stohyee poslaht zuvvahzuddlah dohpzhedoo?

115 Where is the left luggage (baggage claim) office?
Kde je úschovna?
Gde yeh ooskhohvnah?

116 What time do you open/close?
Kdy otvíráte/zavíráte?
Gdy ohtveerahteh/zuvveerahteh?

117 Where are the luggage trolleys (carts)?
Kde jsou vozíky na zavazadla?
Gde ysow vohzeeky nah zuvvazuddlahd?

118 Where are the lockers?
Kde jsou skříňky na zavazadla?
Gdeh soe skrzheenyeki nahzahvahzahdddah?

119 I have lost my locker key.
Ztratil jsem klíč od skříňky.
*Ztrahtil sehm kleech odh
skzheenky.*

On Board

120 Is this seat taken?
Je toto místo volné?
Yeh tohotoh meestoh vohlneeh?

121 Excuse me, you are sitting
in my reserved seat.
Promiňte, to je moje
rezervované místo.
*Prohminyteh, toh yeh mohye
rezervohvahneeh meestoh.*

122 Which station is this?
Která je to stanice?
Ktehraah yeh toh stanitseh?

123 What time is this train/bus/
ferry/flight due to arrive/
depart?
V kolik hodin tenhle vlak/
tenhle autobus/tahle loď/
tohle letadlo přijíždí/odjíždí?
*Fkollick hodyin tenhleh vluck/
tenhleh aootohbuhs/tahhleh
lodye/tohhleh lehtadloh
przhiyeezhdyee/odyeezhdyee?*

124 Will you wake me just
before we arrive?
Probudíte mě než zastavíme?
*Prohbudyteh mnye nezh
zahstahveemeh?*

Customs and Passports

125 Prosím pasy!

Prosseem passy!
Passports, please!

126 I have nothing/wine/spirits
(alcohol)/tobacco to
declare.
Nemám nic/Mám víno/
alkohol/tabák k proclení.
*Nemaahm nits/Maahm veenoh/
alckohol/tabaack kh protslenee.*

127 I shall be staying for . . .
days/weeks/months.
Budu zde . . . dní/týdnů/
měsíců.
*Boodoo zdeh . . . dnee/teednoo/
mnyesseetsoo.*

AT THE TOURIST OFFICE

128 Do you have a map of the
town/area?
Máte mapu města/okolí?
*Mahteh mahpoo mnyestah/
ohkohlee?*

129 Can I reserve
accommodation here?
Mohu si zde rezervovat
ubytování?
*Mohhooseezdeh rezervohvaht
oobytovaanyee?*

130 Do you have a list of
accommodation?
Máte seznam možností
ubytování?
*Mahteh seznam mozhnostyee
ubitohvahnyee?*

ACCOMMODATION

Hotels

131 I have a reservation in the name of . . .
Mám rezervaci na jméno . . .
Mahm rezervatsi nah mehnnoh . . .

132 I wrote to/faxed/telephoned you last month/last week in . . .
Psa (a)/faxoval(a)/telefonoval(a) jsem vám minulý měsíc/minulý týden v . . .
Psal(ah)/fahksoval(ah)/ telefohnoval(ah) sem vahm minuhlee mnyesseets/minuhlee teeden v . . .

133 Do you have any rooms free?
Máte nějaké volné pokoje?
Mahte nyeyakeh volneh pockoyeh?

134 I would like to reserve a single/double room with/ without bath/shower.
Rád bych rezervoval jednolůžkový/dvojlůžkový pokoj s koupelnou/bez koupelny/se sprchou.
Rahd bykh rezervohvahl pockoy ss kowpelnow/bess kowpelny/ seh sperkhow.

135 I would like bed and breakfast/(room and) half board/(room and) full board.
Rád bych pokoj se snídaní/

polopenzí/plnou penzí.
Rahd bykh pockoy seh sneedanee/pohlohpenzee/plnow penzi.

136 How much is it per night?
Kolik to stojí za jednu noc?
Kollick toh stoyee zah yednoo nots?

137 Is breakfast included?
Je to se snídaní?
Ye toh seh sneedahnee?

138 May I see the room?
Smím se na pokoj podívat?
Smeem seh nah pokoy podeevaht?

139 Do you have any cheaper rooms?
Máte lacinější pokoje?
Mahte latsinyeyshee pockoyeh?

140 I would like to take the room.
Vezmu si tento pokoj.
Vezmoo si tento pockoy.

141 I would like to stay for . . . nights.
Rád bych zůstal . . . nocí.
Rahd bykh zoostahl . . . notsee.

142 The shower/light/tap doesn't work.
Sprcha/světlo/kohoutek nefunguje.
Sprhah/svyetloh/kohoetek nefunguyeh.

143 At what time/where is breakfast served?

Kdy a kde se podává snídaně?
Gdy a gde se pohdahvah sneedahnye?

144 **What time do I have to check-out?**
Kdy musím uvolnit pokoj?
Gdy moozem oovolniht pockoy?

145 **Can I have the key to room no . . ?**
Můžu dostat klíč od pokoje číslo . . ?
Moozhuh dohstaht kleech ot pockohyeh cheesloh . . ?

146 **My room number is . . .**
Číslo mého pokoje je . . .
Cheesloh mehoh pockoyeh yeh . . .

147 **Do you accept travellers' cheques/Eurocheques/ credit cards?**
Přijímáte cestovní šeky/ Eurošeky/kreditní karty?
Prziyeemahteh tsestovnyee sheki/ eoorosheki/kreditnyee karti?

148 **May I have the bill please?**
Účet, prosím?
Oochet, prosseem?

149 **Excuse me, I think there is a mistake in this bill.**
Promiňte, myslím, že v tomto účtu je chyba.
Prominyete, misleem zhe ftomtoh oochtuh yeh hibah.

Youth Hostels

150 **How much is a dormitory bed per night?**

Kolik stojí lůžko v noclehárně?
Kollick stoyee loozhkoh v notslehahrnye?

151 **I am/am not an HI member.**
Jsem/nejsem členem HI.
Sem/neysem chlehnehm ee, oopsi-lon, hah, ah.

152 **May I use my own sleeping bag?**
Můžu používat vlastní spacák?
Moozhoo powsheevath vlastnee spatsahck?

153 **What time do you lock the doors at night?**
Kdy v noci zamykáte?
Gdy v notsi zahmykahteh?

Camping

154 **May I camp here for the night/two nights?**
Můžu zde stanovat jednu noc/dvě noci?
Moozhoo zdeh stahnovaht jehdnoo nots/dvye notsi?

155 **Where can I pitch my tent?**
Kde můžu postavit stan?
Gde moozhoo postahvit stahn?

156 **How much does it cost for one night/one week?**
Kolik stojí jedna noc/jeden týden?
Kollick stoyee yednah nots/yeden tyhdehn?

144
↑
156

ACCOMMODATION/EATING AND DRINKING

157 Where can we park our caravan?
Kam můžeme zaparkovat náš obytný přívěs?
Kam moozhemeh zaparrkohvat nahsh obitnee przheevyes?

158 Where are the washing facilities?
Kde jsou umývárny?
Gde sow oomyhvahrny?

159 Is there a restaurant/supermarket/swimming pool on site/nearby?
Je tady/blízko restaurce/supermarket/plovárna?
Yeh tahdyh/bleezkoh restauratseh/supermarkeht/plohvahrnah?

160 Do you have a safety deposit box?
Máte trezor?
Mahteh trehzohr?

EATING AND DRINKING

Cafés and Bars

161 I would like a cup of/two cups of/another coffee/tea.
Prosím šálek/dva šálky kávy/ještě kávu/čaje.
Prosseem shahleck/dvah shahlkyh/yeshtye kahvoo/chaye.

162 With/without milk/sugar.
S mlékem/cukrem. Bez mléka/cukru.
Ss mlaikehm/tsookrehm. Behz mlaikah/tsookroo.

163 I would like a bottle/glass/two glasses of mineral water/red wine/white wine, please.
Prosím láhev/sklenku/dvě sklenky minerální vody/červeného vína/bílého vína.
Prosseem lahhehv/sklehnku/dvye sklehnkyh minehrahlnee voddy/chervehnehoh veenah/beelehhoh veenah.

164 I would like a beer/two beers, please.
Prosím pivo/dvě piva.
Prosseem pivoh/dvye pivah.

165 May I have some ice?
Led, prosím.
Lehd, prosseem.

166 Do you have any matches/cigarettes/cigars?
Máte zápalky/cigarety/doutníky?
Mahte zahpalkyh/tsigartyh/dowtneekyh?

Restaurants

167 Can you recommend a good/inexpensive restaurant in this area?
Můžete doporučit dobrou/lacinou restauraci v okolí?
Moozheteh dohporuhchit dohbrow latsinow restauratsi vh ohkohlee?

168 I would like a table for . . . people.
Přeji si stůl pro . . . osoby.

46

Pzheyee sih stool proh . . .
ohsohby.

169 Do you have a non-smoking area?
Máte nekuřáckou část?
Mahteh nehkuhrzhahtskoe chahst?

170 Waiter/Waitress!
Číšníku/číšnice!
Cheeshneekoo/cheeshnitse!

171 Do you have a set menu/children's menu/wine list?
Máte sestavené menu? dětské menu/ceník nápojů?
Mahteh sehstahveneh menuh? dyetskeh menuh/tseneek nahpojoo?

172 Do you have any vegetarian dishes, please?
Máte, prosím, vegetariánská jídla?
Mahteh, prosseem, veghetahriahnskeh yeedlah?

173 Are there any local specialities?
Máte nějaké místní speciality?
Mahte nyeyakeh meestnyee spetsialiti?

174 Are vegetables included?
Je v tom také zelenina?
Yeh ftom tahkeh zelenyinah?

175 Could I have it well-cooked/medium/rare please?
Mohl(a) bych to dostat dobře/středně/jen lehce propečené, prosím?

Mohl(ah) bikh toh dostat dobrzhe/strzhednye/yen lehtse propetcheneh, prosseem?

176 I would like the set menu, please.
Sestavené menu, prosím.
(Sestahveneh menuh, prosseem.)

177 I would like the set menu, please.
Sestavené menu, prosím.
Sestahveneh menuh, prosseem.

178 We have not been served yet.
Ještě jsme nebyli obslouženi.
Yeshtye smeh nehbyhli obslowzhenih.

179 Excuse me, this is not what I ordered.
Promiňte, ale tohle jsem si neobjednal(a).
Prohminyete, ahleh toh-hle sem si ne-ohbyednal(ah).

180 May I have some/some more bread/water/coffee/tea?
Přeji si/více chleba/vody/kávy/čaje.
Pzheyi sih/veetse khbleba/voddy/chaye.

181 May I have the bill, please?
Účet, prosím?
Oochet, prosseem?

182 Does this bill include service?
Zahrnuje účet obsluhu?
Zahrnooye oochet obsloohoo?

C Z E C H

183
↕
197

183 Do you accept travellers'
cheques (travelers' checks)/
Eurocheques/MasterCard/
US dollars?
Berete cestovní šeky/
Eurošeky/MasterCard/
americké dolary?
*Bereteh tsestovnee shehkyh/
Euroshekyh/Masterkard/
ahmehritskeh dohlaryh?*

184 Can I have a receipt, please?
Můžete mi vystavit účtenku,
prosím?
*Moozhetemi vistahvit
oochtenkuh, prosseem?*

185 Where is the toilet
(restroom), please?
Prosím, kde jsou toalety?
Prosseem, gde sow toaletyh?

On the Menu

186 First courses
Předkrmy
Przhetkrmi

187 Soups
Polévky
Polehvki

188 Main courses
Hlavní jídla
Hlavnyee yeedlah

189 Fish dishes
Rybí pokrmy
Ribee pohkrmi

190 Meat dishes
Masitá jídla
Mahssitah yeedlah

191 Vegetarian dishes
Vegetariánská/Bezmasá jídla
*Vehgehtahrianskah/Bezmahssah
yeedlah*

192 Cheese
Sýry
Seerri

193 Desserts
Moučníky/Zákusky
Moechnyeeki/Zahkooski

194 Specialities
Speciality
Spetsialiti

GETTING AROUND

Public Transport

195 Where is the bus stop/
coach station/nearest metro
(subway) station?
Kde je autobusová zastávka/
autokarová stanice/nejbližší
metro zastávka?
*Gde yeh aoothoboosovah zahstahvkah/
auuthokahrovah stanitseh/neyblizhshee
metroh zahstahvkah?*

196 When is the next/last bus
to . . ?
Kdy jede další/poslední
autobus do . . ?
*Gdy yedeh dalshee/poslednee
aoothobos doh . . ?*

197 How much is the fare to the
city centre (downtown)/
railway (railroad) station/
airport?

Kolik stojí jízdenka do středu města/na železniční nádraží/na letiště?
Kollick stoyee yeezdehnkah doh stzhedoo mystah/nah zheleznichnee nahdrazhee/nah lehtishtye?

198 **Will you ell me when to get off?**
Reknete mi kde vystoupit?
Zheknyeteh mee gdeh vyhstowpith?

199 **Does this bus go to . . ?**
Jede tento autobus do . . ?
Yedeh tentoh aoothoboos doh . . ?

200 **Which number bus goes to . . ?**
Které číslo autobusu jede do . . ?
Ktehreh cheesloh aoothoboosoo yedeh doh . . ?

201 **May I have a single (one-way)/return (round-trip)/day ticket/book of tickets?**
Prosím jízdenku/zpáteční/denní lístek/svazek lístků.
Prosseem yeezdehnkoo/zpahtechnee/dehnee leesteck/svahzeck leestkoo.

Taxis

202 **I would like to go to . . .
How much will it cost?**
Jedu do . . . Kolik to stojí?
Yedoo doh . . . Kollick toh stoyee?

203 **Please stop here.**
Zastavte zde, prosím.
Zahstahvteh zdeh, prosseem.

204 **I would like to order a taxi today/tomorrow/at 2pm to go from . . . to . . .**
Rád bych objednal taxi na dnešek/zítra/ve čtrnáct hodin od . . . do . . .
Rahd bykh ohbyednahl taxi nah dnehsheck/zeetrah/ve shternahtst hoddinh od . . . doh . . .

Asking the Way

205 **Excuse me, do you speak English?**
Promiňte, mluvíte anglicky?
Prohmihnyete, mlooveeteh ahnlitskyh?

206 **Excuse me, is this the right way to . . ?**
Promiňte, jdu tudy správně . . .
Prohminyete, jduh toodi sprahvnye . . .

207 **. . . the cathedral/the tourist information office/the castle/the old town**
. . . ke katedrále/k turistické informační kanceláři/ke hradu/ke starému městu
ke kahtedrahleh/ktooristitskeh inforrmachnyee kahntselahrzhi/ke hradoo/ke stahrehmuh mnyestuh.

**C
Z
E
C
H**

**198
↑
207**

49

CZECH

208
↕
219

208 Can you tell me the way to the railway station/bus station/taxi rank (stand)/city centre (downtown)/beach?
Jak se dostanu na nádraží/autobusové nádraží/stanoviště autotaxi/střed města/pláž?
Yuck seh dostahnoo nah nahdrazhee/aootohboosoveh nahdrahzhee/stahnovishtye aoototaxi/stzhed mnyestah/plazh?

209 First/second/left/right/straight ahead.
První/druhá/nalevo/napravo/rovně.
Pervnee/droohah/nahlevoh/naprahvoh/rovnye.

210 Where is the nearest police station/post office?
Kde je nejbližší policejní stanice/pošta?
Gde yeh neyblizhshee politseynee stanitseh/poshtah?

211 Is it far?
Je to daleko?
Yeh toh dahlekoh?

212 Do I need to take a taxi/catch a bus?
Musím jet taxíkem/autobusem?
Mooseem yeht taxeekehm/aoothoboosehm?

213 Can you point to it on my map?

Ukažte to na mapě.
Ookazhte toh nah mahpye.

214 Thank you for your help.
Děkuji za Vaši pomoc.
Dyekooyi zah vashi pohmots.

SIGHTSEEING

215 Where is the Tourist Information office?
Kde jsou turistické informace?
Gde sow toorististikeh informatseh?

216 Where is the cathedral/church/museum?
Kde je katedrála/kostel/muzeum?
Gde ye kahtehdrahlah/kohstehl/moozeoom?

217 How much is the entrance (admission) charge?
Kolik je vstupné?
Kollick yeh vstoopneh?

218 Is there a reduction for children/students/senior citizens?
Je sleva pro děti/studenty/důchodce?
Yeh slehvah proh dyetee/stoodehnty/dookhodtseh?

219 What time does the next guided tour start?
Kdy jde další skupina s průvodcem?
Gdy ydeh dahlshee skoopinah ss proovohdtsehm?

220 One/two adults/children, please.

Jeden/dva dospělí/děti, prosím.

Yedehn/dvah dohspyelee/dyetee, prosseem.

221 May I take photographs here?

Smím tady fotografovat?

Smeem tahdi fotografohvaht?

ENTERTAINMENT

222 Can you recommend a good bar/nightclub?

Doporučíte dobrý bar/noční podnik?

Dohpohrucheeteh dohbree bahr/nochnee pohdnick?

223 Do you know what is on at the cinema (playing at the movies)/theatre at the moment?

Co dávají v kině/v divadle?

Tsoh dahvahyee vh kihnye/vh divahdleh?

224 I would like to book (purchase) . . . tickets for the matinée/evening performance on Monday.

Rád bych zamluvil . . . vstupenek na pondělní odpolední/večerní představení.

Rahd bykh zahmloovil . . . vstoopehnehck nah pohndyelnee ohdpohlehdnee pzhedstahvehnee.

225 What time does the film/performance start?

Kdy začíná film/představení?

Gdy zacheenah film/pzhedstahvehnee?

MEETING PEOPLE

226 Hello/Goodbye

Nazdar/Na shledanou

Nahzdahr/Nah-skhleddunnow

227 Good morning/good afternoon/good evening/goodnight.

Dobré jitro/dobrý den/dobrý večer/dobrou noc.

Dohbreh yitroh/dohbree den/dohbree vecherr/dohbroe nots.

228 Pleased to meet you.

Těší mě.

Tyehshee mnye.

229 How are you?

Jak se daří?

Yuck seh dazhee?

230 Fine, thank you. And you?

Dobře, děkuji. A vy?

Dobrzhe, dyekuhyi. A vi?

231 My name is . . .

Jmenuji se . . .

Menooyi seh . . .

232 This is my friend/boyfriend/girlfriend/husband/wife/brother/sister.

To je můj přítel/chlapec/dívka/manžel/manželka/bratr/sestra.

Toh jeh mooy pzheetehl/khlahpets/dyeefkah/mahnzhel/mahnzhelkah/brahtr/sehstrah.

233 Where are you travelling to?
Kam jedete?
Kahm yehdehteh?

234 I am/we are going to . . .
Jedu/jedeme do . . .
Yehdoo/yehdehmeh doh . . .

235 How long are you travelling for?
Jak dlouho cestujete?
Yuck dlowhoh tsehstooyeteh?

236 Where do you come from?
Odkud jste?
Odkood steh?

237 I am/we are from . . .
Jsem/jsme z . . .
Sem/sme z . . .

238 We're on holiday.
Jsme tu na dovolené.
Smeh tuh nahdohvohleneh.

239 This is our first visit here.
Jsme tady na návštěvě poprvé.
Smeh tahdi nah nahfshtyevye pohpreveh.

240 Would you like/May I have a cigarette?
Přejete si/Můžu si vzít cigaretu?
Pzheyeteh sih/Moozhuu sih vzeet tsigahrehtoo?

241 I am sorry, but I do not understand.
Promiňte, nerozumím Vám.
Prohminyteh, nehrozoomeem vahm.

242 Please speak slowly.
Mluvte, prosím, pomalu.
Mloofteh, prosseem, pohmahloo.

243 Do you mind if I smoke?
Smím si zapálit?
Smeem sih zahpahlit?

244 Do you have a light?
Můžu si připálit?
Moozhoo sih pzhipahlit?

245 I am waiting for my husband/wife/boyfriend/girlfriend.
Čekám na svého manžela/svou ženu/svého přítele/svou přítelkyni.
Chekahm na svehhoh mahnzhela/svoe zhenuh/svehhoh przheeteleh/svoe przheetelkynyi

TRAVELLING WITH CHILDREN

246 Do you have a high chair/baby-sitting service/cot?
Máte dětskou židli/opatrovatelskou službu/postýlku?
Mahteh dyetskow zhidli/ohpahtrohvahtelskow sloozhboo/posteelkoo?

247 Where is the nursery/playroom?
Kde jsou jesle/dětský pokoj?
Gde sow yesleh/dyetskee pockoy?

248 Where can I warm the baby's bottle?
Kde můžu ohřát lahvičku?

Gde moozhoo ohzhaht lahvichkoo?

COMMUNICATIONS

Post

249 How much will it cost to send a letter/postcard/this package to Britain/Ireland/America/Canada/Australia/New Zealand?
Kolik stojí dopis/pohlednice/tento balík do Británie/Irska/Ameriky/Kanady/Australie/na Nový Zéland?
Kollick stoyee dohpis/pohlehdnitseh/tehntoh bahleeck doh Britahnie/Irskah/Ahmehrickyh/Kahnahdy/Aoostrahliah/nah nohvee zehlahnd?

250 I would like one stamp/two stamps.
Prosím známku/dvě známky.
Prosseem znahmkoo/dvye znahmky.

251 I'd like . . . stamps for postcards to send abroad, please.
Potřebuji . . . poštovní známky na pohlednice do ciziny, prosím.
Potrzhebuhyi . . . pohshtovnyee znahmki nahpohhlednyitse do tsizini, prosseem.

Phones

252 I would like to make a telephone call/reverse the charges to (make a collect call to) . . .
Rád bych zatelefonoval/na účet volaného do . . .
Rahd bykh zahtelephonohvahl/nah oochet vohlahnehoo doh . . .

253 Which coins do I need for the telephone?
Jaké mince potřebuji pro telefon?
Yuckeh mintseh pohtzhebooyee proh telephohn?

254 The line is engaged (busy).
Linka je obsazena.
Linkah yeh obsazhenah.

255 The number is . . .
Číslo je . . .
Cheesloh yeh . . .

256 Hello, this is . . .
Haló, tady je . . .
Hulloh, tahdiye . . .

257 May I speak to . . ?
Mohu mluvit s . . ?
Mohu mluhvit s . . ?

258 He/She is not in at the moment. Can you call back?
Momentálně tady není.
Můžete zavolat později?
Mohmentahlnyeh tahdi nenyee. Moozheteh zahvolat pohzdyeyi?

CZECH

249
↑
258

MONEY

259 I would like to change these travellers' cheques (travelers' checks)/this currency/this Eurocheque.
Rád bych vyměnil tyto cestovní šeky/tuto měnu/tento Eurošek.
Rahd bykh vymnyenil tytoh tsehstovnee shecky/tootoh mnyenoo/tehntoh Ehurohsheck.

260 How much commission do you charge? (What is the service charge?)
Kolik účtujete provize?
Kollick oochtooyeteh prohvizeh?

261 Can I obtain money with my MasterCard?
Můžu vybrat peníze s MasterCard?
Moozhoo vybraht pehneezeh ss MasterCard?

SHOPPING

Names of Shops and Departments

262 Knihkupectví/Papírnictví
Knyihkoopetstvee/Pahpeernyictvee
Bookshop/Stationery

263 Klenotnictví/Dárky
Klehnotnyitstvee/Dahrrki
Jeweller's/Gifts

264 Obuv

Ohbuhf
Shoes

265 Železářství
Zhelezahrzhstvee
Hardware

266 Starožitnosti
Starrozhitnohstyi
Antiques

267 Holič/Kadeřník
Holich/Kahdehrzhnyeek
Hairdressers (men's)/(women's)

268 Tabák
Tahbahk
Tobacconist

269 Pekárna
Pehkahrrnah
Baker's

270 Samoobsluha
Sahmoh-opsloohah
Supermarket

271 Fotografické potřeby
Fotografitskeh pohtrzhebi
Photoshop

272 Hračky
Hrachki
Toys

273 Cestovní kancelář
Tsestovnyee kahntselahrzh
Travel Agent

274 Drogerie/Parfumerie
Drohgueriyeh/Parrfuhmehriye
Toiletries

²⁷⁵ **Desky**
Dahski
Records

In the Shop

²⁷⁶ **What time do the shops open/close?**
Kdy jsou obchody otevřené/zavřené?
Gdy sow obkhody ohtevzheneh/zavzheneh?

²⁷⁷ **Where is the nearest market?**
Kde je nejbližší trh?
Gdeye neyblizhshee treh?

²⁷⁸ **Can you show me the one in the window/this one?**
Můžete mi ukázat to ve výloze/tady to?
Moozhetemi uhkahzat toh veveelozeh/tahdi toh?

²⁷⁹ **Can I try this on?**
Můžu to vyzkoušet?
Moozhoo toh vyzkowshet?

²⁸⁰ **What size is this?**
Jaká je to velikost?
Yuckah yeh toh vehlikohst?

²⁸¹ **This is too large/too small/too expensive.**
Je to příliš velké/příliš malé/příliš drahé.
Yeto przheelish velkeh/przheelish mahleh/przheelish drah-heh.

²⁸² **Do you have any others?**
Máte nějaké jiné?
Mahte nyeyakeh yineh?

²⁸³ **My size is . . .**
Moje velikost je . . .
Moyeh velikohst ye . . .

²⁸⁴ **Where is the changing room/childrens'/cosmetic/ladieswear/menswear/food department?**
Kde jsou tady převlékárny/dětské oddělení/kosmetika/dámské/pánské oddělení/potraviny?
Gde sow tahdy pzhevlehkahrny/dyetskeh otdyelehnee/kohsmehtickah/dahmskeh/pahnskeh otdyelehne/potrahviny?

²⁸⁵ **I would like . . .**
Rád(a) bych . . .
Rahd(ah) bikh . . .

²⁸⁶ **I would like a quarter of a kilo/half a kilo/a kilo of bread/butter/cheese/ham/tomatoes.**
Prosím čtvrt kila/půl kila/kilo chleba/másla/sýra/šunky/rajčat.
Prosseem chtvert kilah/pool kilah/kiloh khlebbah/mahslah/seerah/shoonky/rahychat.

²⁸⁷ **How much is this?**
Kolik to stojí?
Kollick toh stoyee?

²⁸⁸ **I'll take this one, thank you.**
Vezmu si tuhle, děkuji.
Vezmoossi toohle, dyekuyi.

C Z E C H

**289
↑
300**

289 **Do you have a carrier
(shopping) bag?**
Máte sáček?
Mahteh sahcheck?

290 **Do you have anything
cheaper/larger/smaller/of
better quality?**
Máte něco lacinější/větší/
menší/kvalitnější?
*Mahteh nyetsoh latsinyejshee/
vyetshee/menshee/
kvahlitnyeyshee?*

291 **I would like a film for this
camera.**
Rád bych film pro tento aparát.
*Rahd bykh film proh tentoh
aparaht.*

292 **I would like some batteries,
the same size as this old
one.**
Rád bych baterie, stejné
velikosti jako tato stará.
*Rahd bykh bahtehrieh, stehyneh
vehlikohsti yuckoh ttahtoh
stharah.*

293 **Would you mind wrapping
this for me, please?**
Zabalte mi to, prosím.
Zahbahlteh mee toh, prosseem.

294 **Sorry, but you seem to have
given me the wrong
change.**
Promiňte, vrátil jste mi peníze
špatně.
*Prohminyteh, vrahtil steh mee
pehneezeh shpatnye.*

MOTORING

Car hire (Rental)

295 **I have ordered (rented) a car
in the name of . . .**
Zamluvil jsem auto pod
jménem . . .
*Zahmloovil sehm aootoh pohd
mehnehm . . .*

296 **How much does it cost to
hire (rent) a car for one day/
two days/one week?**
Kolik stojí vypůjčení auta na
den/dva dny/na týden?
*Kollick stoyee vypoojchenee
aootah nah den/dvah dnyh/nah
teeden?*

297 **Is the tank already full of
petrol (gas)?**
Je nádrž plná benzínu?
Yeh nahdrsh plnah behnzeenoo?

298 **Is insurance and tax
included? How much is the
deposit?**
Zahrnuje to pojištění a daně?
Kolik je záloha?
*Zahrnooye toh poyeeshtyenee ah
dahneh? Kollick ye zahlohah?*

299 **By what time must I return
the car?**
Do kdy musím vrátit auto?
*Doh gdyh moosseem vrahtit
aootoh?*

300 **I would like a small/family
car with a radio/cassette
player.**

Přeji si malé/rodinné auto s radiem/kazetou.
Pzheyee sih mahleh/roddineh aootoh ss rahdiehm/kazetow.

Asking the Way

301 **Excuse me, can you help me please?**
Promiňte, můžete mi, pomoci, prosím?
Prohminyeteh, moozhetemi pohmohtsi, prohsseem?

302 **How do I reach the motorway/main road?**
Jak se dostanu na dálnici/na hlavní silnici?
Yakseh dohstahnuh nadahlnyitsi/nahlavnyee silnyitsi?

303 **I think I have taken the wrong turning.**
Myslím, že jsem špatně odbočil.
Misleem zhessem shpatnyeh odbohchil.

304 **I am looking for this address.**
Hledám tuto adresu.
Hlehdahm tuhtoh adrehsuh.

305 **I am looking for the . . . hotel.**
Hledám hotel . . .
Hlehdahm hotel . . . .

306 **How far is it to . . . from here?**
Jak daleko je odsud do . . ?

Yak dahlekoh yeh odsuhd doh . . ?

307 **Carry straight on for . . . kilometres.**
Jeď te pořád rovně asi . . . kilometrů.
Yedye-teh porzhahd rovnyeh ahsee . . . kilohmehtroo.

308 **Take the next turning on the right/left.**
Na příští odbočce zahněte doprava/doleva.
Na przheeshtyee odboch-tse zahnyehteh doprahvah/dohlehvah.

309 **Turn right/left at the next crossroads/traffic lights.**
Odbočíte doprava/doleva na nejbližší křižovatce/u nejbližšího semaforu.
Odbohcheeteh dohprahvah/dohlehvah nah neyblish-shee krzhizhovaht-tse/uh neyblish-sheehoh sehmahforuh.

310 **You are going in the wrong direction.**
Jedete špatným směrem.
Yedyete shpahtneem smnyerem.

Parking

311 **How long can I park here?**
Jak dlouho tady můžu parkovat?
Yak dloehoh tahdi moozhu parrkohvaht?

MOTORING

C
Z
E
C
H

312
↑
327

312 **Is there a car park near here?**
Je tady někde blízko parkoviště?
Yeh tahdi nyegdeh bleeskoh parrkohveeshtye?

313 **At what time does this car park close?**
V kolik hodin se tohle parkoviště zavírá?
Fkollick hohdyin se toh-hle parrkohveeshtye zaveerah?

Signs and Notices

314 **Jednosměrný provoz.**
Yednohsmnyernee prohvohs.
One way.

315 **Zákaz vjezdu.**
Zahkaz vyezduh.
No entry.

316 **Parkování zakázáno.**
Parrkohvahnyee zahkahzahnoh.
No parking.

317 **Objížďka**
Obyeezhdyekah
Detour (diversion)

318 **Stůj/Stop.**
Stooy/Stop.
Stop.

319 **Dej přednost v jízdě.**
Dey przhednost vyeezdyeh.
Give way (yield).

320 **Kluzká vozovka/ Nebezpečí smyku.**
Kluhzkah vohzovkah/

Nebespechee smikuh.
Slippery road.

321 **Zákaz předjíždění.**
Zahkaz przhedyeezhdyenyee.
No overtaking.

At the Filling Station

322 **Unleaded (lead-free)/ Standard/Premium**
Bezolovnatý/Normál/Super
Besolovnahtee/Norrmahl/ Suhperr

323 **Fill the tank please.**
Plnou nádrž, prosím.
Pulnoe nahdrzh, prohseem.

324 **Do you have a road map of this area?**
Máte silniční mapu této oblasti?
Mahteh silnyichnyee mahpuh tehtoh oblahstyi?

325 **How much is the car-wash?**
Kolik stojí umytí auta?
Kolik stoyee uhmytyee owtah?

Breakdowns

326 **I've had a breakdown at . . .**
Porouchalo se mi auto u . . .
Poroekhahloh seh mi outoh uh . . .

327 **I am on the road from . . . to . . .**
Jsem na silnici z . . . do . . .
Sehm na silneetsi z . . . doh . . .

58

328 I can't move the car. Can
you send a tow-truck?
Nemohu s autem odjet.
Můžete poslat havarijní
odtahovou službu?
Nehmohhu soutehm odyeht.
Moozhete pohslat
hahvahriynyee ohdtahhovoe
sluhzhbuh?

329 I have a flat tyre.
Píchl(a) jsem pneumatiku.
Peekhl(a) sehm pneuhmahtikuh.

330 The windscreen
(windshield) has smashed/
cracked.
Mám rozbité/prasklé přední
sklo.
Mahm rozbihteh/prahskleh
przhednyee skloh.

331 There is something wrong
with the engine/brakes/
lights/steering/gearbox/
clutch/exhaust.
Něco není v pořádku s
motorem/s brzdami/se
světly/s převodovkou/se
spojkou/s výfukem.
Nyetso nehnyee v pohrzhahdkuh
smohtohrem/s br-zdahmee/
sesvyetly/sprzehvohdohvkoe/se
spoykoe/sveefookem

332 It's overheating.
Přehřívá se to.
Przhehrzheevahsseh toh.

333 It won't start.
Nechce to nastartovat.

Nekhtse toh nahstahrtohvat.

334 Where can I get it repaired?
Kde si to můžu nechat
opravit?
Gdehsi toh moozhu nekhaht
ohprahvit?

335 Can you take me there?
Můžete mě tam zavézt?
Moozhete mnye tahm zahvehst?

336 Will it take long to fix?
Bude oprava trvat dlouho?
Buhde ohprahva turvaht
dloehoh?

337 How much will it cost?
Kolik to bude stát?
Kollick toh boodeh staht?

Accidents

338 Can you help me? There
has been an accident.
Můžete mi pomoct? Stala se
nehoda.
Moozheteh me pomotst? Stahlah
seh nahodah.

339 Please call the police/an
ambulance.
Zavolejte, prosím, policii/
záchranku.
Zahvohlehyteh, prohseem,
pohlitssiyi/zahhrankooh.

340 Is anyone hurt?
Je někdo zraněný?
Jeh nyekdoh zranyehnee?

59

Traffic Offences

341 I'm sorry, I didn't see the sign.

Moc mě to mrzí, neviděl jsem tu značku.

Mohts mnye toh mrrzeeh, nevidyel sem to znachkooh.

342 Must I pay a fine? How much?

Musím zaplatit pokutu? Kolik?

Muhseem zahphlahtyit pohkuhtuh? Kolik?

343 Show me your documents.

Ukažte mi své doklady.

Ookazhte me sveh dohklahdi.

HEALTH

Pharmacy

344 Do you have anything for a stomachache/headache/ sore throat/toothache?

Máte něco proti bolení břicha/hlavy/v krku/zubu?

Mahteh nyetso prohti bohlehnee bzhikha/vh krckoo/zooboo?

345 I need something for diarrhoea (diarrhea)/ constipation/a cold/a cough/insect bites/ sunburn/travel (motion) sickness.

Potřebuji něco proti průjmu/zácpě/rýmě/kašli/poštípání hmyzem/spálení sluncem/cestovní nevolnosti.

Pohtzhehbooyi nyetsoh prohti prooymoo/zahtzpye/reemnye/kashli/poshteenahnee hmyzehm/spahlehnee slontsehm/tsehstovnee nehvohlnohsti.

346 How much/how many do I take?

Kolik toho mám vzít?

Kollick tooho mahm vzeet?

347 How often do I take it/ them?

Jak často to mám brát?

Yuck chashstoh toh mah braht?

348 How much does it cost?

Kolik to stojí?

Kollick toh stoyee?

349 Can you recommend a good doctor/dentist?

Můžete doporučit dobrého lékaře/zubaře?

Moozheteh dopohroochit dohbrehoh lehkazhe/zoobazhe?

350 Is it suitable for children?

Je to vhodné pro děti?

Yeh toh vhohdneh pro dyeti?

Doctor

351 I have a pain here/in my arm/leg/chest/stomach.

Bolí mě tady/v paži/v noze/hrudi/žaludku.

Bohlee mnye tahdy/vh pahzhi/vh nohzeh/hroodi/zhahloodkoo.

352 Please call a doctor, this is an emergency.

Prosím zavolejte doktora, je

to náhlá příhoda.
*Prosseem zahvohleyteh
dohktohrah, yeh toh nahlah
pzheehodah.*

353 I would like to make an appointment to see a doctor.

Rád bych se objednal u
doktora.
*Rahd bykh seh ohbyednahl oo
dohktohrah.*

354 I am diabetic/pregnant.

Mám cukrovku/jsem v jiném
stavu.
*Mahm tsookrovkoo/sem vh
yeenehm stahvoo.*

355 I need a prescription for . . .

Potřebuji předpis na . . .
*Pohtzhehbooyi pzhehdpiss
nah . . .*

356 Can you give me something to ease the pain?

Můžete mi dát něco na
ulehčení bolesti?
*Moozhehteh mee daht nyetso
nah oolehchenee bohlehstee?*

357 I am/he is/she is allergic to penicillin.

Mám alergii/Má alergii/Má
alergii na penicilin.
*Mahm ahlehrguiyi/Mah
ahlehrguiyi/Mah ahlehrguiyi
nah pehnitsileen.*

358 Does this hurt?

Bolí to?
Bohlee toh?

359 You must/he must/she must go to hospital.

Musíte/On musí/Ona musí
do nemocnice.
*Muhsseeteh/On muhsee/Onah
muhsee dohnehmohtsnyitseh.*

360 Take these once/twice / three times a day.

Užívejte je jednou/dvakrát/
třikrát denně.
*Oozheeveyteh yeh yednoe/
dvahkraht/trzhikraht denye.*

361 I am/he is/she is taking this medication.

Užívám/On užívá/Ona užívá
tyhle léky.
*Oozheevahm/On oozheevar/
Onah oozheevar teehleh lahky.*

362 I have medical insurance.

Mám lékařské pojištění.
*Mahm lehkahrzhskeh
poyishtyenyee.*

Dentist

363 I have toothache.

Bolí mě zub.
Bohlee mnye zoob.

364 My filling has come out.

Vypadla mně plomba.
Vypahdlah mnye plohmbah.

365 I do/do not want to have an injection first.
Přeji si/nepřeji si nejdříve injekci.
Pzheyee ssi/nehpzheyee ssi neydzheeveh inyeksti.

EMERGENCIES

366 Help!
Pomoc!
Pohmots!

367 Call an ambulance/a doctor/the police.
Zavolejte sanitku/doktora/policii!
Zahvohleyteh sahnitkoo/docktorah/pohlitsiyee!

368 I have had my travellers' cheques (travelers' checks)/credit cards/purse/handbag/rucksack (knapsack)/luggage/wallet stolen.
Byly mi ukradeny cestovní šeky/kreditní karty/peněženka/kabelka/ruksak/zavazadlo/náprsní taška.
Byly mee ookrahdehny tsehstohvnee shecky/krehditnih kahrty/pennyehzhenkah/kubbelkah/rooksack/zuvvahzuddloh/nahprsnee tashkah.

369 Can you help me, I have lost my daughter/son?
Pomozte mi, ztratil jsem dceru/syna.
Pohmohsteh mee, ztrahtil sem tseroo/seenah.

370 Please go away/leave me alone.
Běžte pryč/nechte mě být.
Byezhteh prych/nekhteh mnye byt.

371 Fire!
Hoří!
Hohrzhee!

372 I want to contact the British/American/Canadian/Irish/Australian/New Zealand/South African consulate.
Rád(a) bych se spojil(a) s britským/americkým/kanadským/irským/australským/novozélandským/jihoafrickým konzulátem.
Rahd(ah) byh seh spohyilah s britskeem/ahmehritskeem/kahnahtskeem/irskeem/aoostralskeem/nohvoh zehlahntskeem/yihoh-ahfritskeem konsuhlahtem.

Introduction

French is spoken as a first language not only in France but also in Monaco, in the French-speaking areas of Belgium (the south and west, and Brussels) and in western Switzerland (including the cities of Geneva and Lausanne), and it is widely spoken in Luxembourg. In all of these regions there will be quite a few people who can understand or speak some English, particularly in the more tourist-frequented localities, but it will pay dividends to at least attempt to speak some French, particularly in France itself.

F R E N C H

Addresses for travel and tourist information

UK: *Maison de la France*, 178 Piccadilly, London W1V 0AL; tel: 0891 244123. *Belgian National Tourist Office*, Premier House, 2 Gayton Rd, Harrow, Middlesex HA1 2XU; tel: (0181) 861 3300. *Swiss National Tourist Office*, Swiss Centre, London W1V 8EE; tel: (0171) 734 1921.

USA: *French Government Tourist Office*, 610 Fifth Avenue, New York, NY 10020-2452; tel: (212) 757-1125. *Belgian National Tourist Office*, 745 Fifth Avenue (Suite 714), New York, NY 10151; tel: (212) 758-8130. *Swiss National Tourist Office*, Swiss Center, 608 Fifth Avenue, New York, NY 10020; tel: (212) 757-5944.

ESSENTIALS

Alphabet

A *ah*	B *beh*
C *seh*	D *de*
E *eur*	F *eff*
G *ge*	H *ash*
I *ee*	J *ji*
K *ka*	L *elle*
M *emme*	N *enne*
O *o*	P *pe*
Q *ku*	R *erre*
S *esse*	T *te*
U *u*	V *ve*
W *dooble ve*	X *iks*
Y *ee grec*	Z *zede*

Basic Words and Phrases

1 Yes **No**
Oui Non
Wee *nawng*

2 Please **Thank you**
S'il vous plaît Merci
Seel voo pleh *Mehrsee*

3 That's O.K. **Perhaps**
Ça va Peut-être
Sahr vahr *Purtehtr*

4 To **From**
à De
ah *der*

5 Here **There**
Ici Là
Eesee *lah*

6 None **Also**
Aucun Aussi
Okang *Ossee*

7 How **When**
Comment Quand
Kommahng *kahng*

8 What **Why**
Quel Pourquoi
kehl *poorkwah*

9 I don't understand.
Je ne comprends pas.
Zher ner kawngprahng pah.

10 I don't speak French.
Je ne parle pas français.
Zher ner pahrl pah frahngsay.

11 Do you speak English?
Vous parlez anglais?
Voopahrlay ahnglay?

12 Can you please write it down?
Pouvez-vous l'écrire s'il vous plaît?
Poovehvoo laycreer seelvooplay?

¹³ **Can you please speak more slowly?**
Pouvez-vous parler plus lentement s'il vous plaît?
Poovehvoo pahrlay plew lahntermahng seelvooplay?

¹⁴ **How much does it/this cost?**
Quel est le prix?
Kehl eh ler pree?

Days

¹⁵ **Monday** **Tuesday**
Lundi Mardi
Langdee *Mahrdee*

¹⁶ **Wednesday** **Thursday**
Mercredi Jeudi
Mehrkrerdee *Zhurdee*

¹⁷ **Friday** **Saturday**
Vendredi Samedi
Vahndrerdee *Sahmdee*

¹⁸ **Sunday** **Morning**
Dimanche Le matin
Deemahngsh *Ler mahtang*

¹⁹ **Afternoon** **Evening**
L'après-midi Le soir
Lahpreh meedee *Ler swahr*

²⁰ **Night** **Week**
La nuit La semaine
Lah nwee *Lah sermehn*

²¹ **Yesterday** **Tomorrow**
Hier Demain
Yehr *Dermang*

Numbers

²² **Zero** **One**
Zéro Un
Zayroa Ang

²³ **Two** **Three**
Deux Trois
Dur *Trwah*

²⁴ **Four** **Five**
Quatre Cinq
Kahtr *Sangk*

²⁵ **Six** **Seven**
six Sept
Seess *Seht*

²⁶ **Eight** **Nine**
Huit Neuf
Weet *Nurf*

²⁷ **Ten** **Eleven**
Dix Onze
Deess *Awngz*

²⁸ **Twelve** **Thirteen**
Douze Treize
Dooz *Trehz*

²⁹ **Fourteen** **Fifteen**
Quatorze Quinze
Kahtorz *Kangz*

³⁰ **Sixteen** **Seventeen**
Seize Dix-sept
Sehz *Deess seht*

³¹ **Eighteen** **Nineteen**
Dix-huit Dix-neuf
Deez weet *Deez nurf*

³² **Twenty** **Twenty-one**
Vingt Vingt et un
Vang *Vang tay ang*

³³ **Twenty-two** **Thirty**
Vingt-deux Trente
Vangt dur *Trahngt*

F
R
E
N
C
H

13
↑
33

FRENCH

34
↕
54

34 Forty   **Fifty**
Quarante   Cinquante
Kahrahngt   *Sangkahnt*

35 Sixty   **Seventy**
Soixante   Soixante-dix
Swahssahngt   *Swassahngt deess*

36 Eighty   **Ninety**
Quatre-vingts   Quatre-vingt-dix
Kahtrer vang   *Kahtrer vang deess*

37 One hundred Five hundred
Cent   Cinq cents
Sahng   *Sang sahng*

38 One thousand One million
Mille   Un million
Meel   *Ang meelyawng*

Time

39 9.00
Neuf heures
Nurv urr

40 9.05
Neuf heures cinq
Nurv urr sangk

41 9.10
Neuf heures dix
Nurv urr deess

42 9.15
Neuf heures et quart
Nurv urr eh kahr

43 9.20
Neuf heures vingt
Nurv urr vang

44 9.25
Neuf heures vingt-cinq
Nurv urr vang sangk

45 9.30
Neuf heures et demie
Nurv urr eh dermee

46 9.35
Dix heures moins vingt-cinq
Dee zurr mwang vang sangk

47 9.40
Dix heures moins vingt
Dee zurr mwang vang

48 9.45
Dix heures moins le quart
Dee zurr mwang le kahr

49 9.50
Dix heures moins dix
Dee zurr mwang deess

50 9.55
Dix heures moins cinq
Dee zurr mwang sangk

51 12.00/Midday/Midnight
Douze heures/Midi/Minuit
Doowz urr/meedee/meenurhee

52 What time is it?
Quelle heure est-il?
Kel urr ehteel?

53 It is . . .
Il est. . .
Eel eh . . .

ARRIVING AND DEPARTING

Airport

54 Excuse me, where is the check-in desk for . . . airline?
Excusez-moi, où est le comptoir
d'enregistrement de . . ?
Ekskewsehmwah, oo eh ler

kongtwahr
dahngrehzheestrehmahng der . . ?

55 **What is the boarding gate/
time for my flight?**
Quelle est la porte
d'embarquement/l'heure
d'embarquement de mon vol?
*Kehl eh lah pohrt
dahngbahrkehmahng/lurr
dahngbahrkehmahng der mawng
vohl?*

56 **How long is the delay likely
to be?**
Le retard est de combien?
Ler rurtahr eh der kawngbyang?

57 **Where is the duty-free shop?**
Où est la boutique hors-taxe?
Oo eh lah bootik ohrtahks?

58 **Which way is the baggage
reclaim?**
Où se trouve l'aire de réception
des bagages?
*Oo ser troov lair der
rehssehpsseeawng deh bahgahzh?*

59 **Where can I get the bus to
the city centre?**
Où puis-je prendre le bus pour
le centre-ville?
*Oo pweezh prahngdr ler bews poor
ler sahngtr veel?*

Train Station

60 **Where is the ticket office/
information desk?**
Où se trouve le guichet/le
bureau de renseignements?
Oo ser troov ler geesheh/ler

bewroa der rahngsehniehmahng?

61 **Which platform does the
train to . . . depart from?**
De quel quai part le train
pour . . ?
Der kehl kay pahr ler trang poor . . ?

62 **Where is platform . . ?**
Où se trouve le quai . . ?
Oo ser troov ler kay . . ?

63 **When is the next train to . . ?**
Quand est le prochain train
pour . . ?
Kahng eh ler proshang trang poor . . ?

64 **Is there a later train to . . ?**
Y-a-t-il un train plus tard pour
. . ?
*Ee ahteel ang trang plew tahr
poor . . ?*

Port

65 **How do I get to the port?**
Pour aller au port, s'il vous
plaît?
Poor ahleh oh por, seelvooplay?

66 **When is the next sailing
to . . ?**
Quand est le prochain départ
pour . . ?
*Kahng eh ler proshang dehpahr
poor . . ?*

67 **Can I catch an earlier ferry
with this ticket?**
Puis-je prendre un ferry plus tôt
avec ce billet?
*Pweezh prahngdrer ang ferry plew
tow ahvehk ser beeyeh?*

F
R
E
N
C
H

55
↕
67

Notices and Signs

68 Voiture-restaurant
Vwature restorahn
Buffet (Dining) Car

69 Autobus
Otoebewss
Bus

70 Eau potable/Eau non potable
Oa poatahbl/Oa nawng poatahbl
Drinking/Non-drinking water

71 Entrée
Ahngtray
Entrance

72 Sortie
Soartee
Exit

73 Renseignements
Rahngsehnyermahng
Information

74 Consigne
Kawngsseeñ
Left Luggage (Baggage Claim)

75 Consigne automatique
Kawngsseeñ oatomahtick
Luggage Lockers

76 Poste
Peost
Post Office

77 Quai
Kay
Platform

78 Gare
Gahr
Railway (Railroad) Station

79 Aéroport
Ahehrohpohr
Airport

80 Port
Pohr
Port

81 Restaurant
Rehstoarahng
Restaurant

82 Fumeurs/non fumeurs
Fewmurh/nawng fewmurh
Smoking/Non-Smoking

83 Téléphone
Taylayphone
Telephone

84 Guichet
Gueechay
Ticket Office

85 Enregistrement des bagages
Ahngrehzheestrehmahng day bahgahzh
Check-in Desk

86 Horaires
Oarayrh
Timetables (Schedules)

87 Toilettes
Twahlayt
Toilets (Restrooms)

88 Hommes
Ommh
Gentlemen

89 Femmes
Dahm
Ladies'

90 Tramway

FRENCH

68
↑
90

Trahmway
Tram (Streetcar)

91 Métro
Maytroa
Underground (Subway)

92 Salle d'attente
Sahldahtahngth
Waiting-Room

Buying a Ticket

**93 I would like a first-class/
second-class single (one-
way)/return (round-trip)
ticket to . . .**
Je voudrais un billet de première
classe/deuxième classe aller/
aller-retour pour . . .
*Zher voodray ang beeyeh
prermyehr/durzyehm klahss
ahlay/ahlay rertoor poor . . .*

**94 Is my rail pass valid on this
train/ferry/bus?**
Est-ce que ma carte ferroviaire
est valable pour ce train/ce
ferry/ce bus?
*Ehss ker mah kahrt fehrohveeair
eh vahlahblh dahng ser trang/ser
ferry/ser bewss?*

**95 I would like an aisle/window
seat.**
Je voudrais être près de l'allée/la
fenêtre.
*Zher voodray aytr pray der
lahlaeh/lah fernaytr.*

96 No smoking/smoking, please.
Non fumeur/fumeur.
Nawng fewmur/fewmur.

**97 We would like to sit
together.**
Nous aimerions être assis
ensemble.
*Noo aymerreeawng ehtr ahssee
ahngsahngbl.*

**98 I would like to make a seat
reservation.**
Je voudrais réserver une place.
*Zher voodray rehzehrveh ewn
plahss.*

**99 I would like to reserve a
couchette/sleeper for one
person/two people/for my
family.**
J'aimerais réserver une
couchette/place de voiture-lit
pour une personne/deux
personnes/pour ma famille.
*Zhaymerray rehzehrveh ewn
kooshayt/plahss der vwature-lee
poor ewn pehrson/dur perhson/
poor mah fahmeeye.*

**100 I would like to reserve a
cabin.**
Je voudrais réserver une cabine.
*Zher voodray rehzehrveh ewn
kahbeen.*

Timetables (Schedules)

101 Arrive
Ahrivh
Arrive

102 S'arrête à
Sahrayth ah
Calls (Stops) at

103 Restauration
Restoarahsseeaawng
Catering Service

104 Changez à
Chahngzay ah . . .
Change at . . .

105 Correspondance
Koarespawngdahngss
Connection

106 Tous les jours
Too ley joorh
Daily

107 Toutes les quarante minutes
Tooth lay kahrahngt menewt
Every 40 Minutes

108 Première classe
Prermeeayrh class
First-Class

109 Toutes les heures
Toot lay zur
Hourly

110 Il est recommandé de réserver sa place
Eel eh rekomahngday der rayzayrvoay sa plahs
Seat reservations are recommended

111 Deuxième classe
Dersieme class
Second-class

112 Supplément à payer
Sewplaymahng ah payay
Supplement Payable

113 Par
Pah
Via

Luggage

114 How much will it cost to send (ship) my luggage in advance?
Quel est le prix pour envoyer mes bagages en avance?
Kehl eh ler pree poor ahngwahllay meh bahgahz ahng ahvahngss?

115 Where is the left luggage (baggage claim) office?
Où se trouve la consigne?
Oo ser troov lah kawngseen?

116 What time do you open/close?
A quelle heure ouvrez-vous/fermez-vous?
Ah kehl ur oovrayvoo/fairmehvoo?

117 Where are the luggage trolleys (carts)?
Où se trouve les chariots à bagages?
Oo ser troov leh shahryo ah bahgahzh?

118 Where are the lockers?
Où se trouve la consigne automatique?
Oo ser troov lah kawngseen awtoematique?

119 I have lost my locker key.
J'ai perdu la clé de mon casier.
Zhay payrdew lah kleh der mawng kahzeeay.

70

ARRIVING/TOURIST OFFICE/ACCOMMODATION

On Board

120 Is this seat taken?
Est-ce que cette place est libre?
Ehsker sayt plahss eh leebr?

121 Excuse me, you are sitting in my reserved seat.
Excusez-moi, vous occupez la place que j'ai réservée.
Ehskewzaymwah voo okewpeh lah plahss ker zay rehzehrveh.

122 Which station is this?
Quelle est cette gare?
Kehl eh sayt gahr?

123 What time is this train/bus/ferry/flight due to arrive/depart?
A quelle heure arrive/part le train/le bus/le ferry?
Ah kehlur ahrivh/pahr ler trang/ler bewss/ler ferry?

124 Will you wake me just before we arrive?
Pouvez-vous me réveiller avant l'arrivée?
Poovay voo mer rehvehlleh ahvahng lahreeveh?

Customs and Passports

125 Les passeports, s'il vous plaît!
Leh pahsspor, seelvooplay!
Passports, please!

126 I have nothing/wine/spirits (alcohol)/tobacco to declare.
Je n'ai rien à déclarer/J'ai du vin/de l'acool/du tabac à déclarer.

Zher neh reeang ah dehklahreh/zhay dew vang/der lahlkol/dew tahbah ah dehklahreh.

127 I shall be staying for . . . days/weeks/months.
Je vais rester . . . jours/semaines/mois.
Zhe veh resteh . . . zoor/sermehn/mwah.

AT THE TOURIST OFFICE

128 Do you have a map of the town/area?
Avez-vous une carte de la ville/région?
Ahveh-voo ewn cart der lah veel/rehjyawng?

129 Can I reserve accommodation here?
Puis-je réserver un logement ici?
Peweezh rehzehrveh ang lozhmahng eesee?

130 Do you have a list of accommodation?
Vous avez une liste d'hôtels?
Voozahveh ewn leesst dohtehl?

ACCOMMODATION

Hotels

131 I have a reservation in the name of . . .
J'ai fait une réservation au nom de . . .
Zheh feh ewn rehsehrvahssyawng o nawng der . . .

132 I wrote to/faxed/telephoned
you last month/last week in . . .
Je vous ai écrit/faxé/téléphoné
le mois dernier/la semaine
dernière.
*Zher voozeh ehkree/faxeh/
tehlehfoneh ler mwah dehrnyeh/
lah sermayn dehrnyair.*

133 Do you have any rooms free?
Vous avez des chambres
disponibles?
*Voozahveh deh shahngbr
deesspohneebl?*

134 I would like to reserve a
single/double room with/
without bath/shower.
Je voudrais réserver une
chambre pour une personne/
pour deux personnes avec/sans
salle de bain/douche.
*Zhe voodray rehsehrveh ewn
shahngbr poor ewn pehrson/poor
dur pehrson avek/sawns sal der
banne/doosh.*

135 I would like bed and
breakfast/(room and) half
board/(room and) full board.
Je voudrais le petit-déjeuner/la
demi-pension/la pension
complète.
*Zher voodray ler pewtee-dehjewoneh/
lah dermee-pahngsyawong/lah
pahngsyawong kawongplait.*

136 How much is it per night?
Quel est le prix pour une nuit?
Khel eh ler pree poor ewn nuwy?

137 Is breakfast included?

Est-ce que le petit-déjeuner est
compris?
*Ehsker ler pertee dehjerneh eh
kawngpree?*

138 May I see the room?
Puis-je voir la chambre?
Pweezh vwahr lah shahngbr?

139 Do you have any cheaper
rooms?
Avez-vous des chambres moins
chères?
Ahvehvoo deh shahngbr mooang shayr?

140 I would like to take the room.
Je prends la chambre.
Zhe prahng lah shangbr.

141 I would like to stay for . . .
nights.
Je voudrais rester . . . nuits.
Zhe voodray resteh . . . newyh.

142 The shower/light/tap doesn't
work.
La douche/la lumière/le robinet
ne marche pas.
*Lah doosh/lah luhmiair/ler
rohbeenay ner marsh pah.*

143 At what time/where is
breakfast served?
A quelle heure/où servez-vous
le petit-déjeuner?
*Ah khel ur/ooh serveh-voo ler
perteedehjerneh?*

144 What time do I have to
check-out?
A quelle heure dois-je laisser la
chambre?
*Ah khel ur dwahz lehseh lah
shahngbr?*

145 Can I have the key to room no
. . ?
Je voudrais la clé de la chambre . . .
*Zher voodray lah klay der lah
shahngbr . . .*

146 My room number is . . .
Le numéro de ma chambre
est . . .
*ler newomehro der mah shahngbr
eh . . .*

147 Do you accept travellers'
cheques/Eurocheques/credit
cards?
Vous acceptez les chèques de
voyage/les Eurochèques/les
cartes de crédit?
*Voos aksepteh leh sheck der
vwoyazh/laze eurosheck/leh kart
der krehdee?*

148 May I have the bill please?
Pouvez-vous me donner la note,
s'il vous plaît?
*Poovehvoo mer doneh lah nott
seelvooplay?*

149 Excuse me, I think there is a
mistake in this bill.
Excusez-moi, mais je crois qu'il
ya a une erreur dans la note.
*Ehskewzaymwah, zhe kwaw ke eel
ee ah oon errer don la not.*

Youth Hostels

150 How much is a dormitory bed
per night?
Quel est le prix d'un lit en
dortoir par nuit?
Kehl eh ler pree dang lee ahng

dortwarr pahr newy?*

151 I am/am not an HI member.
Je suis/Je ne suis pas membre
d'une Auberge de Jeunesse.
*Zhe sewy/zhe ner sewy pah
mahngbr dewn obehrz der
jurnehss.*

152 May I use my own sleeping
bag?
Est-ce que je peux me servir de
mon propre sac de couchage?
*Ehsker zhe pur mer sairvyr der
mawng proprer sahk der
kooshahz?*

153 What time do you lock the
doors at night?
A quelle heure fermez-vous la
porte le soir?
*Ah kehlur fehrmehvoo lah port ler
swahr?*

Camping

154 May I camp here for the
night/two nights?
Puis-je camper ici pour la nuit/
deux nuits?
*Pweehze kahngpeh ysee poor lah
newy/dur newy?*

155 Where can I pitch my tent?
Où puis-je dresser ma tente?
Oo pweehze dresseh mah tahngt?

156 How much does it cost for
one night/week?
Quel est le prix par nuit/par
semaine?
*Kehl eh ler pree pahr newy/pahr
sermayn?*

157 Where can we park our caravan?
Où ouvons-nous garer notre caravane?
Oo poovong noo gahreh nohtr kahrahvahn?

158 Where are the washing facilities?
Où se trouve le bloc sanitaire?
Oo ser troov ler block sanitaire?

159 Is there a restaurant/supermarket/swimming pool on site/nearby?
Y-a-t-il un restaurant/supermarché/piscine sur place/près d'ici?
Yahteel ang restorahng/supermahrsheh/peassinn sewr plahss/pray deessee?

160 Do you have a safety deposit box?
Avez-vous un coffre-fort?
Ahvehvoo ang koffr-for?

EATING AND DRINKING

Cafés and Bars

161 I would like a cup of/two cups of/another coffee/tea.
Je voudrais une tasse de/deux tasses de/encore une tasse de café/thé.
Zher voodray ewn tahss der/der tahss der/oncaw ewn tahss der kafeh/teh.

162 With/without milk/sugar.
Avec/sans lait/sucre.
Ahvek/sahng lay/sewkr.

163 I would like a bottle/glass/two glasses of mineral water/red wine/white wine, please.
Je voudrais une bouteille/un verre/deux verres d'eau minérale/de vin rouge/de vin blanc, s'il vous plaît.
Zhe voodray ewn bootayy/ang vair/der vair doa mynehral/der vang roozh/der vang blahng, sylvooplay.

164 I would like a beer/two beers, please.
Je voudrais une bière/deux bières, s'il vous plaît.
Zhe voodray ewn byair/der byair, sylvooplay.

165 May I have some ice?
Puis-je avoir de la glace?
Pweezh ahvoar der lah glass?

166 Do you have any matches/cigarettes/cigars?
Avez-vous des allumettes/des cigarettes/ des cigares?
Ahveh-voo dehzahlewmaitt/deh cigaraytt/deh ssigar?

Restaurants

167 Can you recommend a good/inexpensive restaurant in this area?
Pouvez-vous recommander un bon restaurant/un restaurant bon marché dans les environs?
Pooveh-voo rekomahngdeh ewn bawng restorahng/ewn restorahng bawng mahrcheh dahng lehzahngvyrawng?

F R E N C H

¹⁶⁸ I would like a table for . . .
people.
Je voudrais une table pour . . .
personnes.
*Zher voodray ewn tabl poor . . .
pehrson.*

¹⁶⁹ Do you have a non-smoking
area?
Vous avez une zone non-
fumeurs?
*Voozahvah ewn zohn nong
fewmur?*

¹⁷⁰ Waiter/Waitress!
Garçon/Mademoiselle, s'il vous
plaît!
*Garssawng, madmwahzel,
sylvooplay!*

¹⁷¹ Do you have a set menu/
children's menu/wine list?
Avez-vous un table d'hôte/un
menu pour enfants/la carte des
vins?
*Ahvehvoo ewn tabler d'ot/ewn
menew poor ahngfahng/lah list
deh vang?*

¹⁷² Do you have any vegetarian
dishes, please?
Avez-vous des plats
végétariens, s'il vous plaît?
*ahvehvoo der plah
vehgehtahryang, sylvooplay?*

¹⁷³ Are there any local
specialities?
Il y a des spécialités locales?
*Eel ee a deh sawng leh
spayseeahleeteh locahl?*

¹⁷⁴ Are vegetables included?

Est-ce que les légumes sont
compris?
*Essker leh lehgewm sawng
kohngpree?*

¹⁷⁵ Could I have it well-cooked/
medium/rare please?
Je le voudrais bien cuit/ à point/
saignant.
*Zher ler voodray beeang kwee/ah
pwang/saynyang.*

¹⁷⁶ What does this dish consist
of?
En quoi consiste ce plat?
Ahng koah kawngsist ser plah?

¹⁷⁷ I would like the set menu,
please.
Je voudrais la carte, s'il vous
plaît.
Zher voodray lah cart, sylvooplay.

¹⁷⁸ We have not been served yet.
Nous n'avons pas été encore
servis.
*Noo nahvawng pahzehteh ahngkor
sehrvee.*

¹⁷⁹ Excuse me, this is not what I
ordered.
Excusez-moi, ce n'est pas ce que
j'ai commandé.
*Ekskewzaymwah, ser nay pah ser
ker zheh komandeh.*

¹⁸⁰ May I have some/some more
bread/water/coffee/tea?
Puis-je avoir du pain/encore du
pain/de l'eau/du café/du thé?
*Pweezh ahvoar dew pang/ahngkor
dew pang/der lo/dew kafeh/dew
teh?*

168
↕
180

FRENCH

181 **May I have the bill, please?**
L'addition, s'il vous plaît!
Laddyssyawng, sylvooplay!

182 **Does this bill include service?**
Est-ce que le service est compris?
Ehsk ler sehrveess eh kawngpree?

183 **Do you accept travellers' cheques (travelers' checks)/ Eurocheques/MasterCard/US dollars?**
Prenez-vous les chèques de voyage/les eurochèques/la Mastercard/les dollars américains?
Prernehvoo leh cheque der vwahahzh/leh eurocheque/lah Mastercard/leh dolar ahmehrykang?

184 **Can I have a receipt, please?**
Je pourrais avoir un reçu sil vous plaît?
Zher pooray avwahr ahng rerssew seelvooplay?

185 **Where is the toilet (restroom), please?**
Où sont les toilettes, s'il vous plaît?
Oo sawng leh twahlaitt, sylvooplay?

On the Menu

186 **First courses**
Entrées
Ahngtray.

187 **Soups**
Soupes
Soup

188 **Main courses**
Plats principaux
Plah prangseepo.

189 **Fish dishes**
Poissons
Pooahsong

190 **Meat dishes**
Viandes
Veeanhd

191 **Vegetarian dishes**
Plats végétariens
Plah vehzhehtahryang

192 **Cheese**
Fromages
Frohmahzh

193 **Desserts**
Desserts
Dehser

194 **Specialities**
Spécialités
Spehsseeahleeteh

GETTING AROUND

Public Transport

195 **Where is the bus stop/coach station/nearest metro (subway) station?**
Où se trouve l'arrêt d'autobus le plus proche/la gare routière/la station de métro la plus proche?
Oo ser troov lahreh dotobewss la plew prosh/lah gahr rootyair/lah stassion der mehtro lah plew prosh?

196 When is the next/last bus to . . ?

A quelle heure est le prochain/ dernier autobus pour . . ?

Ahkehlur eh ler prochang/ dehrneeyeh otobewss poor . . ?

197 How much is the fare to the city centre (downtown)/ railway (railroad) station/ airport?

Quel est le prix du billet pour le centre-ville/la gare/l'aéroport?

Kehl eh ler pree dew beeyeh poor ler sahngtr-veel/lah gahr/ lahehropor?

198 Will you tell me when to get off?

Pouvez-vous me le dire quand je devrai descendre?

Poovehvoo mer deer kahng zher deuvreh dehssahngdr?

199 Does this bus go to . . ?

Est-ce que cet autobus va à . . ?

Ehsk sayt otobewss vah ah . . ?

200 Which number bus goes to . . ?

Quel est le numéro de l'autobus qui va à . . ?

Khel eh ler newmehro de lotobewss kee vah ah . . ?

201 May I have a single (one-way)/return (round-trip)/day ticket/book of tickets?

Puis-je avoir un aller/un aller-retour/un ticket pour la journée/un carnet de tickets?

Pweezh ahvwahr ewn ahleh/ewn ahleh-retoor/ewn tickeh poor lah

joorneh/ewn kahrneh der tickeh?

Taxis

202 I would like to go to . . . How much will it cost?

Je voudrais aller à . . . Quel est le prix?

Zhe voodray ahleh ah . . . kehl eh ler pree?

203 Please stop here.

Arrêtez ici, s'il vous plaît.

Ahrehteh yssy, sylvooplay.

204 I would like to order a taxi today/tomorrow/at 2pm to go from . . . to . . .

Je voudrais réserver un taxi aujourd'hui/demain/à deux heures pour aller de . . . à . . .

Zher voodray rehzehrveh ewn taxi ojoordewee/dermang/ah derzur poor ahleh der . . . ah . . .

Asking the Way

205 Excuse me, do you speak English?

Excusez-moi, parlez-vous anglais?

Ekskewsehmwah, pahrlehvoo ahnglay?

206 Excuse me, is this the right way to . . ?

Excusez-moi, c'est la bonne direction pour . . ?

Ekskewzaymwah, seh lah bon deerekseeawng poor . . ?

77

FRENCH

207 **. . . the cathedral/the tourist information office/the castle/ the old town.**

. . . la cathédrale/l'office de tourisme/le château/la vieille ville.

. . . lah kahtehdrahl/lohfeece de tooreezm/ler chateau/lah veeay veel

208 **Can you tell me the way to the railway (railroad) station/ bus station/taxi rank (stand)/ city centre (downtown)/ beach?**

Pour aller à la gare/gare routière/station de taxis/au centre ville/à la plage, s'il vous plaît?

Poor ahlee ah lah gahr/gahr rootyair/stahssion der taxi/oh sahngtr veel/ah lah plahzh, sylvooplay?

209 **First/second left/right/ straight ahead.**

Première/deuxième à gauche/à droite/tout droit.

Prermeyair/derzeaim ah goash/ah drwaht/too drwah.

210 **Where is the nearest police station/post office?**

Où se trouve le poste de police/ le bureau de poste le plus près?

Oo ser troov ler post der poliss/ler bewro der post ler plew pray?

211 **Is it far?**

C'est loin?

seh looang?

212 **Do I need to take a taxi/catch a bus?**

Faut-il prendre un taxi/un autobus?

Foteel prahngdr ewn taxi/ewn otobewss?

213 **Can you point to it on my map?**

Pouvez-vous me le montrer sur la carte?

Poovehvoo mer ler mawngtreh sewr lah kart?

214 **Thank you for your help.**

Merci pour votre aide.

Mehrsee poor votrayd.

SIGHTSEEING

215 **Where is the Tourist Information office?**

Où se trouve l'office de tourisme?

Oo ser troov loffyss de toorism?

216 **Where is the cathedral/ church/museum?**

Où se trouve la Cathédrale/ l'Église/le Musée?

Oo ser troov lah katehdral/ lehglyz/ler mewzeh?

217 **How much is the entrance (admission) charge?**

Quel est le prix d'entrée?

Khel eh ler pree delahngtreh?

218 **Is there a reduction for children/students/senior citizens?**

Y-a-til une réduction pour les enfants/les étudiants/les

personnes du troisième âge?
*Eeahteel ewn rehdewkssyawng
poor lehzahngfahng/
lehzehtewdyahng/leh pehrson dew
trwahzyehm ahzh?*

219 **What time does the next guided tour start?**
A quelle heure commence la prochaine visite guidée?
Ah kehlur komahngs lah proshain vysyt gueedeh?

220 **One/two adults/children, please.**
Un/deux adulte(s /enfant(s), s'il vous plaît.
Ewn/durzahdewlt/ahngfahng, seel voo play.

221 **May I take photographs here?**
Je peux prendre des photos ici?
Zher per prangdr deh phowtoh eessee?

ENTERTAINMENT

222 **Can you recommend a good bar/nightclub?**
Pouvez-vous me recommander un bar/une boîte de nuit?
Poovehvoo mer rerkomahngdeh ang bahr/ewn boaht der newee?

223 **Do you know what is on at the cinema (playing at the movies)/theatre at the moment?**
Savez-vous ce qu'il y a au cinéma/théâtre en ce moment?
Sahvehvoo ser keelyah o cinema/ tehahtr ahng ser momahng?

224 **I would like to book (purchase) . . . tickets for the matinée/evening performance on Monday.**
Je voudrais réserver . . . places pour la séance en matinée/ soirée lundi.
Zher voodray rehzehrveh . . . plass poor lah sehahngss ahng mahteeneh/swoiray lerndi.

225 **What time does the film/ performance start?**
A quelle heure commence la séance/la représentation?
Ah kehlur komahngss lah sehahngs/lah rerprehzahngtahssyawng?

MEETING PEOPLE

226 **Hello/Goodbye.**
Bonjour/Au revoir.
Bawngzhoor/oa revwahr.

227 **Good morning/good afternoon/good evening/ goodnight.**
Bonjour/bonjour/bonsoir/ bonne nuit.
Bawngzhoor/bawngzhoor/ bawngswahr/bun nwee.

228 **Pleased to meet you.**
Enchanté de faire votre connaissance.
Ahngsahngteh der fair votr konehssahngss.

229 **How are you?**
Comment allez-vous?
Komahng ahlehvoo?

230 Fine, thank you. And you?
Bien merci. Et vous?
Beeang mehrsee. Eh voo?

231 My name is . . .
Je m'appelle. . .
Zher mahpehl . . .

232 This is my friend/boyfriend/
girlfriend/husband/wife/
brother/sister.
C'est un ami/c'est mon ami/
mon amie/mon mari/ma
femme/mon frère/ma soeur.
*Saytangnahmee/say
mawngnahmee/mawngnahmee/
mawng mahree/mah fahm/
mawng frayr/mah surr.*

233 Where are you travelling to?
Où partez-vous en voyage?
Oo pahrtehvoo ahng vwahahzh?

234 I am/we are going to . . .
Je vais/nous allons à . . .
Zher vay/noozahlawng ah . . .

235 How long are you travelling
for?
Combien de temps partez-vous?
*Kawngbeeang der tahng
pahrtehvoo?*

236 Where do you come from?
D'où venez-vous?
Doo vernehvoo?

237 I am/we are from . . .
Je suis/nous sommes de . . .
Zher sewea/noo soam der . . .

238 We're on holiday.
Nous sommes en vacances.
Noo som ahng vahkahngss.

239 This is our first visit here.
C'est la première fois que nous
venons ici.
*Seh lah prermiair fwah ker noo
vernon eeesee.*

240 Would you like/May I have a
cigarette?
Voulez-vous/Puis-je avoir une
cigarette?
*Voolehvoo/pweezhahvwahr ewn
seegahrett?*

241 I am sorry but I do not
understand.
Je suis désolé(e) mais je ne
comprends pas.
*Zher sewee dehzoleh meh zher ner
kawngprahng pah.*

242 Please speak slowly.
Veuillez parler lentement.
Vuryeh pahrleh lahngtmahng.

243 Do you mind if I smoke?
Est-ce que cela vous ennuie si je
fume?
*Ehsker cerlah voo ahngnewee ssi
zher fewm?*

244 Do you have a light?
Avez-vous du feu?
Ahveh-voo dew fur?

245 I am waiting for my husband/
wife/boyfriend/girlfriend.
J'attends mon mari/ma femme/
mon ami/mon amie.
*Zhatahng mawng mahree/mah
fahm/mawngnahmee/
mawngnahmee.*

TRAVELLING WITH CHILDREN

246 Do you have a high chair/
baby-sitting service/cot?
Avez-vous une chaise pour
bébé/un service de garde pour
enfants/un berceau?
*Ahvehvoo ewn shehz poor behbeh/
ang sehrvees der gahrd poor
ahngfahng/ang behrso?*

247 Where is the nursery/
playroom?
Où se trouve la chambre
d'enfants/la salle de jeux?
*Ooser troov lah shahngbr
dahngfahng/lah sall der zur?*

248 Where can I warm the baby's
bottle?
Où puis-je faire réchauffer le
biberon?
*Oo pweezh fair rehshoffeh ler
beebrawng?*

COMMUNICATIONS

Post

249 How much will it cost to send
a letter/postcard/this
package to Britain/Ireland/
America/Australia/
New Zealand/Canada?
Quel est le tarif pour envoyer
une lettre/carte postale/ce
paquet en Grande-Bretagne/
Irlande/Amérique/Australie/
Nouvelle-Zélande/au Canada?
*Kehl eh ler tariff poor
ahngvwahyeh ewn lettr/kahrt
postahl/ser pahkeh ahng grahngd-
brertahnya/irland/amehrick/
ostrahlee/noovel-zehland/oh
kahnahdah?*

250 I would like one stamp/two
stamps.
Je voudrais un timbre/deux
timbres.
*Zher voodray ang tangbr/der
tangbr.*

251 I'd like . . . stamps for
postcards to send abroad,
please.
Je voudrais . . . timbres pour
envoyer des cartes postales à
l'étranger sil vous plaît.
*Zher voodray . . . tangbr poor
ahngvwahyeh deh kahrt postahl
ah lehtrahngzhai seelvooplay*

Phones

252 I would like to make a
telephone call/reverse the
charges to (make a collect
call to) . . .
Je voudrais téléphoner/
téléphoner en PCV à . . .
*Zher voodray telephoneh/telephoneh
ahng PehCehVeh ah . . .*

253 Which coins do I need for the
telephone?
Quelles pièces me faut-il pour
téléphoner?
*Kehl peaehss mer foteel poor
tehlehphoneh?*

F R E N C H

²⁵⁴ **The line is engaged (busy).**
La ligne est occupée.
Lah lyñ eh okewpeh.

²⁵⁵ **The number is . . .**
Le numéro est . . .
Ler newmehro eh . . .

²⁵⁶ **Hello, this is . . .**
Bonjour, c'est . . . à lappareil.
Bawngzhoor, seh . . . ahlahparay.

²⁵⁷ **May I speak to . . ?**
Je voudrais parler à . . .
Zher voodray pahrlay ah . . .

²⁵⁸ **He/She is not in at the moment. Can you call back?**
Il/elle n'est pas là. Pouvez-vous rappeler?
Eel/ehl nay pah lah. Voo poovay rahperlay?

MONEY

²⁵⁹ **I would like to change these travellers' cheques (travelers' checks)/this currency/this Eurocheque.**
J'aimerais changer ces chèques de voyage/ces devises/cet Eurochèque.
Zhaymray shahngzheh seh cheque der vwahahzh/seh derveez/seht eurocheque.

²⁶⁰ **How much commission do you charge? (What is the service charge?)**
Quelle commission prenez-vous?
Kehl komyssyawng prernehvoo?

²⁶¹ **Can I obtain money with my**

MasterCard?
Puis-je avoir de l'argent avec ma MasterCard?
Pweezh ahvwahr der largaang ahvek mah mastercard?

SHOPPING

Names of Shops and Departments

²⁶² **Librairie/Papeterie**
Leebrayree/pahpaytehree
Bookshop/Stationery

²⁶³ **Bijoutier/Cadeaux**
Beezhootehree/Kahdow
Jeweller's/Gifts

²⁶⁴ **Chaussures**
Showsewr
Shoes

²⁶⁵ **Quincaillerie**
Kahngkahyeree
Hardware

²⁶⁶ **Antiquaire**
Ahnteekair
Antiques

²⁶⁷ **Coiffeur (hommes)/(femmes)**
Cwafferr
Hairdressers (men's)/(women's)

²⁶⁸ **Bureau de tabac**
Bewrow der tahbah
Tobacconist

²⁶⁹ **Boulangerie**
Boolahngzheree
Baker's

²⁷⁰ **Supermarché**
Sewpermahrshay

254
↕
270

Supermarket

271 Photographe
Phohtowgraf
Photoshop

272 Jouets
Zhooay
Toys

273 Bureau de voyages
Bureoh der vwoyazh
Travel Agency

274 Articles de toilette
Ahrteekl der twahleht
Toiletries

275 Disques
Deesk
Records

In the Shop

276 What time do the shops open/close?
A quelle heure ouvrent/ferment les magasins?
Ah kehlur oovr/fehrm leh mahgazhang?

277 Where is the nearest market?
Où est le marché le plus proche?
Oo eh ler mahrshay ler plew prosh?

278 Can you show me the one in the window/this one?
Pouvez-vous me montrer celui/celle dans la vitrine/celui-ci/celle-ci?
Poovayvoo mer mohntray serlwee/sel dahng lah veetreen/serlweesi/selsi?

279 Can I try this on?

Puis-je essayer ceci?
Pweezh ehssayeh cerssee?

280 What size is this?
Quelle est cette taille?
Kehleh saytt tahye?

281 This is too large/too small/too expensive.
C'est trop grand/trop petit/trop cher.
Say trohw grahng/trohw pertee/trohw share.

282 Do you have any others?
Vous en avez d'autres?
Voozahngnahvay doatr?

283 My size is . . .
Ma taille (clothes)/ma pointure (shoes) est . . .
Mah tie (clothes)/mah pooahngtewr ay . . .

284 Where is the changing room/childrens/cosmetic/ladieswear/menswear/food department?
Où se trouve le salon d'essayage/le rayon enfants/le rayon produits de beauté/le rayon femmes/le rayon hommes /l'alimentation?
Oo ser troov ler sahlawng dehsayahzh/ler rehyawng ahngfahng/ler rehyawng prodewee der boteh/ler rehyawng fahm/ler rehyawng ohm/lahleemahng-tahsyawng?

285 I would like . . .
Je voudrais . . .
Zher voodray . . .

286 I would like a quarter of a kilo/half a kilo/a kilo of bread/butter/cheese/ham/tomatoes.

e voudrais deux cent cinquante grammes (250g)/un demi-kilo/un kilo de pain/beurre/fromage/jambon/tomates.

Zher voodray dur sahng sangkahngt gram/ahng dermeekilo/ang kilo der pang/burr/frohmahzh/zhahngbawng/tomaht.

287 How much is this?

C'est combien?

Cey combeean?

288 I'll take this one, thank you.

Je prends celui-ci/celle-ci merci.

Zher prahng serlweesi/sehlsee mehrsee.

289 Do you have a carrier (shopping) bag?

Avez-vous un sac?

Ahvehvoo ang sahk?

290 Do you have anything cheaper/larger/smaller/of better quality?

Avez-vous quelque chose de moins cher/plus petit/plus grand/de meilleure qualité?

Ahvehvoo kehlkershos der moang shehr/plew pertee/plew grohnd/der mehyur kaleeteh?

291 I would like a film for this camera.

Je voudrais une pellicule pour cet appareil photo.

Zher voodray ewn pehleekewl poor

sayt ahpahrehye foto

292 I would like some batteries, the same size as this old one.

Je voudrais des piles, comme celle-ci.

Zher voodray deh peel, kom cehlsee.

293 Would you mind wrapping this for me, please?

Pourriez-vous m'envelopper ceci, s'il vous plaît?

Pooreeehvoo mahngverloppeh cersee, seelvooplay?

294 Sorry, but you seem to have given me the wrong change.

Excusez-moi, mais je crois que vous ne m'avez pas rendu le compte.

Excewsehmwah meh zher krwah ker voo ner mahveh pah rahngdew ler kawngt.

MOTORING

Car Hire (Rental)

295 I have ordered (rented) a car in the name of . . .

J'ai réservé une voiture au nom de . . .

Zhay rehzehrveh ewn vwahtewr o nawng der . . .

296 How much does it cost to hire (rent) a car for one day/two days/one week?

Quel est le prix de location d'une voiture pour un jour/deux jours/une semaine?

*Kehl eh ler pree der lokahsyawng
d'ewn vwahtewr poor ang zoor/
der zoor/ewn sermen?*

**297 Is the tank already full of
petrol (gas)?**
Le plein est-il fait?
Ler plang ehtylfeh?

**298 Is insurance and tax
included? How much is the
deposit?**
Est-ce que l'assurance et les
taxes sont comprises? Combien
faut-il donner de caution?
*Ehss ker lahsewrahngss eh leh tax
sawng kawngpreezh? Kawngbyabg
foteel doneh der kossyawng?*

**299 By what time must I return
the car?**
A quelle heure dois-je ramener
la voiture?
*Ah kelur dwahzh rahmerneh lah
vwahtewr?*

**300 I would like a small/family
car with a radio/cassette
player.**
Je voudrais une petite voiture/
une grosse voiture avec radio/
lecteur de cassettes.
*Zher voodray ewn perteet
vwahtewr/ewn gross vwahtewr
ahvehk rahdio/lecturr der kassaytt.*

Asking the Way

**301 Excuse me, can you help me
please?**
Excusez-moi, vous pouvez
m'aider s'il vous plaît?

*Ekskewzaymwah, voo poovay
mahyday seelvooplay*

**302 How do I reach the
motorway/main road?**
Pour aller jusqu'à l'autoroute/la
route principale?
*Poor ahleh zhewskah lowtohroot/
lah root prahngsipahl?*

**303 I think I have taken the
wrong turning.**
Je crois que je me suis trompé
de chemin.
*Zher krawh ker zhay mer trompay
der sheman.*

304 I am looking for this address.
Je cherche cette adresse.
Zher shaersh set adress.

**305 I am looking for the . . .
hotel.**
Je cherche l'hôtel . . .
Zher shaersh lohtel . . .

**306 How far is it to . . .
from here?**
. . . c'est loin d'ici?
. . . say looahng deesee?

**307 Carry straight on for . . .
kilometres.**
Continuez tout droit pendant . .
. kilomètres.
*Kohnteeneway too drooah
pahngdahng . . . kilomehtr.*

**308 Take the next turning on the
right/left.**
Prenez la prochaine rue/route à
droite/à gauche.
*Prernay lah proshen rew/root ah
drwaht/ah goash.*

309 **Turn right/left at the next crossroads/traffic lights.**
Tournez à droite/à gauche au prochain croisement/aux feux.
Toornay ah drwaht/ah goash oh prohshahng krowzmahng/oh phyer.

310 **You are going in the wrong direction.**
Vous allez dans la mauvaise direction.
Vooz ahleh dahng lah mowvehz deerekseeawng.

Parking

311 **How long can I park here?**
Combien de temps est-ce que je peux rester garé ici?
Kawngbeeang der tahng essker zher per restay gahray eessee?

312 **Is there a car park near here?**
Y a-t-il un parking près d'ici?
Eeyahteel ahng parking preh deessee?

313 **At what time does this car park close?**
A quelle heure est-ce que le parking ferme?
Ah kehl urr essker ler parking fehrm?

Signs and Notices

314 **Sens unique**
Sahns uhneek
One way

315 **Sens interdit**
Sahns ahngterdee
No entry

316 **Stationnement interdit**
Stassionmahng ahngterdee
No parking

317 **Déviation**
Dehveeasseeawong
Detour (diversion)

318 **Stop**
Stop
Stop

319 **Cédez la**
Preeohreetay
Give way (yield)

320 **Chaussée glissante**
Showsay gleesahnt
Slippery road

321 **Dépassement interdit**
Daypassmahng ahngterdee
No overtaking

At the Filling Station

322 **Unleaded (lead-free)/Standard/Premium**
Sans plomb/normal/super
Sahng plong/normall/sewpehr

323 **Fill the tank please.**
Le plein s'il vous plaît.
Ler plahng seelvooplay.

324 **Do you have a road map of this area?**
Vous avez une carte de la région?
Voozahvay ewn kahrt der lah rehzheeawong?

325 **How much is the car-wash?**

Le lavage automatique coûte
combien?
*Ler lahvahzh automateek koot
kawngbeeang?*

Breakdowns

326 I've had a breakdown at . . .
Je suis tombé(e) en panne à . . .
Zher sewee tombay ahng pan ah . . .

327 I am on the road from . . . to . . .
Je suis sur la route de . . . à . . .
*Zher sewee sewr lah root der . . .
ah . . .*

328 I can't move the car. Can you
send a tow-truck?
Je ne peux pas déplacer la
voiture. Vous pouvez envoyer
une dépanneuse?
*Zher ner purr pah dehplahsay lah
vwahtewr. Voo poovay
ahngvwahyeh ewn daypahnurze?*

329 I have a flat tyre.
J'ai un pneu crevé.
Zhai ang punerr krervay.

330 The windscreen (windshield)
has smashed/cracked.
Le pare-brise est cassé/fendu.
*Ler pahrbreez ay kahseh/
fahngdew.*

331 There is something wrong
with the engine/brakes/
lights/steering/gearbox/
clutch/exhaust.
Il y a un problème avec le
moteur/les freins/les feux/la
direction/la boîte à vitesses/
l'embrayage/le pot

d'échappement.
*Eeleeyah ang problairm ahvek ler
mowturr/leh frahng/leh fur/lah
deerehkseeawong/lah
bwahtahveetess/lahngbrayyazh/
ler poh dehshahpmahng.*

332 It's overheating.
Le moteur chauffe.
Ler mohturr showf.

333 It won't start.
La voiture ne démarre pas.
Lah vwahtewr ner dehmahr pah.

334 Where can I get it repaired?
Où est-ce que je peux le/la faire
réparer?
*Oo essker zher purr ler/lah fair
rehpahray?*

335 Can you take me there?
Vous pouvez m'y emmener?
Voo poovay mee ahngmernay?

336 Will it take long to fix?
La réparation prendra
longtemps?
*Lah rehpahrasseeawong prahngdrah
lohngtahng?*

337 How much will it cost?
Ça coûtera combien?
Sah kootrah kawngbeeang?

Accidents

338 Can you help me? There has
been an accident.
Vous pouvez m'aider? Il y a eu
un accident.
*Voo poovay mayday? Eelyaew ang
akseedahng.*

F
R
E
N
C
H

326
↑
338

339 Please call the police/an ambulance.
Vous pouvez appeler la police/ une ambulance s'il vous plaît.
Voo poovay ahperleh lah poleess/ ewn ahngbewlahngss seelvooplay.

340 Is anyone hurt?
Y a-t-il des blessés?
Eeahteel deh blaysay?

Traffic Offences

341 I'm sorry, I didn't see the sign.
Je suis désolé(e), je n'ai pas vu le panneau.
Zher sewee dehzoleh, zher nay pah vew ler panow.

342 Must I pay a fine? How much?
Est-ce que je dois payer une amende? Combien?
Ehsker zher dwah payeh ewn amahnd? Kawngbeeang?

343 Show me your documents.
Vos papiers s'il vous plaît.
Vow pahpyeh seelvooplay.

HEALTH

Pharmacy

344 Do you have anything for a stomachache/headache/sore throat/toothache?
Avez-vous quelque chose contre le mal à l'estomac/les maux de tête/le mal de gorge/le mal de dents?

Ahveh-voo kelhkshoz kawngtr ler mal ah lestoma/leh mo der teht/ler mal der gorzh/ler mal der dahng?

345 I need something for diarrhoea (diarrhea)/ constipation/a cold/a cough/ insect bites/sunburn/travel (motion) sickness.
J'ai besoin de quelque chose contre la diarrhée/la constipation/un rhume/la toux/ les piqûres d'insectes/les brûlures de soleil/le mal de la route (car)/de l'air (plane)/de mer (boat).
Zhai berzwoang der kehlkshoz kawngtr lah diarrhae/ang rhoom/ ewn tou/lers peakewr dangsect/leh koo der soleye/ler mal der lah root/der l'air/der mair.

346 How much/how many do I take?
Combien dois-je en prendre?
Kawngbeeang dwahzh ahng prahngdr?

347 How often do I take it/them?
Combien de fois dois-je en prendre?
Kawngbeeang der fwah dwahzh ahng prahngdr?

348 How much does it cost?
Quel est le prix?
Khel eh ler pree?

349 Can you recommend a good doctor/dentist?
Pouvez-vous me recommander un bon médecin/dentiste?

Pooveh-voo mer rerkomahngdeh ang bawng doctur/dahngtist?

350 Is it suitable for children?
Est-ce qu'on peut le donner aux enfants?
Esskawng pew ler doneh ozahnfahn?

Doctor

351 I have a pain here/in my arm/ leg/chest/stomach.
J'ai mal ici/au ras/à la jambe/à la poitrine/à l'estomac.
Zhai mal eessee/o brah/ah lah zhahngb/ah lah pwahtryn/ah lestomah.

352 Please call a doctor, this is an emergency.
Appelez un médecin, s'il vous plaît, c'est urgent.
Ahperleh ewn doctur, seel voo play, sehtewrzhahng.

353 I would like to make an appointment to see a doctor.
Je voudrais prendre rendez-vous chez le médecin.
Zher voodray prahngdr rahngdehvoo sheh ler doctur.

354 I am diabetic/pregnant.
Je suis diabétique/enceinte.
Zher sewee diabetic/ahngsang.

355 I need a prescription for . . .
J'ai besoin d'une ordonnance pour . . .
Zhai berzooang dewnordonahngss poor . . .

356 Can you give me something to ease the pain?
Pouvez-vous me donner quelque chose contre la douleur?
Poovayvoo mer doneh kehlkshoz kawngtr lah doolur?

357 I am/he is/she is allergic to penicillin.
Je suis/il est/elle est allergique à la pénicilline.
Zher sewee/eel ay/ehl ay allerzheek ah lah pehneeseeleen.

358 Does this hurt?
Ça fait mal?
Sah fay mahl?

359 You must/he must/she must go to hospital.
Vous devez/il doit/elle doit aller à l'hôpital.
Voo dervay/eel dwah/ehl dwah ahleh ah lopeetahl.

360 Take these once/twice/three times a day.
Prenez ces médicaments une fois/deux fois/trois fois par jour.
Prernay say medeekahmahng ewn fwah/dur fwah/trwah fwah pahr zhoor.

361 I am/he is/she is taking this medication.
Je prends/il prend/elle prend ces médicaments.
Zher prahng/eel prahng/ehl prahng say medeekahmahng.

F R E N C H

362
↕
372

362 **I have medical insurance.**
J'ai une assurance médicale.
Zhay ewn assurans mehdeekahl.

Dentist

363 **I have toothache.**
J'ai mal aux dents.
Zhai mahl o dahng.

364 **My filling has come out.**
Mon plombage est tombé.
Mawng plawngbahz eh tawngbeh.

365 **I do/do not want to have an injection first.**
Je veux/je ne veux pas qu'on me donne une piqûre avant.
Zher vur/zher nur vur pah ke orn mer don oon peakewr ahvehn.

EMERGENCIES

366 **Help!**
Au secours!
Ossercoor!

367 **Call an ambulance/a doctor/ the police!**
Appelez une ambulance/un docteur/la police!
Ahperleh ewnahngbewlahngss/ang doctur/lah poleess!

368 **I have had my travellers' cheques (travelers' checks)/ credit cards/purse/handbag/ rucksack (knapsack)/ luggage/wallet stolen.**
On m'a volé mes chèques de voyage/mes cartes de crédits/ mon porte-monnaie/mon sac à main/mon sac à dos/mes bagages/mon porte-feuille.
Awng mah voleh meh cheque der vwahahzh/meh carte der crehdite/ mawng portemonneh/mawng sackamahn/mawng sackadoe/meh bahgagzh/mawng portfur-ye.

369 **Can you help me, I have lost my daughter/son?**
Pouvez-vous m'aider, j'ai perdu ma fille/mon fils?
Poovehvoo mehdeh, jeh pehrdew mah feeye/mawng feess?

370 **Please go away/leave me alone.**
Allez-vous en/Laissez-moi tranquille.
Ahlehvoozahng/lehssehmwah trahngkeel.

371 **Fire!**
Au feu!
Oh fur!

372 **I want to contact the British/ American/Canadian/Irish/ Australian/New Zealand/ South African consulate.**
Je veux contacter le Consulat britannique/américain/ canadien/irlandais/australien/ néo-zélandais/sud-africain.
Zher vurr kontaktay ler kohnsewlah breetahneek/ ahmehreekahng/kahnahdyahng/ eerlahnday/austrahleeahng/ nayozaylahngday/ sewdafreekahng.

Introduction

German is the official language of Germany and Austria, and is spoken in the northern and eastern regions of Switzerland, as well as in the East Cantons area of Belgium, near the German border; some areas of northern Italy near Austria have a German-speaking population. German is also spoken in Luxembourg, and is often used as a second language in Central European countries, such as Hungary and the Czech Republic. Considering the wide geographical extent of the language, it is not surprising that considerable regional variation exists in accent and vocabulary (and sometimes spelling).

Addresses for travel and tourist information

UK: *German National Tourist Office*, 65 Curzon St, London W1Y 7PE; tel: (0171) 495 3990. *Austrian National Tourist Office*, 30 St George St, London W1R 0AL; tel: (0171) 629 0461. *Swiss National Tourist Office*, Swiss Centre, London W1V 8EE; tel: (0171) 734 1921.

USA: *German National Tourist Office*, Chanin Building, 122 East 42nd St (52nd Floor), New York, NY 10168-0072; tel: (212) 308-3300. *Austrian National Tourist Office*, 500 Fifth Ave (Suite 2009–2022), New York, NY 10110; tel: (212) 944-6880. *Swiss National Tourist Office*, Swiss Center, 608 Fifth Avenue, New York, NY 10020; tel: (212) 757-5944.

ESSENTIALS

ESSENTIALS

Alphabet

A	Ä
ah	*ah oomlowt*
B	C
bey	*tsey*
D	E
dey	*ey*
F	G
ef	*gey*
H	I
hah	*ee*
J	K
yot	*kah*
L	M
el	*em*
N	O
en	*oh*
Ö	P
oh oomlowt	*pey*
Q	R
koo	*eyr*
S	ß (= double S)
es	*ess-tsett*
T	U
tey	*oo*
Ü	V
oo oomlowt	*fow*
W	X
vey	*iks*
Y	Z
oopsilon	*tset*

Basic Words and Phrases

1. **Yes** **No**
   Ja Nein
   Yah *nine*

2. **Please** **Thank you**
   Bitte Danke
   Bitter *Danke*

3. **That's O.K.** **Perhaps**
   Das stimmt Vielleicht
   Das shtimt *Feellykht*

4. **To** **From**
   Nach Von
   Nakh *fon*

5. **Here** **There**
   Hier dort
   Here *dort*

6. **None** **Also**
   Kein Auch
   Kinee *Aukh*

7. **How** **When**
   Wie Wann
   Vee *Ven*

8. **What** **Why**
   Was Warum
   Vas *Varum*

9. **I don't understand.**
   Ich verstehe Sie nicht.
   Ikh ferhstayher zee nikht.

10. **I don't speak German.**
    Ich spreche kein Deutsch.
    Ikh shprekher kine doitsh.

11. **Do you speak English?**
    Sprechen Sie Englisch?
    Shprekhen zee english?

12 Can you please write it down?
Könnten Sie das bitte aufschreiben?
Kernten zee das bitter owfshryben?

13 Can you please speak more slowly?
Könnten Sie bitte langsamer sprechen?
Kernten zee bitter langzamer shprekhen?

14 How much does it/this cost?
Was kostet es/das?
Vas kostet es/das?

Days

15 Monday — **Tuesday**
Montag — Dienstag
Mohntagh — *Deenstagh*

16 Wednesday — **Thursday**
Mittwoch — Donnerstag
Mitvokh — *Donnerstagh*

17 Friday — **Saturday**
Freitag — Samstag
Frytagh — *Samstagh*

18 Sunday — **Morning**
Sonntag — Morgen
Sontagh — *Morgen*

19 Afternoon — **Evening**
Nachmittag — Abend
Naakhmittag — *Aabend*

20 Night — **Week**
Nacht — Woche
Naakht — *Wokhe*

21 Yesterday — **Tomorrow**
Gestern — Morgen
Gess-tern — *Morgen*

Numbers

22 Zero — **One**
Null — Eins
Nool — *Ines*

23 Two — **Three**
Zwei — Drei
Tsvy — *Dry*

24 Four — **Five**
Vier — Fünf
Feer — *Foonf*

25 Six — **Seven**
Sechs — Sieben
Zex — *Zeeben*

26 Eight — **Nine**
Acht — Neun
Akht — *Noyn*

27 Ten — **Eleven**
Zehn — Elf
Tseyn — *Elf*

28 Twelve — **Thirteen**
Zwölf — Dreizehn
Tsverlf — *Drytseyn*

29 Fourteen — **Fifteen**
Vierzehn — Fünfzehn
Feertseyn — *Foonftseyn*

30 Sixteen — **Seventeen**
Sechzehn — Siebzehn
Zekhtseyn — *Zeeptseyn*

31 Eighteen — **Nineteen**
Achtzehn — Neunzehn
Akhttseyn — *Noinetseyn*

GERMAN

12
↑
31

93

G E R M A N

32 **Twenty**
Zwanzig
Tvantsig

Twenty-one
Einundzwanzig
Ine-oont-tsvantsikh

33 **Twenty-two**
Zweiundzwanzig
Zvioonttvantsikh

Thirty
Dreißig
Drysikh

34 **Forty**
Vierzig
Feertsikh

Fifty
Fünfzig
Foonftsikh

35 **Sixty**
Sechzig
Zekhtsikh

Seventy
Siebzig
Zeebtsikh

36 **Eighty**
Achtzig
Akhtsikh

Ninety
Neunzig
Noyntsikh

37 **One hundred**
Hundert
Hoondert

Five hundred
Fünfhundert
Foonfhoondert

38 **One thousand**
Ein tausend
Ine towsend

One million
Eine Million
Iner millyohn

Time

39 **9.00**
Neun Uhr
Noyn oor

40 **9.05**
Neun Uhr fünf
Noyn oor foonf

41 **9.10**
Neun Uhr zehn
Noyn oor tseyn

42 **9.15**
Neun Uhr fünfzehn

Noyn oor foonftseyn

43 **9.20**
Neun Uhr zwanzig
Noyn oor tvantsikh

44 **9.25**
Neun Uhr fünfundzwanzig
Noyn oor foonf-oont-tsvantsig

45 **9.30**
Neun Uhr drei ig
Noyn oor drytsig

46 **9.35**
Neun Uhr fünfunddreißig
Noyn oor foonf-oont-drysikh

47 **9.40**
Neun Uhr vierzig
Noyn oor feertsikh

48 **9.45**
Neun Uhr fünfunfvierzig
Noyn oor foonf-oont-feertsikh

49 **9.50**
Neun Uhr fünfzig
Noyn oor foonftsikh

50 **9.55**
Neun Uhr fünfundfünfzig
Noyn oor foonf-oont-foonftsikh

51 **12.00/Midday/Midnight**
Mittag/Mitternacht
Mittagh/mitternakht

52 **What time is it?**
Wie spät ist es?
Vee shpeyt is es?

53 **It is . . .**
Es ist . . .
Es ist . . .

Airport

54 **Excuse me, where is the check-in desk for . . . airline?**
Entschuldigung, wo ist der Abfertigungsschalter für . . ?
Entshuldeegen, vo ist dair abfairtigoongs-shalter foor . . ?

55 **What is the boarding gate/ time for my flight?**
Von welchem Flugsteig geht mein Flug ab?/Wann muß ich einsteigen?
Fon velchem floogstyge geyht mine floog ab?/Vann moos ikh eynstygen?

56 **How long is the delay likely to be?**
Wieviel Verspätung hat mein Flug?
Veefeel fershpeytung hat mine floog?

57 **Where is the duty-free shop?**
Wo ist der zollfreie Laden?
Vo ist dair tsollfryer larden?

58 **Which way is the baggage reclaim?**
Wo ist die Gepäckausgabe?
Vo ist dee gepekowsgarber?

59 **Where can I get the bus to the city centre?**
Wo fährt der Bus ins Stadtzentrum ab?
Vo fairt dair boos ins shtat-tsentrum ab?

Train Station

60 **Where is the ticket office/ information desk?**
Wo ist der Fahrkartenschalter/ das Informationszentrum?
Voh ist der faarkartenshalter/das informatsion tsentroom?

61 **Which platform does the train to . . . depart from?**
Von welchem Bahnsteig fährt der Zug nach . . . ab?
Fon velchen baanshtykh fairt der tsook nakh . . . ab?

62 **Where is platform . . ?**
Wo ist Bahnsteig . . ?
Voh ist baanshtykh . . ?

63 **When is the next train to . . ?**
Wann fährt der nächste Zug nach . . ?
Vann fairt der nexter tsook nakh . . ?

64 **Is there a later train to . . ?**
Gibt es einen späteren Zug nach . . ?
Geebt es inen shpaeteren tsook nakh . . ?

Port

65 **How do I get to the port?**
Wie komme ich zum Hafen?
Vee kommer ikh zoom haafen?

66 **When is the next sailing to . . ?**
Wann fährt die nächste Fähre nach . . ?
Van fairt dee nexter fairer nakh . . ?

G
E
R
M
A
N

54
↕
66

GERMAN

67 ↕ 87

67 **Can I catch an earlier ferry with this ticket?**
Kann ich mit diesem Ticket eine frühere Fähre nehmen?
Can ikh mit deesem ticket iner froohere fairer neymen?

Notices and Signs

68 **Speisewagen**
shpyzevaagen
Buffet (Dining) Car

69 **Bus**
Bus
Bus

70 **Trinkwasser/kein Trinkwasser**
treenkvasser/kine treenkvasser
Drinking/Non-drinking water

71 **Eingang**
Ine-gang
Entrance

72 **Ausgang**
Ows-gang
Exit

73 **Information**
Eenformatsion
Information

74 **Gepäckaufbewahrung**
gepeckowfbevaarung
Left Luggage (Baggage Claim)

75 **Schließfächer**
schleessfekher
Luggage Lockers

76 **Postamt**
postamt
Post Office

77 **Bahnsteig**
baanshtykh
Platform

78 **Bahnhof**
baanhof
Railway (Railroad) Station

79 **Flughafen**
Floogharfen
Airport

80 **Hafen**
Harfen
Port

81 **Restaurant**
restohrong
Restaurant

82 **Raucher/Nichtraucher**
raukher/nikhtraukher
Smoking/Non-smoking

83 **Telefon**
taylefohn
Telephone

84 **Fahrkartenschalter**
faarkartenshalter
Ticket Office

85 **Abfertigungsschalter**
Abfairtigoongs-shalter
Check-in Desk

86 **Fahrplan**
faarplaan
Timetable (Schedule)

87 **Toiletten**
toletten
Toilets (Restrooms)

88 Herren
Herren
Gentlemen

89 Damen
Daamen
Ladies'

90 Straßenbahn
Shtraasenbaan
Tram (Streetcar)

91 Die U-Bahn
Dee Oo-baan
Underground (Subway)

92 Warteraum
Varterowm
Waiting Room

Buying a Ticket

93 I would like a first-class/ second-class/single (one- way)/return (round-trip) ticket to . . .
Ich möchte bitte eine (einfache Fahrkarte)/Rückfahrkarte (Rundfahrkarte) erster Klasse/ zweiter Klasse nach . . .
Eek merkhter bitter iner inefakhe faarkaarte/rookfaarkaarte airster classer/tsvyter classer nakh . . .

94 Is my rail pass valid on this train/ferry/bus?
Gilt mein Rail Pass für diesen Zug/diese Fähre/diesen Bus?
Guilt mine rail pass foor deesen tsug/deese fairer/deesen boos?

95 I would like an aisle/window seat.

Bitte einen Sitzplatz am Fenster/Durchgang.
Bitter inen plaats am fenster/ doorkhgang.

96 No smoking/smoking, please.
Raucher/Nichtraucher.
Raukher/nikhtraukher.

97 We would like to sit together.
Wir möchten gerne zusammen sitzen.
Veer merkhten gairner tsoozammen zitsen.

98 I would like to make a seat reservation.
Ich möchte gern einen Platz reservieren.
Ikh merkhter gairn inen plats resairveeren.

99 I would like to reserve a couchette/sleeper for one person/two people/for my family.
Ich möchte eine Schlafwagen-/ Liegewagenreservierung für eine Person/zwei Personen/ meine Familie.
Ikh merkhter ine shlaafvaagen-/ leegevaagen-reserveerung foor iner pairzohn/tsvy pairzohnen/miner fameelyer.

100 I would like to reserve a cabin.
Ich möchte gern eine Kabine reservieren.
Ikh merkhther gairn iner cabeener resairveeren.

G
E
R
M
A
N

88
↕
100

97

Timetables (Schedules)

101 Ankunft
Ankunft
Arrive

102 Hält in . . . an
Helt in . . . an
Calls (Stops) at

103 Mini bar
Minibar
Catering Service

104 In . . . umsteigen
In . . . oomshtygen
Change at . . .

105 Anschluß
Aanshluss
Connection

106 Täglich
Tayglikh
Daily

107 Alle . . . Minuten
Aller . . . minooten
Every 40 Minutes

108 Erste Klasse
Airster classer
First-class

109 Stündlich
Shtundlikh
Hourly

**110 Sitzplatzreservierung
empfohlen**
Zitsplats-reserveerung empvoolen
Seat reservations are
recommended

111 Zweite Klasse
Tsvyte classe
Second class

112 Zuschlagspflichtig
tsooshlaags-pfleechteeg
Supplement Payable

113 über
Oober
Via

Luggage

**114 How much will it cost to
send (ship) my luggage in
advance?**
Wieviel kostet es mein Gepäck
vorauszuschicken?
*Veefeel kostet es mine gepeck
forowss-tsoosheeken?*

**115 Where is the left luggage
(baggage claim) office?**
Wo ist die
Gepäckaufbewahrung?
Voo ist dee gepeck-owfbevaarung?

**116 What time do you open/
close?**
Um wieviel Uhr machen Sie
auf/zu?
*Oom veefeel oor makhen zee owf/
tsoo?*

**117 Where are the luggage
trolleys (carts)?**
Wo finde ich die Gepäckwagen?
Voo feende ikh dee gepeckvaagen?

118 Where are the lockers?
Wo sind die Schließfächer?
Vo seent dee shlees-fekher?

119 I have lost my locker key.
Ich habe den Schlüssel für mein Schließfach verloren.
Ikh haaber den shloossel foor mine shleesfakh ferlooren.

On Board

120 Is this seat taken?
Ist dieser Platz besetzt?
Ist deezer plats bezetst?

121 Excuse me, you are sitting in my reserved seat.
Entschuldigen Sie bitte, aber Sie sitzen auf meinem reservierten Platz.
Entshuldigen zee bitter, aber zee zitsen owf minem rezerveerten plats.

122 Which station is this?
Wie heißt dieser Bahnhof?
Vee hysst deezer baanhof?

123 What time is this train/bus/ ferry/flight due to arrive/ depart?
Wann kommt dieser Zug/dieser Bus/diese Fähre/dieser Flug an?/Wann geht dieser Zug/ dieser Bus/diese Fähre/dieser Flug?
Van kommt deeser tsug/deeser boos/deeser fairer/deeser floog an?/ Van geyt deeser tsug/deeser boos/ deeser fairer/deeser floog?

124 Will you wake me just before we arrive?
Bitte wecken Sie mich kurz bevor wir ankommen.

Bitter vekken zee meekh koorts before veer ankommen.

Customs and Passports

125 Ihren Reisepass bitte!
Passports, please!
Eeren ryzerpass, bitter!

126 I have nothing/wine/spirits (alcohol)/tobacco to declare.
Ich habe nichts/keinen Wein/ keinen Schnaps/keinen Tabak zu verzollen.
Ikh haabe neekhst/kinen vine/ kinen shnapps/kinen tabak tsoo fertsollen.

127 I shall be staying for . . . days/weeks/months.
Ich werde für . . . Tage/ Wochen/Monate bleiben.
Ikh verder foor . . . taager/ wokhen/mohnate blyben.

AT THE TOURIST OFFICE

128 Do you have a map of the town/area?
Haben Sie eine Stadtkarte/ Landkarte?
Haaben zee iner shtatkaarter/ landkaarter?

129 Can I reserve accommodation here?
Kann ich hier eine Unterkunft reservieren?
Can ikh here iner oonterkoonft reserveeren?

130 Do you have a list of accommodation?
Haben Sie ein Unterkunftsverzeichnis?
Haben see ine unterkunfts-fertsychnis?

ACCOMMODATION

Hotels

131 I have a reservation in the name of . . .
Ich habe eine Reservierung foor . . .
Ikh haabe iner reserveerung foor . . .

132 I wrote to/faxed/telephoned you last month/last week in . . .
Ich habe Ihnen letzten Monat/die letzte Woche im . . . geschrieben/ein Fax geschickt/angerufen
Ikh haber eenen letsten mohnat/dee letste wokhe im . . . geshreeben/ine fax gesheekt/angeroofen

133 Do you have any rooms free?
Haben Sie Zimmer frei?
Haben zee tsimmer fry?

134 I would like to reserve a single/double room with/without bath/shower.
Ich möchte ein Einzelzimmer/Doppelzimmer mit/ohne Bad/Dusche reservieren.
Ikh merkhter ine inetsel-tsimmer/doppel-tsimmer meet/oohner baad/doosher reserveeren.

135 I would like bed and breakfast/(room and) half board/(room and) full board.
Ich möchte Übernachtung mit Frühstück/Halbpension/Vollpension.
Ikh merkhter oobernakhtung meet frooshtook/halbpensiohn/follpensiohn.

136 How much is it per night?
Wieviel kostet das pro Nacht?
Veefeel kostet das pro nakht?

137 Is breakfast included?
Einschließlich Frühstück?
Ineshleesslykh frooshtook?

138 May I see the room?
Kann ich das Zimmer bitte sehen?
Can ikh das tsimmer bitter sehen?

139 Do you have any cheaper rooms?
Haben Sie billigere Zimmer?
Haaben see beeligerer tsimmer?

140 I would like to take the room
Ich nehme das Zimmer, bitte.
Ikh nehmer das tsimmer, bitter.

141 I would like to stay for . . . nights.
Ich möchte für . . . Nächte bleiben.
Ikh merkhter foor . . . nekhte blyben

142 The shower/light/tap doesn't work.
Die Dusche/das Licht/der Wasserhahn funktioniert nicht.
Dee doosher/das licht/dair vasserharn foonktsioneert nikht.

143 **At what time/where is breakfast served?**
Um wieviel Uhr/wo wird Frühstück serviert?
Omm veefeel oor/vo veerd frooshtook serveert?

144 **What time do I have to check out?**
Um wieviel Uhr müssen wir das Zimmer verlassen?
Oom veefeel oor moossen veer das tsimmer ferlassen?

145 **Can I have the key to room no . . ?**
Könnten Sie mir bitte den Schlüssel für Zimmer Nummer . . . geben?
Kernten zee mere bitter dayn shloosel foor tsimmer noomer . . . geyben?

146 **My room number is . . .**
Meine Zimmernummer ist . . .
Miner tsimmer-noomer ist . . .

147 **Do you accept travellers' cheques/Eurocheques/credit cards?**
Nehmen Sie Reiseschecks/ Euroschecks/Kreditkarten an?
Neymen zee ryzersheks/oirosheks/ credeetcarten an?

148 **May I have the bill please?**
Die Rechnung, bitte?
Dee rekhnung, bitter?

149 **Excuse me, I think there is a mistake in this bill.**
Entschuldigung, ich glaube auf dieser Rechnung ist ein Fehler.
Entshuldeegen, ikh glowbe owf deeser rekhnoong ist ine feyler.

Youth Hostels

150 **How much is a dormitory bed per night?**
Wieviel kostet ein Bett im Schlafsaal pro Nacht, bitte?
Veefeel kostet ine bet eem shlaafzaal pro nakht, bitter?

151 **I am/am not an HI member.**
Ich bin ein/kein Mitglied des internationaler Jugendherbergsverbands.
Ikh been ine/kine meetgleed des internatsionaaler yoogent- hairbairgs-ferbands.

152 **May I use my own sleeping bag?**
Kann ich meinen eigenen Schlafsack benutzen?
Can ikh minen ygenen shlaafzack benootsen?

153 **What time do you lock the doors at night?**
Um wieviel Uhr wird abends abgeschlossen?
Oom veefeel oor weerd abends abgeshlossen?

Camping

154 **May I camp here for the night/two nights?**
Kann ich für eine Nacht/zwei Nächte hier campen?
Can ikh foor ine/tsvy nekhte here campen?

GERMAN

143
↕
154

155 **Where can I pitch my tent?**
Wo kann ich mein Zelt
aufstellen?
Voo can ikh mine tselt owfshtellen?

156 **How much does it cost for
one night/week?**
Wieviel kostet es für eine
Nacht/Woche?
*Veefeel kostet es foor iner nakht/
wokhe?*

157 **Where can we park our
caravan?**
Wo können wir unseren
Wohnwagen parken?
*Vo kernen veer oonseren
vohnvargen parken?*

158 **Where are the washing
facilities?**
Wo sind die Waschräume?
Voo seent dee vashroyme?

159 **Is there a restaurant/
supermarket/swimming pool
on site/nearby?**
Gibt ein Restaurant/einen
Supermarkt/ein Schwimmbad in
der Nähe dieses
Campingplatzes?
*Geebt es ine restohrong/inen
zoopermarkt/ine shvimmbad in
der neyher deezes campingplatses?*

160 **Do you have a safety deposit
box?**
Haben Sie eine
Sicherheitsverwahrung?
*Haaben see iner zeekherhytes-
fervaarung?*

EATING AND DRINKING

Cafés and Bars

161 **I would like a cup of/two
cups of/another coffee/tea.**
Eine Tasse/Zwei Tassen/noch
eine Tasse Kaffee/Tee, bitte.
*Ikh merkter iner tasser/tsvy
tassen kafey/tey, bitter.*

162 **With/without milk/sugar**
Mit/ohne Milch/Zucker.
Meet/ohner milkh/tsukker.

163 **I would like a bottle/glass/
two glasses of mineral water/
red wine/white wine, please**
Ich möchte eine Flasche/ein
Glas/zwei Gläser
Mineralwasser/Rotwein/
Weißwein, bitte.
*Ikh merkhter iner flasher/ine glas/
tsvy glayzer mineraalvasser/
rohtvine/vice-vine, bitter.*

164 **I would like a beer/two
beers, please.**
Ein Bier/Zwei Biere, bitte.
Ine beer/tsvy beerer, bitter.

165 **May I have some ice?**
Kannich etwas Eis haben?
Can ikh etvas ice haaben?

166 **Do you have any matches/
cigarettes/cigars?**
Haben Sie Streichhölzer/
Zigaretten/Zigarren?
*Haaben see shtrykhherltser/
tseegaretten/tseegarren?*

Restaurants

167 Can you recommend a good/
inexpensive restaurant in this
area?

Können Sie ein gutes/nicht zu
teueres Restaurant in dieser
Gegend empfehlen?

*Kernen zee ine gootes/nikht tsoo
toyeress restohrong in deezer
geygent empfeylen?*

168 I would like a table for . . .
people.

Ein Tisch für . . . Personen, bitte.

Ine teesh foor . . . perzohnen, bitter.

169 Do you have a non-smoking
area?

Haben Sie einen Bereich für
Nichtraucher?

*Haben zee inen berykh foor
nikhtrowkher?*

170 Waiter/Waitress!

Herr Ober/Fräulein, bitte!

Hair ohber/froyline, bitter!

171 Do you have a set menu/
children's menu/wine list?

Haben Sie eine Tageskarte/
Kinderspeisekarte/Weinkarte?

*Haaben zee iner tahgeskaarter/
keender-shpyzekaarter/
vinekaarter?*

172 Do you have any vegetarian
dishes, please?

Gibt es bei Ihnen vegetarische
Gerichte, bitte?

*Geebt es by eenen vegetareesher
gereekhter, bitter?*

173 Are there any local
specialities?

Gibt es örtliche Spezialitäten?

Geebt es ortlikhe specialitayten?

174 Are vegetables included?

Ist Gemüse dabei?

Ist gemoose darbye?

175 Could I have it well-cooked/
medium/rare please?

Ich möchte es bitte durch/halb
durch/englisch gebraten.

*Ikh merkhter es bitter doorkh/halb
doorkh/english gebrarten.*

176 What does this dish consist of?

Was für ein Gericht ist es?

Vas foor ine gereekht ist es?

177 I would like the set menu,
please.

Das Tageskarte, bitte.

Das tahgeskaarte, bitter.

178 We have not been served yet.

Wir warten noch auf
Bedienung.

Veer varten nokh owf bedeenung.

179 Excuse me, this is not what I
ordered.

Entschuldigung, das habe ich
nicht bestellt.

*Entshuldeegen, das haber ikh nikht
beshtelt.*

180 May I have some/some more
bread/water/coffee/tea?

Kann ich noch etwas Brot,
Wasser/Kaffee/Tee haben?

*Can ikh etvas/nokh etvas broht/
vasser/kaffey/tey haaben?*

103

**G
E
R
M
A
N**

**181
↑
195**

181 May I have the bill, please?
Die Rechnung, bitte?
Dee rekhnung, bitter?

182 Does this bill include service?
Ist diese Rechnung einschließlich Bedienung?
Ist deeze rekhnung ine-shleessleekh bedeenung?

183 Do you accept travellers' cheques (travelers' checks)/Eurocheques/MasterCard/US dollars?
Nehmen sie Reiseschecks/uroschecks/MasterCard/US Dollars?
Naymen zee Ryzersheks/Eurosheks/MasterCard/US Dollars?

184 Can I have a receipt, please?
Könnte ich bitte eine Quittung haben?
Kernter ikh bitter ine kwitoong harben?

185 Where is the toilet (restroom), please?
Wo sind die Toiletten, bitte?
Voo zeent dee toletten, bitter?

On the Menu

186 First courses
Vorspeisen
Fore-shpysen

187 Soups
Suppen
Sooppen

188 Main courses
Hauptgerichte
Howpt-gerikhte

189 Fish dishes
Fischgerichte
Fish-gerikhte

190 Meat dishes
Fleischgerichte
Flyesh-gerikhte

191 Vegetarian dishes
Vegetarische Gerichte
Vegetairishe gerikhte

192 Cheese
Käse
Keyse

193 Desserts
Desserts
Desayrs

194 Specialities
Spezialitäten
Specialitayten

GETTING AROUND

Public Transport

195 Where is the bus stop/coach station/nearest metro (subway) station?
Wo ist die nächste Bushaltestelle/der nächste Busbahnhof/die U-Bahnhaltestelle, bitte?
Voo ist die nexter bushaltersteller/der nexter busbaanhof/dee nexter Oo-baahn-halter-shteller?

196 When is the next/last bus to . . ?
Wann fährt der nächste/letzte Bus nach . . ?
Vann fairt der nexter/letster bus nakh . . ?

197 How much is the fare to the city centre (downtown)/railway (railroad) station/airport?
Wieviel kostet es zur Stadtmitte/zum Bahnhof/Flughafen?
Veefeel kostet es tsoor shtatmitte/tsoom baanhof/flooghaafen?

198 Will you tell me when to get off?
Sagen Sie mir bitte wann ich aussteigen muß?
Zaagen zee meer bitter vann ikh owsstygen moos?

199 Does this bus go to . . ?
Fährt dieser Bus nach . . ?
Fairt deezer bus nakh . . ?

200 Which number bus goes to . . ?
Welcher Bus fährt nach . . ?
Velkher bus fairt nakh . . ?

201 May I have a single (one-way)/return (round-trip)/day ticket/book of tickets?
Ich möchte eine einfache Fahrkarte/Rückfahrkarte/Rundfahrkarte/Tageskarte/ein Fahrkartenheft?
Ikh merkhter iner inefakher faarkaarter/ruekfaarkaarter/

tagheskaarter/iner faarkaartenheft?

Taxis

202 I would like to go to . . .
How much will it cost?
Ich möchte nach . . . fahren, wieviel kostet das?
Ikh merkhter nakh . . . faaren, veefeel kostet das?

203 Please stop here.
Bitte anhalten.
Bitter anhalten.

204 I would like to order a taxi today/tomorrow/at 2pm to go from . . . to . . .
Ich möchte gerne ein Taxi für heute/morgen/zwei Uhr bestellen um von . . . nach . . . zu fahren.
Ikh merkhter gairner ine Taxi foor hoyter morgen/tsvy oor bestellen oom fon . . . nakh . . . zu faaren.

Asking the Way

205 Excuse me, do you speak English?
Entschuldigen Sie, sprechen Sie Englisch?
Entshuldigen zee, shprekhen zee english?

206 Excuse me, is this the right way to . . ?
Entschuldigung, bin ich hier richtig für . . ?
Entshuldeegen, bin ikh here rikhtig foor . . ?

207 ... the cathedral/the tourist information office/the castle/ the old town
... den Dom/die Touristeninformation/das Schloß/die Altstadt?
... den dorm, dee tooristen-informatsion/das shloss/dee altshtat?

208 Can you tell me the way to the railway station/bus station/taxi rank (stand)/city centre (downtown)/beach?
Können sie mir bitte sagen wie ich zum Bahnhof/zum Busbahnhof/zum TaxiRank/zur Stadtmitte/zum Strand komme?
Kernen zee meer bitter zaagen, vee ikh tsoom baanhof/tsoom busbaanhof/tsoom taxirank/tsoor shtatmitter/tsoom shtrant kommer?

209 First/second left/right/ straight ahead.
Die erste Straße links/rechts/ geradeaus.
Dee airste shtraasser leenks/ rekhts/geraader-ows.

210 Where is the nearest police station/post office?
Wo ist die nächste Polizeiwache/das nächste Postamt?
Voo ist dee nexter politsywakhe/ das nexter postamt?

211 Is it far?
Ist es weit?
Ist es vyte?

212 Do I need to take a taxi/a bus?
Muß ich eine Taxi/einen Bus nehmen?
Moos ikh iner taxi/inen bus nayhmen?

213 Can you point to it on my map?
Können Sie es mir bitte auf der Karte zeigen?
Kernen see es meer bitter owf der kaarte tsygen?

214 Thank you for your help.
Vielen Dank für Ihre Hilfe.
Feelen dank foor eehrer heelfe.

SIGHTSEEING

215 Where is the Tourist Information office?
Wo ist das TouristenInformationsbüro?
Voo ist das touristen-informatisons-booro?

216 Where is the cathedral/ church/museum?
Wo ist der Dom/die Kirche/das Museum?
Voh ist der dohm/dee keerkhe/das moozeyum?

217 How much is the entrance (admission) charge?
Was kostet der Eintritt?
Vas kostet der inetreet?

218 Is there a reduction for children/students/senior citizens?
Gibt es eine Ermäßigung für Kinder/Studenten/Rentner?

Geebt es iner ermeyssigung foor kinder/shtudenten/rentner?

219 What time does the next guided tour start?
Um wieviel Uhr ist die nächste Führung?
Oom veefeel oor ist dee nexter foohrung?

220 One/two adults/children, please.
Ein Erwachsener/zwei Erwachsene/Kinder, bitte.
Ine ervaxener/tsvy ervaxener/kinder, bitter.

221 May I take photographs here?
Darf man hier fotografieren?
Darf man here fotografeeren?

ENTERTAINMENT

222 Can you recommend a good bar/nightclub?
Können Sie eine gute Bar/einen guten Nachtklub empfehlen?
Kernen zee iner gooter bar/inen gooten nakhtklub empfehlen?

223 Do you know what is on at the cinema (playing at the movies)/theatre at the moment?
Was spielt im Augenblick im Kino/Theater?
Vass shpeelt im augenbleek im keeno/teyaater?

224 I would like to book (purchase) . . . tickets for the matinée/evening

performance on Monday.
Ich möchte gerne Eintrittskarten für die Frühvorstellung am Montag bestellen.
Ikh merkhter gairner inetreetskaarten foor dee frooforshtellung am mohntagh beshtellen.

225 What time does the film/performance start?
Um wieviel Uhr fängt der Film/die Vorstellung an?
Oom veefeel oor fengt der film/dee forshtellung an?

MEETING PEOPLE

226 Hello/Goodbye.
Hallo/Auf Wiedersehen.
Hallo/Owf Veederzeyhen.

227 Good morning/good afternoon/good evening/goodnight.
Guten Morgen/guten Tag/guten Abend/gute Nacht.
Gooten morgen/gooten targ/gooten arbent/goote nakht.

228 Pleased to meet you.
Es freut mich Sie kennenzulernen.
Es froyt mikh zee kennen-tsoo-lernen.

229 How are you?
Wie geht es Ihnen?
Vee gayht es eehnen?

230 Fine, thank you. And you?
Gut danke, und Ihnen?
Goot, danker, oond eenen?

GERMAN

231 My name is . . .
Mein Name ist . . .
Mine naamer ist . . .

232 This is my friend/boyfriend/
girlfriend/husband/wife/
brother/sister.
Dies ist mein Freund/mein
Freund/meine Freundin/mein
Mann/meine Frau/mein Bruder/
meine Schwester.
*Dees ist mine froynd/mine froynd/
miner froindeen/mine man/miner
frow/mine brooder/miner shvester.*

233 Where are you travelling to?
Wohin reisen Sie?
Voheen ryzen zee?

234 I am/we are going to . . .
Ich fahre/wir fahren nach . . .
Ikh faare/weer faaren nakh . . .

235 How long are you travelling
for?
Wie lange reisen Sie?
Vee lange ryzen zee?

236 Where do you come from?
Woher kommen Sie?
Vohair kommen zee?

237 I am/we are from . . .
Ich komme/wir kommen aus . . .
Ikh kommer/veer kommen aus . . .

238 We're on holiday.
Wir machen Urlaub.
Veer makhen oorlowb.

239 This is our first visit here.
Wir sind zum ersten Mal hier.
Veer sind tsum airsten marl here.

240 Would you like a ciagrette?/
May I have a cigarette?
Möchten Sie eine Zigarette/
Kann ich bitte eine Zigarette
haben?
*Merkhten zee iner tsigaretter/Can
ikh bitter iner tsigaretter haaben?*

241 I am sorry but I do not
understand.
Es tut mir leid, aber ich verstehe
es nicht.
*Es toot meer lite, aaber ikh
ferstayher es nikht.*

242 Please speak slowly.
Sprechen Sie bitte langsam.
Sprekhen zee bitter langzam.

243 Do you mind if I smoke?
Darf ich rauchen?
Darf ikh raukhen?

244 Do you have a light?
Haben Sie Feuer bitte?
Haaben see foyer bitter?

245 I am waiting for my husband/
wife/boyfriend/girlfriend.
Ich warte auf meinen Mann/
meine Frau/meinen Freund/
meine Freundin.
*Ikh varter owf minen mann/miner
frow/minen froind/miner froindin.*

TRAVELLING WITH CHILDREN

246 Do you have a high chair/
babysitting service/cot?
Haben Sie einen Kinderstuhl/
Babysitter/ein Kinderbett?
*Haaben zee inen kindershtool/
Babysittier/ine kinderbet?*

108

247 Where is the nursery/playroom?
Wo ist das Kinderzimmer/pielzimmer?
Voh ist das kindertsimmer/speeltsimmer?

248 Where can I warm the baby's bottle?
Wo kann ich die Milchflasche für das Baby aufwärmen?
Voh can ikh die Milkflasher foor das Baby owf-vairmen?

COMMUNICATIONS

Post

249 How much will it cost to send a letter/postcard/this package to Britain/Ireland/America/Canada/Australia/New Zealand?
Wieviel kostet ein Brief/eine Postkarte/dieses Paket nach England/Irland/Amerika/Kanada/Australien/Neuseeland?
Veefeel kostet ine breef/iner postkaarter/deezes pakayt nakh England/Eerland/America/Canada/Owstralee-en/Noyzeyland.

250 I would like one stamp/two stamps.
Ich möchte eine/zwei Briefmarke(n).
Ikh merkhter iner/tsvy breefmarke(n).

251 I'd like . . . stamps for postcards to send abroad, please.
Ich möchte . . . Briefmarken für Postkarten ins Ausland bitte.
Ikh merkhter . . . breefmarken foor postkarten ins owslund bitter.

Phones

252 I would like to make a telephone call/reverse the charges to (make a collect call to) . . .
Ich möchte einen Anruf/ein RGespräch nakh . . . machen
Ikh merkhter inen aanroof/ine eyr-geshprekh nakh . . . makhen

253 Which coins do I need for the telephone?
Welche Münzen brauche ich für dieses Telefon?
Velkhe moontsen browkhe ikh foor deezes teylefohn?

254 The line is engaged (busy).
Die Nummer ist besetzt.
Dee noommer ist bezetst.

255 The number is . . .
Die Nummer ist . . .
Dee noommer ist . . .

256 Hello, this is . . .
Hallo, hier spricht . . .
Hallo, here shprikht . . .

**G
E
R
M
A
N**

²⁵⁷ May I speak to . . ?
Kann ich bitte mit . . .
sprechen?
*Kann ikh bitter mit . . .
shprekhen?*

²⁵⁸ He/She is not in at the
moment. Can you call back?
Er/Sie ist im Moment nicht da.
Könnten Sie später noch einmal
anrufen?
*Air/Zee ist im morment nikht dar.
Kernten zee shpeter nokh inemarl
anroofen?*

MONEY

²⁵⁹ I would like to change these
travellers' cheques (travelers'
checks)/this currency/this
Eurocheque.
Ich möchte gerne diese
Reiseschecks/dieses Geld/
diesen Euroscheck wechseln.
*Ikh merkhter gairner deezer
ryzersheks/deezes gelt/deezen
Euroshek vexeln.*

²⁶⁰ How much commission do
you charge (What is the
service charge)?
Wie hoch ist Ihre Provision?
Vee hokh ist eere provizion?

²⁶¹ Can I obtain money with my
MasterCard?
Kann ich mit meiner
MasterCard Geld bekommen?
*Can ikh meet miner MasterCard
gelt bekommen?*

SHOPPING

Names of Shops and Departments

²⁶² Buchgeschäft/Schreibwaren
Bookhgesheft/Shribevahren
Bookshop/Stationery

²⁶³ Schmuckgeschäft/Geschenke
Shmookgesheft/Geshenker
Jeweller's/Gifts

²⁶⁴ Schuhe
Shooher
Shoes

²⁶⁵ Eisenwaren
Eyesenvahren
Hardware

²⁶⁶ Antiquitäten
Anteekweeteyten
Antiques

²⁶⁷ Friseur (Herren)/(Damen)
Freesoor (hairren)/(darmen)
Hairdressers (men's)/(women's)

²⁶⁸ Tabakwarengeschäft
Tabakvahrengesheft
Tobacconist

²⁶⁹ Bäckerei
Bekkereye
Baker's

²⁷⁰ Supermarkt
Soopermarkt
Supermarket

²⁷¹ Fotogeschäft
Fotogesheft
Photoshop

257
↕
271

272 **Spielwaren**
Speelvahren
Toys

273 **Reisebüro**
Ryesebooro
Travel Agent

274 **Toilettenartikel**
Toiletenarteekel
Toiletries

275 **Schallplatten**
Shallplatten
Records

In the Shop

276 **What time do the shops open/close?**
Um wieviel Uhr öffnen/
schließen die Geschäfte?
*Oom veefeel oor erffnen/shleessen
dee geshefter?*

277 **Where is the nearest market?**
Wo ist der nächste Markt?
Vo ist dair nekster markt?

278 **Can you show me the one in the window/this one?**
Zeigen Sie mir bitte den im
Fenster/diesen da?
*Tsyegen zee mere bitter den im
fenster/deezen dar?*

279 **Can I try this on?**
Kann ich das anprobieren?
Can ikh das anprobeeren?

280 **What size is this?**
Welche Größe ist dieses Stück?
Velkhe grersser ist deezes shtook?

281 **This is too large/too small/too expensive.**
Es ist zu groß/zu klein/zu teuer.
Es ist tsu gross/tsu kline/tsu toyer.

282 **Do you have any others?**
Haben Sie noch andere?
Haben zee nokh anderer?

283 **My size is . . .**
Ich habe Größe . . .
Ikh haber grerser . . .

284 **Where is the changing room/children's/cosmetic/ladieswear/menswear/food department?**
Wo ist der Umkleideraum/
Kinder- /Damen- /
Herrenkleidungs- /
Lebensmittel-abteilung?
*Voh ist der oomklyderowm/dee
kinder/daamen/herenklydungs/
leybensmittel abtylung?*

285 **I would like . . .**
Ich hätte gern . . .
Ikh hetter gairn . . .

286 **I would like a quarter of a kilo/half a kilo/a kilo of bread/butter/cheese/ham/tomatoes.**
Ich möchte gerne ein viertel
Kilo/halbes Kilo/ein Kilo Brot/
Butter/Käse/Schinken/
Tomaten.
*Ikh merkhter gairner ine feertel
keelo/halbes keelo/ine keelo broht/
bootter/kayzer/sheenken/tomaten.*

GERMAN

272
↕
286

287 How much is this?
Wieviel kostet das?
Veefeel kostet das?

288 I'll take this one, thank you.
Ich nehme das, dankeschön.
Ikh neymer das, dankershern.

289 Do you have a carrier (shopping) bag?
Haben Sie eine Tragetasche?
Haaben zee iner traager-tasher?

290 Do you have anything cheaper/larger/smaller/of better quality?
Haben Sie etwas billigeres/größeres/kleineres/Haben Sie eine bessere Qualität?
Haaben zee etvas billigeress/grersseress/klineress/Haaben zee iner bessere qualitaet?

291 I would like a film for my camera.
Ich möchte einen Film für meinen Fotoapparat.
Ikh merkhter inen film foor minen fotoaparat.

292 I would like some batteries, the same size as this old one.
Ich möchte einige Batterien, die gleiche Größe wie die alten.
Ikh merkhter iyniger batteree-en, dee glykhe grersser vee dee alten.

293 Would you mind wrapping this for me, please?
Können Sie es bitte einpacken?
Kernen zee es bitter ine-pakken?

294 Sorry, but you seem to have given me the wrong change.

Entschuldigung, aber Sie scheinen einen Fehler mit dem Wechselgeld gemacht zu haben.
Entshuldigung, aber zee shinern inen fayler mit dem vekhselgeld gemahkt tsoo haaben.

MOTORING

Car Hire (Rental)

295 I have ordered (rented) a car in the name of . .
Ich habe einen Wagen für . . . bestellt.
Ikh haaber inen vaagen foor . . . beshtellt.

296 How much does it cost to hire (rent) a car for one day/two days/one week?
Was kostet es einen Wagen für einen Tag/zwei Tage/eine Woche zu mieten?
Vas kostet es inen vaagen foor inen taagh/tsvy taager/iner wokher tsoo meeten?

297 Is the tank already full of petrol (gas)?
Ist der Tank voll?
Ist der tank foll?

298 Is insurance and tax included? How much is the deposit?
Ist die Versicherung und Steuer inbegriffen? Wieviel muß man anzahlen?
Ist dee ferzeekherung oont shtoyer inbegreeffen? Veefeel moos man aantsahlen?

299 By what time must I return the car?

Um wieviel Uhr muß ich den Wagen zurückbringen?

Oom veefeel oor moos ikh den vaagen tsoo-rookh bringen?

300 I would like a small/family car with a radio/cassette player.

Ich möchte einen kleinen/ Familienwagen mit Radio und Kassettenspieler.

Ikh merkhter inen klinen/fameelien vaagen mit radio oont cassettenshpeeler.

Asking the Way

301 Excuse me, can you help me please?

Entschuldigung, könnten Sie mir bitte helfen?

Entshuldeegen, kernten zee mere bitter helfen?

302 How do I reach the motorway/main road?

Wie komme ich zur Autobahn/ zur Hauptstraße?

Vee kommer ikh tsur owtobarn/ tsur howpt-shtrarser?

303 I think I have taken the wrong turning.

Ich glaube, ich bin falsch abgebogen.

Ikh glowber, ikh bin falsh abgeborgen.

304 I am looking for this address.

Ich suche diese Adresse.

Ikh sookher deeser ardresse.

305 I am looking for the . . . hotel.

Ich suche das . . . Hotel.

Ikh sookher das . . . hotel.

306 How far is it to . . . from here?

Wie weit ist es bis . . . von hier?

Vee vite ist es bees . . . fon here?

307 Carry straight on for . . . kilometres.

Fahren Sie . . . Kilometer geradeaus.

Faren zee . . . keelometer gerarde ows.

308 Take the next turning on the right/left.

Biegen Sie die nächste Straße rechts/links ab.

Beegen zee dee nekste shtrarser rekhts/links ab.

309 Turn right/left at the next crossroads/traffic lights.

Biegen Sie an der nächsten Kreuzung/Ampel rechts/links ab.

Beegen zee un dair neksten kroitsung/ampel rekhts/links ab.

310 You are going in the wrong direction.

Sie fahren in die falsche Richtung.

Zee faren in dee falsher richtung.

Parking

311 How long can I park here?
Wie la ge darf man hier parken?
Vee langer darf man here parken?

312 Is there a car park near here?
Gibt es einen Parkplatz in der Nähe?
Geebt es inen parkplats in dair neher?

313 At what time does this car park close?
Wann schließt dieser Parkplatz?
Van shleest deeser parkplats?

Signs and Notices

314 Einbahnstraße.
Ine-barn-shtraser.
One way.

315 Zutritt/Einfahrt verboten.
Tsutreet/Inefart ferbohten.
No entry.

316 Parkverbot.
Park-ferboht.
No parking.

317 Umweg (Umleitung)
Oomweyg (oomlytung)
Detour (diversion)

318 Halt.
Halt.
Stop.

319 Vorfahrt beachten.
Forfart beakhten.
Give way (yield).

320 Straßenglätte.
Shtrasen-gletter.
Slippery road.

321 Überholen verboten.
Ooberhohlen ferbohten.
No overtaking.

At the Filling Station

322 Unleaded (lead-free)/ Standard/Premium
Bleifrei/Normal/Super
Blye-frye/normahl/super

323 Fill the tank please.
Volltanken, bitte.
Foll-tanken, bitter.

324 Do you have a road map of this area?
Haben Sie eine Straßenkarte für diese Gegend?
Haben zee iner shtrasen-karte foor deeser gegent?

325 How much is the car-wash?
Was kostet die Autowäsche?
Vas kostet dee owtowesher?

Breakdowns

326 I've had a breakdown at . . .
Ich habe eine Panne bei . . .
Ikh haber ine panner bye . . .

327 I am on the road from . . . to . . .
Ich bin auf der Straße von . . . nach . . .
Ikh bin owf dair shtrase fon . . . nakh . . .

328 I can't move the car. Can you send a tow-truck?
Mein Auto ist kaputt. Können Sie einen Abschleppwagen schicken?
Mine owto ist kapoot. Kernnen zee inen Abshlep-vagen shiken?

329 I have a flat tyre.
Mein Reifen ist platt.
Mine ryefen ist platt.

330 The windscreen (windshield) has smashed/cracked.
Die Windschutzscheibe ist kaputt/gesprungen.
Dee vindshoots-shyeber ist kapoot/geshprungen.

331 There is something wrong with the engine/brakes/lights/steering/gearbox/clutch/exhaust.
Ich habe Probleme mit dem Motor/der Bremse/dem Licht/der Steuerung/dem Getriebe/der Kupplung/dem Auspuff.
Ikh haber probleyme mit dem motor/dair bremser/dem licht/dair shtoyerung/dem getreeber/dair koopploong/dem owspooff.

332 It's overheating.
Der Motor ist überhitzt.
Dair motor ist ooberhitst.

333 It won't start.
Es springt nicht an.
Es shpringt nikht an.

334 Where can I get it repaired?
Wo kann ich es reparieren lassen?
Vo can ikh es repareeren lassen?

335 Can you take me there?
Können Sie mich dort hinbringen?
Kernen zee mikh dort hinbringen?

336 Will it take long to fix?
Dauert die Reparatur lange?
Dowert dee reparatoor languer?

337 How much will it cost?
Was wird es kosten?
Vas veerd es kosten?

Accidents

338 Can you help me? There has been an accident.
Können Sie mir helfen? Es ist ein Unfall passiert.
Kernen zee mere helfen? Es ist ine oonfal paseert.

339 Please call the police/an ambulance.
Bitte rufen Sie die Polizei/einen Krankenwagen.
Bitter roofen zee dee politsye/inen krankenvagen.

340 Is anyone hurt?
Ist jemand verletzt?
Ist yemant fairletst?

Traffic Offences

341 I'm sorry, I didn't see the sign.
Tut mir leid, ich habe das Schild nicht gesehen.
Toot mere lyed, ikh haber das shilt nikht gesayhen.

G
E
R
M
A
N

328
↕
341

342 Must I pay a fine? How much?
Gibt das einen Strafzettel? Wieviel?
Geebt das inen shtraf-tsettel? Veefeel?

343 Show me your documents.
Zeigen Sie mir Ihre Papiere.
Tsyegen zee mere eere papeerer.

HEALTH

Pharmacy

344 Do you have anything for a stomachache/headache/sore throat/toothache?
Haben Sie etwas für Magen-schmerzen/Kopfschmerzen/Halsschmerzen/Zahn-schmerzen?
Haaben zee etvas foor maagenshmertsen/kopfshmertsen/hals-shmertsen/tsahnschmertsen?

345 I need something for diarrhoea (diarrhea)/constipation/a cold/a cough/insect bites/sunburn/travel (motion) sickness.
Ich benötige etwas für Durchfall/Verstopfung/eine Erkältung/einen Husten/Insektenstiche/Sonnenbrand/Reisekrankheit.
Ikh benertiger etvas foor doorkhfall/fershtopfung/iner erkeltung/inen hoosten/insektenshteekhe/zonnenbrand/ryzerkrankhite.

346 How much/how many do I take?
Wieviel/wieviele soll ich nehmen?
Veefeel/veefeeler soll ikh neymen?

347 How often do I take it/them?
Wie oft soll ich es/sie nehmen?
Vee oft soll ikh es/zee neymen?

348 How much does it cost?
Wieviel kostet das?
Veefeel kostet das?

349 Can you recommend a good doctor/dentist?
Können Sie einen guten Arzt/Zahnarzt empfehlen?
Kernen see meer inen gooten artst/tsaanartst empfehlen?

350 Is it suitable for children?
Ist es gut mit Kindern?
Ist es goot mit kindern?

Doctor

351 I have a pain here/in my arm/leg/chest/stomach.
Ich habe hier Schmerzen/an meinem Arm/Bein/an meiner Brust/an meinem Magen.
Ikh haaber shmertsen here/an minem arm/bine/an miner broost/an minem maagen.

352 Please call a doctor, this is an emergency.
Rufen Sie bitte einen Arzt, es ist ein Notfall.
Roofen zee bitter inen artst, es ist ine nohtfall.

353 I would like to make an appointment to see a doctor.
Ich möchte einen Arzttermin vereinbaren.
Ikh merkhter inen artst-termeen ferinebaaren.

354 I am diabetic/pregnant.
Ich bin ein Diabetiker/ich bin schwanger.
Ikh been ine deeabetiker/ikh been shvanger.

355 I need a prescription for . . .
Ich benötige ein Rezept foor . . .
Ikh benertiger ine retsept foor . . .

356 Can you give me something to ease the pain?
Können Sie mir etwas gegen die Schmerzen geben?
Kernen zee meer etvas geygen dee shmertsen geyben?

357 I am/he is/she is allergic to penicillin.
Ich bin/er ist/sie ist allergisch auf Penizillin.
Ikh bin/air ist/zee ist allergish owf penitsileen.

358 Does this hurt?
Tut das weh?
Toot das way?

359 You must/he must/she must go to hospital.
Sie müssen/er muß/sie muß ins Krankenhaus.
Zee moossen/air mousse/zee mous ins krankenhouse.

360 Take these once/twice /three times a day.

Nehmen Sie diese einmal/ zweimal/dreimal täglich.
Naymen zee deeser inemal/ tsvyemal/drymal teyglikh.

361 I am/he is/she is taking this medication.
Ich nehme/er nimmt/sie nimmt diese Medikamente.
Ikh naymer/air nimmt/zee nimmt deeser medikamenter.

362 I have medical insurance.
Ich habe eine Krankenversicherung.
Ikh haber ine kranken-fersikheroong.

Dentist

363 I have toothache.
Ich habe Zahnschmerzen.
Ikh haabe tsahn-shmertsen.

364 My filling has come out.
Eine Füllung ist herausgefallen.
Iner fooloong ist herowsgefallen.

365 I do/do not want to have an injection first.
Ich will eine/keine Spritze haben.
Ikh vill iner/kiner shpreetse haaben.

EMERGENCIES

366 Help!
Hilfe!
Heelfe!

G E R M A N

367
↕
37

367 **Call an ambulance/a doctor/
the police!**
Rufen Sie bitte einen
Krankenwagen/einen Arzt/die
Polizei!
*Roofen zee bitter inen
krankenvaagen/inen artst/dee
politsye!*

368 **I have had my travellers'
cheques (travelers' checks)/
credit cards/purse/handbag/
rucksack (knapsack)/
luggage/wallet stolen.**
Man hat mir meine
Reiseschecks/Kreditkarten/
meinen Geldbeutel/meine
Handtasche/meinen Rucksack/
mein Gepäck/meine Brieftasche
gestohlen.
*Man hat meer miner ryzersheks/
creditkaarten/minen geldboytel/
miner handtasher/minen
ruckzack/mine gepeck/miner
breeftasher geshtohlen.*

369 **Can you help me, I have lost
my daughter/son?**
Können Sie mir bitte helfen, ich
habe meine Tochter/meinen
Sohn verloren?
*Kernen zee meer bitter helfen, ikh
haabe miner tokhter/minen zohn
ferloren?*

370 **Please go away/leave me
alone.**
Lassen Sie mich bitte in Ruhe!
Lassen see meekh bitter in roohe!

371 **Fire!**
Feuer!
Foyer!

372 **I want to contact the British/
American/Canadian/Irish/
Australian/New Zealand/
South African consulate.**
Ich möchte mich mit dem
britischen/amerikanischen/
kanadischen/irischen/
australischen/neuseeländischen/
südafrikanischen Konsulat in
Verbindung setzen.
*Ikh merkhter mikh mit dem
britishen/amerikanishen/
karnardishen/eereeshen/
owstralishen/noysaylendishen/
soodafrikanishen konsoolat in
ferbeendoong setsen.*

118

Introduction

Greek is a language with a 3000-year history, and modern written Greek would be readable, and probably to a large degree comprehensible, by an ancient Athenian. The non-roman script is the most difficult aspect of the language for the visitor, although many street signs and notices have both the Greek characters and a transliteration into the roman alphabet. This is in itself a source of potential confusion, however, as there is no one accepted way of writing a Greek word in roman script, so any Greek text can have a variety of spellings in the roman alphabet.

The spoken language has fewer pitfalls, although beware that the word for 'yes' sounds like English 'nay', whereas a Greek who nods his head up and down is probably saying 'no', this being the equivalent of shaking the head. English is widely spoken in tourist areas, and French is an official second language, but be prepared to speak Greek when off the beaten track.

G
R
E
E
K

Addresses for travel and tourist information

UK: *National Tourist Organisation of Greece*, 4 Conduit St, London W1R 0DJ; tel: (0171) 734 5997.
USA: *National Tourist Organisation of Greece*, Olympic Tower, 645 Fifth Ave (5th Floor), New York, NY 10022; tel: (212) 421-5777.

ESSENTIALS

ESSENTIALS

Alphabet

A, α	B, β
alpha	vita
Γ, γ	Δ, δ
gamma	delta
E, ε	Z, ζ
epsilon	zeeta
H, η	Θ, θ
eeta	theeta
I, ι	K, κ
iota	kappa
Λ, λ	M, μ
lamda	mi
N, ν	Ξ, ξ
ni	xi
O, o	Π, π
omikron	pi
P, ρ	Σ, σ
ro	sigma
T, τ	Y, υ
taf	ipsilon
Φ, φ	X, χ
fi	hi
Ψ, ψ	Ω, ω
psi	omega

Basic Words and Phrases

1 Yes   No
Ναι   Οχι
Ne   Ohi

2 Please   Thank you
Παρακαλώ   Ευχαριστώ

Parakalo   Efharisto

3 That's O.K.   Perhaps
Εντάξει   Ισως
Entaxi   Isos

4 To   From
Προς   Από
Pros   Apo

5 Here   There
Εδώ   Εκεί
Edo   Eki

6 None   Also
Τίποτα   Επίσης
Tipota   Episis

7 How   When
Πώς   Πότε
Pos   Pote

8 What   Why
Τι   Πού;
Ti   Pu?

9 I don't understand.
Δεν καταλαβαίνω.
Den katalaveno

10 I don't speak Greek.
Δεν μιλώ Ελληνικά.
Den milo Ellinika

11 Do you speak English?
Μιλάτε Αγγλικά;
Milate Anglika?

12 Can you please write it down?
Μπορείτε σας παρακαλώ να
το γράψετε;
Borite sas parakalo na to grapsete?

13 Can you please speak more
slowly?

Μπορείτε σας παρακαλώ να
μιλάτε πιο αργά;
*Borite sas parakalo na milate pio
arga?*

14 **How much does it/this cost?**
Πόσο κοστίζει αυτό;
Poso kostizi afto?

Days

15 **Monday** **Tuesday**
Δευτέρα Τρίτη
Deftera *Triti*

16 **Wednesday** **Thursday**
Τετάρτη Πέμπτη
Tetarti *Pembti*

17 **Friday** **Saturday**
Παρασκευή Σάββατο
Paraskevi *Savvato*

18 **Sunday** **Morning**
Κυριακή Πρωί
Kiriaki *Proi*

19 **Afternoon** **Evening**
Απόγευμα Βράδυ
Apogevma *Vradi*

20 **Night** **Week**
Νύχτα Εβδομάδα
Nihta *Evdomada*

21 **Yesterday** **Tomorrow**
Χτες Αύριο
Htes *Avrio*

Numbers

22 **Zero** **One**
Μηδέν Ενα
Miden *Ena*

23 **Two** **Three**
Δύο Τρία
Dio *Tria*

24 **Four** **Five**
Τέσσερα Πέντε
Tessera *Pente*

25 **Six** **Seven**
Εξι Επτά
Exi *Epta*

26 **Eight** **Nine**
Οκτώ Εννέα
Okto *Ennea*

27 **Ten** **Eleven**
Δέκα Εντεκα
Deka *Endeka*

28 **Twelve** **Thirteen**
Δώδεκα Δεκατρία
Dodeka *Dekatria*

29 **Fourteen** **Fifteen**
Δεκατέσσερα Δεκαπέντε
Dekatessera *Dekapente*

30 **Sixteen** **Seventeen**
Δεκαέξι Δεκαεπτά
Dekaexi *Dekaepta*

31 **Eighteen** **Nineteen**
Δεκαοχτώ Δεκαεννέα
Dekaokto *Dekaennea*

32 **Twenty** **Twenty-one**
Είκοσι Είκοσι ένα
Ikosi *Ikosi ena*

33 **Twenty-two** **Thirty**
Είκοσι δύο Τριάντα
Ikosi dio *Trianta*

**G
R
E
E
K**

**14
↕
33**

34 Forty   Fifty
Σαράντα   Πενήντα
Saranta   *Peninta*

35 Sixty   Seventy
Εξήντα   Εβδομήντα
Exinta   *Evdominta*

36 Eighty   Ninety
Ογδόντα   Ενενήντα
Ogdonta   *Eneninta*

37 One hundred Five hundred
Εκατό   Πεντακόσια
Ekato   *Pentakosia*

38 One thousand One million
Χίλια   Ενα εκατομμύριο
Hilia   *Ena ekatommirio*

Time

39 9.00
Εννέα
Ennea

40 9.05
Εννέα και πέντε
Ennea ke pente

41 9.10
Εννέα και δέκα
Ennea ke deka

42 9.15
Εννέα και τέταρτο
Ennea ke tetarto

43 9.20
Εννέα και είκοσι
Ennea ke ikosi

44 9.25
Εννέα και είκοσι πέντε
Ennea ke ikosi pente

45 9.30
Εννέα και μισή
Ennea ke misi

46 9.35
Δέκα πάρα είκοσι πέντε
Deka para ikosi pente

47 9.40
Δέκα πάρα είκοσι
Deka para ikosi

48 9.45
Δέκα πάρα τέταρτο
Deka para tetarto

49 9.50
Δέκα πάρα δέκα
Deka para deka

50 9.55
Δέκα πάρα πέντε
Deka para pente

51 12.00/Midday/Midnight
Δώδεκα/Μεσημέρι/
Μεσάνυχτα
Dodeka/Mesimeri/Mesanihta

52 What time is it?
Τί ώρα είναι;
Ti ora ine?

53 It is . . .
Είναι . . .
Ine . . .

ARRIVING AND DEPARTING

Airport

54 Excuse me, where is the
check-in desk for . . . airline?
Με συγχωρείτε, πού είναι ο
έλεγχος αποσκευών και

εισιτηρίων για την
αερογραμμή . . ;
*Me sinhorite, pu ine o elenhos
aposkevon kai isitirion ya tin
aerogrammi . . ?*

**55 What is the boarding gate/
time for my flight?**
Ποια είναι η θύρα/ώρα
επιβίβασης για την πτήση μου;
*Pia ine i thira/ora epivivasis ya tin
ptisi mu?*

**56 How long is the delay likely
to be?**
Πόσο προβλέπεται να
διαρκέσει η καθυστέρηση;
*Poso provlepete na diarkesi i
kathisterisi?*

57 Where is the duty-free shop?
Πού είναι το κατάστημα
αφορολόγητων;
Pu ine to katastima aforoloyiton?

**58 Which way is the baggage
reclaim?**
Πού είναι η αίθουσα
αποσκευών;
Pu ine i ethusa aposkevon?

**59 Where can I get the bus to
the city centre?**
Από πού μπορώ να πάρω το
λεωφορείο για το κέντρο
της πόλης;
*Apo pu boro na paro to leoforio ya
to kentro tis polis?*

Train Station

**60 Where is the ticket office/
information desk?**

Πού είναι το γραφείο
εισιτηρίων/το γραφείο
πληροφοριών;
*Pu ine to grafio isitirion/to grafio
pliroforion?*

**61 Which platform does the
train to . . . depart from?**
Από ποια πλατφόρμα
αναχωρεί το τραίνο για
την . . ;
*Apo pia platforma anahori to
treno ya tin . . ?*

62 Where is platform . . ?
Πού είναι η πλατφόρμα . . ;
Pu ine i platforma . . ?

63 When is the next train to . . ?
Πότε είναι το επόμενο
τραίνο για την . . ;
Pote ine to epomeno treno ya tin . . ?

64 Is there a later train to . . ?
Υπάρχει αργότερα τραίνο
για την . . ;
Iparhi argotera treno ya tin . . ?

Port

65 How do I get to the port?
Πώς μπορώ να πάω στο
λιμάνι;
Pos boro na pao sto limani?

**66 When is the next sailing
to . . ?**
Ποια είναι η επόμενη
πλεύση για την . . ;
Pia ine i epomeni plefsi ya tin . . ?

67 Can I catch an earlier ferry
with this ticket?
Με αυτό το εισιτήριο
μπορώ να επιβιβαστώ σε
φέρρυ που φεύγει νωρίτερα;
*Me avto to isitirio boro na
epivivasto se ferry pu fevyi
noritera?*

Notices and Signs

68 Αμαξοστοιχία με μπουφέ
Amaxostihia me Buffet
Buffet (Dining) Car

69 Λεωφορείο
Leoforio
Bus

70 Πόσιμο/μη πόσιμο νερό
Posimo/mi posimo nero
Drinking/Non-drinking water

71 Είσοδος
Isodos
Entrance

72 Έξοδος
Exodos
Exit

73 Πληροφορίες
Plirofories
Information

74 Χώρος Αποσκευών
Horos Aposkevon
Left Luggage

75 Θυρίδες Αποσκευών
Thirides Aposkevon
Luggage Lockers

76 Ταχυδρομείο
Tahidromio

Post Office

77 Πλατφόρμα/Εξέδρα
Platforma/Exedra
Platform

78 Σιδηροδρομικός Σταθμός
Sidirodromikos Stathmos
Railway (Railroad) Station

79 Αεροδρόμιο
Aerodromio
Airport

80 Λιμάνι
Limani
Port

81 Εστιατόριο
Estiatorio
Restaurant

82 Για Καπνιστές/Για μη
καπνιστές
Ya kapnistes/ya mi kapnistes
Smoking/Non-smoking

83 Τηλέφωνο
Tilephono
Telephone

84 Γραφείο Εισιτηρίων
Grafio Isitirion
Ticket Office

85 Έλεγχος Αποσκευών &
Εισιτηρίων
Elenhos Aposkevon ke Isitirion
Check-in Desk

86 Δρομολόγιο
Dromologio
Timetable (Schedule)

87 Αποχωρητήρια
Apohoritiria

Toilets (Restrooms)

88 **Ανδρών**
Andron
Gentlemen

89 **Γυναικών**
inekon
Ladies'

90 **Τραμ**
Tram
Tram (Streetcar)

91 **Υπόγειος Σιδηρόδρομος**
Ipoyios Sidirodromos
Underground (Subway)

92 **Αίθουσα Αναμονής**
Ethusa Anamonis
Waiting Room

Buying a Ticket

93 I would like a first-class/
second-class single (one-
way)/return (round-trip)
ticket to . . .
Θα ήθελα πρώτης θέσεως/
δευτέρας θέσεως απλό/μετ'
επιστροφής εισιτήριο για
την . . .
*Tha ithela protis theseos/defteras
theseos/aplo/met epistrofis isitirio
ya tin . . .*

94 Is my rail pass valid on this
train/ferry/bus?
Το σιδηροδρομικό
εισιτήριο που έχω ισχύει
για αυτό το τραίνο/φέρρυ/
λεωφορείο;

*To sidirodromiko isitirio pu eho
ishii ya afto to treno/ferry/
leoforio?*

95 I would like an aisle/window
seat.
Θα ήθελα μια θέση δίπλα
στο διάδρομο/παράθυρο.
*Tha ithela mia thesi dipla sto
diadromo/parathiro.*

96 No smoking/smoking, please.
Απαγορεύεται το
κάπνισμα/επιτρέπεται το
κάπνισμα, παρακαλώ.
*Apagorevete to kapnisma/
epitrepete to kapnisma, parakalo.*

97 We would like to sit
together.
Θα θέλαμε να καθίσουμε
μαζί.
Tha thelame na kathisoume mazi.

98 I would like to make a seat
reservation.
Θα ήθελα να κρατήσω μία
θέση.
Tha ithela na kratiso mia thesi.

99 I would like to reserve a
couchette/sleeper for one
person/two people/my
family.
Θα ήθελα να κρατήσω
κουκέτα/κλινάμαξα για ένα
άτομο/δύο άτομα/την
οικογένειά μου.
*Tha ithela na kratiso kuketa/
klinamaxa ya ena atomo/dio
atoma/tin ikoyenia mu.*

G
R
E
E
K

88
↕
99

100 I would like to reserve a cabin.
Θα ήθελα να κρατήσω μία
καμπίνα.
Tha ithela na kratiso mia kabina.

Timetables (Schedules)

101 Αφίξεις
Afixis
Arrive

102 Σταματά στο
Stamata sto
Calls (Stops) at

103 Υπηρεσία Εστίασης
Ipiresia estiasis
Catering Service

104 Αλλάζει στο
Allazi sto
Change at

105 Σύνδεση
Sindesi
Connection

106 Καθημερινά
Kathimerina
Daily

107 Κάθε σαράντα (40) λεπτά
Kathe saranta (40) lepta
Every 40 minutes

108 Πρώτης θέσεως
Protis Theseos
First-class

109 Κάθε ώρα
Kathe ora
Hourly

110 Συστήνονται κρατήσεις θέσεων

Sistinonte kratisis theseon
Seat reservations are recommended

111 Δευτέρας Θέσεως
Defteras Theseos
Second-class

112 Συμπληρωματικό Ποσό
Simpliromatiko Poso
Supplement Payable

113 Μέσω
Meso
Via

Luggage

114 How much will it cost to send (ship) my luggage in advance?
Πόσο θα μου στοιχίσει να
στείλω εκ των προτέρων τις
αποσκευές μου;
Poso tha mu stihisi na stilo ek ton proteron tis aposkeves mu?

115 Where is the left luggage (baggage claim) office?
Πού είναι το γραφείο
αποσκευών;
Pu ine to grafio aposkevon?

116 What time do you open/ close?
Τί ώρα ανοίγετε/κλείνετε;
Ti ora aniyete/klinete?

117 Where are the luggage trolleys (carts)?
Πού είναι τα τρόλλεϋ των
αποσκευών;
Pu ine ta trolley ton aposkevon?

118 Where are the lockers?
Πού είναι οι θυρίδες;
Pu ine i thirides?

119 I have lost my locker key.
Εχασα το κλειδί της
θυρίδας μου.
Ehasa to klidi tis thiridas mu.

On Board

120 Is this seat taken?
Μήπως αυτή η θέση είναι
ελεύθερη;
Mipos afti i thesi ine eleftheri?

121 Excuse me, you are sitting in
my reserved seat.
Με συγχωρείτε, αλλά
κάθεστε στην κρατημένη
μου θέση.
*Me sinhorite, alla katheste stin
kratimeni mu thesi.*

122 Which station is this?
Ποιος σταθμός είναι αυτός;
Pios stathmos ine aftos?

123 What time is this train/bus/
ferry/flight due to arrive/
depart?
Τι ώρα αναμένεται να
φθάσει/αναχωρήσει το
τραίνο/λεωφορείο/φέρρυ/
πτήση;
*Ti ora anamenete na fthasi/
anahorisi to treno/leoforio/ferry/
ptisi?*

124 Will you wake me just before
we arrive?
Μπορείτε να με ξυπνήσετε
προτού φτάσουμε;

*Borite na me xipnisete protu
ftasume?*

Customs and Passports

125 Τα διαβατήριά σας,
παρακαλώ!
Ta diavatiria sas, parakalo!
Passports, please!

126 I have nothing/wine/spirits
(alcohol)/tobacco to declare.
Δεν έχω τίποτα να δηλώσω/
κρασί/οινοπνευματώδη/
καπνό.
*Den eho tipota na diloso/krasi/
inopnevmatodi/kapno.*

127 I shall be staying for . . .
days/weeks/months.
Θα μείνω για . . . ημέρες/
εβδομάδες/μήνες.
*Tha mino ya . . . imeres/
evdomades/mines.*

AT THE TOURIST OFFICE

128 Do you have a map of the
town/area?
Μήπως έχετε χάρτη της
πόλης/περιοχής;
*Mipos ehete harti tis polis/
periohis?*

129 Can I reserve accommodation
here?
Μπορώ να κρατήσω
δωμάτια εδώ;
Boro na kratiso domatia edo?

G
R
E
E
K

118
↕
129

130 Do you have a list of accommodation?
Εχετε κάποια λίστα δωματίων που νοικιάζονται;
Ehete kapia lista domation pu nikiazonte?

ACCOMMODATION

Hotels

131 I have a reservation in the name of . . .
Εχω κράτηση στο όνομα . . .
Eho kratisi sto onoma . . .

132 I wrote to/faxed/telephoned you last month/last week in . . .
Σας έγραψα/έστειλα φαξ/ τηλεφώνησα τον/την περασμένο(η) μήνα/ εβδομάδα . . .
Sas egrapsa/estila fax/tilephonisa ton/ tin perasmeno(i) mina/evdomada . . .

133 Do you have any rooms free?
Εχετε ελεύθερα δωμάτια;
Ehete elefthera domatia?

134 I would like to reserve a single/double room with/ without bath/shower.
Θα ήθελα να κρατήσω ένα μονό/διπλό δωμάτιο με/ χωρίς μπάνιο/ντους.
Tha ithela na kratiso ena mono/ diplo domatio me/horis banio/ dush.

135 I would like bed and breakfast/(room and) half board/(room and) full board.
Θα ήθελα δωμάτιο με πρόγευμα/δωμάτιο με δύο φαγητά/δωμάτιο με φαγητά.
Tha ithela domatio me proyevma/ domatio me dio fayita/domatio me fayita.

136 How much is it per night?
Πόσο στοιχίζει τη νύχτα;
Poso stihizi ti nihta?

137 Is breakfast included?
Περιλαμβάνει και πρόγευμα;
Perilamvani ke proyevma?

138 May I see the room?
Μπορώ να δω το δωμάτιο;
Boro na do to domatio?

139 Do you have any cheaper rooms?
Μήπως έχετε φτηνότερα δωμάτια;
Mipos ehete ftinotera domatia?

140 I would like to take the room.
Θα ήθελα να πάρω αυτό το δωμάτιο.
Tha ithela na paro afto to domatio.

141 I would like to stay for . . . nights.
Θα ήθελα να μείνω για . . . νύχτες.
Tha ithela na mino ya . . . nihtes.

142 The shower/light/tap doesn't work.
Το ντους/ηλεκτρικό/βρύση δεν λειτουργεί.
To dush/ilektriko/vrisi den lituryi.

143 At what time/where is breakfast served?
Τι ώρα/πού σερβίρεται το πρόγευμα;
Ti ora/pu servirete to proyevma?

144 What time do I have to check-out?
Τι ώρα πρέπει να αδειάσω το δωμάτιο;
Ti ora prepi na adiaso to domatio?

145 Can I have the key to room no . . ?
Μπορείτε να μου δώσετε το κλειδί για το δωμάτιο αριθ.
. . . ;
Borite na mu dosete to klidi ya to domatio arithmos . . ?

146 My room number is . . .
Ο αριθμός του δωματίου μου είναι . . .
O arithmos tu domatiu mu ine . . .

147 Do you accept travellers' cheques/Eurocheques/credit cards?
Δέχεστε ταξιδιωτικές επιταγές/Ευρωεπιταγές/ πιστωτικές κάρτες;
Deheste taxidiotikes epitayes/ Evroepitayes/pistotikes kartes?

148 May I have the bill, please?
Μπορώ να έχω το λογαριασμό, παρακαλώ;
Boro na eho to logariasmo, parakalo?

149 Excuse me, I think there is a mistake in this bill.
Με συγχωρείτε, νομίζω πως

υπάρχει κάποιο λάθος στο λογαριασμό.
Me sinhorite, nomizo pos iparhi kapio lathos sto logariasmo.

Youth Hostels

150 How much is a dormitory bed per night?
Πόσο κάνει ένα κρεβάτι κοιτώνα τη νύχτα;
Poso kani ena krevati kitona ti nihta?

151 I am/am not an HI member.
Είμαι/δεν είμαι μέλος της HI.
Ime/den ime melos tis HI.

152 May I use my own sleeping bag?
Μπορώ να χρησιμοποιήσω το δικό μου σλήπινγκ μπαγκ;
Boro na hrisimopiiso to diko mu sleeping bag?

153 What time do you lock the doors at night?
Τί ώρα κλείνετε τις πόρτες τα βράδια;
Ti ora klinete tis portes ta vradia?

Camping

154 May I camp here for the night/two nights?
Μπορώ να κάνω κάμπιγκ εδώ για τη νύχτα/δύο νύχτες;
Boro na kano camping edo ya ti nihta/dio nihtes?

155 Where can I pitch my tent?
Πού μπορώ να στήσω την
τέντα μου;
Pu boro na stiso tin tenta mu?

156 How much does it cost for
one night/one week?
Πόσο στοιχίζει για μία
νύχτα/μία εβδομάδα;
*Poso stihizi ya mia nihta/mia
evdomada?*

157 Where can we park our
caravan?
Πού μπορούμε να
παρκάρουμε το τροχόσπιτό
μας;
*Pu borume na parkarume to
trochospito mas?*

158 Where are the washing
facilities?
Πού είναι οι ευκολίες
πλυσίματος;
Pu ine i efkolies plisimatos?

159 Is there a restaurant/
supermarket/swimming pool
on site/nearby?
Υπάρχει μήπως
εστιατόριο/υπεραγορά/
πισίνα εδώ/εδώ κοντά;
*Iparhi mipos estiatorio/iperagora/
pisina edo/edo konta?*

160 Do you have a safety deposit
box?
Μήπως έχετε θυρίδα
ασφαλείας αντικειμένων;
*Mipos ehete thirida asfalias
antikimenon?*

EATING AND DRINKING

Cafés and Bars

161 I would like a cup of/two
cups of/another coffee/tea.
Θα ήθελα ένα φλιτζάνι/δύο
φλιτζάνια/ακόμη ένα καφέ/
τσάι.
*Tha ithela ena flitzani/dio
flitzania/akomi ena kafe/tsai.*

162 With/without milk/sugar.
Με/χωρίς γάλα/ζάχαρη.
Me/horis gala/zahari.

163 I would like a bottle/glass/
two glasses of mineral water/
red wine/white wine, please.
Θα ήθελα ένα μπουκάλι/
ποτήρι/δύο ποτήρια
μεταλλικό νερό/κόκκινο
κρασί/άσπρο κρασί,
παρακαλώ.
*Tha ithela ena bukali/potiri/dio
potiria metalliko nero/kokkino
krasi/aspro krasi, parakalo.*

164 I would like a beer/two
beers, please.
Θα ήθελα μια μπύρα/δύο
μπύρες, παρακαλώ.
*Tha ithela mia bira/dio bires,
parakalo.*

165 May I have some ice?
Μπορώ να έχω λίγο πάγο;
Boro na eho ligo pago?

166 Do you have any matches/
cigarettes/cigars?
Μήπως έχετε σπίρτα/
τσιγάρα/πούρα;

Mipos ehete spirta/tsigara/pura?

Restaurants

167 Can you recommend a good/
inexpensive restaurant in this
area?
Μπορείτε να μου
συστήσετε ένα καλό/φτηνό
εστιατόριο σε αυτή την
περιοχή;
*Borite na mu sistisete ena kalo/
ftino estiatorio se afti tin periohi?*

168 I would like a table for . . .
people.
Θα ήθελα ένα τραπεζάκι για
. . . άτομα.
*Tha ithela ena trapezaki gia . . .
atoma.*

169 Do you have a non-smoking
area?
Εχετε ορισμένη περιοχή
για αυτούς που δεν
καπνίζουν;
*Ehete orismeni periohi ya aftus pu
den kapnizun?*

170 Waiter/Waitress!
Γκαρσόν/Σερβιτόρα!
Garson/Servitora!

171 Do you have a set menu/
children's menu/wine list?
Εχετε σετ μενού/παιδικό
μενού/κατάλογο κρασιών;
*Ehete set menu/pediko menu/
katalogo krasion?*

172 Do you have any vegetarian
dishes, please?

Μήπως έχετε πιάτα για
χορτοφάγους, παρακαλώ;
*Mipos ehete piata ya hortofagous,
parakalo?*

173 Are there any local
specialities?
Εχετε κάτι το ειδικό που
συνηθίζεται τοπικά;
*Ehete kati to idiko pu sinithizete
topika?*

174 Are vegetables included?
Χορταρικά και λαχανικά
συμπεριλαμβάνονται;
*Hortarika ke lahanika
simperilamvanonte?*

175 Could I have it well-cooked/
medium/rare please?
Μπορώ να το έχω καλά/
μέτρια/ελάχιστα ψημένο,
παρακαλώ;
*Boro na to eho kala/metria/
elahista psimeno, parakalo?*

176 What does this dish consist
of?
Από τι αποτελείται αυτό το
πιάτο;
Apo ti apotelite afto to piato?

177 I would like the set menu,
please.
Θα ήθελα το σετ μενού,
παρακαλώ.
Tha ithela to set menu, parakalo.

178 We have not been served yet.
Δεν σερβιριστήκαμε
ακόμη.
Den serviristikame akomi.

179 Excuse me, this is not what I ordered.
Με συγχωρείτε, δεν είναι αυτό που παράγγειλα.
Me sinhorite, den ine afto pu paragila.

180 May I have some/some more bread/water/coffee/tea?
Μπορώ να έχω λίγο/ακόμη λίγο ψωμί/νερό/καφέ/τσάι;
Boro na eho ligo/akomi ligo psomi/nero/kafe/tsai?

181 May I have the bill, please?
Μπορώ να έχω το λογαριασμό, παρακαλώ;
Boro na eho to logariasmo, parakalo?

182 Does this bill include service?
Ο λογαριασμός περιλαμβάνει και σέρβις;
O logariasmos perilamvani ke service?

183 Do you accept travellers' cheques (travelers' checks)/Eurocheques/MasterCard/US dollars?
Μήπως παίρνετε ταξιδιωτικές επιταγές/Ευρωεπιταγές/Μάστερ Καρτς/Αμερικανικά Δολλάρια;
Mipos pernete taxidiotikes epitayes/Evroepitayes/MasterCard/Amerikanika dollaria?

184 Can I have a receipt, please?
Μπορώ να έχω την απόδειξη, παρακαλώ;
Boro na eho tin apodixi, parakalo?

185 Where is the toilet (restroom), please?
Πού είναι η τουαλέτα, παρακαλώ;
Pu ine i tualeta, parakalo?

On the Menu

186 First courses
Πρώτα φαγητά
Prota fayita

187 Soups
Σούπες
Supes

188 Main courses
Κύρια φαγητά
Kiria fayita

189 Fish dishes
Φαγητά με ψάρι
Fayita me psari

190 Meat dishes
Φαγητά με κρέας
Fayita me kreas

191 Vegetarian dishes
Είδη χορτοφαγίας
Idi hortofayias

192 Cheese
Τυριά
Tiria

193 Desserts
Επιδόρπιο
Epidorpio

194 Specialities
Πιάτο της ημέρας
Piato tis imeras

GETTING AROUND

Public Transport

195 Where is the bus stop/coach station/nearest metro (subway) station?
Πού είναι η στάση λεωφορείων/ο σταθμός των πούλμαν/το πλησιέστερο μετρό;
Pu ine i stasi leoforion/o stathmos ton pullman/to plisiestero metro?

196 When is the next/last bus to . . ?
Πότε είναι το επόμενο/τελευταίο λεωφορείο για την . . ;
Pote ine to epomeno/telefteo leoforio ya tin . . ?

197 How much is the fare to the city centre (downtown)/railway (railroad) station/airport?
Πόσο κάνει το εισιτήριο για το κέντρο της πόλης/το σιδηροδρομικό σταθμό/το αεροδρόμιο;
Poso kani to isitirio ya to kentro tis polis/to sidirodromiko stathmo/to aerodromio?

198 Will you tell me when to get off?
Μου λέτε πού να κατέβω;
Mu lete pu na katevo?

199 Does this bus go to . . ?
Αυτό το λεωφορείο πάει στο . . ;
Afto to leoforio pai sto . . ?

200 Which number bus goes to . . ?
Ποιο λεωφορείο πηγαίνει στο . . ;
Pio leoforio piyeni sto . . ?

201 May I have a single (one-way)/return (round-trip)/day ticket/book of tickets?
Μπορώ να έχω μονό/μετ' επιστροφής/ημερήσιο εισιτήριο/βιβλίο εισιτηρίων;
Boro na eho mono/met epistrofis/imerisio isitirio/vivlio isitirion?

Taxis

202 I would like to go to . . . How much will it cost?
Θα ήθελα να πάω στο . . ., πόσο θα μου στοιχίσει;
Tha ithela na pao sto . . ., poso tha mu stihisi?

203 Please stop here.
Παρακαλώ σταματάυε εδώ.
Parakalo stamatate edo.

204 I would like to order a taxi today/tomorrow/at 2pm to go from . . . to . . .
Θα ήθελα να παραγγείλω ταξί σήμερα/αύριο/στις 2 μ.μ. να με πάρει από το . . . στο . . .
Tha ithela na parangilo taxi simera/avrio/stis 2 to apoyevma na me pari apo to . . . sto . . .

G
R
E
E
K

195
↕
204

Asking the Way

205 Excuse me, do you speak English?
Με συγχωρείτε, μήπως μιλάτε Αγγλικά;
Me sinhorite, mipos milate Anglika?

206 Excuse me, is this the right way to . . ?
Με συγχωρείτε, μπορείτε να μου πείτε πώς θα πάω στο/στη . . ;
Me sinhorite, borite na mu pite pos tha pao sto/sti . . ?

207 . . . the cathedral/the tourist information office/the castle/the old town
. . . καθεδρικό ναό/τουριστικό γραφείο πληροφοριών/κάστρο/παλιά πόλη
. . . kathedriko nao/turistiko grafio pliroforion/kastro/palia poli

208 Can you tell me the way to the railway (railroad) station/bus station/taxi rank (stand)/city centre (downtown)/beach?
Μπορείτε να μου πείτε το δρόμο προς τον σιδηροδρομικό σταθμό/σταθμό λεωφορείων/στάση ταξί/το κέντρο της πόλεως/την πλαζ;
Borite na mu pite ton dromo pros ton sidirodromiko stathmo/stathmo leoforion/stasi taxi/to kentro tis poleos/tin plaz?

209 First/second/left/right/straight ahead.
Πρώτη/δεύτερη στροφή/αριστερά/δεξιά/ευθεία.
Proti/defteri strofi/aristera/dexia/efthia.

210 Where is the nearest police station/post office?
Πού είναι ο πλησιέστερος αστυνομικός σταθμός/το ταχυδρομείο;
Pu ine o plisiesteros astinomikos stathmos/to tahidromio?

211 Is it far?
Είναι μακριά;
Ine makria?

212 Do I need to take a taxi/catch a bus?
Χρειάζομαι να πάρω ταξί/λεωφορείο;
Hriazome na paro taxi/leoforio?

213 Can you point to it on my map?
Μπορείτε να μου το υποδείξετε στο χάρτη;
Borite na mu to ipodixete sto harti?

214 Thank you for your help.
Σας ευχαριστώ για τη βοήθειά σας.
Sas efharisto ya ti voithia sas.

SIGHTSEEING

215 Where is the Tourist Information office?
Πού είναι το Γραφείο Τουρισμού;
Pu ine to grafio Turismu?

²¹⁶ **Where is the cathedral/ church/museum?**
Πού είναι η Μητρόπολη/ Εκκλησία/το Μουσείο;
Pu ine i mitropoli/ekklisia/to musio?

²¹⁷ **How much is the entrance (admission) charge?**
Πόσο κάνει η είσο ος;
Poso kani i isodos?

²¹⁸ **Is there a reduction for children/students/senior citizens?**
Μήπως υπάρχει έκπτωση για παιδιά/φοιτητές/ ηλικιωμένους;
Mipos iparhi ekptosi ya pedia/ fitites/ilikiomenus?

²¹⁹ **What time does the next guided tour start?**
Τί ώρα αρχίζει η επόμενη περιοδεία με ξεναγό;
Ti ora arhizi i epomeni periodia me xenago?

²²⁰ **One/two adults/children, please.**
Ενα/δυό ενήλικες/παιδιά, παρακαλώ.
Ena/dio enilikes/pedia, parakalo.

²²¹ **May I take photographs here?**
Επιτρέπεται η λήψη φωτογραφιών εδώ;
Epitrepete i lipsi photographion edo?

ENTERTAINMENT

²²² **Can you recommend a good bar/nightclub?**
Μπορείτε να μου συστήσετε ένα καλό μπαρ/ νυχτερινό κέντρο;
Borite na mu sistisete ena kalo bar/nihterino kentro?

²²³ **Do you know what is on at the cinema (playing at the movies)/theatre at the moment?**
Ξέρετε τι παίζεται τώρα στο σινεμά/στο θέατρο;
Xerete ti pezete tora sto cinema/sto theatro?

²²⁴ **I would like to book (purchase) . . . tickets for the matinée/evening performance on Monday.**
Θα ήθελα να κρατήσω . . . εισιτήρια για απογευματινή/βραδινή παράσταση τη Δευτέρα.
Tha ithela na kratiso . . . isitiria ya apoyevmatini/vradini parastasi ti Deftera.

²²⁵ **What time does the film/ performance start?**
Τί ώρα αρχίζει το φιλμ/η παράσταση;
Ti ora arhizi to film/i parastasi?

MEETING PEOPLE

²²⁶ **Hello/Goodbye.**
Γειά σας/Χαίρετε.
Ya sas/Herete.

G
R
E
E
K

216
↕
226

²²⁷ **Good morning/good afternoon/good evening/goodnight.**
Καλημέρα/χαίρετε/καλησπέρα/καληνύχτα.
Kalimera/herete/kalispera/kalinihta.

²²⁸ **Pleased to meet you.**
Χαίρω πολύ.
Hero poli.

²²⁹ **How are you?**
Τι κάνετε;
Ti kanete?

²³⁰ **Fine, thank you. And you?**
Πολύ καλά, ευχαριστώ. Κι εσείς;
Poli kala, efharisto. Ki esis?

²³¹ **My name is . . .**
Ονομάζομαι . . .
Onomazome . . .

²³² **This is my friend/boyfriend/girlfriend/husband/wife/brother/sister.**
Σας συστήνω το φίλο μου/το φίλο μου/τη φίλη μου/το σύζυγό μου/τη σύζυγό μου/τον αδελφό μου/την αδελφή μου.
Sas sistino to filo mu/to filo mu/ti fili mu/to sizigo mu/ti sizigo mu/ton adelfo mu/tin adelfi mu.

²³³ **Where are you travelling to?**
Για πού ταξιδεύετε;
Ya pu taxidevete?

²³⁴ **I am/we are going to . . .**
Πάω/πάμε στο . . .
Pao/pame sto . . .

²³⁵ **How long are you travelling for?**
Για πόσο καιρό θα ταξιδέψετε;
Ya poso kero tha taxidepsete?

²³⁶ **Where do you come from?**
Από πού είστε;
Apo pu iste?

²³⁷ **I am/we are from . . .**
Είμαι/είμαστε από την . . .
Ime/imaste apo tin . . .

²³⁸ **We're on holiday.**
Είμαστε σε διακοπές.
Imaste se diakopes.

²³⁹ **This is our first visit here.**
Είναι η πρώτη μας επίσκεψη εδώ.
Ine i proti mas episkepsi edo.

²⁴⁰ **Would you like/May I have a cigarette?**
Θα θέλατε/Μπορώ να έχω ένα τσιγάρο;
Tha thelate/Boro na eho ena tsigaro?

²⁴¹ **I am sorry, but I do not understand.**
Λυπάμαι, μα δεν καταλαβαίνω.
Lipame, ma den katalaveno.

²⁴² **Please speak slowly.**
Παρακαλώ, μιλάτε αργά.
Parakalo, milate arga.

²⁴³ **Do you mind if I smoke?**
Θα σας πείραζε αν κάπνιζα;
Tha sas piraze an kapniza?

²⁴⁴ **Do you have a light?**
Μήπως έχετε φωτιά;
Mipos ehete fotia?

245 I am waiting for my husband/
wife/boyfriend/girlfriend.
Περιμένω τον/την/το/τη
άντρα/γυναίκα/φίλο/φίλη
μου.
*Perimeno ton/tin/to/ti/antra/
gineka/filo/fili mu.*

TRAVELLING WITH CHILDREN

246 Do you have a high chair/
baby-sitting service/cot?
Μήπως έχετε καρέκλα
μωρού/υπηρεσία μπέιμπυ
σίττιγκ/παιδικό κρεβάτι;
*Mipos ehete karekla moru/ipiresia
baby-sitting/pediko krevati?*

247 Where is the nursery/
playroom?
Πού είναι το νηπιαγωγείο/
η αίθουσα παιχνιδιών;
*Pu ine to nipiagoyio/i ethusa
pehnidion?*

248 Where can I warm the baby's
bottle?
Πού μπορώ να ζεστάνω το
μπουκάλι του μωρού;
*Pu boro na zestano to bukali tu
moru?*

COMMUNICATIONS

Post

249 How much will it cost to send
a letter/postcard/this
package to Britain/Ireland/
America/Canada/Australia/
New Zealand?

Πόσο θα στοιχίσει να
στείλω μια επιστολή/καρτ
ποστάλ/αυτό το πακέτο στη
Βρετανία/Ιρλανδία/
Αμερική/Καναδά/Νέα
Ζηλανδία;
*Poso tha stihisi na stilo mia
epistoli/card postale/afto to paketo
sti Vretania/Irlandia/Ameriki/
Canada/Nea Zilandia?*

250 I would like one stamp/two
stamps.
Θα ήθελα ένα
γραμματόσημο/δύο
γραμματόσημα.
*Tha ithela ena grammatosimo/dio
grammatosima.*

251 I'd like . . . stamps for
postcards to send abroad,
please.
Θα ήθελα . . .
γραμματόσημα για
καρτποστάλ να τις στείλω
στο εξωτερικό, παρακαλώ.
*Tha ithela . . . gramatosima ya
card postale na tis stilo sto
exoteriko, parakalo.*

Phones

252 I would like to make a
telephone call/reverse the
charges to (make a collect call
to) . . .
Θα ήθελα να τηλεφωνήσω/
να αντιστρέψω το κόστος
στο . . .
*Tha ithela na tilefoniso/na
antistrepso to kostos . . .*

253 **Which coins do I need for the telephone?**
Ποια κέρματα χρειάζομαι για το τηλέφωνο;
Pia kermata hriazome ya to tilefono?

254 **The line is engaged (busy).**
Η γραμμή είναι κατειλημμένη.
I grami ine katilimeni.

255 **The number is . . .**
Ο αριθμός είναι . . .
O arithmos ine . . .

256 **Hello, this is . . .**
Εμπρός, είμαι . . .
Empros, ime . . .

257 **May I speak to . . ?**
Μπορώ να μιλήσω στον/στην . . ;
Boro na miliso ston/stin . . ?

258 **He/She is not in at the moment. Can you call back?**
Δεν είναι εδώ αυτή τη στιγμή. Μπορείτε να ξανακαλέσετε;
Den ine edo avti ti stigmi. Borite na xanakalesete?

MONEY

259 **I would like to change these travellers' cheques (travelers' checks)/this currency/this Eurocheque.**
Θα ήθελα να εξαργυρώσω αυτές τις ταξιδιωτικές επιταγές/αυτό το συνάλλαγμα/αυτή την Ευρωεπιταγή.
Tha ithela na exaryiroso aftes tis taxidiotikes epitayes/afto to sinallagma/afti tin Evroepitayi.

260 **How much commission do you charge? (What is the service charge?)**
Τί προμήθεια επιβάλλετε;
Ti promithia epivallete?

261 **Can I obtain money with my MasterCard?**
Μπορώ να τραβήξω λεφτά με την Μάστερκαρτ μου;
Boro na travixo lefta me tin MasterCard mu?

SHOPPING

Names of Shops and Departments

262 **Βιβλιοπωλείο/Χαρτοπωλείο**
Vivliopolio/Hartopolio
Bookshop/Stationery

263 **Κατάστημα Κοσμημάτων/Δώρων**
Katastima Kosmimaton/Thoron
Jeweller's/Gifts

264 **Υποδήματα**
Ipodimata
Shoes

265 **Είδη Κιγκαλερίας**
Idi Kingalerias
Hardware

266 **Αντίκες**
Antikes
Antiques

²⁶⁷ **Κομμωτήριο (ανδρών)/ (γυναικών)**
Komotirio (andron)/(ginekon)
Hairdressers (men's)/(women's)

²⁶⁸ **Καπνοπωλείο**
Kapnopolio
Tobacconist

²⁶⁹ **Αρτοποιείο**
Artopiio
Baker's

²⁷⁰ **Σουπερμάρκετ**
Supermaket
Supermarket

²⁷¹ **Φωτογραφείο**
Photographio
Photoshop

²⁷² **Παιχνίδια**
Pehnidia
Toys

²⁷³ **Ταξιδιωτικός Πράκτορας**
Taxidiotikos Praktoras
Travel Agent

²⁷⁴ **Είδη Τουαλέτας**
Idi Tualetas
Toiletries

²⁷⁵ **Δίσκοι**
Diski
Records

In the Shop

²⁷⁶ **What time do the shops open/close?**
Τι ώρα ανοίγουν/κλείνουν τα καταστήματα;
Ti ora anigun/klinun ta katastimata?

²⁷⁷ **Where is the nearest market?**
Πού είναι η κοντινότερη αγορά;
Pu ine i kontinoteri agora?

²⁷⁸ **Can you show me the one in the window/this one?**
Μπορείτε να μου δείξετε κάτι που είδα στη βιτρίνα/ αυτό εδώ;
Borite na mu dixete kati pu ida sti vitrina/afto edo?

²⁷⁹ **Can I try this on?**
Μπορώ να το δοκιμάσω;
Boro na to dokimaso?

²⁸⁰ **What size is this?**
Τι μέγεθος είναι;
Ti meyethos ine?

²⁸¹ **This is too large/too small/ too expensive.**
Είναι πολύ μεγάλο/μικρό/ ακριβό.
Ine poli megalo/mikro/ akrivo.

²⁸² **Do you have any others?**
Εχετε άλλα;
Ehete ala?

²⁸³ **My size is . . .**
Το νούμερό μου είναι . . .
To numero mu ine . . .

G R E E K

267 ↑ 283

284 Where is the changing room/ childrens'/cosmetic/ ladieswear/menswear/food department?

Πού είναι το δοκιμαστήριο/το παιδικό τμήμα/το τμήμα καλλυντικών/γυναικείων/ ανδρικών/τροφίμων.

Pu ine to dokimastirio/to pediko tmima/to tmima kalintikon/ ginekion/andrikon/trofimon?

285 I would like . . .

Θα ήθελα . . .

Tha ithela . . .

286 I would like a quarter of a kilo/half a kilo/a kilo of bread/butter/cheese/ham/ tomatoes.

Θα ήθελα ένα τέταρτο κιλό/ μισό κιλό/ένα κιλό ψωμί/ βούτυρο/τυρί/ζαμπόν/ τομάτες.

Tha ithela ena tetarto kilo/miso kilo/ena kilo psomi/vutiro/tiri/ zambon/tomates.

287 How much is this?

Πόσο κάνει αυτό;

Poso kani afto?

288 I'll take this one, thank you.

Θα πάρω αυτό εδώ, ευχαριστώ.

Tha paro afto edo, efharisto.

289 Do you have a carrier (shopping) bag?

Εχετε μία σακούλα;

Ehete mia sakula?

290 Do you have anything cheaper/larger/smaller/of better quality?

Εχετε τίποτα φτηνότερο/ μεγαλύτερο/μικρότερο/ καλύτερης ποιότητας;

Ehete tipota ftinotero/megalitero/ mikrotero/kaliteris piotitas?

291 I would like a film for this camera.

Θα ήθελα ένα φιλμ για αυτή την φωτογραφική μηχανή.

Tha ithela ena film ya afti tin fotografiki mihani.

292 I would like some batteries, the same size as this old one.

Θα ήθελα μερικές μπαταρίες, του ίδιου μεγέθους, όπως αυτή η παλιά.

Tha ithela merikes bataries, tu idiu meyethus, opos afti i palia.

293 Would you mind wrapping this for me, please?

Θα μπορούσατε να μου το τυλίξετε, παρακαλώ;

Tha borusate na mu to tilixete, parakalo?

294 Sorry, but you seem to have given me the wrong change.

Συγνώμη, αλλά φαίνεται ότι μου δώσατε λάθος ρέστα.

Signomi, alla fenete oti mu dosate lathos resta.

MOTORING

Car Hire (Rental)

295 I have ordered (rented) a car in the name of . . .
Παράγγειλα αυτοκίνητο στο όνομα . . .
Parangila aftokinito sto onoma . . .

296 How much does it cost to hire (rent) a car for one day/ two days/one week?
Πόσο στοιχίζει να ενοικιάσω αυτοκίνητο για ία μέρα/δύο μέρες/μία εβδομάδα;
Poso stihizi na enikiaso aftokinito ya mia mera/dio meres/mia evdomada?

297 Is the tank already full of petrol (gas)?
Μήπως το ντεπόζιτο είναι ήδη γεμάτο με βενζίνη;
Mipos to deposito ine idi yemato me venzini?

298 Is insurance and tax included? How much is the deposit?
Περιλαμβάνει ασφάλεια και φόρο; Πόσα είναι η προκαταβολή;
Perilamvani asfalia ke foro? Posa ine prokatavoli?

299 By what time must I return the car?
Μέχρι πότε πρέπει να επιστρέψω το αυτοκίνητο;
Mehri pote prepi na epistrepso to aftokinito?

300 I would like a small/family car with a radio/cassette player.
Θα ήθελα ένα μικρό/ οικογενειακό αυτοκίνητο με ράδιο/κασετόφωνο.
Tha ithela ena mikro/ikoyeniako aftokinito me radio/kassetofono.

Asking the Way

301 Excuse me, can you help me please?
Με συγχωρείτε, μπορείτε σας παρακαλώ να με βοηθήσετε;
Me sinchorite, borite sas parakalo na me voithisete?

302 How do I reach the motorway/main road?
Από πού μπορώ να πάω στον αυτοκινητόδρομο/ κύριο δρόμο;
Apo pu boro na pao ston aftokinitodromo/kirio dromo?

303 I think I have taken the wrong turning.
Νομίζω πως πήρα λάθος στροφή.
Nomizo pos pira lathos strofi.

304 I am looking for this address.
Ψάχνω για αυτή τη διεύθυνση.
Psachno ya afti ti diefthinsi.

305 I am looking for the . . . hotel.
Ψάχνω για το ξενοδοχείο . . .
Psahno ya to xenodohio . . .

306 How far is it to ... from here?
Πόσο μακριά είναι από εδώ
το ...
Poso makria ine apo edo to ...

307 Carry straight on for ...
kilometres.
Προχωρήστε κατευθείαν
για ... χιλιόμετρα.
*Prohoriste katefthia ya ...
hiliometra.*

308 Take the next turning on the
right/left.
Στρίψετε στην επόμενη
στροφή δεξιά/αριστερά.
*Stripsete stin epomeni strofi dexia/
aristera.*

309 Turn right/left at the next
crossroads/traffic lights.
Στρίψετε δεξιά/αριστερά
στο(α) επόμενο(α)
σταυροδρόμι/φανάρια
κυκλοφορίας.
*Stripsete dexia/aristera sto(a)
epomeno(a) stavrodromi/fanaria
kikloforias.*

310 You are going in the wrong
direction.
Έχετε πάρει την αντίθετη
κατεύθυνση.
Ehete pari tin antitheti katefthinsi.

Parking

311 How long can I park here?
Για πόσο διάστημα μπορώ
να παρκάρω εδώ;
*Ya poso diastima boro na parkaro
edo?*

312 Is there a car park near here?
Υπάρχει χώρος
σταθμεύσεως κάπου εδώ;
*Iparhi horos stathmefseos kapu
edo?*

313 At what time does this car
park close?
Τι ώρα κλείνει ο χώρος
σταθμεύσεως;
Ti ora klini o horos stathmefseos?

Signs and Notices

314 Μονόδρομος
Monodromos
One way

315 Απαγορεύεται η είσοδος
Apagorevete i isodos
No entry

316 Απαγορεύεται η
στάθμευση
Apagorevete i stathmefsi
No parking

317 Παρακαμπτήριος
Parakamptirios
Detour (diversion)

318 Σταμάτημα/Stop
Stamatima/Stop
Stop

319 Δώσε προτεραιότητα
Dose protereotita
Give way (yield)

320 Ολισθηρός δρόμος
Olisthiros dromos
Slippery road

321 Απαγορεύεται η
υπέρβαση

G
R
E
E
K

306
↕
321

Apagorevete i ipervasi
No overtaking

At the Filling Station

322 Unleaded (lead-free)/
Standard/Premium
Αμόλυβδη/Απλή (Regular)/
Σούπερ (Super).
Amolivdi/Apli/Super.

323 Fill the tank please.
Γεμίστε το ντεπόζιτο
παρακαλώ.
Gemiste to depozito parakalo.

324 Do you have a road map of
this area?
Εχετε χάρτη οδικού δικτύου
αυτής της περιοχής;
*Ehete harti odiku diktiu aftis tis
periohis?*

325 How much is the car-wash?
Πόσο κοστίζει το πλύσιμο
αυτοκινήτου;
Poso kostizi to plisimo aftokinitu?

Breakdowns

326 I've had a breakdown at . . .
Το αυτοκίνητο χάλασε
στη . . .
To aftokinito halase sti . . .

327 I am on the road from . . . to . . .
Είμαι στο δρόμο από . . .
στο/στη . . .
Ime sto dromo apo . . . sto/sti . . .

328 I can't move the car. Can you
send a tow-truck?
Δεν μπορώ να κινήσω το

αυτοκίνητο. Μπορείτε να
στείλετε ρυμουλκό;
*Den boro na kiniso to aftokinito.
Borite na stilete rimulko?*

329 I have a flat tyre.
Εχω ξεφουσκωμένο
λάστιχο.
Eho xefuskomeno lastiho.

330 The windscreen (windshield)
has smashed/cracked.
Το παρμπρίζ έσπασε/
ράγισε.
To parbriz espase/ragise.

331 There is something wrong
with the engine/brakes/
lights/steering/gearbox/
clutch/exhaust.
Κάτι δεν πάει καλά με τη/
τα μηχανή/φρένα/φώτα/
τιμόνι/ταχύτητες/
συμπλέκτη/εξάτμιση.
*Kati den pai kala me ti/ta mihani/
frena/fota/timoni/tahitites/
siblekti/exatmisi.*

332 It's overheating.
Υπερθερμαίνεται.
Iperthermenete.

333 It won't start.
Δεν ξεκινά.
Den xekina.

334 Where can I get it repaired?
Πού μπορώ να το
επισκευάσω;
Pu boro na to episkevaso?

335 Can you take me there?
Μπορείτε να με πάτε εκεί;
Borite na me pate eki?

G
R
E
E
K

322
↑
335

336 Will it take long to fix?
Πόση ώρα θα κάνετε να το
επισκευάσετε;
*Posi ora tha kanete na to
episkevasete?*

337 How much will it cost?
Πόσο θα κοστίσει;
Poso tha kostisi?

Accidents

338 Can you help me? There has
been an accident.
Μπορείτε να με βοηθήσετε;
Εχει συμβεί κάποιο ατύχημα.
*Borite na me voithisete? Ehi simvi
kapio atihima.*

339 Please call the police/an
ambulance.
Παρακαλώ καλέσετε την
αστυνομία/ασθενοφόρο.
*Parakalo kalesete tin astinomia/
asthenoforo.*

340 Is anyone hurt?
Εχει τραυματιστεί κανείς;
Ehi travmatisti kanis?

Traffic Offences

341 I'm sorry, I didn't see the
sign.
Συγγνώμη, δεν πρόσεξα την
πινακίδα.
Signomi, den prosexa tin pinakida.

342 Must I pay a fine? How
much?
Πρέπει να πληρώσω
πρόστιμο; Πόσα;
Prepi na pliroso prostimo? Posa?

343 Show me your documents.
Δείξτε μου τα χαρτιά σας.
Dixte mu ta hartia sas.

HEALTH

Pharmacy

344 Do you have anything for a
stomachache/headache/sore
throat/toothache?
Εχετε κάτι για
στομαχόπονο/πονοκέφαλο/
ερεθισμένο λαιμό/
πονόδοντο;
*Ehete kati ya stomahopono/
ponokefalo/erethismeno lemo/
ponodonto?*

345 I need something for
diarrhoea (diarrhea)/
constipation/a cold/a cough/
insect bites/sunburn/travel
(motion) sickness.
Χρειάζομαι κάτι για τη
διάρροια/δυσκοιλιότητα/
κρύο/βήχα/δαγκώματα
εντόμων/ηλιοκαύματα/
ναυτία.
*Hriazome kati ya ti diarria/
dispepsia/krio/vinha/dangomata
entomon/iliokavmata/naftia.*

346 How much/how many do I
take?
Πόσο/Πόσα να παίρνω;
Poso/posa na perno?

347 How often do I take it/them?
Κάθε πόση ώρα να το/τα
παίρνω;
Kathe posi ora na to/ta perno?

348 How much does it cost?
Πόσο κοστίζει;
Poso kostizi?

349 Can you recommend a good
doctor/dentist?
Μπορείτε να μου
συστήσετε ένα καλό
γιατρό/οδοντογιατρό;
*Borite na mu sistisete ena kalo
yatro/odontoyatro?*

350 Is it suitable for children?
Είναι κατάλληλο για
παιδιά;
Ine katallilo ya pedia?

Doctor

351 I have a pain here/in my arm/
leg/chest/stomach.
Πονάω εδώ/στο βραχιονά
μου/στη γάμπα/στο
στήθος/στο στομάχι.
*Ponao edo/sto vrahiona mu/sti
gamba/sto stithos/sto stomahi.*

352 Please call a doctor, this is an
emergency.
Παρακαλώ τηλεφωνήστε
ένα γιατρό, είναι επείγουσα
κατάσταση.
*Parakalo tilefoniste ena yatro, ine
epigusa katastasi.*

353 I would like to make an
appointment to see a doctor.
Θα ήθελα να κλείσω
ραντεβού για να δω τον
γιατρό.
*Tha ithela na kliso rantevu ya na
tho ton yatro.*

354 I am diabetic/pregnant.
Είμαι διαβητικός/έγκυος.
Ime diavitikos/engios.

355 I need a prescription for . . .
Θέλω συνταγή για . . .
Thelo sintayi ya . . .

356 Can you give me something
to ease the pain?
Μπορείτε να μου δώσετε
κάτι για να καταπραϋνει
τον πόνο;
*Borite na mu dosete kati gia na
katapraini ton pono?*

357 I am/he is/she is allergic to
penicillin.
Είμαι/είναι/αλλεργικός(ή)
στην πενικιλίνη.
Ime/ine/alergikos(i) stin penicilini.

358 Does this hurt?
Πονάει;
Ponai?

359 You must/he must/she must
go to hospital.
Πρέπει να πάτε/πάει στο
νοσοκομείο.
Prepi na pate/pai sto nosokomio.

360 Take these once/twice /three
times a day.
Παίρνετε αυτά μία φορά/
δύο/τρεις φορές την ημέρα.
*Pernete afta mia fora/dio/tris fores
tin imera.*

361 I am/he is/she is taking this
medication.
Παίρνω/παίρνει αυτό το
φάρμακο.
Perno/perni afto to pharmako.

G
R
E
E
K

348
↑
361

G
R
E
E
K

362 **I have medical insurance.**
Εχω ασφάλεια
νοσοκομειακής
περίθαλψης.
*Echo asfalia nosokomiakis
perithalpsis.*

Dentist

363 **I have toothache.**
Νοιώθω πονόδοντο.
Niotho ponodonto.

364 **My filling has come out.**
Βγήκε το σφράγισμα.
Vgike to sfrayisma.

365 **I do/do not want to have an
injection first.**
Θέλω/δεν θέλω να έχω
πρώτα ένεση.
Thelo/den thelo na eho prota enesi.

EMERGENCIES

366 **Help!**
Βοήθεια!
Voithia!

367 **Call an ambulance/a doctor/
the police!**
Τηλεφωνήστε για
ασθενοφόρο/γιατρό/
αστυνομία !
*Tilefoniste yia asthenoforo/yatro/
astinomia!*

368 **I have had my travellers'
cheques (travelers' checks)/
credit cards/purse/handbag/
rucksack (knapsack)/
luggage/wallet stolen.**
Μου κλέψανε τις

ταχυδρομικές μου επιταγές/τις
πιστωτικές μου κάρτες/το
τσαντάκι μου/τη τσάντα μου/
τον εκδρομικό σάκο/τις
αποσκευές/το πορτοφόλι μου.
*Mu klepsane tis tahidromikes mu
epitayes/tis pistotikes mu kartes/to
portofoli mu/tin tsanta mu/ton
ekdromiko sako/tis aposkeves/to
portofoli mu.*

369 **Can you help me, I have lost
my daughter/son?**
Μπορείτε να με βοηθήσετε,
έχασα τη θυγατέρα μου/τον
γιο μου;
*Borite na me voithisete, ehasa ti
thigatera mu/ton yo mu?*

370 **Please go away/leave me
alone.**
Παρακαλώ φύγετε/αφήστε
με μόνη.
Parakalo fiyete/afiste me moni.

371 **Fire!**
Πυρκαγιά!
Pirkaya!

372 **I want to contact the British/
American/Canadian/Irish/
Australian/New Zealand/
South African consulate.**
Θέλω να επικοινωνήσω με το
Βρετανικό/Αμερικανικό/
Καναδικό/Ιρλανδικό/
Αυστραλιανό/Νέας Ζηλανδίας/
Νοτίου Αφρικής Προξενείο.
*Thelo na epikinoniso me to
Vretaniko/Amerikaniko/Kanadiko/
Irlandiko/Avstraliano/Neas
Zilandias/Notiu Afrikis Proxenio.*

146

Introduction

Hungarian, or Magyar, is distantly related to Finnish and Estonian, but is utterly unlike the languages of the other main linguistic groups of Europe. English is spoken to a fair degree, at least in tourist areas. German is even more widespread as a second language. Hungarian is undoubtedly a difficult language to master, and Hungarians are well aware of this, but you should nevertheless try to learn a few greetings, as silence when entering a shop, for instance, is considered rude.

In Hungarian, prepositions are replaced by suffixes. Each suffix has two forms, choose one that sounds harmonious with the noun/place name.

There is no specific gender in the Hungarian language, therefore there is no difference in the words for 'he/she/it'.

**H
U
N
G
A
R
I
A
N**

Addresses for travel and tourist information

UK: *IBUSZ (Hungarian National Tourist Office)*, c/o Danube Travel, 6 conduit St, London W1R 9TG; tel: (0171) 493 0263.
USA: *IBUSZ (Hungarian Travel North American Division)*, 1 Parker Plaza, Suite 1104, Fort Lee, NJ 07024; tel: (201) 592-8585.

ESSENTIALS

Letters

A	Á
o	*ah*
B	C
bay	*tsay*
CS	D
chay	*day*
E	É
eh	*ay*
F	G
eff	*gay*
GY	H
dj	*hah*
I	J
ee	*yay*
K	L
kah	*el*
LY	M
yeu	*em*
N	NY
en	*nee-uh*
O	Ó
o	*aw*
Ö	Ő
uh	*ur*
P	Q
pay	*q*
R	S
air	*esh*
SZ	T
ess	*tay*
TY	U

tch	*oo*
Ú	Ü
ooh	*ew*
Ű	V
eew	*vay*
W	X
doop-lo vay	*ex*
Y	Z
eep-see-lon	*zat*
ZS	
zhay	

Basic Words and Phrases

1. **Yes** — **No**
   Igen — Nem
   igen — *nem*

2. **Please** — **Thank you**
   Kérem szépen — Köszönöm
   kay-rem say-pan — *kuh-suh-nuhn*

3. **That's O.K.** — **Perhaps**
   Rendben van. — Esetleg
   rhend-ben von — *eh-shet-leg*

4. **To** — **From**
   Fele — Onnan
   fah-lah — *on-non*

5. **Here** — **There**
   Itt — Ott
   it — *ot*

6. **None** — **Also**
   Semelyik — Szintén
   sheh-may-yeek — *seen-tayn*

7. **How** — **When**
   Hogyan — Mikor
   ho-djon — *mee-kor*

8. **What** — **Why**

Mit	Miért
mit	*mee-ayrt*

9 I don't understand.
Nem értem.
nem ayr-tehm

10 I don't speak Hungarian.
Nem tudok magyarul.
nem too-dok mo-djo-rool.

11 Do you speak English?
Beszél angolul?
beh-sayl on-go-lool

12 Can you please write it down?
Kérem le tudná ezt írni?
kay-rehm leh tood-nay ehz eeyr-ni

13 Can you please speak more slowly?
Kérem beszéljen lassabban?
kay-rehm beh-sayl-yen losh-shob-bon

14 How much does it/this cost?
Ez mennyibe kerül?
ehz mehnn-yee-beh keh-rewl

Days

15 Monday — **Tuesday**
Hétfő — Kedd
heyt-fur — *kehdd*

16 Wednesday — **Thursday**
Szerda — Csütörtök
sehr-dah — *chew-tohr-tuhk*

17 Friday — **Saturday**
Péntek — Szombat
payn-tehk — *soom-bot*

18 Sunday — **Morning**
Vasárnap — Délelőtt

vo-shahr-nop	*dayl-eh-lurtt*

19 Afternoon — **Evening**
Délután — Este
dayl-oo-tahn — *esh-teh*

20 Night — **Week**
Éjjel — Hét
eey-yehl — *hayt*

21 Yesterday — **Tomorrow**
Tegnap — Holnap
tehg-nop — *hol-nop*

Numbers

22 Zero — **One**
Nulla — Egy
nool-lo — *edj*

23 Two — **Three**
Kettő — Három
keht-tur — *hah-rom*

24 Four — **Five**
Négy — Öt
naydj — *uht*

25 Six — **Seven**
Hat — Hét
hot — *hayt*

26 Eight — **Nine**
Nyolc — Kilenc
nn-yolts — *kee-lehnts*

27 Ten — **Eleven**
Tíz — Tizenegy
teez — *tee-zehn-edj*

28 Twelve — **Thirteen**
Tizenkettő — Tizenhárom
tee-zehn-keht-tur — *tee-zehn-hah-rom*

29 Fourteen — **Fifteen**
Tizennégy — Tizenöt
tee-zehn-naydj — *tee-zehn-uht*

30 Sixteen
Tizenhat
tee-zehn-hot

Seventeen
Tizenhét
tee-zehn-hayt

31 Eighteen
Tizennyolc
tee-zehn-n-yolts

Nineteen
Tizenkilenc
tee-zehn-kee-lehnts

32 Twenty
Húsz
hoos

Twenty-one
Huszonegy
hoo-son-edj

33 Twenty-two
Huszonkettő
hoo-son-keht-tur

Thirty
Harminc
hor-mints

34 Forty
Negyven
nehdj-vehn

Fifty
Ötven
uht-vehn

35 Sixty
Hatvan
hot-von

Seventy
Hetven
heht-vehn

36 Eighty
Nyolcvan
n-yolts-von

Ninety
Kilencven
kee-lehnts-vehn

37 One hundred
Egyszáz
edj-sahz

Five hundred
Ötszáz
oht-sahz

38 One thousand
Egyezer
edj-eh-zehr

One million
Egy millió
edj meel-li-aw

Time

39 9.00
Kilenc óra
kee-lehnts aw-ro

40 9.05
Kilenc óra öt perc
kee-lehnts aw-ro uht pertz

41 9.10
Kilenc óra tíz perc
kee-lehnts aw-ro teez pertz

42 9.15
Negyed tíz
neh-djehd teez

43 9.20
Kilenc óra húsz perc
kee-lehntz aw-ro hoos pertz

44 9.25
Kilenc óra huszonöt perc
kee-lehntz aw-ro hoo-son-uht pertz

45 9.30
Fél tíz
fayl teez

46 9.35
Kilenc óra harmincöt perc
kee-lehntz aw-ro hor-mints-uht pertz

47 9.40
Kilenc óra negyven perc
kee-lehntz aw-ro nehdj-vehn pertz

48 9.45
Háromnegyed tíz
hah-rom-neh-djehd teez

49 9.50
Kilenc óra ötven perc
kee-lehntz aw-ro uht-ven pertz

50 9.55
Kilenc óra ötvenöt perc
kee-lehntz aw-ro uht-vehn-uht pertz

51 12.00/Midday/Midnight
Tizenkét óra/Dél/Éjfél
tee-zen-kayt aw-ro/dayl/ay-fayl

52 What time is it?
Hány óra van?

hahnn-y aw-ro von

53 It is . . .

... óra van.

... *aw-ro von*

ARRIVING AND DEPARTING

Airport

54 Excuse me, where is the check-in desk for . . . airline?

Bocsánat, hol találom a . . . légitársaság utaskezelő pultját?

bo-chah-not, hol to-lah-lom o . . . lay-gee-tahr-sho-shahg oo-tosh-keh-zeh-lur poolt-yaht

55 What is the boarding gate/ time for my flight?

Melyik az én gépem beszálló kapuja?/Mikor indul a gépem?

meh-yeek oz ayn gay-pehm beh-sahl-law ko-poo-ya?/mee-kor in-dool o gay-pehm?

56 How long is the delay likely to be?

Mennyi a várható késés?

mehnn-y-ee o vahr-ho-taw kay-shaysh?

57 Where is the duty-free shop?

Hol van a Duty-Free üzlet?

hol von o duty-free ewz-leht?

58 Which way is the baggage reclaim?

Merre van a poggyász kiváltó?

mehr-rheh von o podj-djahs ki-vahl-taw

59 Where can I get the bus to the city centre?

Honnan indul a busz a városközpontba?

hon-non in-dool o bus o vah-rosh-kuhz-pont-bo

Train Station

60 Where is the ticket office/ information desk?

Hol van a jegypénztár/ információ?

hol von o yedj-pehnz-tahr/in-for-mah-tsi-aw

61 Which platform does the train to . . . depart from?

Melyik vágányról indul a vonat . . . -ba/-be?

meh-yeek vah-gahn-yrawl in-dool o vo-not . . . -bo/-beh

62 Where is platform . . . ?

Hol van a . . . -os/es vágány?

hol von o . . . -osh/ash vah-gahn

63 When is the next train to . . ?

Mikor indul a következő vonat . . . -ba/-be?

mee-kor in-dool o kuh-veht-keh-zur vo-not . . . -bo/-beh

64 Is there a later train to . . ?

Van egy későbbi vonat is . . . -ba/-be?

von edj kay-shurb-bi vo-not eesh . . . -bo/-beh

Port

65 How do I get to the port?

Hogy jutok el a kikötőbe?

hodj yoo-tok ehl o kee-kuh-tur-beh

66 When is the next sailing to . . ?
Mikor indul a következő hajó . .
. -ba/-be?
*mee-kor in-dool o kuh-veht-keh-
zur ho-yaw . . . -bo/-beh*

67 Can I catch an earlier ferry
with this ticket?
Ezzel a jeggyel egy korábbi
kompra is felszállhatok?
*ehz-zehl o yehdj-ehl edj ko-rahb-
bee komp-ro ish fehl-sahl-ho-tok*

Notices and Signs

68 Büfé
buh-fay
Buffet (Dining Car)

69 Autóbusz
o-oo-taw-boos
Bus

70 Ivóvíz/Nem ivóvíz
ee-vaw-veez/nem ee-vaw-veez
Drinking/Non-drinking water

71 Bejárat
beh-yah-rot
Entrance

72 Kijárat
kee-yah-rot
Exit

73 Információ
in-for-mah-tsee-aw
Information

74 Poggyász Kiváltó
podj-djahs kee-vahl-taw
Left Luggage (Baggage Claim)

75 Kulcsra zárható
csomagmegőrző szekrény
koolch-ro zahr-ho-taw cho-mog-

mehg-ur-zur sehk-raynn-y
Luggage Lockers

76 Posta/Postahivatal
posh-to/posh-to-hee-vo-tol
Post Office

77 Peron/Vágány
peh-ron/vah-gahn-y
Platform

78 Vasútállomás/Vonatállomás
*vo-shoot-ahl-lo-mahsh/vo-not-ahl-
lo-mahsh*
Railway (Railroad Station)

79 Repülőtér
re-pew-lur-tayr
Airport

80 Hajókikötő/Hajóállomás
*ho-yaw-kee-kuh-tur/ho-yaw-ahl-
lo-mahsh*
Port

81 Étterem/Vendéglő
ayt-teh-rehm/vehn-dayg-lur
Restaurant

82 Dohányzó/Nem-Dohányzó
*do-hahnn-yzaw/nem do-hahnn-
yzaw*
Smoking/Non-Smoking

83 Telefon
teh-leh-fon
Telephone

84 Jegypénztár
yedj-paynz-tahr
Ticket Office

85 Utaskezelő Pult
oo-tosh-keh-zeh-lur poolt
Check-in Desk

86 Menetrend
meh-neht-rehnd
Timetable (Schedule)

87 WC
vay-tsay
Toilets (Restrooms)

88 Férfiak
fayr-fee-ok
Gentlemen

89 Nők
nurk
Ladies'

90 Villamos
veel-lo-mosh
Tram (Streetcar)

91 Metro
meht-raw
Underground (Subway)

92 Váróterem
vah-raw-teh-rehm
Waiting-Room

Buying a Ticket

93 I would like a first-class/
second-class single (one-
way)/return (round-trip)
ticket to . . .
Kérek egy elsőosztályú/
másodosztályú egyszeri
utazásra szóló/retúr jegyet . . . -
ba/-be.
*kay-rehk edj ehl-shur-os-tah-yooh/
mah-shod-os-tah-yooh edj-seh-ree
oo-to-zahsh-ro saw-law/reh-toohr
yeh-djeht . . . -bo/-beh*

94 Is my rail pass valid on this
train/ferry/bus?

A jegyem erre a vonatra/
kompra/buszra is érvényes?
*o yeh-djehm er-reh o vo-not-ro/
komp-ro/boos-ro eesh ayr-vayn-
yehsh*

95 I would like an aisle/window
seat.
A közlekedő folyosó/ablak
melletti ülést kérném.
*o kuhz-leh-keh-dur fo-yo-shaw/
oblok mehl-leht-tee ew-laysht
kehr-nehm*

96 No smoking/smoking, please.
Kérem ne dohányozzanak/
Dohányozni szabad.
*kay-rehm neh do-hahnn-yoz-zo-
nok/do-hahnn-yoz-ni so-bod.*

97 We would like to sit
together.
Szeretnénk egymás mellett ülni.
*seh-reht-naynk edj-mahsh mehl-
lehtt ewl-ni.*

98 I would like to make a seat
reservation.
Szeretnék ülőhelyet foglalni.
*seh-reht-nayk ew-lur-heh-yeht fog-
lol-ni.*

99 I would like to reserve a
couchette/sleeper for one
person/two people/for my
family.
Szeretnék egy couchettet/
hálókocsit foglalni egy személyre/
két személyre/a családomnak.
*seh-reht-nayk edj coo-shehtt-eht/
hah-law-ko-cheet fog-lol-ni edj
seh-may-reh/kayt seh-may-reh/o
cho-lah-dom-nok.*

100 I would like to reserve a cabin.
Egy kabint szeretnék foglalni.
edj co-beent seh-reht-nayk fog-lolni.

Timetables (Schedules)

101 Érkezés
ayr-keh-zaysh
Arrive

102 Megáll . . . -ban/-ben
mehg-ahll . . . -bon/-behn
Calls (Stops at . . .)

103 Étkezési Lehetőség
ayt-keh-zay-shee le-heh-tur-shayg
Catering Service

104 Átszállás . . . -ban/-ben
aht-sahl-lahsh . . . -bon/-behn
Change at . . .

105 Csatlakozás
chot-lo-ko-zahsh
Connection

106 Napi
no-pee
Daily

107 Negyven percenként
nehdj-vehn pert-zehn-kaynt
Every 40 Minutes

108 Első-osztály
el-shur os-tahy
First-Class

109 óránként
aw-rahn-kaynt
Hourly

110 Ajánlott a helyfoglalás
o-yahn-lott o hehy-fog-lo-lahsh

Seat reservations are recommended

111 Másodosztály
mah-shod-os-tahy
Second-class

112 Fizetendő Pótdíj
fee-zeh-tehn-dur pawt-deey
Supplement Payable

113 útvonalon
ooht-vo-no-lon
Via

Luggage

114 How much will it cost to send (ship) my luggage in advance?
Mennyibe kerül előreküldeni a poggyászomat?
mehnn-yee-beh keh-rewl eh-lur-re-kewl-deh-nee o podj-djah-so-mot

115 Where is the left luggage (baggage claim) office?
Merre van a talált csomagok irodája?
mehr-reh von o to-lahlt cho-mo-gok eero-dah-yah

116 What time do you open/close?
Mikor nyitnak/zárnak?
mee-kor nn-yeet-nok/zahr-nok

117 Where are the luggage trolleys (carts?)
Hol találom a poggyász trolikat?
hol to-lah-lom o podj-djahs tro-lee-kot

118 Where are the lockers?
Hol találom a kulcsra zárható

csomagmegőrző szekrényeket?
hol to-lah-lom o koolch-ro zahr-
ho-taw cho-mog-mehg-ur-zur
sehk-raynn-yeh-keht

119 I have lost my locker key.
Elvesztettem a csomagmegőrző
kulcsát.
el-vehs-teht-tehm o cho-mog-
mehg-ur-zur kool-chaht

On Board

120 Is this seat taken?
Foglalt ez a hely?
fog-lolt ehz o hehy

121 Excuse me, you are sitting in
my reserved seat.
Bocsánatot kérek, de ön az én
foglalt helyemen ül.
bo-chah-no-tot kay-rehk, deh uhn
oz ayn fog-lolt heh-yeh-mehn ewl

122 Which station is this?
Ez melyik állomás?
ehz meh-yeek ahl-lo-mahsh

123 What time is this train/bus/
ferry/flight due to arrive/
depart?
Ez a vonat/busz/komp/repülő
mikor érkezik/indul ?
ehz o vonot/boos/komp/reh-pew-
lur mee-kor ayr-keh-zeek/in-dool

124 Will you wake me just before
we arrive?
Felébresztene közvetlenül a
megérkezésünk előtt?
fehl-ayb-rehs-teh-neh kuhz-veht-
leh-newl o mehg-ayr-keh-zay-
shewnk eh-lurtt

Customs and Passports

125 Passports, please!
Kérjük az útleveleket!
kayr-yewk oz ooht-leh-veh-leh-
keht

126 I have nothing to declare. I
have wine/spirits (alcohol)/
tobacco to declare.
Semmi elvámolni valóm sincs.
Bor/szesz/dohányáru elvámolni
valóm van.
shehm-mee ehl-vah-mol-ni vo-
lawm sheench. bor/sehs/do-hahnn-
y-ah-rooh ehl-vah-mol-ni vo-lawm
von

127 I shall be staying for . . .
days/weeks/months.
. . . napig/hétig/hónapig
maradok.
. . . no-pig/hay-tig/haw-nopig
morodok

AT THE TOURIST OFFICE

128 Do you have a map of the
town/area?
Van egy városi/helyi térképe?
von edj vah-ro-shee/heh-yee tayr-
kay-peh

129 Can I reserve accommodation
here?
Lehet itt szállást foglalni?
leh-heht itt sahl-lahsht fog-lol-ni

130 Do you have a list of
accommodation?
Van önnek egy szállás listája?
von uhn-nehk edj sahl-lahsh lish-
tah-yo

H
U
N
G
A
R
I
A
N

119
↑
130

ACCOMMODATION

ACCOMMODATION

Hotels

I have a reservation in the name of . . .
Szobát foglaltam . . . néven.
so-baht fog-lol-tom . . . nay-vehn

I wrote to/faxed/telephoned you last month/last week in . . .
Irtam/faxot küldtem/ telefonáltam önnek a múlt hónapban/héten . . . -án/-én
eer-tom/fox-ot kewld-tehm/teh-leh- fo-nahl-tom uhn-nehk o moolt haw- nop-bon/hay-tehn . . . ahn/ehn

Do you have any rooms free?
Van szabad szobájuk?
von so-bod so-bah-yook

I would like to reserve a single/double room with/ without bath/with/without shower.
Szeretnék foglalni egy egyágyas/kétágyas szobát fürdőszobával/fürdőszoba nélkül/zuhanyozóval/ zuhanyozó nélkül.
seh-reht-naynk fog-lolni edj edj- ah-djos/kayt-ahd-jos so-baht fewr- dur-so-bahvol/fewr-dur-so-bah nayl-kewl/zoo-honn-yozaw-vol/ zoo-honn-yozaw nayl-kewl.

I would like bed and breakfast/room and half board/room and full board.
Szeretnék egy szobát reggelivel/Szeretnék egy szobát reggelivel és vacsorával/

Szeretnék egy szobát teljes ellátással.
seh-reht-nayk edj so-baht rehg- gehlee-vehl/seh-reht-nayk edj so- baht rehg-geh-lee-vehl aysh vo- cho-rah-vol/seh-reht-nayk edj so- baht tehl-yehsh ehl-lah-tahsh-shol.

How much is it per night?
Mennyibe kerül egy éjjelre?
mehnn-yee-beh keh-rewl edj ay-yehl- reh

Is breakfast included?
Az árban a reggeli is benne van?
oz ahr-bon o rehg-geh-li ish behn-neh von

May I see the room?
Megnézhetem a szobát?
mehg-nayz-hehtehm o so-baht

Do you have any cheaper rooms?
Van olcsóbb szobájuk?
von ol-chawbb so-bah-yook

I would like to take the room.
Szeretném kivenni a szobát.
seh-reht-naym ki-vehn-ni o so- baht

I would like to stay for . . . nights.
Szeretnék . . . éjjelt maradni.
seh-reht-nayk . . . ay-yehlt mo- rod-ni

The shower/light/tap doesn't work.
A zuhany/villany/csap nem működik.
o zoo-honn-y/veel-lonn-y/chop nem meew-kuh-dik

156

143 At what time/where is breakfast served?

Hány órakor/hol lehet reggelizni?

hahnn-y aw-rokor/hol leh-eht rehg-geh-leez-ni

144 What time do I have to check-out?

Hány órakor kell átadnom a szobát?

hahnn-y aw-ro-kor kehll aht-od-nom o so-baht

145 Can I have the key to room no . . ?

Megkaphatnám a . . . -os számu szoba kulcsát.

meg-kop-hot-nahm o . . . -osh sah-moo so-bah kool-chaht

146 My room number is . . .

A szobaszámom . . .

o so-bo-sah-mom . . .

147 Do you accept travellers' cheques/Eurocheques/credit cards?

Elfogadnak Traveller's csekket/ Euro-csekket/hitelkártyát?

el-fo-god-nok travellers chehk-keht/ euro-chehk-keht/hee-tehl-kahrt-yaht

148 May I have the bill please?

Megkaphatnám a számlát?

meg-kop-hot-nahm o sahm-laht

149 Excuse me, I think there is a mistake in this bill.

Elnézést kérek, de azt hiszem hiba van a számlában.

ehl-nay-zay-sht kay-rehk, deh ozt hee-sehm hee-bo von o sahm-lah-bon

Youth Hostels

150 How much is a dormitory bed per night?

Mennyibe kerül a hálóteremben egy ágy egy éjjelre?

mehnn-yee-beh keh-rewr o hah-law-teh-rehm-behn edj ahdj ehdj ay-yehl-reh

151 I am/am not an HI member.

HI tag vagyok/Nem vagyok HI tag.

HI tog vo-djok/nem vo-djok HI tog.

152 May I use my own sleeping bag?

Használhatom a saját hálózsákomat?

hos-nahl-ho-tom o sho-yaht hah-law-zhah-ko-mot

153 What time do you lock the doors at night?

Hány órakor zárják be a kaput éjjelre?

hahnn-y aw-rokor zahr-yahk beh o ko-poot ay-yehl-reh

Camping

154 May I camp here for the night/two nights?

Campingezhetünk itt egy éjjelre/két éjjelre?

com-pin-gehz-heh-tuhnk itt edj ay-yehl-reh/kayt ay-yehl-reh

155 Where can I pitch my tent?

Hol verhetem fel a sátramat?

hol vehr-heh-tehm fehl o saht-ro-mot

156 How much does it cost for
one night/week?
Mennyibe kerül egy éjjelre/egy
hétre?
*mehnn-yee-beh keh-rewr edj ay-
yehl-reh/edj hayt-reh*

157 Where can we park our caravan?
Hol állíthatjuk le a
lakókocsinkat?
*hol ahl-leet-hot-yook leh o lo-kaw-
ko-cheen-kot*

158 Where are the washing
facilities?
Hol van a mosakodási
lehetőség?
*hol von o mo-sho-ko-dah-shi leh-
heh-tur-shayg*

159 Is there a restaurant/
supermarket/swimming pool
on site/nearby?
Van étterem/szupermarket/
uszoda a területen/környéken?
*von ayt-teh-rehm/soo-pehr-mor-
keht/oo-sodo o teh-rew-leh-tehn/
kuhr-nn-yay-kehn*

160 Do you have a safety deposit
box?
Van önöknek értékmegőrzőjük?
*von uh-nuhk-nehk ayr-tayk-meg-
ur-zur-yewk*

EATING AND DRINKING

Cafés and Bars

161 I would like a cup of/two
cups of/another coffee/tea.
Szeretnék kérni egy csésze/két
csésze/mégegy kávét/teát.

*seh-reht-nayk kayr-ni edj chay-
seh/kayt chay-seh/mayg-edj kah-
vayt/teh-aht*

162 With milk/sugar. Without
milk/sugar.
Tejjel/Cukorral. Tej nélkül/
Cukor nélkül.
*tehy-yehl/tsoo-kor-rol.
tehy nayl-kewl/tsoo-kor nayl-kewl.*

163 I would like a bottle/glass/
two glasses of mineral water/
red wine/white wine, please.
Szeretnék kérni egy üveg/egy
pohár/két pohár ásvány vizet/
vörös bort/fehér bort.
*seh-reht-nayk kayr-ni edj ew-
vehg/edj po-hahr/kayt po-hahr
ahsh-vahnn-y vee-zeht/vuh-ruhsh
bort/feh-hayr bort.*

164 I would like a beer/two
beers, please.
Szeretnék kérni egy sört/két sört.
*seh-reht-nayk kayr-ni edj sh-uhrt/
kayt sh-uhrt*

165 May I have some ice?
Kaphatok jeget?
kop-ho-tok yeh-geht

166 Do you have any matches/
cigarettes/cigars?
Van gyufája/cigarettája/szivarja?
*von djoo-fah-yo/tsee-go-reht-
tahyo/see-vor-yo*

Restaurants

167 Can you recommend a good/
inexpensive restaurant in this
area?
Tud egy jó/olcsó éttermet

ajánlani ezen a környéken?
tood edj yaw/ol-chaw ayt-tehr-meht o-yahn-loni eh-zehn o kuhr-nn-yay-kehn

168 I would like a table for . . . people.
Szeretnék egy asztalt . . . főre.
seh-reht-nayk edj os-tolt . . . fur-reh

169 Do you have a non-smoking area?
Van itt nem dohányzó rész?
von itt nem do-hahnn-yzaw rays

170 Waiter/Waitress!
Pincér/Pincérnő!
pin-cayr/pin-cayr-nur

171 Do you have a set menu/children's menu/wine list?
Van komplett menüjük/gyermek menüjük/itallapjuk?
von komp-lett meh-new-yewk/djehr-mehk meh-new-yewk/ee-tol-lop-yook

172 Do you have any vegetarian dishes, please?
Van vegetariánus ételük?
von veh-geh-to-ri-ah-noosh ay-teh-lewk

173 Are there any local specialities?
Van valamilyen helyi specialitásuk?
von volo-mee-yehn heh-yi shpe-tsi-o-lee-tah-shook

174 Are vegetables included?
A zöldségek is benne vannak az árban?

o *zuhld-shay-gehk ish behn-neh von-nok oz ahr-bon*

175 Could I have it well-cooked/medium/rare please?
Kérhetem a húst jól átsülten/közepesen sülten/angolosan sülten?
kayr-heh-tehm o hoosht yawl aht-shewl-tehn/kuh-zeh-peh-shehn shewl-tehn/on-golo-shon shewl-tehn

176 What does this dish consist of?
Miből készült ez az étel?
mee-bur kay-sewlt ehz oz ay-tehl

177 I would like the set menu, please.
Szeretném kérni a komplett menüt.
seh-reht-naym kayr-ni o komp-lett meh-neewt

178 We have not been served yet.
Még nem szolgáltak ki minket.
mayg nem sol-gahl-tok kee meen-keht

179 Excuse me, this is not what I ordered.
Elnézést kérek, de nem ezt rendeltem.
ehl-nay-zaysht kay-rehk, deh nem ehzt rehn-dehl-tem

180 May I have some/some more bread/water/coffee/tea?
Kérhetek kenyeret/még kenyeret/vizet/kávét/teát?
kayr-heh-tehk kehnn-yeh-reht/mayg kehnn-yeh-reht/vee-zeht/kah-vayt/teh-aht?

H U N G A R I A N

**168
↑
180**

181 **May I have the bill, please?**
Szeretném kérni a számlát.
seh-reht-naym kayr-ni o sahm-laht

182 **Does this bill include service?**
A számla a felszolgálási díjat is
tartalmazza?
*o sahm-lah o fehl-sol-gah-lah-shi
dee-yot ish tor-tol-moz-zo*

183 **Do you accept travellers'
cheques (travelers' checks)/
Eurocheques/MasterCard/US
dollars?**
Elfogadnak travellers'csekket/
Euro-csekket/Master Cardot/
Amerikai Dollárt?
*el-fo-god-nok travellers chehk-
keht/euro-chehk-keht/master card-
ot/a-meh-ree-koi dol-lahrt*

184 **Can I have a receipt, please?**
Kérhetek nyugtát erről?
*kayr-heh-tehk nn-yoog-taht ehr-
rurl*

185 **Where is the toilet
(restroom), please?**
Megmondaná hol találom a WC-t?
*mehg-mon-do-nah hol to-lah-lom
o vay-tsayt*

On the Menu

186 **First courses**
Előételek
eh-lur-ay-teh-lehk

187 **Soups**
Levesek
leh-veh-shehk

188 **Main courses**
Főételek

fur-ay-teh-lehk

189 **Fish dishes**
Halételek
hol-ay-teh-lehk

190 **Meat dishes**
Húsételek
hoosh-ay-teh-lehk

191 **Vegetarian dishes**
Vegetariánus ételek
*veh-geh-to-ree-ah-noosh ay-teh-
lehk*

192 **Cheese**
Sajtok
shoy-tok

193 **Desserts**
Édességek
ay-dehsh-shay-gehk

194 **Specialities**
Specialitások
shpeh-tzi-o-li-tah-shok

GETTING AROUND

Public Transport

195 **Where is the bus stop/coach
station/nearest metro
(subway) station?**
Hol van a buszmegálló/
autóbusz állomás/legközelebbi
metro állomás?
*hol von o boos-mehg-ahl-law/o-
oo-taw-boos ahl-lo-mahsh/leg-
kuh-zeh-lehb-bi meht-raw ahl-lo-
mahsh.*

196 When is the next/last bus to . . ?
Mikor indul a következő/utolsó
busz . . . -ba/-be?
mee-kor in-dool o kuh-veht-keh-
zur boos . . . -bo/-beh

197 How much is the fare to the
city centre (downtown)/
railway (railroad station/
airport?
Mennyibe kerül a menetjegy a
városközpontba/
vasútállomáshoz/repülőtérre?
mehnn-yee-beh keh-rewl o meh-
neht-yehdj o vah-rosh-kuhz-pont-
bah/vo-shoot-ahl-lo-mahsh-hoz/
reh-pew-lur-tayr-reh

198 Will you tell me when to get
off?
Szólna, mikor kell leszállnom?
sawl-no mee-kor kehll leh-sahll-
nom

199 Does this bus go to . . ?
Ez a busz megy . . . -ba/-be?
ehz o boos mehdj . . . -bo/-beh

200 Which number bus goes to . . ?
Hányas busz megy . . . -ba/-be?
hahnn-yos boos mehdj . . . -bo/-
beh

201 May I have a single (one-
way)/return (round-trip)/day
ticket/book of tickets?
Szeretnék kéni egy egyszeri
utazásra szóló/retúr/napi
jegyet/jegycsomagot.
seh-reht-nayk kayr-ni edj edj-seh-ree
oo-to-zahsh-ro saw-law/reh-toor/
nopi ye-djeht/yedj-cho-mo-got

Taxis

202 I would like to go to . . .
How much will it cost?
Szeretnék eljutni . . . -ba/-be.
Mibe fog ez kerülni?
seh-reht-nayk ehl-yoot-ni . . . -bo/-
beh Mee-beh fog ehz keh-rewl-ni

203 Please stop here.
Kérem itt álljon meg.
kay-rehm itt ahll-yon mehg

204 I would like to order a taxi
today/tomorrow/at 2pm to
go from . . . to . . .
Szeretnék rendelni egy taxit
mára/holnapra/délután 2 órára
hogy elvigyen . . . -ból/-bő1 . . .
-ba/-be.
seh-reht-nayk rehn-dehl-ni ehdj
toxit mah-ro/hol-nop-ro/dayl-oo-
tahn kayt aw-rah-ro hodj ehl-vee-
djehn . . . -bawl/burl . . . -bo/-beh

Asking the Way

205 Excuse me, do you speak
English?
Bocsánat, beszél angolul?
bo-chah-not, beh-sayl on-go-lool

206 Excuse me, is this the right
way to . . ?
Bocsánat, erre kell menni . . . -
ba/-be?
bo-chah-not, ehr-reh kehll mehn-ni
. . . -bo/-beh

207 . . . the cathedral/the tourist
information office/the castle/
the old town
   . . . a katedrális/a turista
információs iroda/a kastély/az
óváros
   . . . .o ko-tehd-rah-leesh/o too-rish-
to in-for-mah-tsi-awsh ee-ro-do/o
kosh-tay/oz aw-vah-rosh

208 Can you tell me the way to
the railway (railroad station)/
bus station/taxi rank (stand)/
city centre (downtown)/
beach?
   Meg tudná mondani hogy jutok
el a vasútállomáshoz/
buszmegállóhoz/taxiállomáshoz/
városközpontba/tengerpartra?
   mehg tood-nah mon-doni hodj yoo-tok
ehl o vo-shoot-ahl-lo-mahsh-hoz/boos-
mehg-ahl-law-hoz/toxi-ahl-lo-mahsh-
hoz/vah-rosh-kuhz-pont-bo/tehn-
gehr-port-ra

209 First/second left/right/
straight ahead.
   Első/második balra/jobbra/
egyenesen előre.
   eehl-sur/mah-sho-dik bol-ro/yobb-
ro/edj-eh-neh-shen eh-lur-re

210 Where is the nearest police
station/post office?
   Hol van a legközelebbi
rendőrőrs/postahivatal?
   hol von o lehg-kuh-zeh-lehb-bi
rehn-dur-uhrsh/posh-to-hee-vo-tol

211 Is it far?
   Messze van?
   mehs-seh von

212 Do I need to take a taxi/catch
a bus?
   Taxival/Busszal kell mennem?
   toxi-vol/boos-sol kehll mehn-nehm

213 Can you point to it on my
map?
   Megmutatná ezt a térképen?
   mehg-moo-tot-nah ehzt o tayr-
kay-pehn

214 Thank you for your help.
   Köszönöm a segítségét.
   kuh-suh-nuhm o sheh-geet-shay-
gayt

SIGHTSEEING

215 Where is the Tourist
Information office?
   Hol van a Turista Információs
Iroda?
   hol von o too-reesh-to in-for-mah-
tsee-awsh ee-ro-do

216 Where is the cathedral/
church/museum?
   Hol van a katedrális/templom/
múzeum?
   hol von o ko-tehd-rah-leesh/
tehmp-lom/mooh-zeh-oom

217 How much is the entrance
(admission) charge?
   Mennyibe kerül a belépődíj?
   mehnn-yee-beh keh-rewl o beh-lay-
pur-deey

218 Is there a discount for children/
students/senior citizens?
   Adnak árengedményt
gyermekeknek/
egyetemistáknak/
nyugdíjasoknak?

od-nok ahr-ehn-gehd-maynn-yt
djehr-meh-kehk-nehk/e-djeh-teh-
meesh-tahk-nok/nn-yoog-dee-yo-
shok-nok

219 **What time does the next guided tour start?**
Mikor indul a következő csoport idegennyelvű vezetővel?
mee-kor in-dool o kuh-veht-keh-zur cho-port ee-deh-gehn-nn-yel-veew veh-zeh-tur-vehl

220 **One/two adults/children, please.**
Egy/Két felnőtt/gyermek jegyet kérek.
edj/kayt fehl-nurtt/djehr-mehk ye-djeht kay-rehk

221 **May I take photographs here?**
Lehet itt fényképezni?
leh-heht itt faynn-y-kay-pehz-ni

ENTERTAINMENT

222 **Can you recommend a good bar/nightclub?**
Tudna ajánlani egy jó bárt/éjjeli szórakozóhelyet?
tood-no o-yahn-loni edj yaw bahrt/ay-yeli saw-ro-ko-zaw-heh-yeht

223 **Do you know what is on at the cinema (playing at the movies)/theatre at the moment?**
Meg tudná mondani, most mit játszanak a moziban/szinházban?
mehg tood-nah mon-doni, mosht mit yaht-sonok o mo-zee-bon/seen-hahz-bon

224 **I would like to book (purchase) . . . tickets for the matinée/evening performance on Monday.**
Szeretnék . . . jegyet foglalni venni a hétfő délutáni/esti előadásra.
seh-reht-nayk . . . yeh-djeht fog-lolni o hayt-fur dayl-oo-tah-ni/ehsh-tee eh-lur-o-dahsh-ro

225 **What time does the film/performance start?**
Mikor kezdődik a film/az előadás ?
mee-kor kehz-dur-dik o film/oz eh-lur-o-dahsh

MEETING PEOPLE

226 **Hello/Goodbye.**
Helló/Viszontlátásra
hehl-law/vee-sont-lah-tahsh-ro

227 **Good morning/good afternoon/good evening/goodnight.**
Jó reggelt/jó napot/jó estét/jó éjszakát.
yaw rehg-gehlt/yaw no-pot/yaw ehsh-tayt/yaw ay-y-so-kaht

228 **Pleased to meet you.**
Örülök hogy találkoztunk.
uh-rew-luhk hodj to-lahl-koz-toonk

229 **How are you?**
Hogy van?
hodj von

230 **Fine, thank you. And you?**
Köszönöm, jól. És ön?
kuh-suh-nuym yawl. aysh uhn

231 My name is . . .
A nevem . . .
o neh-vehm . . .

232 This is my friend/boyfriend/
girlfriend/husband/wife/
older brother/younger brother/
older sister/younger sister.
Ez a barátom/udvarlóm/barátnőm/
férjem/feleségem/bátyám/öcsém/
nővérem/hugom.
*ehz o bo-rah-tom/ood-vor-lawm/
bo-raht-nurm/fayr-yehm/feh-leh-
shay-gehm/baht-yahm/uh-
chaym/nur-vay-rehm/hoo-gom*

233 Where are you travelling to?
Hova utazik?
ho-vo oo-to-zik

234 I am going to . . . /we are
going to . . .
Én . . . -ba/-be utazom/Mi . . . -
ba/-be utazunk.
*ayn . . . -bo/-beh oo-to-zom/mee . .
. -bo/-beh oo-to-zoonk*

235 How long are you travelling
for?
Meddig utazik?
mehd-deeg oo-to-zik

236 Where do you come from?
Honnan jött?
hon-non yuhtt

237 I am from . . ./we are from . . .
Én . . . -ból/-ből jöttem/Mi . . . -
ból/-ből jöttünk.
*ayn . . . -bawl/-burl yuht-tehm/
mee . . . -bawl/-burl yuht-tewnk*

238 We're on holiday.
Szabadságon vagyunk.
so-bod-shah-gon vo-djoonk

239 This is our first visit here.
Most vagyunk itt először.
mosht vo-djoonk itt eh-lur-suhr

240 Would you like a cigarette?/
May I have a cigarette?
Kér egy cigarettát?/ Kérhetek
egy cigarettát?
*kayr edj tsee-go-reht-taht//kayr-
heh-tehk edj tsee-go-reht-taht*

241 I am sorry but I do not
understand.
Sajnálom, de nem értem.
soj-nah-lom, deh nem ayr-tehm

242 Please speak slowly.
Kérem, beszéljen lassabban.
*kay-rehm, beh-sayl-yehn losh-
shob-bon*

243 Do you mind if I smoke?
Zavarja ha dohányzom?
zo-vor-yo ho do-hahnn-y-zom

244 Do you have a light?
Kérhetek tüzet?
kayr-heh-tehk tew-zeht

245 I am waiting for my husband/
wife/boyfriend/girlfriend.
A férjemre/feleségemre/
udvarlómra/barátnőmre várok.
*o fayr-yehm-reh/feh-leh-shay-
gehm-reh/ood-vor-lawm-ro/bo-
raht-nurm-reh vah-rok*

TRAVELLING WITH CHILDREN

246 Do you have a high chair/
baby-sitting service/cot?
Van önöknek etetőszékük/
gyermek-vigyázó szolgálatuk/
gyermekágyuk?

von uh-nuhk-nehk eh-teh-tur-say-kewk/djehr-mehk-vee-djah-zaw sol-gah-lo-took/djehr-mehk-ah-djook

247 Where is the nursery/playroom?

Hol van az ovoda/játékszoba?
hol von oz o-vo-do/yah-tayk-so-bo

248 Where can I warm the baby's bottle?

Hol tudom megmelegíteni a baby cumis-üvegét?
hol too-dom mehg-meh-leh-gee-teh-ni o baby coo-meesh-ew-veh-gayt

COMMUNICATIONS

Post

249 How much will it cost to send a letter/postcard/this package to Britain/Ireland/America/Canada/Australia/New Zealand?

Mennyibe kerül egy levél/képeslap/ez a csomag Angliába/Irországba/Amerikába/Kanadába/Ausztráliába/Új Zélandba?
mehnn-yee-be keh-rewl edj leh-vayl/kay-pehsh-lop/ehz o cho-mog ong-li-ahba/eer-or-sahg-bo/o-meh-ri-kah-bo/ko-no-dah-bo/oust-rah-liah-bo/ooy zay-londbo

250 I would like one stamp/two stamps.

Szeretnék egy bélyeget/két bélyeget.
seh-reht-nayk edj bay-yeh-geht/kayt bay-yeh-geht.

251 I'd like . . . stamps for postcards to send abroad, please.

Külföldre küldendő képeslapra szeretnék . . . bélyeget kérni.
kewl-fuhld-reh kewl-dehn-dur kay-pehsh-lopro seh-reht-nayk . . . bay-yeh-geht kayr-ni

Phones

252 I would like to make a telephone call/reverse the charges (make a collect call) to . . .

Szeretnék telefonálni/R beszélgetést kérni . . . -ba/-be.
sehreht-nayk teh-leh-fo-nahl-ni/ehrr beh-sayl-geh-taysht kayr-ni . . . -bol/-beh

253 Which coins do I need for the telephone?

Milyen érmével működik a telefon?
mee-yehn ayr-may-vehl meew-kuh-dik o teh-leh-fon

254 The line is engaged (busy).

Foglalt a vonal.
fog-lolt o vo-nol

255 The number is . . .

A szám . . .
a sahm . . .

256 Hello, this is . . .

Halló, itt . . . beszél.
hol-law, itt . . . beh-sayl

257 May I speak to . . ?

Beszélhetnék . . . . . . -val/-vel?
be-sayl-heht-nayk . . . -vol/-vehl

H U N G A R I A N

258 He/She is not in at the moment. Can you call back?
Pillanatnyilag nincs a helyén. Visszaszólna később?
peel-lo-not-nn-yee-log neench o heh-yayn. vees-so-sawl-no kay-shurbb

MONEY

259 I would like to change these travellers' cheques (travelers' checks)/this currency/this Eurocheque.
Szeretném beváltani ezeket a Travellers csekkeket/ezt a valutát/ezt az Euro csekket.
seh-reht-naym beh-vahl-toni eh-zeh keht o travellers chehk-keh-keht/ehzt o vo-loo-taht/ehzt oz euro chehk-keht

260 How much commission do you charge? (What is the service charge?)
Mennyit számolnak fel jutalékként?
mehnn-yeet sah-mol-nok fehl yoo-to-layk-kaynt

261 Can I obtain money with my MasterCard?
Válthatok ki pénzt a MasterCard-ommal?
vahlt-ho-tok ki paynzt o mastercard-om-mol

SHOPPING

Names of Shops and Departments

262 Könyvüzlet/Irószerbolt
kuhnn-yv-ewz-leht/ee-raw-sehr-bolt
Bookshop/Stationery

263 Ékszerész/Ajándéküzlet
ayk-seh-rays/o-jahn-dayk-ewz-leht
Jeweller's/Gifts

264 Cipők
tsee-purk
Shoes

265 Vaskereskedés
vosh-keh-rehsh-keh-daysh
Hardware

266 Antikvárium
on-teek-vah-ree-oom
Antiques

267 Férfi/Női Fodrász
fayr-fi/nur-i fod-rahs
Hairdressers (men's)/(women's)

268 Dohányáruda/Dohányüzlet
do-hahnn-y-ah-roo-do/do-hahnn-y-ewz-leht
Tobacconist

269 Pékség/Kenyérüzlet
payk-shayg/keh-nn-yayr-ewz-leht
Baker's

270 Szupermarket
supermarket
Supermarket

271 Ofotért/Fotóüzlet
o-fo-tayrt/fo-taw-ewz-leht
Photoshop

272 Játéküzlet/Játékbolt
yah-tayk-ewz-leht/yah-tayk-bolt
Toys

273 Utazási Iroda/IBUSZ
oo-to-zah-shi ee-rodo/ee-boos
Travel Agent

274 Illatszerek
eel-lot-seh-rehk
Toiletries

275 Lemezek
leh-meh-zehk
Records

In the Shop

276 What time do the shops open/close?
Mikor nyitnak/zárnak az üzletek?
mee-kor n-y-eet-nok/zahr-nok oz ewz-leh-tehk

277 Where is the nearest market?
Hol van a legközelebbi piac?
hol von o lehg-kuh-zeh-lehb-bi pee-ots

278 Can you show me the one in the window/this one?
Megmutatná nekem az ablakban levőt/ezt?
mehg-moo-tot-nah neh-kehm oz ob-lok-bon leh-vurt/ehzt

279 Can I try this on?
Felpróbálhatom?
fehl-praw-bahl-ho-tom

280 What size is this?
Mekkora méret ez?
mehk-koro may-reht ehz

281 This is too large/too small/too expensive.
Ez túl nagy/túl kicsi/túl drága.
ehz tool nodj/tool kee-chi/tool drah-go

282 Do you have any others?
Van még más is?
von mayg máhsh eesh

283 My size is . . .
. . . -os/-es a méretem.
. . . -osh/-ehsh o may-reh-tehm

284 Where is the changing room/childrens/cosmetic/ladieswear/menswear/food department?
Hol van a próbafülke/a gyermek osztály/a kozmetikai osztály/a nőiruha osztály/a férfiruha orszály/az élemiszer osztály?
hol von o praw-bo-fewl-keh/o djehr-mehk os-tahy/o koz-meh-tee-koi os-tahy/o nur-y-roo-ho os-tahy/o fayr-fee-roo-ho os-tahy/oz ay-lehl-mee-sehr os-tahy

285 I would like . . .
Szeretnék egy . . . -t.
seh-reht-nayk edj . . . -t

286 I would like a quarter of a kilo/half a kilo/a kilo of bread/butter/cheese/ham/tomatoes.
Kérek egy negyed kiló/fél kiló/kiló kenyeret/vajat/sajtot/sonkát/paradicsomot.
kay-rehk edj neh-djehd kee-law/fayl kee-law/kee-law keh-nn-yeh-reht/vo-jot/soy-tot/son-kaht/poro-dee-cho-mot

287 How much is this?
Ez mennyibe kerül?
ehz mehnn-yee-beh keh-rewl

288 I'll take this one, thank you.
Ezt megveszem, köszönöm.
ehzt mehg-veh-sehm, kuh-suh-nuhm

HUNGARIAN

274
↕
288

167

289 Do you have a carrier (shopping) bag?
Kérhetek egy nylonzacskót?
kayr-heh-tehk edj nehy-lon-zoch-kawt

290 Do you have anything cheaper/larger/smaller/of better quality?
Van önnek olcsóbb/nagyobb méretű/kissebb méretű/jobb minőségű áruja?
von uhn-nehk ol-chawbb/nod-jobb may-reh-teew/kee-shehbb may-reh-teew/yobb mee-nur-shay-geew ah-roo-yo

291 I would like a film for this camera.
Ehhez a fényképezőgéphez szeretnék filmet venni.
eh-hehz o faynn-y-kay-peh-zur-gayp-hehz seh-reht-nayk feel-meht vehn-ni

292 I would like some batteries, the same size as this old one.
Ugyanolyan méretű elemet szeretnék venni, mint ez a régi.
oodjon-ol-yon may-reh-teew eh-leh-meht seh-reht-nayk vehn-ni, meent ehz o ray-gi

293 Would you mind wrapping this for me, please?
Becsomagolná nekem ezt, kérem?
beh-cho-mogol-nah neh-kehm ehzt, kay-rehm

294 Sorry, but you seem to have given me the wrong change.
Elnézést kérek, de azt hiszem rosszul adott vissza.
ehl-nay-zaysht kay-rehk, deh ozt hee-sehm ros-sool o-dott vees-so

MOTORING

Car Hire (Rental)

295 I have ordered (rented) a car in the name of . . .
Egy autót béreltem . . . néven.
ejd o-oo-tawt bay-rehl-tehm . . . nay-vehn

296 How much does it cost to hire (rent) a car for one day/two days/one week?
Mennyibe kerül egy autó bérlése egy napra/két napra/egy hétre?
mehnn-yee-beh keh-rewl edj o-oo-taw bayr-lay-sheh edj nop-ro/kayt nop-ro/edj hayt-reh

297 Is the tank already full of petrol (gas)?
Az autó fel van már tankolva?
oz o-oo-taw fehl von mahr ton-kol-vo

298 Is insurance and tax included? How much is the deposit?
A biztosítás és az adó is az árban benne van? Mennyi letétet kérnek?
o beez-to-shee-tahsh ays oz o-daw eesh oz ahr-bon behn-neh von? mehnn-yee leh-tay-teht kayr-nehk

299 By what time must I return the car?
Mikorra kell visszahoznom az autót?

*mee-kor-rah kehll vees-so-hoz-nom
oz o-oo-tawt*

300 **I would like a small/family
car with a radio/cassette player.**
Szeretnék egy kisméretű/családi
autót rádióval/magnóval.
*seh-reht-nayk edj keesh-may-reh-
teew o-oo-tawt rah-dee-aw-vol/
mog-naw-vol*

Asking the Way

301 **Excuse me, can you help me
please?**
Bocsánatot kérek, segítene
nekem?
*bo-chah-no-tot kay-rehk, sheh-gee-
teh-neh neh-kehm*

302 **How do I reach the
motorway/main road?**
Hogy jutok el az autópályára/a
főútvonalra?
*hodj yoo-tok ehl oz o-oo-taw-pah-
yah-ro/o fur-oot-vo-nol-ro?*

303 **I think I have taken the
wrong turning.**
Azt hiszem rossz helyen
fordultam be.
*ozt hee-sehm ross heh-yehn for-
dool-tom beh*

304 **I am looking for this address.**
Ezt a címet keresem.
ehzt o cee-meht keh-reh-shem

305 **I am looking for the . . . hotel.**
A . . . szállót keresem.
o . . . sahl-lawt keh-reh-shem

306 **How far is it to . . . from
here?**

Milyen messze van a . . . innen?
*mee-yehn mehs seh von o . . . in-
nehn*

307 **Carry straight on for . . .
kilometres.**
Menjen egyenesen . . . kilométert.
*mehn-yehn eh-djeh-neh-shehn . . .
kee-lo-may-tehrt*

308 **Take the next turning on the
right/left.**
Forduljon be a következő
sarkon jobbra/balra.
*ford-ool-jon beh o kuh-veht-keh-
zur shor-kon yobb-ro/bol-ro*

309 **Turn right/left at the next
crossroads/traffic lights.**
Forduljon jobbra/balra a
következő útkereszteződésnél/
közlekedési lámpánál.
*for-dool-yon yobb-ro/bol-ro o kuh-
veht-keh-zur ooht-keh-rehs-teh-
zur-daysh-nayl/kuhz-leh-keh-day-
shi lahm-pah-nahl*

310 **You are going in the wrong
direction.**
Ön rossz fele megy.
uhn ross feh-leh mehdj

Parking

311 **How long can I park here?**
Meddig parkolhatok itt?
mehd-dig por-kol-ho-tok itt

312 **Is there a car park near here?**
Van itt a közelben egy parkoló?
*von itt o kuh-zehl-behn edj por-ko-
law*

313 At what time does this car park close?
Mikor zár be ez a parkoló?
mee-kor zahr beh ehz o por-ko-law

Signs and Notices

314 Egyirányú utca
edj-ee-rahnn-y-ooh oot-tzo
One way

315 Behajtani tilos
be-hoj-toni tee-losh
No entry.

316 Parkolni tilos.
por-kol-ni tee-losh
No parking

317 Útelterelés
oot-ehl-teh-reh-laysh
Detour (diversion)

318 Állj
ahlly
Stop.

319 Elsőbbségadás kötelező
ehl-shurbb-shayg-o-dahsh kuh-teh-leh-zur
Give way (yield).

320 Csúszós út
choo-sawsh oot
Slippery road

321 Előzni tilos
eh-lurz-ni tee-losh
No overtaking.

At the Filling Station

322 Unleaded (lead-free)/ Standard/Premium
Ólommentes benzin/

Normálbenzin/Szuperbenzin
aw-lom-mehn-tehsh behn-zeen/ normahl-behn-zeen/soo-pehr-behn-zeen

323 Fill the tank please.
Kérem töltse tele a tankot.
kay-rehm tuhlt-sheh teh-leh o ton-kot

324 Do you have a road map of this area?
Van önnek erről a környékről autótérképe?
von uhn-nehk ehr-rurl o kuhr-nn-y-ayk-rurl o-oo-taw-tayr-kay-peh

325 How much is the car-wash?
Mennyibe kerül az autómosás?
mehnn-yee-beh keh-rewl oz o-oo-taw-mo-shah-sh

Breakdowns

326 I've had a breakdown at . . .
Meghibásodott az autónk . . . -nál/-nél.
mehg-hee-bah-sho-dott oz o-oo-tawonk . . . -nahl/-nayl

327 I am on the road from . . . to . . .
A . . . -tól . . . -ig vezető úton vagyok.
o . . . -tawl . . . -ig veh-zeh-tur ooh-ton vod-jok

328 I can't move the car. Can you send a tow-truck?
Lerobbant az autóm. Tudna küldeni egy autómentőt?
leh-rob-bont oz o-oo-tawm. tood-no kewl-deh-ni edj o-oo-taw-mehn-turt

329 I have a flat tyre.
Defektet kaptam.
deh-fehk-teht kop-tom

330 The windscreen (windshield)
has smashed/cracked.
A szélvédő széttörött/megrepedt.
*o sayl-vay-dur sayt-tuh-ruhtt/
mehg-reh-pehdt*

331 There is something wrong
with the engine/brakes/
lights/steering/gearbox/
clutch/exhaust.
Valami baj van a motorral/
fékekkel/lámpákkal/
kormánnyal/sebességváltóval/
kipuffogó csővel.
*vo-lomi boy von o motor-rol/fay-
kehk-kehl/lahm-pahk-kol/kor-
mahnn-y-ol/sheh-behsh-shayg-
vahl-taw-vol/kee-poof-fo-gaw
chur-vehl*

332 It's overheating.
A kocsi túlmelegszik.
o ko-chi tool-meh-lehg-sik

333 It won't start.
Az autó nem indul be.
oz o-oo-taw nem in-dool beh

334 Where can I get it repaired?
Hol tudom megjavíttatni?
hol too-dom mehg-yo-veet-tot-ni

335 Can you take me there?
El tudna vinni engem odáig?
*el tood-no veen-ni ehn-gehm o-
dah-eeg*

336 Will it take long to fix?
Sokáig tart míg megjavítják ?
*sho-kah-ig tort meeg mehg-yo-
veet-jahk*

337 How much will it cost?
Mennyibe fog kerülni?
mehnn-yee-beh fog keh-rewl-ni

Accidents

338 Can you help me? There has
been an accident.
Tudna segíteni? Baleset történt.
*tood-no sheh-gee-teh-ni? bol-eh-
sheht tuhr-taynt*

339 Please call the police/an
ambulance.
Kérem hívja a rendőrséget/
mentőket.
*kay-rehm heev-yo o rehn-dur-
shay-geht/mehn-tur-keht*

340 Is anyone hurt?
Megsebesült valaki?
meg-she-beh-shewlt vo-loki

Traffic Offences

341 I'm sorry, I didn't see the
sign.
Bocsánatot kérek, de nem
láttam a táblát.
*bo-chah-notot kay-rehk, deh nem
laht-tom o tahb-laht*

342 Must I pay a fine? How much?
Kell büntetés fizetnem?
Mennyit?
*kehll bewn-teh-taysht fee-zeht-
nehm? mehnn-yeet*

343 Show me your documents.
Mutassa az okmányait.
moo-tosh-sho oz ok-mah-nn-y-oit

171

HEALTH

At the Pharmacy

344 Do you have anything for a
stomachache/headache/sore
throat/toothache?
Tudna adni valamit
gyomorfájásra/fejfájásra/
torokfájásra/fogfájásra?
tood-no odni vo-lo-meet djo-mor-
fah-yahsh-ro/fehy-fah-yahsh-ro/
torok-fah-yah-shro/fog-fah-yash-ro

345 I need something for
diarrhoea (diarrhea)/
consti ation/a cold/a cough/
insect bites/sunburn/travel
(motion) sickness.
Kérek valamit hasmenésre/
székrekedésre/megfázásra/
köhögés ellen/rovarcsípésre/
leégés ellen/utazás közbeni
hányinger ellen
kay-rehk vo-lo-mit hosh-meh-
naysh-reh/sayk-reh-keh-daysh-
reh/meg-fah-zahsh-ro/kuh-huh-
gays el-lehn/ro-vor-chee-paysh-
reh/le-ay-gaysh el-lehn/oo-to-
zahsh kuhz-beh-ni hahnn-y-in-
gehr el-lehn

346 How much/how many do I
take?
Mennyit/hány darabot kell
bevennem?
mehnn-yeet/hahnn-y do-ro-bot
kehll beh-vehn-nehm

347 How often do I take it/them?
Milyen gyakran kell ezt/ezeket
bevennem?
mee-yehn djok-ron kehll ehzt/eh-
zeh-keht beh-vehn-nehm

348 How much does it cost?
Mennyibe kerül?
mehnn-yee-beh keh-ruhl

349 Can you recommend a good
doctor/dentist?
Tud ajánlani egy jó doktort/
fogorvost?
tood o-yahn-loni edj jaw dok-tort/
fog-or-vosht

350 Is it suitable for children?
Gyermekeknek is való?
djer-meh-kehk-nehk ish volaw

Doctor

351 I have a pain here/in my arm/
leg/chest/stomach.
Fájdalmat érzek itt/a karomban/
a lábamban/a mellkasomban/a
gyomromban.
fahy-dolmot ayr-zehk itt/o ko-
rom-bon/o lah-bom-bon/a mehll-
ko-shom-bon/a djom-rom-bon

352 Please call a doctor, this is an
emergency.
Kérem azonnal hívjon orvost,
sürgősségi esetről van szó.
kay-rehm o-zon-nol heev-yon or-
vosht, shewr-gur-sh-shay-gi eh-
shet-rurl von saw

353 I would like to make an
appointment to see a doctor.
Szeretnék bejelentkezni az
orvoshoz.
seh-reht-nayk beh-yeh-lehnt-kehz-
ni oz or-vosh-hoz

HUNGARIAN

344
↕
353

172

³⁵⁴ **I am diabetic/pregnant.**
Cukorbeteg/terhes vagyok.
tsoo-kor-beh-tehg/tehr-hesh vod-yok

³⁵⁵ **I need a prescription for . . .**
Egy receptre van szükségem . . .
-ra/-re.
edj reh-tzehpt-reh von sewk-shay-gehm . . . -ro/-reh

³⁵⁶ **Can you give me something to ease the pain?**
Tudna valami fájdalomcsillapítót adni?
tood-no vo-lo-mee fahy-do-lom-chil-lo-pee-taw odni

³⁵⁷ **I am allergic to penicillin. He/she is allergic to pencillin.**
Allergiás vagyok a penicillinre.
Ő allergiás a penicillinre.
ol-lehr-gee-ahsh vod-yok o peh-ni-tzi-lin-reh. Ur ol-lehr-gee-ahsh o peh-ni-tzi-lin-reh.

³⁵⁸ **Does this hurt?**
Ez fáj?
ehz fahy

³⁵⁹ **You must go to hospital. He/she must go to hospital.**
önnek kórházba kell mennie.
Neki kórházba kell mennie.
Uhn-nehk kawr-hahz-bo kehll mehn-ni-eh. Neh-ki kawr-hahz-bo kehll mehn-ni-eh.

³⁶⁰ **Take these once/twice/three times a day.**
Ezt naponta egyszer/kétszer/háromszor kell bevenni.
ehzt no-pon-to edj-sehr/kayt-sehr/hah-rom-sor kehll beh-ven-ni

³⁶¹ **I am taking this medication. He is/she is taking this medication.**
Én ezt a gyógyszert szedem.
Ő ezt a gyógyszert szedi.
ayn ehzt o djawdj-sehrt seh-dehm Ur ehzt o djawdj-sehrt seh-dee

³⁶² **I have medical insurance.**
Van betegbiztosításom.
von beh-tehg-beez-to-shee-tah-shom

Dentists

³⁶³ **I have toothache.**
Fáj a fogam.
fahy o fo-gom

³⁶⁴ **My filling has come out.**
Kiesett a tömés a fogamból.
kee-eh-shehtt o toh-maysh o fo-gom-bawl

³⁶⁵ **I do/do not want to have an injection first.**
Először kérek/nem kérek injekciót.
eh-lur-suhr kay-rehk/nem kay-rehk ee-nyehk-tzee-awt

EMERGENCIES

³⁶⁶ **Help!**
Segítség!
sheh-geet-shayg

³⁶⁷ **Call an ambulance/a doctor/the police!**
Hívja azonnal a mentőket/az orvost/a rendőrséget!
heev-jo ozon-nol o mehn-tur-keht/oz or-vosht/o rehn-dur-shay-geht

173

368 I have had my travellers' cheques (travelers' checks)/ credit cards/purse/handbag/ rucksack (knapsack)/ luggage/wallet stolen.

Ellopták a Travellers csekkjeimet/a hitelkártyáimat/a pénztárcámat/a táskámat/a hátizsákomat/a poggyászomat/ az irattárcámat.

el-lop-tahk o travellers chehk-ye-hee-meht/o hee-tehl-kahrt-yah-ee-mot/o paynz-tahr-tzah-mot/o tahsh-kah-mot/o hah-tee-zhah-ko-mot/o podj-djah-so-mot/oz ee-rot-tahr-tzah-mot.

369 Can you help me, I have lost my daughter/son?

Tudna segíteni, nem találom a lányomat/fiamat?

tood-no sheh-gee-teh-ni, nem to-lah-lom o lah-nn-y-omot/fee-o-mot

370 Please go away/leave me alone.

Kérem menjen innen/hagyjon békében.

kay-rehm mehn-yehn in-nehn/ hod-jon bay-kay-behn

371 Fire!

Tűz van!

teewz von

372 I want to contact the British/ American/Canadian/Irish/ Australian/New Zealand/ South African consulate.

Fel akarom hívni a Brit/ Amerikai/Kanadai/ír/ Ausztráliai/Új Zélandi/Dél Afrikai konzulátust.

fehl o-korom heev-ni o brit/o-meh-ree-koi/ko-nodoi/eer/o-oost-rah-lee-o-i/ooy zay-lon-di/dayl of-ree-koi kon-zoo-lah-toosht

Introduction

Italian, of all the 'Romance' languages the closest to the original Latin, is spoken throughout the Italian peninsula and surrounding islands, and in the southern cantons of Switzerland. Local dialects vary greatly from standard Italian, which is to be expected in a country that consisted of a large number of small independent states for most of its history, but the pure form of the language, derived from the dialect of Tuscany, is understood and spoken everywhere. English is spoken wherever tourists congregate in numbers, but away from those areas you will have to speak Italian. However, it is not the most difficult of languages to pick up, especially because its spelling is entirely regular, with no unexpected quirks of pronunciation, and accented characters are few.

ITALIAN

Addresses for travel and tourist information

UK: *Italian State Tourist Board*, 1 Princes St, London W1R 8AY; tel: (0171) 408 1254.
USA: *Italian Government Travel Office (ENIT)*, 630 Fifth Ave (Suite 1565), Rockefeller Center, New York, NY 10111; tel: (212) 245-4822/2324.

ESSENTIALS

Alphabet

The letters J (i lungo), K (cappa),
W (vu doppia), X (ics) and Y
(ipsilon) are used only to spell
foreign words and names.

A	B
a	*bee*
C	D
chi	*dee*
E	F
eyy	*effe*
G	H
gee	*acca*
I	L
ee	*elle*
M	N
emme	*enne*
O	P
o	*pea*
Q	R
ku	*erre*
S	T
esse	*tee*
U	V
oo	*voo*
Z	
zeta	

Basic Words and Phrases

1 **Yes**   **No**
  Sì   No
  See   *Noh*

2 **Please**   **Thank you**

Per favore   Grazie
Perr fahvawreh   *Grahtsyeh*

3 **That's O.K.**   **Perhaps**
  Va bene   Forse
  Vah behneh   *Forrseh*

4 **To**   **From**
  A   da
  ah   *dah*

5 **Here**   **There**
  Qui   là
  Kwee   *lah*

6 **None**   **Also**
  Nessuno   Anche
  Nessoonaw   *Ahnkeh*

7 **How**   **When**
  Come   quando
  Cawme   *kwahndaw*

8 **What**   **Why**
  che   perché
  keh   *perrkeh*

9 **I don't understand.**
  Non capisco.
  Nawn kahpeescaw

10 **I don't speak Italian.**
   Non parlo italiano.
   Nawn parrlaw itahlyahnaw

11 **Do you speak English?**
   Parla inglese?
   Parrla eenglehzeh?

12 **Can you please write it
   down?**
   Potrebbe scriverlo, per favore?
   *Pawtrebbeh screevehrrlaw, perr
   fahvawreh?*

13 **Can you please speak more
   slowly?**

Potrebbe parlare più
lentamente, per favore?
*Pawtrebbeh pahrrlahrreh pyoo
lehntahmehnteh, perr fahvawreh?*

14 How much does it/this cost?
Quant'è/quanto costa?
Kwahntèh/kwahntah kawstah?

Days

15 Monday **Tuesday**
Lunedì Martedì
Loonehdee *Marrtehdee*

16 Wednesday **Thursday**
Mercoledì Giovedì
Merrcawlehdee *Jawvehdee*

17 Friday **Saturday**
Venerdì Sabato
Venerrdee *Sàbahtaw*

18 Sunday **Morning**
Domenica Mattino
Dawméhneeca *Mahtteenaw*

19 Afternoon **Evening**
Pomeriggio Sera
Pawmehreedjaw *Sehra*

20 Night **Week**
Notte Settimana
Notteh *Setteemahna*

21 Yesterday **Tomorrow**
Ieri Domani
Yeree *Dawmahnee*

Numbers

22 Zero **One**
Zero Uno
Tsehraw *Oonaw*

23 Two **Three**

Due **Tre**
Dweh *Treh*

24 Four **Five**
Quattro Cinque
Kwahttraw *Cheenkweh*

25 Six **Seven**
Sey Sette
Say *Setteh*

26 Eight **Nine**
Otto Nove
Ottaw *Noveh*

27 Ten **Eleven**
Dieci Undici
Dyehchee *Oondeechee*

28 Twelve **Thirteen**
Dodici Tredici
Dawdeechee *Tréhdeechee*

29 Fourteen **Fifteen**
Quattordici Quindici
Kwahttòrrdeechee *Kweendeechee*

30 Sixteen **Seventeen**
Sedici Diciassette
Sédeechee *Deechassetteh*

31 Eighteen **Nineteen**
Diciotto Diciannove
Deechottaw *Deechannoveh*

32 Twenty **Twenty-one**
Venti Ventuno
Ventee *Ventoonaw*

33 Twenty-two **Thirty**
Ventidue Trenta
Venteedweh *Trenta*

34 Forty **Fifty**
Quaranta Cinquanta
Kwahrahnta *Cheenkwahnta*

ITALIAN

14
↕
34

35 Sixty   **Seventy**
Sessanta   Settanta
Sessahnta   *Settahnta*

36 Eighty   **Ninety**
Ottanta   Novanta
Ottahnta   *Novahnta*

37 One hundred Five hundred
Cento   Cinquecento
Chentaw
Cheenkwechentaw

38 One thousand One million
Mille   Un milione
Meelleh   *Oon meellyawneh*

Time

39 9.00
Nove
Noveh

40 9.05
Nove e cinque
Noveh eh cheenkweh

41 9.10
Nove e dieci
Noveh eh dyehchee

42 9.15
Nove e quindici
oveh eh kweendechee

43 9.20
Nove e venti
Noveh eh ventee

44 9.25
Nove e venticinque
Noveh eh venteecheenkweh

45 9.30
Nove e trenta
Noveh eh trenta

46 9.35
Nove e trentacinque
Noveh eh trentacheenkweh

47 9.40
Nove e quaranta
Noveh eh kwahranta

48 9.45
Nove e quarantacinque
Noveh eh kwahrantacheenkweh

49 9.50
Nove e cinquanta
Noveh eh cheenkwahnta

50 9.55
Nove e cinquantacinque
Noveh eh cheenkwahntacheenkweh

51 12.00/Midday/Midnight
Dodici/Mezzogiorno/
mezzanotte
*Dohdychee/metsawjorrnaw/
metsanotteh*

52 What time is it?
Che ore sono?
Keh awreh sawnaw?

53 It is . . .
Sono le . . .
Sawnaw leh . . .

ARRIVING AND DEPARTING

Airport

**54 Excuse me, where is the
check-in desk for . . . airline?**
Mi scusi, dov'è il banco
accettazioni per la linea aerea . . ?
*Mee scoozee, dawvèh eel bahnkaw
ahchettatsyawnee perr lah
leenayah ah-aerrhayah . . ?*

55 **What is the boarding gate/ time for my flight?**
Qual'è il cancello di imbarco/ orario del mio volo?
Kwaalèh eel kahnchehlaw dee ihmbahrcaw/awrahreeaw deel meeoh vawloh?

56 **How long is the delay likely to be?**
Qual'è il ritardo previsto?
Kwaalhè eel rreehtahrdaw prehveestaw?

57 **Where is the duty-free shop?**
Dov'è il duty-free?
Dawvèh eel duty-free?

58 **Which way is the baggage reclaim?**
Dove si trova il recupero bagagli?
Dawveh see trawvah eel rehkupehrraw bahgahlyee?

59 **Where can I get the bus to the city centre?**
Dove posso prendere l'autobus per il centro?
Dawveh pawssaw prendereh lahutobhuss perr eel chentraw?

Train Station

60 **Where is the ticket office/ information desk?**
Dov'è la biglietteria/l'ufficio informazioni?
Dawvèh lah beelyetteryha/ looffeechaw eenformahtseeawnee?

61 **Which platform does the train to . . . depart from?**
Da quale marciapiede parte il treno per . . ?

Dah kwahleh marchyahpyedeh parteh eel trehnaw perr . . ?

62 **Where is platform . . ?**
Dov'è il marciapiede . . ?
Dawvèh eel marchyahpyedeh . . ?

63 **When is the next train to . . ?**
A che ora arriva il prossimo treno per . . ?
Ah keh awrah arreevah eel prosseemaw trehnaw perr . . ?

64 **Is there a later train to . . ?**
C'è un altro treno per . . ?
Chèh oon ahltraw trehnaw perr . . ?

Port

65 **How do I get to the port?**
Come arrivo al porto?
Cawmeh arrevaw ahl pawrrtaw?

66 **When is the next sailing to . . ?**
Quand'è la prossma partenza per . . ?
Kwandèh lah prawssema parrtentsa perr . . ?

67 **Can I catch an earlier ferry with this ticket?**
Posso prendere un traghetto che parta prima con questo biglietto?
Pawssaw prendereh oon trahgettaw keh pahrrtah preemah kawn kwestaw beelyettaw?

Notices and Signs

68 **Carrozza rinfreschi**
Carrotsa reenfreskee
Buffet (Dining) Car

69 **Autobus**
Ahootawboos
Bus

70 **Acqua potabile/non potabile**
Aqua pawtahbeeleh/non pawtahbeeleh
Drinking/Non-drinking water

71 **Entrata**
Entrahta
Entrance

72 **Uscita**
Oosheeta
Exit

73 **Informazioni**
Eenformahtsyawnee
Information

74 **Bagaglio depositato**
Bahgalyaw depawseetahtaw
Left Luggage (Baggage Claim)

75 **Armadietti per bagagli**
Armahdyettee perr baghgalee
Luggage Lockers

76 **Ufficio postale**
Ooffeechaw pawstahleh
Post Office

77 **Marciapiede**
Marchyahpyedeh
Platform

78 **Stazione ferroviaria**
Stahtsyawneh ferrawvyarya
Railway (Railroad) Station

79 **Aeroporto**
Ahaerrhawpawrrtaw
Airport

80 **Porto**
Pawrrtaw
Port

81 **Ristorante**
Reestawrahnteh
Restaurant

82 **Per fumatori/non fumatori**
Perr foomahtawree/non foomahtawree
Smoking/Non-Smoking

83 **Telefono**
Telèfawnaw
Telephone

84 **Biglietteria**
Beelyetterya
Ticket Office

85 **Banco accettazioni**
Bahnkaw ahchettahtsyawnee
Check-in Desk

86 **Orario**
Awraryaw
Timetable (Schedule)

87 **Tolette**
Tawletteh
Toilets (Restrooms)

88 **Signori**
Seenyawree
Gentlemen

89 **Signore**
Seenyawreh
Ladies'

90 **Tram**
Trahm
Tram (Streetcar)

91 **Metropolitana**
Metrawpawleetahna
Underground (Subway)

ITALIAN

69
↕
91

180

92 Sala d'attesa
Sahla dahttehsa
Waiting Room

Buying a Ticket

93 I would like a first-class/
second-class single (one-
way)/return (round-trip)
ticket to . . .
Vorrei un biglietto di sola
andata/andata e ritorno di
prima classe/di seconda classe
per . . .
*Vawrray oon beelyettaw dee
sawlah ahndahta/ahndahta eh
reetawrnaw dee preema classeh/
dee seconda classeh perr . . .*

94 Is my rail pass valid on this
train/ferry/bus?
Il mio abbonamento è valido su
questo treno/traghetto/
autobus?
*Eel meeoh abhawnahmentaw èh
vahleedhaw soo kwestaw
trehnaw/trahgehtaw/
ahootawboos?*

95 I would like an
aisle/window seat.
Vorrei un posto vicino al
corridoio/al finestrino.
*Vawrray oon pawstaw
veecheenaw ahl correedoyaw/ahl
feenestreenaw.*

96 No smoking/smoking,
please.
Per favore nello
scompartimento per fumatori/
non fumatori.
*Perr fahvawreh nehllo
scomparteementaw peer
foomahtawree /non foomahtawree.*

97 We would like to sit
together.
Vorremmo sedere accanto.
*Vawrremmaw sehdehreh
ahckahntaw.*

98 I would like to make a seat
reservation.
Vorrei prenotare un posto.
*Vawrray prehnawtahrreh oon
pawstaw.*

99 I would like to reserve a
couchette/sleeper for one
person/two people/for my
family.
Vorrei prenotare una cuccetta/
una cabina per una persona/due
persone/per la mia famiglia.
*Vawrray prehnawtareh oona
coocchetta/oona cahbeena perr
oona perrsawna/dweh
perrsawneh/perr lah myah
fahmeelya.*

100 I would like to reserve a
cabin.
Vorrei prenotare una cabina.
*Vawrray prehnawtahrreh oonah
kahbeenah.*

Timetables (Schedules)

101 Arrivare
Arreevahreh
Arrive

102 Ferma a
Ferrma ah
Calls (Stops) at

I
T
A
L
I
A
N

92
↕
102

103 Servizio
d'approvvigionamento
*Serveetsyaw
dahpprawvveejawnahmentaw*
Catering Service

104 Cambiare a
Cahmbyareh ah
Change at

105 Coincidenza
Coincheedentsa
Connection

106 Giornaliero
Jawrnahlyeraw
Daily

107 Ogni quaranta minuti
Awnee kwahrahnta meenootee
Every 40 Minutes

108 Prima classe
Preema classeh
First Class

109 Ogni ora
Awnee awra
Hourly

110 Si raccomanda la
prenotazione dei posti
*See rahckawmahnda la
prehnawtatsyawneh day pawstee*
Seat reservations are
recommended

111 Seconda classe
Secawnda classeh
Second Class

112 Supplemento esigibile
Soopplehmentaw eseejeebeeleh
Supplement Payable

113 Via
Veeha
Via

Luggage

114 How much will it cost to send
(ship) my luggage in
advance?
Quanto costa la spedizione
anticipata del mio bagaglio?
*Kwahntaw cawstah la
spehdeetsyawneh ahnteecheepahta
del myaw bahgalyaw?*

115 Where is the left luggage
(baggage claim) office?
Dov'è il deposito bagagli?
*Dawvèh eel dehpawseetaw
bahgahlee?*

116 What time do you open/
close?
A che ora aprite/chiudete?
*Ah keh awra ahpreeteh/
kewdehteh?*

117 Where are the luggage
trolleys (carts)?
Dove sono i carrelli
portabagagli?
*Dawveh sawnaw ee carrellee
porrtahbahgalee?*

118 Where are the lockers?
Dove sono gli armadietti?
*Dawveh sawnaw lyee
ahrmahdyetteh?*

119 I have lost my locker key.
Ho perso la chiave del mio
armadietto.
*Aw perrsaw lah kyahveh del
myaw armahdyettaw.*

182

On Board

120 Is this seat taken?
È libero questo posto?
Èh leebehraw kwestaw pawstaw?

121 Excuse me, you are sitting in
my reserved seat.
Scusi, Lei siede nel mio posto
riservato.
*Scoozee, Lay syedeh nel myaw
pawstaw reeservahtaw.*

122 Which station is this?
Che stazione è?
Keh stahtsyawneh èh?

123 What time is this train/bus/
ferry/flight due to arrive/
depart?
A che ora è previsto l'arrivo/
partenza di questo treno/
autobus/volo?
*Ah keh awrah èh prehveestaw
lahrreevaw/pahrrtehntsah dee
kwestaw trehnaw/ ahootawboos/
vawlaw?*

124 Will you wake me just before
we arrive?
Mi sveglia poco prima
dell'arrivo?
*Mee svelyah pawcaw preema
dellarreevaw?*

Customs and Passports

125 Passaporti per favore!
Passaporrtee perr fahvawreh!
Passports, please!

126 I have nothing/wine/spirits
(alcohol)/tobacco to declare.
Non ho nulla da dichiarare/ho

vino/alcolici/tabacco da
dichiarare.
*Non aw noollah dah deekyarareh/
aw veenaw/ahlcoleechee/
tahbahckaw dah deekyarareh.*

127 I shall be staying for . . .
days/weeks/months.
Mi tratterrò per . . . giorni/
settimane/mesi.
*Mee trahtterraw perr . . . jawrnee/
setteemahneh/mehzee.*

128 Do you have a map of the
town/area?
Ha una mappa della città/della
zona?
*Ah oona mahppa della cheettàh/
della zawna?*

129 Can I reserve accommodation
here?
Posso prenotare qui l'alloggio?
*Pawssaw prenotahre kwee
lallodjaw?*

130 Do you have a list of
accommodation?
Ha un elenco di alloggi?
Ah oon ehlehnkaw dee ahlawdjee?

Hotels

131 I have a reservation in the
name of . . .
Ho una prenotazione per . . .
*Aw oona prehnawtahtsyawneh
perr . . .*

I
T
A
L
I
A
N

120
↕
131

132 I wrote to/faxed/telephoned you last month/last week in . . .
Vi ho scritto/inviato un fax/telefonato il mese scorso/la settimana scorsa a . . .
Vee haw skreehtaw/eenveeahtaw oon fax/tehlehfonahtaw eel mehseh skawhrsaw/lah sehteemahnah skawrsah ah . . .

133 Do you have any rooms free?
Avete camere libere?
Ahvehteh kahmehreh leebehreh?

134 I would like to reserve a single/double room with/without bath/shower.
Vorrei prenotare una camera singola/matrimoniale con/senza bagno/doccia.
Vawrray prehnawtahreh oona cahmehra seengawlah/mahtreemawnyahleh con/sentsa bahnyaw/ occha

135 I would like bed and breakfast/(room and) half board/(room and) full board.
Vorrei una camera con colazione/con mezza pensione/pensione completa.
Vawrray oona cahmehra con cawlahtsyawneh/con metsa pensyawneh/pensyawneh complehta.

136 How much is it per night?
Quant'è per notte?
Kwahntèh perr notteh?

137 Is breakfast included?
È compresa la colazione?
Èh comprehsa lah cawlatsyawneh?

138 May I see the room?
Posso vedere la camera?
Pawssaw vehdehreh lah cahmehra?

139 Do you have any cheaper rooms?
Ha delle camere più economiche?
Ah delleh cahmehreh pyoo ehcawonohmikeh?

140 I would like to take the room
Vorrei la camera.
Vawrray lah cahmehra.

141 I would like to stay for . . . nights.
Vorrei alloggiare per . . . notti.
Vawrray allawdjahreh perr . . . nottee.

142 The shower/light/tap doesn't work.
La doccia/luce/rubinetto non funziona.
Lah dawcheeah/loocheh/roobeenehttaw nawn foontsyawnah.

143 At what time/where is breakfast served?
A che ora/dove viene servita la colazione?
Ah keh awra/dawveh vyeneh serrveeta lah cawlahtsyawneh?

144 What time do I have to check-out?
A che ora devo lasciare libera la camera?
Ah keh awra dehvaw lahshareh leebehra lah cahmehra?

145 Can I have the key to room no . . ?
Posso avere la chiave della camera numero . . ?

I
T
A
L
I
A
N

132
↕
145

Payssaw ahvehreh lah keeyahveh
dehlah noohmehraw . . ?

146 My room number is . . .
La mia camera ha il numero . . .
*Lah myah cahmehra ah eel
noomehraw . . .*

147 Do you accept travellers'
cheques/Eurocheques/credit
cards?
Accettate assegni turistici/
euroassegni/carte di credito?
*Achetahteh asehnyee
tooreesteechee/ehooraw-ahsehnyee/
kahrrteh dee krehdeehtaw?*

148 May I have the bill please?
Mi dà il conto per favore?
*Mee dah eel cawntaw perr
fahvaworeh?*

149 Excuse me, I think there is a
mistake in this bill.
Mi scusi, credo ci sia un errore
nel conto.
*Mee scozee, kredaw chee syah oon
errawreh nel cawntaw.*

Youth Hostels

150 How much is a dormitory bed
per night?
Quant'è un letto in dormitorio
per notte?
*Kwahntèh oon lettaw een
dormeetawryaw perr notteh?*

151 I am/am not an HI member.
Sono/non sono membro
dell'Associazione Internazionale
Ostelli della Gioventù.
*Sawnaw/non sawnaw membraw
dell Assawchahtsyawne*

Eenterrnahtsyawnahleh ostelee
della Jovehntoo.

152 May I use my own sleeping
bag?
Posso usare il mio sacco a pelo?
*Pawssaw oozahreh eel myaw
saccaw ah pehlaw?*

153 What time do you lock the
doors at night?
A che ora chiudete le porta la
notte?
*Ah keh awra kewdehte leh porrteh
lah notteh?*

Camping

154 May I camp here for the
night/two nights?
Posso accamparmi qui per la
notte/due notti?
*Pawssaw accahmparmee kwee perr
lah notteh/dweh nottee?*

155 Where can I pitch my tent?
Dove posso piantare la tenda?
*Dawveh pawssaw pyahntareh lah
tenda?*

156 How much does it cost for
one night/week?
Qual'è la tariffa per una notte/
una settimana?
*Kwalèh lah tahreeffa perr oona
notteh/oona setteemahna?*

157 Where can we park our
caravan?
Dove possiamo parcheggiare la
roulotte?
*Dawveh pawseeyahmaw
pahrkehdjyahreh lah roolhawt?*

158 Where are the washing facilities?
Dove sono le lavanderie?
Dawveh sawnaw leh lavahndehryeh?

159 Is there a restaurant/supermarket/swimming pool on site/nearby?
C'è un ristorante/un supermercato/una piscina al campeggio/nelle vicinanze?
Chèh oon reestawrahnteh/oon sooperrmerrcahtaw/oona peesheena ahl cahmpedjaw/nelleh veecheenahntseh?

160 Do you have a safety deposit box?
Ha una cassaforte?
Ah oona cassahforrteh?

EATING AND DRINKING

Cafés and Bars

161 I would like a cup of/two cups of/another coffee/tea.
Vorrei una tazza di/due tazze di/un altro caffè/tè.
Vawrray oona tatsa dee/dweh tatseh dee/oon ahltraw caffèh/teh.

162 With/without milk/sugar.
Con/senza latte/zucchero.
Con/sentsa latteh/tsoockehraw.

163 I would like a bottle/glass/two glasses of mineral water/red wine/white wine, please.
Per cortesia, vorrei una bottiglia/un bicchiere/due bicchieri d'acqua minerale/vino rosso/vino bianco.

Peer corrtehzya, vawrray oona botteelya/oon beeckyereh/dweh beeckyeree daqua meenehrahleh/veenaw rawssaw/veenaw byahncaw.

164 I would like a beer/two beers, please.
Per cortesia, vorrei una birra, due birre.
Perr corrteshzya, vawrray oona beerra, dweh beerreh.

165 May I have some ice?
Può darmi del ghiaccio?
Poohòh darrmee del ghyacchaw?

166 Do you have any matches/cigarettes/cigars?
Vendete fiammiferi, sigarette/sigari?
Vendehteh fyammeefehree, seegahretteh, séegaree?

Restaurants

167 Can you recommend a good/inexpensive restaurant in this area?
Può raccomandarmi un buon ristorante/un ristorante economico in questa zona?
Poohòh raccomahndarmee oon boohòn reestawrahnteh/oon reestawrahnteh ehcawnawmeecaw een kwesta zawna?

168 I would like a table for . . . people.
Vorrei un tavolo per . . . persone.
Vawrray oon tahvawlaw perr . . . perrsawneh.

169 Do you have a non-smoking area?
Avete un'area non fumatori?
Ahvehteh oonahrreyah nawn foomahttawree?

170 Waiter/Waitress!
Cameriere/cameriera!
Cahmehryereh/cahmehryera!

171 Do you have a set menu/children's menu/wine list?
Ha un menù fisso/un menù per bambini/una lista dei vini?
Ah oon mehnoo feessaw/oon mehnoo perr bambeenee/oona leesta day veenee?

172 Do you have any vegetarian dishes, please?
Per favore, ha dei piatti vegetariani?
Perr fahvawreh, ah day pyattee vehgehtahryanee?

173 Are there any local specialities?
Avete qualche specialità locale?
Ahvehteh kwalkeh spehchiahleehtah lawkahleh?

174 Are vegetables included?
Sono incluse anche le verdure?
Sawnaw eenclooseh ahnkeh leh vehrdooreh?

175 Could I have it well-cooked/medium/rare please?
Potrei averlo ben cotto/mediamente cotto/poco cotto, per favore?
Pawtray ahvehrlaw behn cawtaw/mehdeeyahmehnteh cawtaw/pawcaw cawtaw perr fahvawreh?

176 What does this dish consist of?
Quali sono gli ingredienti di questo piatto?
Kwahlee sawnaw lee eengrehdyehntee dee kwestaw pyattaw?

177 I would like the set menu, please.
Vorrei il menù fisso.
Vawrray eel mehnoo feessaw.

178 We have not been served yet.
Non ci hanno ancora serviti.
Non chee annaw ahncawra serrveetee.

179 Excuse me, this is not what I ordered.
Mi scusi, questo non è quello che ho ordinato.
Mee scozee, kwehstaw nawn eh kwellaw keh haw awrdeehnahtaw.

180 May I have some/some more bread/water/coffee/tea?
Può darmi del/dell'altro pane/caffè/tè?
Puòh darrmee del/dellahltraw pahneh/caffèh/tèh?

181 May I have the bill, please?
Mi dà il conto, per favore?
Mee dah eel cawntaw, perr fahvawreh?

182 Does this bill include service?
Il conto include il servizio?
Eel cawntaw eencloodeh eel serrveetsyaw?

169
↑
182

183 Do you accept travellers' cheques (travelers' checks)/Eurocheques/MasterCard/US dollars?

Accettate assegni turistici/euroassegni/MasterCard/dollari USA?

Acchettahteh assenee tooreesteechee/ehoorawassenee/MasterCard/dollahree OO EZ AY?

184 Can I have a receipt, please?

Potrei avere la ricetta, per favore?

Pawtray ahvehreh lah reechettah, perr fahvawreh?

185 Where is the toilet (restroom), please?

Dov'è la toletta, per cortesia?

Dawvèh lah tawletta, perr corrtehzya?

On the Menu

186 First courses
Primi piatti
Preemee pyattee

187 Soups
Zuppe
Zooppeh

188 Main courses
Piatti principali
Pyattee preencheepahlee

189 Fish dishes
Piatti di pesce
Pyattee dee pesheh

190 Meat dishes
Piatti di carne
Pyattee dee kahrneh

191 Vegetarian dishes
Piatti vegetariani
Pyattee vehjehtaryanee

192 Cheese
Formaggio
Fawrmahdyiaw

193 Desserts
Dessert
Dehssehrt

194 Specialities
Specialità
Spehcheeyahleehtàh

GETTING AROUND

Public Transport

195 Where is the bus stop/coach station/nearest metro (subway) station?
Dov'è la fermata degli autobus/la stazione delle corriere/la più vicina stazione della metropolitana?
Dawvèh lah ferrmahta delee ahootawboos/lah stahtsyawneh delleh corryereh/lah pyoo veecheena stahtsyawneh della metropawleetahna?

196 When is the next/last bus to . . ?
A che ora è il prossimo/l'ultimo autobus per . . ?
Ah keh awra èh eel prawssemaw/loolteemaw ahootawboos perr . . ?

197 How much is the fare to the city centre (downtown)/railway (railroad) station/airport?

Qual'è la tariffa per il centro città/la stazione ferroviaria/l'aeroporto?
Kwahlèh lah tahreeffa perr eel chentraw cheettàh/lah stahtsyawne ferrawvyarya/l'aheraoporrtaw?

198 **Will you tell me when to get off?**
Può dirmi quando devo scendere?
Poohòh deerrmee kwahndaw dehvaw shendehreh?

199 **Does this bus go to . . ?**
Quest'autobus va a . . ?
Kwest ahootawboos vah ah . . ?

200 **Which number bus goes to . . ?**
Qual'è il numero dell'autobus per . . ?
Kwahlèh eel noomehraw dell ahootawboos perr . . ?

201 **May I have a single (one-way)/return (round-trip)/day ticket/book of tickets?**
Vorrei un biglietto di sola andata/di andata e ritorno valido per un giorno/un blocchetto di biglietti.
Vawrray oon beelyettaw dee sawla ahndahta/dee ahndahta eh reetorrnaw vahleedaw perr oon jawrrnaw/oon blawckettaw dee beelyettee.

Taxis

202 **I would like to go to . . . How much will it cost?**
Vorrei andare a . . . , quant'è?

Vawrray ahnahre ah . . . kwahntèh?

203 **Please stop here.**
Fermi qui, per cortesia.
Ferrmee koohee perr corrtehzya.

204 **I would like to order a taxi today/tomorrow/at 2pm to go from . . . to . . .**
Vorrei prenotare un tassì per oggi/per domani/per le quattordici che mi porti da . . . a . . .
Vawrray prehnawtahreh oon tassee perr odjee/perrdawmahnee/perr leh kwahttorrdeechee keh mee porrtee dah . . . ah . . .

Asking the Way

205 **Excuse me, do you speak English?**
Mi scusi, parla inglese?
Mee scoozee, parrla eenglehzeh?

206 **Excuse me, is this the right way to . . ?**
Mi scusi, è questa la strada per . .
Mee scoozee, eh kwehstah lah strahda perr . . ?

207 **. . . the cathedral/the tourist information office/the castle/the old town.**
. . . la cattedrale/l'ufficio informazioni turistiche/il castello/la città vecchia.
. . . lah kahttehdrahleh/looffeechaw eenforrmahtsyawnee tooreesteekeh/eel kahstehllaw/lah cheettàh vehkyah.

I T A L I A N

198
↑
207

208 Can you tell me the way to the railway (railroad) station/bus station/taxi rank (stand)/city centre (downtown)/beach?
Sa indicarmmi la strada per andare alla stazione ferroviaria/alla stazione degli autobus/al posteggio di auto pubbliche/al centro città/alla spiaggia?
Sah eendeecarrmee lah strahda perr ahndareh ahlla stahtsyawneh ferrawvyarya/ahlla stahtsyawneh delee ahootawboos/ahl pawstedjaw dee ahootaw poobbleekeh/ahl chentraw cheettàh/ahlla spyadjya?

209 First/second left/right/straight ahead.
Prenda la prossima/la seconda a sinistra/a destra/Vada sempre diritto.
Prehnda lah prawsseema/lah secawnda ah seeneestra/ah destra/vahda sempreh deereettaw.

210 Where is the nearest police station/post office?
Dov'è la più vicino posto di polizia/ufficcio postale?
Dawvèh eel pyoo veecheenaw pawstaw dee pawleetsya/ooffechaw pawstahle?

211 Is it far?
È lontano
Èh lawntahnaw?

212 Do I need to take a taxi/catch a bus?
Devo prendere un tassì/l'autobus?

Dehvaw prendehreh oon tassee/lahootawboos?

213 Can you point to it on my map?
Può indicarmelo sulla mappa?
Poohòh eendeecarrmehlaw soolla mappa?

214 Thank you for your help.
Grazie dell'aiuto.
Grahtsyeh dell ahyootaw.

SIGHTSEEING

215 Where is the Tourist Information office?
Dov'è l'Ufficio informazioni turistiche?
Dawvèh l'ooffeechaw eenformmahtsyawnee tooreesteekeh?

216 Where is the cathedral/church/museum?
Dov'è la cattedrale/la chiesa/il museo?
Dawvèh lah cattehdrahleh/lah kyehza/eel moozehaw?

217 How much is the entrance (admission) charge?
Qual'è la tariffa d'ingresso?
Kwahlèh lah tahreeffa deengressaw?

218 Is there a reduction for children/students/senior citizens?
I bambini/gli studenti/i pensionati hanno diritto a una riduzione?
Ee bahmbeenee/lee stoodentee/ee pensyawnahtee annaw deereettaw ah oona reedootsyawneh?

219 **What time does the next guided tour start?**
A che ora ha inizio la prossima visita guidata?
Ah keh awra ah eeneetsyaw lah prosseemah veeseeta goohedahta?

220 **One/two adults/children, please.**
Un adulto/due adulti/due bambini, per favore
Oon ahdooltaw/dweh ahdooltee/dweh bahmbeenee, perr fahvawreh

221 **May I take photographs here?**
Posso fare fotografie qui?
Payssaw fahreh fotografyeh kwee?

ENTERTAINMENT

222 **Can you recommend a good bar/nightclub?**
Può raccomandarmi un buon bar/locale notturno?
Poohòh rahccawmahdarrmee oon bwòn barr/lawcahleh nawttoorrnaw?

223 **Do you know what is on at the cinema (playing at the movies)/theatre at the moment?**
Conosce il programma del cinema/teatro?
Cawnawsheh eel prawgramma del ceenema/tehatraw?

224 **I would like to book (purchase) . . . tickets for the matinee/evening performance on Monday.**
Vorrei prenotare . . . posti per la matinée/lo spettacolo serale di lunedì.
Vawrray prehnawtahre . . . pawstee perr lah mateenéh/law spettahcawlaw sehrahleh dee loonehdee.

225 **What time does the film/ performance start?**
A che ora incomincia il film/lo spettacolo?
Ah keh awra eencawmeencha eel film/law spettahcawlaw?

MEETING PEOPLE

226 **Hello/Goodbye.**
Salve/arrivederci
Sahlveh/arreevehderrchee

227 **Good morning/good afternoon/good evening/ goodnight.**
Buon giorno/buon pomeriggio/ buona sera/buona notte.
Booawn geeyawrnaw/booawn pawmehreehdjaw/booawnah sehrah/booawnah nawtteh.

228 **Pleased to meet you.**
Piacere
Pyahchehreh

229 **How are you?**
Come sta?
Cawmeh stah?

230 **Fine, thank you. And you?**
Bene, grazie. E lei?
Behneh grahtsyeh. Eh ley?

231 **My name is . . .**
Mi chiamo . . .
Mee kyahmaw . . .

I
T
A
L
I
A
N

219
↕
231

232 This is my friend/
boyfriend/girlfriend/
husband/wife/brother/
sister.
Le presento il mio amico/il mio
ragazzo/la mia ragazza/mio
marito/mia moglie/mio fratello/
mia sorella.
Leh prehsentaw eel myaw
ahmeecaw/eel myaw rahgatsaw/
lah myah rahgatsa/myaw
mahreetaw/myah mawlyeh/
myaw frahtèllaw/myah sawrella.

233 Where are you travelling to?
Dov'è diretto?
Dawvèh deerettaw?

234 I am/we are going to . . .
Vado/andiamo a . . .
Vahdaw/ahndyahmaw ah . . .

235 How long are you travelling
for?
Per quanto tempo sarà in
viaggio?
Perr kwahntaw tempaw sahràh
een veehadjaw?

236 Where do you come from?
Da dove viene?
Dah dawveh vyehneh?

237 I am/we are from . . .
Vengo/veniamo da . . .
Vehngaw/vehnyahmaw dah . . .

238 We're on holiday.
Siamo in vacanza.
Seeyahmaw een vahkahntsah.

239 This is our first visit here.
Questa è la nostra prima visita
qui.

Kwehstah eh lah nawstrah
preemah veeseetah kwee.

240 Would you like/May I have a
cigarette?
Vuole una sigaretta?/Potrebbe
darmi una sigaretta?
Voohòleh oona seegahretta?/
Pawtrebbeh darrmee oona
seegahretta?

241 I am sorry but I do not
understand.
Mi scusi, non capisco.
Mee scoozee, non cahpeescaw.

242 Please speak slowly.
La prego di parlare lentamente.
Lah prehgaw dee parrlahreh
lentahmenteh.

243 Do you mind if I smoke?
Le spiace se fumo?
Leh speehacheh seh foomaw?

244 Do you have a light?
Mi fa accendere?
Me fah acchendereh?

245 I am waiting for my
husband/wife/boyfriend/
girlfriend.
Sto aspettando mio marito/
moglie/fidanzato/fidanzata.
Staw ahspehtahndaw meeaw
mahreetaw/mawlyeh/
feedahntsahtaw/feedahntsahtah.

TRAVELLING WITH CHILDREN

246 Do you have a high chair/
baby-sitting service/cot?
Ha un seggiolone/dei baby-
sitter/un lettino?

Ah oon sedjawlawneh/day baby-sitter/oon letteenaw?

247 Where is the nursery/playroom?
Dov'è la camera dei bambini/la stanza dei giochi?
Dawvèh lah cahmera day bahmbeenee/las stantsa day jawkee?

248 Where can I warm the baby's bottle?
Dove posso riscaldare il biberon?
Dawveh pawssaw reescahldareh eel beebehròn?

COMMUNICATIONS

Post

249 How much will it cost to send a letter/postcard/this package to Britain/Ireland/America/Canada/Australia/New Zealand?
Qual'è la tariffa per l'invio di una lettera/cartolina postale/di questo pacco in Gran Bretagna/Irlanda/America/Canada/Australia/Nuova Zelanda?
Kwahlèh lah tahreeffa perr l'eenvyaw dee oona lettehra/carrtawleena pawstahle/dee kwehstaw pahccaw een Grahn Brehtanya/Eerrlahnda/Ahmehreeca/Cahnada/Ahoostrahlia/Noohawva Tsehlahnda?

250 I would like one stamp/two stamps.

Vorrei un francobollo/due francobolli.
Vawrray oon frahncawbawllaw/dweh francawbawllee.

251 I'd like . . . stamps for postcards to send abroad, please.
Vorrei . . . dei francobolli per delle cartoline da inviare all'estero, per favore.
Vawrray . . . dey frahnkawbawlee perr dehleh kahrtawleeneh dah eenveeyahreh ahlehstehraw, perr fahvawreh.

Phones

252 I would like to make a telephone call/reverse the charges to (make a collect call to) . . .
Vorrei fare una telefonata/a carico del destinatario a . . .
(Vawrray fahreh oona telefawnahta/ah càhreecaw del desteenahtahryaw ah . . .

253 Which coins do I need for the telephone?
Che monete devo usare con quest'apparecchio?
Keh mawnehteh dehvaw oozahreh con kwestaw appareckyaw?

254 The line is engaged (busy).
La linea è occupata.
Lah leeneha èh occoopahta.

255 The number is . . .
Il numero è . . .
Eel noomehraw èh . . .

256 Hello, this is . . .
Pronto, sono . . .
Prawntaw, sawnaw . . .

257 May I speak to . . ?
Potrei parlare con . . . ?
Pawtray pahrlahreh kon . . ?

258 He/She is not in at the
moment. Can you call back?
Ora non c'è. Può richiamare?
*Awrrah nawn cheh. Poohòh
reekyahmahreh?*

MONEY

259 I would like to change these
travellers' che ues (travelers'
checks)/this currency/this
Eurocheque.
Vorrei cambiare questi assegni
turistici/questa valuta/questo
euroassegno.
*Vawrray cahmbyahreh kwestee
assenee tooreesteechee/kwesta
vahloota/kwestaw
ehoorawassenyaw.*

260 How much commission do
you charge (What is the
service charge)?
Qual'è la vostraprovvigione?
*Kwalèh lah vostra
prawvveejawneh?*

261 Can I obtain money with my
MasterCard?
Posso incassare contanti con il
Mastercard?
*Pawssaw eencassahreh
cawntahntee con eel Mastercard?*

SHOPPING

Names of Shops and Departments

262 Libreria/Cartoleria
Leebrehreeyah/Kahrtawlehreeyah
Bookshop/Stationery

263 Gioielleria/Articoli da regalo
*Djaweeyehlehreeyah/Ahrteekawlee
dah rehgahlaw*
Jeweller's/Gifts

264 Scarpe
Skahrpeh
Shoes

265 Ferramenta
Fehrrahmehntah
Hardware

266 Antiquario
Ahnteehkwahryaw
Antiques

267 Parrucchiere (per uomini)/
(per donne)
*Pahrrookyehreh (perr ooawmeenee)
(perr dawneh)*
Hairdressers (men's)/(women's)

268 Tabaccaio
Tahbahkaiyaw
Tobacconist

269 Panificio
Pahneefeechyaw
Baker's

270 Supermercato
Soopehrmehrkahtaw
Supermarket

ITALIAN

256
↕
270

271 Fotografo
Fotografaw
Photoshop

272 Giocattoli
Djawkahttawlee
Toys

273 Agenzia di viaggi
Ahjehntsyah dee veeyahdjee
Travel Agent

274 Articoli da toletta
Ahrteekawlee dah tawlettah
Toiletries

275 Dischi
Deeskee
Records

In the Shop

276 What time do the shops open/close?
A che ora aprono/chiudono i negozi?
Ah keh awra àhprawnaw/ kewdawnaw ee nehgotsee?

277 Where is the nearest market?
Dov'è il mercato più vicino?
Dawvèh eel mehrkahtaw pyoo veecheehnaw?

278 Can you show me the one in the window/this one?
Può mostrarmi quello in vetrina/questo?
Poohòh mawstrahrmee kwehllaw een vehtreenah/kwehstaw?

279 Can I try this on?
Posso provarlo?
Pawssaw prawvarrlaw?

280 What size is this?
Di che misura è?
Dee keh meezoora eh?

281 This is too large/too small/ too expensive.
Questo è troppo grande/troppo piccolo/troppo caro.
Kwestaw eh trawpaw grahndeh/ trawpaw peekawlaw/trawpaw kahraw.

282 Do you have any others?
Ne avete degli altri?
Neh ahvehteh delyee ahltree?

283 My size is . . .
La mia taglia è . . .
Lah meeyah tahlyah eh . . .

284 Where is the changing room/ childrens/cosmetic/ ladieswear/menswear/food department?
Dov'è lo spogliatoio/il reparto bambini/cosmetici/ abbigliamento femminile/ abbigliamento maschile/ alimentari?
Dawvèh law spawlyahtoyaw/eel rehparrtaw bahmbeenee/ cosmeteechee abbeelyahmentaw femmeeneeleh/ abbeelyahmentaw maskeeleh/ahleemehntahree?

285 I would like . . .
Vorrei . . .
Vawrray . . .

²⁸⁶ I would like a quarter of a kilo/half a kilo/a kilo of bread/butter/cheese/ham/tomatoes.

Vorrei due etti e mezzo/mezzo chilo/un chilo di pane/burro/formaggio/prosciutto/pomodori.

Vawrray dweh ehttee eh metsaw/metsaw keelaw/oon keelaw dee pahneh/boorraw/forrmahdjaw/prawshoottaw/pawmawdoree.

²⁸⁷ How much is this?

Quant'è?

Kuahntèh?

²⁸⁸ I'll take this one, thank you.

Prenderò questo, grazie.

Prehndehröh kwestaw, grahtsyeh.

²⁸⁹ Do you have a carrier (shopping) bag?

Ha un sacchetto di plastica?

Ah oon sahckettaw dee plahsteeca?

²⁹⁰ Do you have anything cheaper/larger/smaller/of better quality?

Ha un articolo meno caro/più grande/più piccolo/di migliore qualità?

Ah oon arrteecawlaw mehnaw cahraw/pyoo grahndeh/pyoo peeckawlaw/dee meelyawreh kwahleetàh?

²⁹¹ I would like a film for this camera.

Vorrei una pellicola per questa macchina fotografica.

Vawrray oona pelleecawla perr kwesta màckeena fawtawgràhfeeca.

²⁹² I would like some batteries, the same size as this old one.

Vorrei delle pile della stessa grandezza di quella vecchia.

Vawrray delleh peeleh della stehssah grahndetsa dee kwella veckya.

²⁹³ Would you mind wrapping this for me, please?

Le dispiacerebbe impacchett-armele?

Leh deespyahcherebbeh eempahckett-arrmehleh?

²⁹⁴ Sorry, but you seem to have given me the wrong change.

Scusi, si è sbagliato nel darmi il resto se non erro.

Scoozee, se eh sbahlyahtaw nel darrmee eel restaw seh non erraw.

MOTORING

Car Hire (Rental

²⁹⁵ I have ordered (rented) a car in the name of . . .

Ho ordinato una vettura per . . .

Aw orrdeenahtaw oona vettoora perr . . .

²⁹⁶ How much does it cost to hire (rent) a car for one day/two days/one week?

Quant'è il nolo di una vettura per un giorno/due giorni/una settimana?

Kwahntèh eel nawlaw dee oona vettoora perr oon jornaw/dweh joornee/oona setteemahna?

297 Is the tank already full of petrol (gas)?
Il serbatoio è pieno di benzina?
Eel serbahtoyaw èh pyehnaw dee bentseena?

298 Is insurance and tax included? How much is the deposit?
L'assicurazione e l'imposta sono comprese? Quant'è la caparra?
Lasseecoorahtsyawne eh leempawsta sawnaw cawmprehseh? Kwahnteh lah cahparra?

299 By what time must I return the car?
A che ora devo ritornare la vettura?
Ah keh awra devaw reetormahreh lah vettoora?

300 I would like a small/family car with a radio/cassette player.
Vorrei una piccola vettura/una familiare con radio/mangianastri.
Vawrray oona peeccawla vettoora/oona fahmeelyareh con rahdyaw/mahnjanastree.

Asking the Way

301 Excuse me, can you help me please?
Mi scusi, può aiutarmi per favore?
Mee scoozee, poohòh ahyiootahrmee, perr fahvawreh?

302 How do I reach the motorway/main road?
Come si arriva all'autostrada/strada principale?
Cawmeh see ahrreevah alahootawstrahdah/strahdah preencheepahleh?

303 I think I have taken the wrong turning.
Penso di aver preso la svolta sbagliata.
Pehnsaw dee avehr prehsaw lah svawltah sbahlyahtah.

304 I am looking for this address.
Sto cercando questo indirizzo.
Staw cherkahndaw kwestaw eendeereetsaw.

305 I am looking for the ... hotel.
Sto cercando l'hotel ...
Staw cherkahndaw lotehl ...

306 How far is it to ... from here?
Quanto dista ... da qui?
Kwantaw deestah ... dah kwee?

307 Carry straight on for ... kilometres.
Vada dritto per ... chilometri.
Vahdah dreetaw perr ... .keehlawmehtree.

308 Take the next turning on the right/left.
Prenda la prossima svolta a destra/sinistra.
Prehndah lah prawseehmah svawltah ah dehstrah/seeneestrah.

309 Turn right/left at the next crossroads/traffic lights.
Giri a destra/sinistra al prossimo incrocio/semaforo.
Djyree ah dehstrah/seeneestrah ahl prawseemaw eencrawchyaw/sehmahfawraw.

³¹⁰ **You are going in the wrong direction.**
Sta andando nella direzione sbagliata.
Stah ahndahndaw nehllah deerehtsyawneh sbahlyahtah.

Parking

³¹¹ **How long can I park here?**
Per quanto tempo posso parcheggiare qui?
Pehr kwantaw tehmpaw payssaw pahrkehdjahreh kwee?

³¹² **Is there a car park near here?**
C'è un parcheggio da queste parti?
Cheh oon pahrkehdjaw dah kwesteh pahrtee?

³¹³ **At what time does this car park close?**
A che ora chiude il parcheggio?
Ah keh awrah keeyoodeh eel pahrkehdjaw?

Signs and Notices

³¹⁴ **Senso unico.**
Sehnsaw ooneekaw.
One way.

³¹⁵ **Divieto di accesso.**
Deeveeyehtaw dee ahchehssaw.
No entry.

³¹⁶ **Divieto di sosta.**
Deeveeyehtaw dee sawstah.
No parking.

³¹⁷ **Deviazione**
Dehveeyahtsyawneh.
Detour (diversion

³¹⁸ **Stop.**
Stop.
Stop.

³¹⁹ **Dare precedenza.**
Dahreh prehchehdehntsah.
Give way (yield).

³²⁰ **Strada sdrucciolevole.**
Strahdah sdroocheeyawlehvawleh.
Slippery road.

³²¹ **Divieto di sorpasso.**
Deeveeyehtaw dee sawrpahssaw.
No overtaking.

At the Filling Station

³²² **Unleaded (lead-free)/ Standard/Premium**
Carburante senza piombo/ normale/super
Kahrboorahnteh sehntsah peeyawmbaw/nawrmahleh/soopehrr

³²³ **Fill the tank please.**
Il pieno, per favore.
Eel peeyehnaw perr fahvawreh.

³²⁴ **Do you have a road map of this area?**
Avete una carta stradale di quest'area?
Ahvehteh oonah kahrtah strahdahleh dee kwestahreyah?

³²⁵ **How much is the car-wash?**
Quanto costa l'autolavaggio?
Kwahntaw kawstah lahootawlahvahdjyoh.

Breakdowns

³²⁶ **I've had a breakdown at . . .**
Ho avuto un guasto a . . .

*Haw ahvootaw oon gwastaw
ah . . .*

327 I am on the road from . . . to . . .
Sono sulla stra a da . . . a . . .
*Sawnaw soollah strahdah
dah . . . ah . . .*

328 I can't move the car. Can
you send a tow-truck?
Non posso spostare l'auto.
Potrebbe mandare un carro
attrezzi?
*Nawn pawssaw spawstahreh
lahootaw. Pawtrebbeh
mahndahreh oon kahrraw
ahtretzee?*

329 I have a flat tyre.
Ho una ruota a terra.
Haw oonah rooawtah ah tehrrah.

330 The windscreen (windshield)
has smashed/cracked.
Il parabrezza si è sfondato/
incrinato.
*Eel pahrahbretzah see eh
sfawndahtaw/eenkreenahtaw.*

331 There is something wrong
with the engine/brakes/
lights/steering/gearbox/
clutch/exhaust.
C'è qualcosa che non va con il
motore/i freni/le luci/lo sterzo/
il cambio/la frizione/lo scarico.
*Cheh kwahlkawsah keh nawn vah
kawn eel mawtawreh/ee frehnee/
leh loochee/law stehrtsaw/eel
kahmbeeyaw/lah freetsyawneh/
law skahreehkaw.*

332 It's overheating.
E' surriscaldato.

Eh soorreeskahldhataw.

333 It won't start.
Non parte.
Nawn pahrteh.

334 Where can I get it repaired?
Dove posso ripararla?
Dawveh pawssaw reepahrarlah?

335 Can you take me there?
Mi ci potrebbe accompagnare?
*Mee chee pawtrebbeh
ahkawmpahnyareh?*

336 Will it take long to fix?
Ci vorrà molto tempo per
ripararla?
*Chee vawrràh mawltaw
tehmpaw perr reepahrahrlah?*

337 How much will it cost?
Quanto mi costerà?
Kwantaw mee kawstehràh?

Accidents

338 Can you help me? There has
been an accident.
Potrebbe aiutarmi? C'è stato un
incidente.
*Pawtrebbeh ahyiootahrmee? Cheh
stahtaw oon eencheedehnteh.*

339 Please call the police/an
ambulance.
Per favore, chiami la polizia/
un'ambulanza.
*Perr fahvawreh keeyahmee lah
pawleetseeyah/oonamboolahntsah.*

340 Is anyone hurt?
Ci sono feriti?
Chee sawnaw fehreetee?

Traffic Offences

341 I'm sorry, I didn't see the sign.
Mi scusi, non ho visto il cartello.
Mee scoozee, nawn haw veestaw eel kahrtehllaw.

342 Must I pay a fine? How much?
Devo pagare una multa? Quant'è?
Dehvaw pahgareh oonah mooltah? Kwantèh?

343 Show me your documents.
Mi mostri i documenti.
Mee mawstree ee dawcoomehntee.

HEALTH

Pharmacy

344 Do you have anything for a stomachache/headache/sore throat/toothache?
Ha un preparato per il mal di stomaco/mal di testa/mal di gola/mal di denti?
Ah oon prehpahrahtaw perr eel mahl dee stohmahcaw/mahl dee testa/mahl dee gawla/mahl dee dehntee?

345 I need something for diarrhoea (diarrhea)/ constipation/a cold/a cough/insect bites/sunburn/ travel (motion) sickness.
Ho bisogno di un rimedio per la diarrea/la stitichezza/il raffreddore/la tosse/le punture di insetti/l'eritema solare/il mal di viaggio.
Aw beesawnyaw dee oon reemehdyaw perr lah dyahrreha/ lah steeteeketsa/eel rahffredawreh/ lah tawsseh/leh poontooreh dee eensehttee/lehreetehma sawlahreh/ eel mahl dee vyahdjaw.

346 How much/how many do I take?
Quanto/quanti ne devo prendere?
Kwahntaw/kwahntee neh dehvaw préndehreh?

347 How often do I take it/ them?
Ogni quanto devo prenderlo/ prenderli?
Awnee kwahntaw dehvaw prenderrlaw/prenderrlee?

348 How much does it cost?
Quanto costa?
Kwahntaw cawsta?

349 Can you recommend a good doctor/dentist?
Può raccomandarmi un buon medico/dentista?
Poohò rhaccawmahndarrmee oon boohòn méhdeecaw/denteesta?

350 Is it suitable for children?
È adatto per i bambini?
Èh ahdahttaw perr ee bahmbeenee?

Doctor

351 I have a pain here/in my arm/leg/chest/stomach.

Ho un dolore qui/nel braccio/nella gamba/nel petto/nello stamco.
Aw oon dawlawreh kwee/nel bracchaw/nella gahmba/nel pettaw/nellaw stohmahcaw.

352 Please call a doctor, this is an emergency.
La prego di chiamare un medico. È un'emergenza.
Lah prehgaw dee kyahmahreh oon mèdeecaw. Èh oonemerrgentsa.

353 I would like to make an appointment to see a doctor.
Vorrei prendere un appuntamento con un medico.
Vawrray prendehre oon ahppoontahmentaw con oon mèdeecaw.

354 I am diabetic/pregnant.
Sono diabetica/incinta.
Sawnaw dyahbèhteeca/eencheenta.

355 I need a prescription for . . .
Ho bisogno di una ricetta per . . .
Aw beesohnyaw dee oona reechetta perr . . .

356 Can you give me something to ease the pain.
Può prescrivermi qualcosa che allevii il dolore?
Poohòh prehscreeverrmee kwahlcawsa keh allevee eel dawlawreh?

357 I am/he is/she is allergic to penicillin.
Sono/egli è/ella è allergico (masc.)/allergica (fem.) alla penicillina.

Sawnaw/ehlyee eh/ehlah eh allehrjeekaw/allehrjeekah ahlah pehneecheeleenah.

358 Does this hurt?
Questo fa male?
Kwestaw fah mahleh?

359 You must/he must/she must go to hospital.
Lei deve/egli deve/ella deve andare in ospedale.
Ley dehveh/ehlyee dehveh/ehlah dehveh ahndahreh een awspehdahleh.

360 Take these once/twice/three times a day.
Prenda queste una volta/due volte/tre volte al giorno.
Prehndah kwesteh oonah vawltah/dooweh vawlteh/treh vawlteh ahl djeeyawrnaw.

361 I am/he is/she is taking this medication.
Sto/egli sta/ella sta prendendo questa medicina.
Staw/ehlyee stah/ehlah stah prehndehndaw kwestah mehdeecheenah.

362 I have medical insurance.
Ho un'assicurazione medica.
Haw oonahseekoorahtsyawneh mehdeekah.

Dentist

363 I have toothache.
Ho mal di denti.
Aw mahl dee dentee.

364 My filling has come out.
È uscita l'otturazione.
Èh oosheeta lawttoorahtsyawneh.

365 I do/do not want to have an injection first.
Voglio/non voglio l'anestetico.
Vawlyaw/non vawlyaw lahnestehteecaw.

EMERGENCIES

366 Help!
Aiuto!
Ahyootaw!

367 Call an ambulance/a doctor/ the police!
Chiamate un'ambulanza/un medico/la polizia!
Kyahmahteh oon ahmboolahntsa/ oon mehdeecaw/la pawleetsya!

368 I have had my travellers' cheques (travelers' checks)/ credit cards/purse/handbag/ rucksack (knapsack)/ luggage/wallet stolen.
Mi hanno rubato gli assegni turistici/le carte di credito/il borsellino/la borsetta/lo zaino/ il bagaglio/il portafoglio.
Mee annaw roobahtaw lee assenee tooreesteechee/leh carrteh dee crédeetaw/eel borrsellenaw/lah borrsetta/law tsaheenaw/eel bahgalyaw/eel porrtafawlyaw.

369 Can you help me, I have lost my daughter/son?
Può aiutarmi? Ho perduto mia figlia/mio figlio.
Poohòh ahyootarrmee? Aw perrdootaw myah feelya/myaw feelyaw.

370 Please go away/leave me alone.
Se ne vada/mi lasci in pace!
Seh neh vahda/me lahshee een pahcheh!

371 Fire!
Al fuoco!
Ahl fooawcaw!

372 I want to contact the British/American/ Canadian/Irish/Australian/ New Zealand/South African consulate.
Voglio contattare il consolato britannico/americano/canadese/ irlandese/australiano/ neozelandese/sudafricano.
Vawlyaw kawntattahreh eel kawnsawlahtaw breetahnneekaw/ ahmehreekahnaw/kahnahdehseh/ eerlahndehseh/ ahoostrahleeyahnaw/ nehawzehlahndehseh/ soodahfrikahnaw.

ITALIAN

364
↑
372

Introduction

The official language of Poland, Polish is a Slavic tongue and therefore related to Russian, Czech and many other Eastern European languages. English is spoken to some extent in larger cities, particularly by younger people, though older inhabitants are more likely to speak German or French as a second language. Russian is understood but unpopular.

Addresses for travel and tourist information

UK: *Orbis (Polish National Tourist Office),* 246 King St, London W6 0RF; tel: (0181) 741 5541.
USA: *Orbis (Polish National Tourist Office),* 500 Fifth Ave, New York, NY 10110; tel: (212) 867-5011.

ESSENTIALS

Alphabet

A *ah*	B *bey*
C *tsey*	D *dey*
E *ey*	F *ef*
G *gye*	H *hah*
I *ea*	J *yot*
K *kah*	L *el*
M *em*	N *en*
O *oh*	P *pey*
Q *koo*	R *air*
S *es*	T *tey*
U *oo*	V *fow*
W *voo*	X *iks*
Y *eegrec*	Z *zet*

Basic Words and Phrases

1 **Yes**
Tak
Tak
No
nie
nye

2 **Please**
Proszę
Proshem
Thank you
Dziękuję
Jenkooyem

3 **That's O.K.**
To jest O.K.
Toe yest O.K.
Perhaps
Może
Mozhe

4 **To**
Do
Doe
From
Z
Z

5 **Here**
Tu
Too
There
Tam
Tam

6 **None**
Nic
Neets
Also
Także
Takzhe

7 **How**
Jak
Yak
When
Kiedy
Kyedy

8 **What**
Co
Tso
Why
Dlaczego
Dlachego

9 **I don't understand.**
Nie rozumiem
Nye rhozoomyem

10 **I don't speak Polish.**
Nie mówię po polsku.
Nye movyem po polsku.

11 **Do you speak English?**
Czy pan (pani) mówi po angielsku?

Chi pan (pani) movee po angielskoo?

12 Can you please write it down?
Proszę napisać.
Proshem napisach.

13 Can you please speak more slowly?
Proszę mówić wolniej.
Proshem moveech volnyey.

14 ow much does it/this cost?
Ile to kosztuje?
Eele to koshtooye?

Days

15 Monday   **Tuesday**
Poniedziałek   Wtorek
Poniejawek   *Vtorek*

16 Wednesday   **Thursday**
Środa   Czwartek
Shroda   *Chvartek*

17 Friday   **Saturday**
Piątek   Sobota
Pyontek   *Sobota*

18 Sunday   **Morning**
Niedziela   Rano
Niejela   *Rano*

19 Afternoon   **Evening**
Po południu   Wieczór
Po powoodnyoo   *Vyechoor*

20 Night   **Week**
Noc   Tydzień
Nots   *Tyjen*

21 Yesterday   **Tomorrow**
Wczoraj   Jutro
Vchoray   *Yootro*

Numbers

22 Zero   **One**
Zero   Jeden
Zero   *Yeden*

23 Two   **Three**
Dwa   Trzy
Dva   *Tshee*

24 Four   **Five**
Cztery   Pięć
Chteree   *Pyench*

25 Six   **Seven**
Sześć   Siedem
Sheshch   *Siedem*

26 Eight   **Nine**
Osiem   Dziewięć
Oshem   *Dzieviench*

27 Ten   **Eleven**
Dziesięć   Jedenaście
Jeshench   *Yedenashchiem*

28 Twelve   **Thirteen**
Dwanaście   Trzynaście
Dvanashchiem   *Tsheenashchiem*

29 Fourteen   **Fifteen**
Czternaście   Piętnaście
Chternashchiem   *Pyentnashchiem*

30 Sixteen   **Seventeen**
Szesnaście   Siedemnaście
Shesnasschiem   *Shiedemnashchiem*

31 Eighteen   **Nineteen**
Osiemnaście   Dziewiętnaście
Oshemnashchiem   *Jevietnashchiem*

P
O
L
I
S
H

12
↑
31

32 **Twenty**
Dwadzieścia
Dvajeshshcha

Twenty-one
Dwadzieścia jeden
Dvajeshchia yeden

33 **Twenty-two**
Dwadzieścia dwa
Dvajeshchia dva

Thirty
Trzydzieści
Tsheejeshchee

34 **Forty**
Czterdzieści
Chterjeshchee

Fifty
Pięćdziesiąt
Pyenjeshiont

35 **Sixty**
Sześćdziesiąt
Sheshjeshiont

Seventy
Siedemdziesiąt
Shiedemjesiont

36 **Eighty**
Osiemdziesiąt
Osiemjeshiont

Ninety
Dziewięćdziesiąt
Jevienjeshiont

37 **One hundred**
Sto
Sto

Five hundred
Pięćset
Pyenchset

38 **One thousand**
Tysiąc
Tyshionc

One million
Milion
Million

Time

39 **9.00**
Dziewiąta
Jevionta

40 **9.05**
Dziewiąta pięć
Jevionta pyench

41 **9.10**
Dziewiąta dziesięć
Jevionta jeshench

42 **9.15**
Dziewiąta piętnaście
Jevionta pyentnashchiem

43 **9.20**
Dziewiąta dwadzieścia
Jevionta dvajeshchia

44 **9.25**
Dziewiąta dwadzieścia pięć
Jevionta dvajeshchia piench

45 **9.30**
Dziewiąta trzydzieści
Jevionta tsheejeshchee

46 **9.35**
Dziewiąta trzydzieści pięć
Jevionta tsheejeshchee pyench

47 **9.40**
Dziewiąta czterdzieści
Jevionta chterjeshchee

48 **9.45**
Dziewiąta czterdzieści pięć
Jevionta chterjeshchee pyench.

49 **9.50**
Dziewiąta pięćdziesiąt
Jevionta pyenjeshiont

50 **9.55**
Dziewiąta pięćdziesiąt pięć
Jevionta pyenjeshiont pyench

51 **12.00/Midday/Midnight**
Dwunasta/Południe/Północ
Dvoonasta/Powoodnye/Poownots

52 **What time is it?**
Która godzina?
Ktoora gojeena?

53 **It is . . .**
Jest . . .
Yest . . .

ARRIVING AND DEPARTING

Airport

54 **Excuse me, where is the check-in desk for . . . airline?**
Przepraszam, gdzie jest stanowisko linii . . ?
Psheyprasham, gje yest stanovizko leenyi . . ?

55 **What is the boarding gate/ time for my flight?**
Gdzie jest wyjście na/O której jest . . . mój lot?
Gje yest veeyshche na/o ktoorey yest . . . mooy lot?

56 **How long is the delay likely to be?**
Jakie będzie opóźnienie?
Yakhe benjeh opoozhnyenye?

57 **Where is the duty-free shop?**
Gdzie jest sklep wolno-cłowy
Gje yest sklep volnoh-tzlovy?

58 **Which way is the baggage reclaim?**
Gdzie jest odbiór bagażu?
Gje yest odbyoor bagazhoo?

59 **Where can I get the bus to the city centre?**
Gdzie jest autobus do centrum?
Gje yest owtohbus do tzentrum?

Train Station

60 **Where is the ticket office/ information desk?**
Gdzie jest kasa/informacja?
Gje yest kasa/informatsya?

61 **Which platform does the train to . . . depart from?**
Z którego peronu odchodzi pociąg do . . ?
Z ktoorego peronu odhojee pochiong do . . ?

62 **Where is platform . . ?**
Gdzie jest peron . . ?
Gje yest peron . . ?

63 **When is the next train to . . ?**
Kiedy odchodzi następny pociąg do . . ?
Kyedy odhojee nastempny pociong do . . ?

64 **Is there a later train to . . ?**
Czy jest późniejszy pociąg do . . ?
Chi yest poozhnieyshee pociong do . . ?

Port

65 **How do I get to the port?**
Jak się dostać do portu?
Yak siem dostach doh portoo?

66 **When is the next sailing to . . ?**
Kiedy odchodzi następny prom do . . ?
Kyedy odhojee nastempny prom doh . . ?

67 **Can I catch an earlier ferry with this ticket?**
Czy ten bilet jest ważny na wcześniejszy prom?
Chi ten beelet yest vazhnee na wchesnyeyshi prom?

P
O
L
I
S
H

54
↑
67

207

Notices and Signs

68 **Wagon restauracyjny**
Vagon restauratsiny
Buffet (Dining) Car

69 **Autobus**
Owtoboos
Bus

70 **Woda pitna/nie do picia**
Voda pitna/nye do pitcha
Drinking/Non-drinking water

71 **Wejście**
Veishchye
Entrance

72 **Wyjście**
Veeyshchye
Exit

73 **Informacja**
Informatsya
Information

74 **Przechowalnia bagażu**
Pshehovalnya bagazhoo
Left Luggage (Baggage Claim)

75 **Schowki na bagaż**
S'hovky na bagazh
Luggage Lockers

76 **Poczta**
Pochta
Post Office

77 **Peron**
Peron
Platform

78 **Dworzec kolejowy**
Dvozhets koleyovy
Railway (Railroad) Station

79 **Port lotniczy**
Port lotneechi
Airport

80 **Port**
Port
Port

81 **Restauracja**
Restauratsya
Restaurant

82 **Dla palących/niepalących**
Dla palontsyh/nyepalontsych
Smoking/Non-Smoking

83 **Telefon**
Telefon
Telephone

84 **Kasa biletowa**
Kasa biletova
Ticket Office

85 **Odprawa**
Odprava
Check-in Desk

86 **Rozkład jazdy**
Rozkwad yazdy
Timetable (Schedule)

87 **Toalety**
Toalety
Toilets (Restrooms)

88 **Mężczyźni**
Menzhtchyzni
Gentlemen

89 **Dla kobiet**
Dla kobyet
Ladies'

POLISH

**68
↕
89**

68
↕
89

90 Tramwaj
Tramvay
Tram (Streetcar)

91 Metro
Metro
Underground (Subway)

92 Poczekalnia
Potchekalnya
Waiting room

Buying a Ticket

**93 I would like a first-class/
second-class single (one-
way)/return (round-trip)
ticket to . . .**
Proszę o bilet pierwszej klasy/
drugiej klasy w jedną stronę/
powrotny do . . .
*Proshe o bilet pyervoshey/droogyey
klasy v yednom strone/povrotny
doh . . .*

**94 Is my rail pass valid on this
train/ferry/bus?**
Czy ten bilet ważny jest na ten
pociąg/prom/autobus?
*Chi ten beelet yest vazhnee nah ten
pochong/prom/owtohbus?*

**95 I would like an aisle/window
seat.**
Proszę o miejsce przy przejściu/
oknie.
*Proshe o mieystse pshee
psheyshchu/oknye.*

96 No smoking/smoking, please.
Palenie wzbronione/
dozwolone.

Palenye vzbronione/dozvolone.

**97 We would like to sit
together.**
Chcemy siedzieć razem.
Htsemy shiejech razem.

**98 I would like to make a seat
reservation.**
Chcę zamówić miejscówkę
*Htsem zahmooveech myeys-
tsoovkeh.*

**99 I would like to reserve a
couchette/sleeper for one
person/two people/for my
family.**
Chcę zarezerwować kuszetkę/
miejsce sypialne dla jednej
osoby/dwóch osób/rodziny.
*Hcem zarezervovach kooshetkem/
mieystse sipyalne dla yedney
osoby/dvooh osoob/rojiny.*

**100 I would like to reserve a
cabin.**
Chcę zamówić kabinę.
Htsem zahmooveech cabin-eh.

Timetables (Schedules)

101 Przyjazd
Pshiyazd
Arrive

102 Zatrzymuje się w
Zatzhimuye shiem v
Calls (Stops) at

103 Usługi gastronomiczne
Uswoogy gastronomichne
Catering Service

**P
O
L
I
S
H**

**90
↕
103**

209

104 Przesiadka w
Psheshadka v
Change at

105 Połączenie
Powonchenye
Connection

106 Codziennie
Tsojennye
Daily

107 Co 40 minut
Tso 40 minut
Every 40   inutes

108 Pierwsza klasa
Pyerovsha klasa
First-class

109 Co godzinę
Tso gojinem
Hourly

110 Zaleca się rezerwację miejsc
Zaletsa shiem rezervatsye mieysts
Seat reservations are
recommended

111 Druga klasa
Drooga klasa
Second-class

112 Dodatkowa opłata
Dodatkova opwata
Supplement Payable

113 Przez
Pshez
Via

Luggage

**114 How much will it cost to send
(ship) my luggage in
advance?**
Ile kosztuje nadanie rzeczy na
bagaż?
*Eele koshtooye nadanye zhechi na
bagazh?*

**115 Where is the left luggage
(baggage claim) office?**
Gdzie jest przechowalnia bagażu?
Gje jest pshehovalnya bagazhoo?

**116 What time do you open/
close?**
O której otwieracie/zamykacie?
*O ktoorey otvyerachie/
zamykachie?*

**117 Where are the luggage
trolleys (carts)?**
Gdzie są wózki bagażowe?
Gje som voozky bagazhove?

118 Where are the lockers?
Gdzie są schowki?
Gje som s-hovkee?

119 I have lost my locker key.
Zgubiłem klucz do schowka.
Zgoobiwem klooch do s'hovka.

On Board

120 Is this seat taken?
Czy to miejsce jest wolne?
Chi to mieystse yest volne?

**121 Excuse me, you are sitting in
my reserved seat.**
Przepraszam, to jest moje

zarezerwowane miejsce.
*Psheprasham, toe yest moye
zarezervovane mieystse.*

122 Which station is this?
Jaka to stacja?
Yaka to statsya?

**123 What time is this train/bus/
ferry/flight due to arrive/
depart?**
O której przyjeżdża/odjeżdża
pociąg/autobus/prom? (O
której jest przylot/odlot?)
*O ktoorey pshijezdzha/odyezdzha
pochong/owtohbus/prom? (O
ktoorey yest pshillot/odlot?)*

**124 Will you wake me just before
we arrive?**
Proszę mnie zbudzić przed
przyjazdem.
*Proshem mnye zbujeech pshed
pshyiazdem.*

Customs and Passports

125 Proszę o paszporty!
Proshem o pashporty!
Passports, please!

**126 I have nothing/wine/spirits
(alcohol)/tobacco to declare.**
Nie mam do zgłoszenia
niczego/wina/alkoholu/tytoniu.
*Nye mam doe zgwoshenya
nichego/vina/alkoholu/titonyoo.*

**127 I shall be staying for . . .
days/weeks/months.**
Będę tu . . . dni/tygodni/
miesięcy.

*Bendem too . . . dnee/tygodnee/
miesyentsy.*

AT THE TOURIST OFFICE

**128 Do you have a map of the
town/area?**
Czy macie plan miasta/rejonu?
Chi matsie plan miasta/reyonoo?

**129 Can I reserve accommodation
here?**
Czy mogę tutaj zarezerwować
zakwaterowanie?
*Chi mogem tutay zarezeroovach
zakvaterovanye?*

**130 Do you have a list of
accommodation?**
Gdzie można się zatrzymać?
Gje mozhna sheh zahtcheemach?

ACCOMMODATION

Hotels

**131 I have a reservation in the
name of . . .**
Mam rezerwację na
nazwisko . . .
Mam rezervatsyem na nazvisko . . .

**132 I wrote to/faxed/telephoned
you last month/last week in . . .**
Pisałem(am)/faxowałem(am)/
telefonowałem(am) w zeszłym
miesiącu/zeszłego tygodnia/w . . .
*Peesawem(am)/faxovawem(am)/
telefonovavem(am) v zeshweem
myeshontzoo/zeshwego teegodnya/
v . . .*

P
O
L
I
S
H

122
↕
132

ACCOMMODATION

133 **Do you have any rooms free?**
Czy są wolne pokoje?
Chi som wolneh pokoye?

134 **I would like to reserve a single/double room with/without bath/shower.**
Chcę zarezerwować pokój pojedynczy/podwójny, z łazienką/prysznicem, bez łazienki/prysznicu.
Htsem zarezervovach pokooy poyedynchy/podvooyny, z wazienkom/pryshnitsem/bez wazienki/pryshnicoo.

135 **I would like bed and breakfast/(room and) half board/(room and) full board.**
Chcę pokój ze śniadaniem/z dwoma posiłkami/zpełnym wyżywieniem.
Hcem pokooy ze sniadanyem/z dwoma poshiwkamy/z pewnym vizhivyenyem.

136 **How much is it per night?**
Ile kosztuje jedna noc?
Eele koshtooye yedna nots?

137 **Is breakfast included?**
Czy jest w to wliczone śniadanie?
Chi yest v to vlichoney shniadanye?

138 **May I see the room?**
Czy mogę zobaczyć ten pokój?
Chi mogem zobachich ten pokooy?

139 **Do you have any cheaper rooms?**

Czy macie tańsze pokoje?
Chi machie tanishe pokoje?

140 **I would like to take the room**
Wezmę ten pokój.
Vezmem ten pokooy.

141 **I would like to stay for . . . nights.**
Chcę się zatrzymać na . . . nocy.
Htsem shiem zatzhimach na . . . notsy.

142 **The shower/light/tap doesn't work.**
Prysznic/światło/kran nie działa.
Prishnitz/shvyatwo/kran nye dzhawa.

143 **At what time/where is breakfast served?**
O której godzinie/gdzie jest śniadanie?
O ktoorey gojeenye/gje yest shnyadanye?

144 **What time do I have to check-out?**
O której godzinie mam opróżnić pokój?
O ktoorey gojeenye mam oproozhnich pokooy?

145 **Can I have the key to room no . . ?**
Proszę o klucz do pokoju numer . . .
Proshem o klooch doh pokoyoo noomer . . .

146 **My room number is . . .**
Numer mojego pokoju jest . . .

Noomer moyego pokoyoo yest . . .

**147 Do you accept travellers'
cheques/Eurocheques/credit
cards?**
Czy przyjmujecie czeki
podróżne/Euroczeki/karty
kredytowe?
*Chi pshiymuyecheh chekee
podroozhne/Eurochekee/karti
kreditoveh?*

148 May I have the bill please.
Proszę o rachunek.
Proshem o rahoonek.

**149 Excuse me, I think there is a
mistake in this bill.**
Przepraszam, wydaje mi się, że
jest pomyłka w rachunku.
*Psheprasham, veedayeh me sheh,
zhe yest pomiwka w rahoonkoo.*

Youth Hostels

**150 How much is a dormitory bed
per night?**
Ile kosztuje łóżko we wspólnej
sypialni, na jedną noc?
*Eele koshtooye woozhko ve
vspoolney sypyalnee, na yednom
nots?*

**151 I am/am not an HI
member.**
Należę/nie należę do HI.
Nalezhem/nye nalezhem do hah, ea.

**152 May I use my own sleeping
bag?**
Czy mogę używać własny
śpiwór?

*Chi mogem uzhivach vwasny
shpivoor?*

**153 What time do you lock the
doors at night?**
O której zamykacie drzwi na
noc?
*O ktoorey zamykatsye djvee na
nots?*

Camping

**154 May I camp here for the
night/two nights?**
Czy mogę się tu kampingować
przez jedną noc/dwie noce?
*Chi mogem too kampingovach
pshes jednom nots/dvye notse?*

155 Where can I pitch my tent?
Gdzie mogę rozbić namiot?
Gje mogem rozbich namyot?

**156 How much does it cost for
one night/week?**
Ile wynosi opłata za jedną noc/
za tydzień?
*Eele vynoshi opwata za yednom
nots/za tyjyen?*

**157 Where can we park our
caravan?**
Gdzie możemy postawić
przyczepę?
*Gje mozhemi postaveech
pshichepeh?*

**158 Where are the washing
facilities?**
Gdzie można się umyć?
Gje mozhna shiem oomych?

147
↑
158

POLISH

159 Is there a restaurant/
supermarket/swimming pool
on site/nearby?
Czy jest na miejscu/w pobliżu
restauracja/supersam/basen
kąpielowy?
*Chi yest na mieystsu/v poblizhoo
restauratsya/supersam/basen
kompielovy?*

160 Do you have a safety deposit
box?
Czy jest tu sejf?
Chi yest too seyf?

EATING AND DRINKING

Cafés and Bars

161 I would like a cup of/two
cups of/another coffee/tea.
Proszę o jedną/dwie/jeszcze
jedną kawę/herbatę.
*Proshem o yednom/dvye/yeshche
yednom kavem/herbatem.*

162 With/without milk/sugar.
Z mlekiem/bez mleka/z
cukrem/bez cukru.
*Z mlekyem/bez mleka/z tsukrem/
bez tsookroo.*

163 I would like a bottle/glass/
two glasses of mineral water/
red wine/white wine, please.
Proszę o butelkę/szklankę/dwie
szklanki wody mineralnej/
czerwonego wina/białego wina.
*Proshem o bootelkem/shklankem/
dvye shklankee vody mineralney/
chervonego vina/biawego vina.*

164 I would like a beer/two
beers, please.
Proszę o piwo/dwa piwa.
Proshem o pivo/dva piva.

165 May I have some ice?
Proszę o lód.
Proshem o lood.

166 Do you have any matches/
cigarettes/cigars?
Czy są zapałki/papierosy/
cygara?
*Chi som zapawki/papyerosy/
tsygara?*

Restaurants

167 Can you recommend a good/
inexpensive restaurant in this
area?
Czy możecie mi polecić dobrą/
niedrogą restaurację w pobliżu?
*Chi mozheche me polechich
dobrom/nyedrogom restauratsye v
poblizhoo?*

168 I would like a table for . . .
people.
Proszę o stolik dla . . . osób.
Proshem o stolik dla . . . osoob.

169 Do you have a non-smoking
area?
Czy są miejsca dla niepalących?
*Chi som myeystsa dla
nyepalontzeeh?*

170 Waiter/Waitress!
Kelner/Kelnerka!
Kelner/Kelnerka!

171 Do you have a set menu/
children's menu/wine list?
Czy mogę prosić o zestaw potraw/
menu dla dzieci/listę win?
*Chi mo em proshich o zestav
potrav/menu dla jechee/listem vin?*

172 Do you have any vegetarian
dishes, please?
Czy są dania jarskie?
Chi som danya yarskye?

173 Are there any local
specialities?
Czy są jakieś specjalności lokalne?
*Chi som jakyesh
spetzyahlnoshchee lokalneh?*

174 Are vegetables included?
Czy to razem z jarzynami?
Chi toh razem z yazhinyamee?

175 Could I have it well-cooked/
medium/rare please?
Poproszę wysmażone dobrze/
średnio/czerwone.
*Poproshem vysmazhoneh dobzeh/
shrednyo/chervoneh.*

176 What does this dish consist of?
Co to za potrawa?
Tso toe za potrava?

177 I would like the set menu,
please.
Proszę o zestaw potraw.
Proshem o zestav potrav.

178 We have not been served yet.
Nie obsłużono nas jeszcze.
Nye obswoozhono nas yeshche.

179 Excuse me, this is not what I
ordered.

Przeparaszam, nie to
zamówiłem(am).
*Psheprasham, nye to
zamooviwem(am).*

180 May I have some bread/
water/coffee/tea?
May I have some more
bread/water/coffee/tea?
Proszę o chleb/wodę/kawę/
herbatę?
Proszę o więcej chleba/wody/
kawy/herbaty?
*Proshem o hleb/vodem/kavem/
herbatem?*
*Proshem o vyentzey hleba/vodee/
kavee/herbatee?*

181 May I have the bill, please?
Proszę o rachunek.
Proshem o rahoonek.

182 Does this bill include service?
Czy jest w to wliczona obsługa?
Chi yest v toe vlichona obswooga?

183 Do you accept travellers'
cheques (travelers' checks)/
Eurocheques/MasterCard/US
dollars?
Czy przyjmujecie czeki
podróżne/Euroczeki/
MasterCard/dolary USA?
*Chi pshiymooyechie cheky
podroozhne/Eurocheky/
MasterCard/ dolary USA?*

184 Can I have a receipt, please?
Pokwitowanie poproszę
Pokveetovanye poproshem.

185 Where is the toilet
(restroom), please?
Gdzie jest toaleta?
Gje yest toaleta?

On the Menu

186 First courses
Pierwsze dania
Pyerwshe danya

187 Soups
Zupy
Zoopi

188 Main courses
Główne dania
Gwoowneh danyah

189 Fish dishes
Dania rybne
Danya ribneh

190 Meat dishes
Dania mięsne
Danya myensneh

191 Vegetarian dishes
Dania jarskie
Danya yarskye

192 Cheese
Ser
Ser

193 Desserts
Desery
Desseree

194 Specialities
Specjalności
Specyalnoshchee

GETTING AROUND

Public Transport

195 Where is the bus stop/coach
station/nearest metro
(subway) station?
Gdzie jest przystanek
autobusowy/dworzec
autobusowy/najbliższa stacja
metra?
*Gje yest pshystanek autoboosovy/
dworzec autobusowy/najblizhsha
statsya metra?*

196 When is the next/last bus
to . . ?
Kiedy odchodzi następny/
ostatni autobus do . . ?
*Kyedy odhojee ostatnee autoboos
doh . . ?*

197 How much is the fare to the
city centre (downtown)/
railway (railroad) station/
airport?
Ile kosztuje przejazd do
centrum/na dworzec kolejowy/
na lotnisko?
*Eele koshtooye psheyazd do
centroom/na dvozhets koleyovy/
na lotnisko?*

198 Will you tell me when to get
off?
Proszę mi powiedzieć kiedy
mam wysiąść.
*Proshem mi povyejech kyedy mam
vyshonshch.*

P
O
L
I
S
H

185
↕
198

199 Does this bus go to . . ?
Czy ten autobus jedzie
do . . ?
Chi ten autoboos yejee doh . . ?

200 Which number bus goes
to . . ?
Który numer jedzie do . . ?
Ktoory numer yedzhye doh . . ?

201 May I have a single (one-
way)/return (round-trip)/day
ticket/book of tickets?
Proszę o bilet w jedną stronę/
powrotny/całodzienny/karnet
biletowy?
*Proshem o bilet v yednom
stronem/povrotny/tzawojennee/
karnet biletovy?*

Taxis

202 I would like to go to . . .
How much will it cost?
Chcę jechać do . . . , ile to
będzie kosztować?
*Htsem yehach doh . . . , ile toe
benjey koshtovach?*

203 Please stop here.
Proszę się tu zatrzymać.
Proshem shiem too zatzhimach.

204 I would like to order a taxi
today/tomorrow/at 2pm to
go from . . . to . . .
Chę zamówić taksówkę na
dzisiaj/jutro/na drugą po
południu, na przejazd z . . .
do . . .
Htsem zamoovich taxoovkem na

*jishyay/na yootro/na droogom po
powoodnyoo, na psheyazd z . . .
doh . . .*

Asking the Way

205 Excuse me, do you speak
English?
Przepraszam, czy mówi Pan/
Pani (*woman*) po angielsku?
*Psheprasham, chi moovi pan/
panee po angyelskoo?*

206 Excuse me, is this the right
way to . . ?
Przepraszam, czy to jest droga
do . . ?
*Psheprasham, chi to yest drogah
doh . . ?*

207 . . . the cathedral/the tourist
information office/the castle/
the old town
. . . katedry/biura turystycznego/
zamku/starego miasta
*katedree/byura tooristichnego/
zamkoo/stahrego myasta*

208 Can you tell me the way to
the railway (railroad) station/
bus station/taxi rank (stand)/
city centre (downtown)/
beach?
Jak dojść do dworca
kolejowego/autobusowego/
postoju taksówek/centrum/na
plażę?
*Yak doyshch do dwortsa
koleyovego/autoboosovego/
postooyo taxoovek/centroom/na
plazhem?*

209 **First/second left/right/ straight ahead.**
Pierwsza/druga w lewo/w prawo/prosto.
Pyervsha/drooga v levo/v pravo/ prosto.

210 **Where is the nearest police station/post office?**
Gdzie jest najbliższy posterunek policji/poczta?
Gje yest nayblizhshy posteroonek politsyee/pochta?

211 **Is it far?**
Czy to daleko?
Chi to daleko?

212 **Do I need to take a taxi/ catch a bus?**
Czy muszę wziąć taksówkę/ jechać autobusem?
Chi mooshem wzionshch taksoovkem/jehach autoboosem?

213 **Can you point to it on my map?**
Czy może mi Pan/Pani (woman) pokazać na mapie?
Chi mozhe mi pan/pany pokazach na mapye?

214 **Thank you for your help.**
Dziękuję za pomoc.
Jenkooyem za pomots.

SIGHTSEEING

215 **Where is the Tourist Information office?**
Gdzie jest Informacja Turystyczna?

Gje yest informatsya tooristichna?

216 **Where is the cathedral/ church/museum?**
Gdzie jest katedra/kościół/ muzeum?
Gje yest katedra/koshchoow/ mooseum?

217 **How much is the entrance (admission) charge?**
Ile wynosi opłata za wstęp?
Eele vynoshee opwata za vstemp?

218 **Is there a reduction for children/students/senior citizens?**
Czy jest zniżka dla dzieci/ studentów/emerytów?
Chi yest znizhka dla jechee/ studentoof/emeritoof?

219 **What time does the next guided tour start?**
O której zaczyna się następny obchód z przewodnikiem?
O ktoorey zachina shiem nastempny obhood z pshevodnikyem?

220 **One/two adults/children, please.**
Jeden/dwa bilety dla dorosłych/dzieci.
Yeden/dva bilety dla doroswyh/ jechee.

221 **May I take photographs here?**
Czy można tu fotografować?
Chi mozhna tu fotografovach?

ENTERTAINMENT

222 Can you recommend a good bar/nightclub?
Czy możecie mi polecić dobry bar/nocny lokal?
Chi mozhechie me polechich dobry bar/notsny lokal?

223 Do you know what is on at the cinema (playing at the movies)/theatre at the moment?
Co grają teraz w kinach/teatrach?
Tso grayom teraz w kinakh/teatrakh?

224 I would like to book (purchase) . . . tickets for the matinee/evening performance on Monday
Chcę zamówić . . . biletów na popołudniowe/wieczorne przedstawienie, w poniedziałek.
Khtsem zamoovich . . . biletoov na popowoodnyove/vyechorney pshedsytavyenye, v ponyedzyawek.

225 What time does the film/performance start?
O której zaczyna się spektakl?
O ktoorey zachina shiem spektakl?

MEETING PEOPLE

226 Hello/Goodbye.
Hallo/Do widzenia.
Hallo/Do vidzenia.

227 Good morning/good afternoon/good evening/goodnight.

Dzień dobry/dzień dobry/dobry wieczór/dobranoc
Djen dobri/ djen dobri/dobri vyechoor/dohbranotz

228 Pleased to meet you.
Miło mi poznać.
Miwo me poznach.

229 How are you?
Jak się Pan (Pani) ma?
Yak shem Pan (Panee) mah?

230 Fine, thank you. And you?
Bardzo dobrze, dziękuję. A Pan(Pani)?
Bardzho dobrzhe, djenkooye. Ah Pan (Panee)?

231 My name is . . .
Nazywam się . . .
Nazyvam shiem . . .

232 This is my friend/boyfriend/girlfriend/husband/wife/brother/sister.
To mój przyjaciel/moja sympatia/moja sympatia/mój mąż/moja żona/mój brat/moja siostra.
Toe mooy psheyatsyel/moya psheyatsyoowka/moya simpatya/mooy monj/moya zhona/moy brat/moya syostra.

233 Where are you travelling to?
Gdzie jedziesz?
Gje yejesh?

234 I am/we are going to . . .
Jadę/jedziemy do . . .
Yadem/yejemy doh . . .

P
O
L
I
S
H

222
↕
234

219

235 How long are you travelling
for?
Na jak długo jesteś w podrbży?
*Na yak dwoogo yestesh v
odroozhee?*

236 Where do you come from?
Skąd jesteś?
Skond yestesh?

237 I am/we are from . . .
Jestem/jesteśmy z . . .
Yestem/yesteshme z . . .

238 We're on holiday.
Jesteśmy na wakacjach.
Yesteshme na vakatzyah.

239 This is our first visit here.
To jest nasz pierwszy pobyt.
To yest nash pyerwshee pobeet.

240 Would you like/May I have a
cigarette?
Czy chcesz/Czy mogę prosić o
papierosa?
*Chi khcesh/Chi mogem proshich o
papyerosa?*

241 I am sorry but I do not
understand.
Przykro mi, ale nie rozumiem.
Pshikro me, aly nye rozoomiem.

242 Please speak slowly.
Proszę mówić powoli.
Proshem moovich povolee.

243 Do you mind if I smoke?
Czy mogę zapalić?
Chi mogem zapalich?

244 Do you have a light?
Czy mogę prosić o ogień?

Chi mogem prosheech o ogien?

245 I am waiting for my husband/
wife/boyfriend/girlfriend.
Czekam na mego męża/moją
żonę/mego chłopca/moją
dziewczynę.
*Chekam na megoh menzha/
moyom zhoneh/megoh hwoptza/
moyom dzhevchineh.*

TRAVELLING WITH CHILDREN

246 Do you have a high chair/
baby-sitting service/cot?
Czy macie krzesło dla dziecka/
usługi czuwania nad dzieckiem/
łóżeczko dziecinne?
*Chi matsye ksheswo dla jetska/
uswoogi choovanya nad jetskiem/
woozhechko jechinney?*

247 Where is the nursery/
playroom?
Gdzie jest pokój dziecinny/
pokój zabaw dla dzieci?
*Gje yest pokooy jechinny/pokooy
zabav dla jechee?*

248 Where can I warm the baby's
bottle?
Gdzie mogę zagrzać butelkę dla
dziecka?
*Gje mogem zagzhach bootelkem
dla jetska?*

COMMUNICATIONS

Post

249 How much will it cost to
send a letter/postcard/this

package to Britain/Ireland/America/Canada/Australia/New Zealand?

Ile kosztuje wysyłka listu/pocztówki/tej paczki do Anglii/Irlandii/Ameryki/Kanady/Australii/Nowej Zelandii?

Eele koshtooye vysywka listoo/poochtoovky/tey pachki do Anglee/Yrlandee/Amerykee/Kanady/Australee/Novey Zelandee?

250 I would like one stamp/two stamps.

Proszę o jeden znaczek/dwa znaczki.

Proshem o yeden znachek/dva znachkee.

251 I'd like . . . stamps for postcards to send abroad, please.

Proszę o . . . znaczków na karty pocztowe na zagranicę.

Proshem o . . . znachkoov na kartee pochtove na zagranitzheh.

Phones

252 I would like to make a telephone call/reverse the charges to (make a collect call to) . . .

Chcę zadzwonić/na koszt abonenta do . . .

Ktsem zadzvonich/na kosht abonenta, doh . . .

253 Which coins do I need for the telephone?

Jakie muszę mieć monety do tego telefonu?

Yakye mushem miech monety doh tego telephonoo?

254 The line is engaged (busy).

Linia jest zajęta.

Linya yest zayenta.

255 The number is . . .

Numer jest . . .

Noomer yest . . .

256 Hello, this is . . ?

Halo, tu mówi . . .

Hello, tu moovee . . .

257 May I speak to . . ?

Czy mogę mówić z . . .

Chi mogem mooveech z . . .

258 He/She is not in at the moment. Can you call back?

Jego/jej niema w tej chwili. Proszę zadzwonić jeszcze raz.

Yego/yey nyema v tey hveelee. Proshem zadhzvoneech yeshche raz.

MONEY

259 I would like to change these travellers' cheques (travelers' checks)/this currency/this Eurocheque.

Chcę wymienić te czeki podróżne/tą walutę/ten Euroczek.

Khcem vymienich te chekee podroozhne/tom valootem/ten Eurochek.

P
O
L
I
S
H

250
↕
259

**P
O
L
I
S
H**

**260
↑
277**

²⁶⁰ How much commission do
you charge (What is the
service charge)?
Ile liczycie za wymianę?
Eele lichytsye za vymianem?

²⁶¹ Can I obtain money with my
MasterCard?
Czy mogę dostać pieniądze na
MasterCard?
*Chi mogem dostach pyenyondze
na MasterCard?*

SHOPPING

Names of shops and Departments

²⁶² Księgarnia/Materiały
papiernicze
*Kshengarnia/materyawee
papyerneecheh*
Bookshop/Stationery

²⁶³ Jubiler/Upominki
Yoobiler/Oopominkee
Jeweller's/Gifts

²⁶⁴ Sklep z obuwiem
Sklep z oboovyem
Shoes

²⁶⁵ Artykuły gospodarstwa
domowego
Artikoowe gospodarstva domovego
Hardware

²⁶⁶ Antykwariat
Anticvaryat
Antiques

²⁶⁷ Fryzjer (męski)/(damski)
Frizyer (menskee)/(damskee

Hairdressers (men's)/(women's

²⁶⁸ Kiosk z papierosami
Kiosk z papyerohsammy
Tobacconist

²⁶⁹ Piekarnia
Pyekarnya
Baker's

²⁷⁰ Supermarket
Soopermarkyet
Supermarket

²⁷¹ Foto Optyk
Photo-optic
Photoshop

²⁷² Zabawki
Zabavkee
Toys

²⁷³ Biuro podróży
Bureau podroozhi
Travel Agent

²⁷⁴ Perfumeria/Drogeria
Perfoomerya/Drogerya
Toiletries

²⁷⁵ Sklep muzyczny
Sklep moozichnee
Records

In the Shop

²⁷⁶ What time do the shops
open/close?
O której otwierają/zamykają
sklepy?
*O ktoorey otvyerayom/
zamykayom sklepy?*

²⁷⁷ Where is the nearest market?
Gdzie jest najbliższy targ?

Gje yest nayblizhshi targ?

278 Can you show me the one in the window/this one?
Proszę pokazać mi ten z wystawy/ten.
Proshem pokazach me ten z vistavee/ten.

279 Can I try this on?
Czy mogę to przymierzyć?
Chi mogem to pshimiezhich?

280 What size is this?
Jaki to rozmiar?
Yakee toe rozmyar?

281 This is too large/too small/too expensive.
To jest za duże/za małe/za drogie.
Toh yest za doozhe/za mawe/za drogye.

282 Do you have any others?
Czy są inne?
Chi som inneh?

283 My size is . . .
Noszę numer . . . .
Noshem noomer . . .

284 Where is the changing room/childrens/cosmetic/ladieswear/menswear/food department?
Gdzie jest szatnia/ubrania dla dzieci/kosmetyki/ubrania damskie/ubrania męskie/żywność?
Gje yest shatnia/ubrania dla jechee/kosmetyki/ubrania damskiey/ubrania menskiey/zhyvnoshch?

285 I would like . . .
Chciałbym (chciałabym)
Htzchawbim (htzchawabim) . . .

286 I would like a quarter of a kilo/half a kilo/a kilo of bread/butter/cheese/ham/tomatoes.
Proszę o ćwierć kilo/pół kilo/kilo chleba/masła/sera/szynki/pomidorów.
Proshem o chvyerch kilo/poow kilo/kilo hleba/maswa/sera/shinky/pomidoroov.

287 How much is this?
Ile to kosztuje?
Eele toe koshtooye?

288 I'll take this one, thank you.
Poproszę ten. Dziękuję.
Poproshem ten. Dzhenkooyeh.

289 Do you have a carrier (shopping) bag?
Czy mogę prosić o torbę?
Chi mogem proshich o torbem?

290 Do you have anything cheaper/larger/smaller/of better quality?
Czy macie coś tańszego/większego/mniejszego/w lepszej jakości?
Chi machye tsosh tanshego/vienkshego/mneyshego/v lepshey yakoshchee?

291 I would like a film for this camera.
Potrzebuję film do aparatu.
Potshebooyem film doe aparatoo.

P
O
L
I
S
H

278
↑
291

223

292 I would like some batteries, the same size as this old one.
Potrzebuję baterie, takie same jak te stare.
Potshebooyem baterye, takye same yak te starey.

293 Would you mind wrapping this for me, please?
Proszę mi to zapakować.
Proshem me toe zapakovac.

294 Sorry, but you seem to have given me the wrong change.
Przepraszam, ale źle mi Pan wydał.
Psheprasham, aley zlye me Pan vydaw.

MOTORING

Car Hire (Rental

295 I have ordered (rented) a car in the name of . .
Zamówiłem samochód na nazwisko . . .
Zamooviwem samohood na nazvisko . . .

296 How much does it cost to hire (rent) a car for one day/two days/one week?
Ile kosztuje wynajęcie samochodu na jeden dzień/dwa dni/tydzień?
Eele koshtooye vynayenchye samohodoo na yeden jen/dva dnyee/tyjen?

297 Is the tank already full of petrol (gas)?
Czy zbiornik jest pełny?
Chi zbyornik yest pewny?

298 Is insurance and tax included? How much is the deposit?
Czy to obejmuje ubezpieczenie i podatek? Ile wynosi depozyt?
Chi toe obeymooye ubezpyechenye ee podatek? Eele koshtooye depozyt?

299 By what time must I return the car?
Do której godziny mam zwrócić samochód?
Doe ktoorey gojeeny mam zvroochich samohood?

300 I would like a small/family car with a radio/cassette player.
Chcę mały/większy samochód z radiem/magnetofonem kasetowym.
Ktsem mawy/vienkshy samohood z radyem/magnetophonem kasetovym.

Asking the Way

301 Excuse me, can you help me please?
Przepraszam, czy może mi Pan(Pani) pomoc?
Psheprasham, chi mozeh me Pan(Pani) pomotz?

302 How do I reach the
motorway/main road?
Którędy do autostrady/głównej
drogi?
*toorendy do autostrady/
gwoovney drogi?*

303 I think I have taken the
wrong turning.
Chyba źle skręciłem(am)
Heeba zhle skrencheewem(am).

304 I am looking for this address.
Szukam tego adresu.
Shookam tego adresoo.

305 I am looking for the . . . hotel.
Szukam hotelu . . .
Shookam hoteloo . . .

306 How far is it to . . .
from here?
Jak daleko stąd do . . .
Yak dalekoh stond doh . . .

307 Carry straight on for . . .
kilometres.
. . . kilometrów prostą drogą.
. . . kilomtroov prostom drogom.

308 Take the next turning on the
right/left.
Następna przecznica w prawo/
w lewo
*Nastempna pshechneetzha v
pravo/v levo*

309 Turn right/left at the next
crossroads/traffic lights.
Trzeba skręcić w prawo/w lewo
na następnym skrzyżowaniu/
przy następnych światłach

Tcheba skrenchich v pravo/v levo
na nastempneem
sksheezhovanyoo/pshee
nastempneeh shvyatwah.

310 You are going in the wrong
direction.
Pan(Pani) jedzie w złym
kierunku.
*Pan(Pani) yedzhe v zweem
kyeroonkoo.*

Parking

311 How long can I park here?
Jak długo można tu parkować?
*Yak dwoogo mozhna tu
parkovach?*

312 Is there a car park near here?
Czy jest parking w pobliżu?
Chi yest parking v pobleezhoo?

313 At what time does this car
park close?
O której zamyka się parking?
O ktoorey zameeka shem parking?

Signs and Notices

314 Jeden kierunek
Yeden kyeroonek
One way

315 Zakaz wjazdu
Zakaz vyazdoo
No entry

316 Nie parkować
Nye parkovach
No parking

317 Objazd
Obyahzd
Detour (diversion)

318 Stop
Stop
Stop

319 Pierwszeństwo ruchu
Pyervshenstvo roohoo
Give way (yield)

320 Śliska nawierzchnia
Shleeska navyerzhnya
Slippery road

321 Zakaz wymijania
Zakaz vimeeyanya
No overtaking

At the Filling Station

**322 Unleaded (lead-free)/
Standard/Premium**
Bez-ołowiowa (bez ołowiu)/
Normalna/wysoko oktanowa
*Bez-owoviova(bez owovyou)/
Normalna/visokoh oktanova*

323 Fill the tank please.
Do pełna, poproszę.
Do pewna, poproshem.

**324 Do you have a road map of
this area?**
Czy jest mapa drogowa tej
okolicy?
*Chi yest mapa drogova tey
okolitzee?*

325 How much is the car-wash?
Ile kosztuje auto-myjnia?
Eele koshtooye awtoh-meeynya?

Breakdowns

326 I've had a breakdown at . . .
Samochód mi się zepsuł na . . .
*Samohood me shem zepsoow
na . . .*

**327 I am on the road from . . .
to . . .**
Jestem w drodze z . . .
do . . .
*Yestem v drodzhe z . . .
doh . . .*

**328 I can't move the car. Can
you send a tow-truck?**
Nie mogę ruszyć samochodu.
Proszę przysłać pomoc
drogową
*Nye mogem rooshich samohodoo.
Proshem pshiswach pomotz
drogovom.*

329 I have a flat tyre.
Mam płaską oponę.
Mam pwaskom oponeh

**330 The windscreen (windshield)
has smashed/cracked.**
Szyba się stłukła/pękła.
Sheba shem stwookwah/penkhwa.

**331 There is something wrong
with the engine/brakes/
lights/steering/gearbox/
clutch/exhaust.**
Mam problem z silnikiem/
hamulcami/światłami/układem
kierowniczym/skrzynią
biegów/sprzęgłem/tłumikiem.
*Mam problem z shilneekyem/
hamooltzame/shvyatwamee/*

ookwadem kyerovneechem/
skhshinyom byegoow/
spshengwem/twoomikyem.

332 It's overheating.
Przegrzewa się.
Pshegzheva sheh.

333 It won't start.
Nie chce ruszyć.
Nye htse rooshich.

334 Where can I get it repaired?
Gdzie mogę naprawić?
Gje mogem napraveech?

335 Can you take me there?
Czy może mnie Pan(Pani) tam
zaprowadzić?
*Chi mozhe mnye Pan(Pani) tam
zaprovadzheech?*

336 Will it take long to fix?
Jak długo potrwa naprawa?
Yak dwoogoh potrva naprava?

337 How much will it cost?
Ile będzie kosztowało?
Eele bendzhe koshtovawoh?

Accidents

**338 Can you help me? There has
been an accident.**
Proszę mi pomoc. Chodzi o
wypadek.
*Proshem mi pomtz. Hodzhi o
vipadek.*

**339 Please call the police/an
ambulance.**
Proszę zawezwać policję/
pogotowie.

*Proshem zavezvach policyem/
pogotohvye.*

340 Is anyone hurt?
Czy ktoś jest ranny?
Chi ktosh yest rannee?

Traffic Offences

**341 I'm sorry, I didn't see the
sign.**
Przepraszam, nie widziałem(am)
znaku.
*Psheprasham, nye
vidzhyawem(am) znakoo.*

**342 Must I pay a fine? How
much?**
Czy muszę zapłacić mandat?
Ile?
*Chi mushem zapwacheech
mandat? Eele?*

343 Show me your documents.
Dokumenty poproszę.
Dokumenti poproshem.

HEALTH

Pharmacy

**344 Do you have anything for a
stomachache/headache/sore
throat/toothache?**
Czy jest coś na ból żołądka/ból
głowy/ból gardła/ból zęba?
*Chi yest tzosh na bool zholondka/
bool gwovy/bool gardwa/bool
zemba?*

345 I need something for
diarrhoea (diarrhea)/
constipation/a cold/a cough/
insect bites/sunburn/travel
(motion) sickness.
Potrzebuję czegoś na biegunkę/
zaparcie/przeziębienie/kaszel/
ukąszenie owada/opaleniznę/
morską chorobę.
*Potshebooyem tsosh na
biegoonkem/zaparchee/
pshezyembyenye/kashel/
ukonshenye ovada/opaleniznem/
morskom horobem.*

346 How much/how many do I
take?
Ile mam zażyć?
Eele mam zazhych?

347 How often do I take it/them?
Jak często mam to brać?
Yak chensto mam toe brach?

348 How much does it cost?
Ile to kosztuje?
Eele toe koshtooye?

349 Can you recommend a good
doctor/dentist?
Czy możecie mi polecić
dobrego lekarza/dentystę?
*Chi mozhetsye me polechich
dobrego lekaja/dentystem?*

350 Is it suitable for children?
Czy nadaje się dla dzieci?
Chi nadaye shye dla jechee?

Doctor

351 I have a pain here/in my
arm/leg/chest/stomach.
Boli mnie tu/w ramieniu/
nodze/piersiach/żołądku.
*Bolee mnye too/v ramyenew/
nodzey/piershiah/zhowondkoo.*

352 Please call a doctor, this is an
emergency.
Proszę wezwać lekarza, to jest
nagły wypadek.
*Proshem wezwoch lekazha, toe yest
nagwy vypadek.*

353 I would like to make an
appointment to see a doctor.
Chcę zamówić wizytę lekarską.
*Khcem zamoovich vizytem
lekarskom.*

354 I am diabetic/pregnant.
Jestem cukrzykiem/w ciąży.
Yestem tsukshykiem/v tsionjy.

355 I need a prescription for . . .
Potrzebuję receptę na . . .
Potshebooyem retseptem na . . .

356 Can you give me something
to ease the pain?
Czy może mi Pan/Pani (woman)
dać jakiś środek
przeciwbólowy?
*Chi mozhe me Pan/Pany dach
yakish shrodek pshechivboolovy?*

357 I am/he is/she is allergic to
penicillin.
Ja jestem/on jest/ona jest
uczulony/a na penicylinę.

*Ya yestem/on yest/ona yest
uchoolonee/a na penitzileenem.*

358 Does this hurt?
Czy to boli?
Chi to bolee?

359 You must/he must/she must go to hospital.
Pan(Pani)/on/ona musi pójść do szpitala.
Pan(Pani)/on/ona mooshe pooyshch doh shpitalah.

360 Take these once/twice /three times a day.
Proszę zażywać to raz/dwa/ trzy razy dziennie.
Proshem zazhivach toh raz/dwa/ tshee razee djenye.

361 I am/he is/she is taking this medication.
Ja zażywam/on zażywa/ona zażywa to lekarstwo.
Ya zazheevam/on zazheeva/ona zazheeva toh lekarstvoh.

362 I have medical insurance.
Mam ubezpieczenie lekarskie.
Mam oobezpyechenye lekarskye.

Dentist

363 I have toothache.
Boli mnie ząb.
Boly mnie zomb.

364 My filling has come out.
Wyleciała mi plomba.
Vyletsyawa me plomba.

365 I do/do not want to have an injection first.
Proszę najpierw o zastrzyk/nie chcę zastrzyku.
Proshem naipyero o zastsheek/nye khcem zastsheekoo.

EMERGENCIES

366 Help!
Pomocy!
Pomotsy!

367 Call an ambulance/a doctor/ the police!
Prosze wezwać karetkę pogotowia/lekarza/policję!
Proshem zavezwach karetkem pogotovya/lekazha/politsyem!

368 I have had my travellers' cheques (travelers' checks)/ credit cards/purse/handbag/ rucksack (knapsack)/ luggage/wallet stolen.
Skradziono mi czeki podróżne/ karty kredytowe/portmonetkę/ torebkę/plecak/bagaż/portfel.
Skrajono me chekee podroozhne/ karty kreditovey/pormonetkem/ torebkem/pletsak/bagazh/portfel.

369 Can you help me, I have lost my daughter/son?
Czy może mi Pan (Pani) pomóc, Zgubiłam córkę/syna?
Chi mozheh me Pan (Panee), Zgoobiwam tsoorkem/syna?

P
O
L
I
S
H

358
↕
369

229

370 Please go away/leave me
alone.
Proszę odejść/zostawić mnie w
spokoju.
*Proshem odeyshch/zostavich mnye
v spokoyoo.*

371 Fire!
Pożar!
Pozhar!

372 I want to contact the British/
American/Canadian/Irish/
Australian/New Zealand/

South African consulate.
Chcę się skontaktować z
konsulatem brytyjskim/
amerykańskim/kanadyjskim/
irlandzkim/australijskim/nowo-
zelandzkim/RPA.
*Htsem shem skontaktovach z
konsulatem britiyskeem/
americanskeem/canadeeyskeem/
irlandzkhim/awstraleeyskim/
novo-zelandzhkhim/er-pe-ah.*

Introduction

Portuguese is spoken throughout Portugal. In tourist areas a certain amount of English is spoken. Portuguese is a descendant of Latin, like Italian, Spanish and French, and a knowledge of any of these other languages will help you to understand a lot of written Portuguese. Spoken Portuguese, however, can be quite difficult for a beginner to comprehend and to speak, and you may need to ask to have things written down for you more often than in other Western European countries. If you have to resort to speaking a second language, try English or even French rather than Spanish.

Written prices can be misunderstood, particularly by North American visitors, unless you realise that $ stands for escudo, the Portuguese unit of currency; the sign is put where the decimal point would normally be, so that e.g. 200$50 would mean 200 escudos and 50 centavos (a centavo is one-hundredth of an escudo).

Addresses for travel and tourist information

UK: *Portuguese National Tourist Office*, 22/25A Sackville St, London W1X 1DE; tel: (0171) 494 1441.
USA: *Portuguese National Tourist Office*, 590 Fifth Ave (4th Floor), New York, NY 10036-4704; tel: (212) 3544403.

ESSENTIALS

Alphabet

A	B
ah	*bay*
C	D
say	*day*
E	F
e	*efi*
G	H
jay	*agah*
I	J
ee	*jota*
K	L
kahpa	*eli*
M	N
emi	*eni*
O	P
o	*pay*
Q	R
kay	*erre*
S	T
esi	*tay*
U	V
oo	*vay*
W	X
vay dooplo	*sheesh*
Y	Z
eepselohn	*zay*

Basic Words and Phrases

1 Yes No
Sim Não
seem *nown*

2 Please Thank you
Por favor Obrigado/a
poor favohr *ohbreegahdoo/a*

3 That's O.K. Perhaps
Está bem Talvez
istah bayng *tahlvaysh*

4 To From
Para De
para *di*

5 Here There
Aqui Ali
akee *alee*

6 None Also
Nenhum (a) Também
nenyoom (a) *tangbayng*

7 How When
Como Quando
kohmoo *kwahndoo*

8 What Why
O que Porquê
oo ki *poorkay*

9 I don't understand.
Não entendo
nown ayngtayngdoo

10 I don't speak Portuguese.
Não sei falar [nome da
linguagem]
nown say falahr . . .

11 Do you speak English?
Fala Inglês?
fahla eenglaysh?

**12 Can you please write it
down?**
Por favor, pode escrever isso?
*poor favohr pohd ishkrivayr
eessoo?*

13 **Can you please speak more slowly?**
Por favor, pode falar mais devagar?
poor favohr, pohd falahr myish devagahr?

14 **How much does it/this cost?**
Quanto custa isto?
kwantoo kooshta ishtoo?

Days

15 **Monday** **Tuesday**
Segunda-feira Terça-feira
sigoongda-fayra tayrsa-fayra

16 **Wednesday** **Thursday**
Quarta-feira Quinta-feira
kwahrta-fayra keengta-fayra

17 **Friday** **Saturday**
Sexta-feira Sábado
sayshta-fayra sahbadoo

18 **Sunday** **Morning**
Domingo Manhã
doomeengoo manyang

19 **Afternoon** **Evening**
Tarde Noite
tahrd noyt

20 **Night** **Week**
Noite Semana
noyt simana

21 **Yesterday** **Tomorrow**
Ontem Amanhã
ohngtayng ahmanyang

Numbers

22 **Zero** **One**
Zero Um
zeroo oong

23 **Two** **Three**
Dois Três
doysh traysh

24 **Four** **Five**
Quatro Cinco
kwahtroo seengkoo

25 **Six** **Seven**
Seis Sete
saysh set

26 **Eight** **Nine**
Oito Nove
oytoo nov

27 **Ten** **Eleven**
Dez Onze
desh ohngz

28 **Twelve** **Thirteen**
Doze Treze
dohz trayz

29 **Fourteen** **Fifteen**
Catorze Quinze
katohrz keengz

30 **Sixteen** **Seventeen**
Dezasseis Dezassete
dizasaysh dizaset

31 **Eighteen** **Nineteen**
Dezoito Dezanove
dizoytoo dizanov

32 **Twenty** **Twenty-one**
Vinte Vinte e um
veengt veengt ee oong

P
O
R
T
U
G
U
E
S
E

13
↑
32

33 **Twenty-two** **Thirty**
Vinte e dois Trinta
veengt ee doysh *treengta*

34 **Forty** **Fifty**
Quarenta Cinquenta
kwarayngta *seengkwayngta*

35 **Sixty** **Seventy**
Sessenta Setenta
sisayngta *sitayngta*

36 **Eighty** **Ninety**
Oitenta Noventa
oytayngta *noovayngta*

37 **One hundred** **Five hundred**
Cem Quinhentos
sayng *keenyengtoos*

38 **One thousand** **One million**
Mil Um milhão
meel *oong meelyowng*

Time

39 **9.00**
Nove horas
nov orash

40 **9.05**
Nove e cinco
nov ee seengkoo

41 **9.10**
Nove e dez
nov ee desh

42 **9.15**
Nove e um quarto
nov ee oong kwahrtoo

43 **9.20**
Nove e vinte
nov ee veengt

44 **9.25**
Nove e vinte e cinco
nov ee veengt ee seengkoo

45 **9.30**
Nove e meia
nov ee maya

46 **9.35**
Nove e trinta e cinco
nov ee treengta ee seengkoo

47 **9.40**
Nove e quarenta
nov ee kwarayngta

48 **9.45**
Nove e quarenta e cinco
nov ee kwarayngta ee seengkoo

49 **9.50**
Nove e cinquenta
nov ee seengkwayngta

50 **9.55**
Nove e cinquenta e cinco
nov ee seengkwaynta ee seengkoo

51 **12.00/Midday/Midnight**
Doze horas/Meio dia/Meia noite
dohzi orash/mayoo-deea/maya-noyt

52 **What time is it?**
Que horas são?
ki orash sowng?

53 **It is . . .**
É/São . . .
eh/sowng . . .

ARRIVING AND DEPARTING

Airport

54 **Excuse me, where is the
check-in desk for . . . airline?**

Desculpe, onde é o balcão de
check-in da . . . (companhia
aérea)?
*dishkoolp, ohngdee eh oo
bahlkowngdi check-een da . . .*

55 **What is the boarding gate/
time for my flight?**
Qual é a porta/hora para o meu
voo?
*kwal e a porta/ora para oo mayo
vo'oo*

56 **How long is the delay likely
to be?**
De quanto será o atraso?
di kwanto sirah oo atrahzoo

57 **Where is the duty-free shop?**
Onde é a loja duty-free?
ohngdee eh a lohzha duty-free?

58 **Which way is the baggage
reclaim?**
Onde é a recolha de bagagem?
*ohngdee eh a rrecohlya di
bagahzhayng*

59 **Where can I get the bus to
the city centre?**
Onde posso tomar o autocarro
para o centro da cidade?
*ohngd possoo toomahr oo
owtohkahrroo para o sayngtroo da
seedahdi*

Train Station

60 **Where is the ticket office/
information desk?**
Onde é a bilheteira/o balcão de
informações?
ohngdee eh a beelyaytayra/oo

bahlkowng di eenfoormasoyesh

61 **Which platform does the
train to . . . depart from?**
De que linha parte o comboio
para . . .
*di ke leenya pahrt oo kohmboyoo
para . . .*

62 **Where is platform . . ?**
Onde é a linha . . ?
ohngdee eh a leenya . . .

63 **When is the next train to . . ?**
Quando é o próximo combóio
para . . ?
*kwandoo eh oo prohseemoo
kohngboyo para . . .*

64 **Is there a later train to . . ?**
Há um combóio mais tarde
para . . ?
*ah oong kohngboyo myish tahrd
para . . .*

Port

65 **How do I get to the port?**
Como posso ir para o porto?
kohmoo possoo eer para oo pohrto

66 **When is the next sailing to . . ?**
Quando é o próximo barco
para . . ?
*kwandoo eh oo prohseemoo
bahrkoo para . . ?*

67 **Can I catch an earlier ferry
with this ticket?**
Posso apanhar um barco mais
cedo com este bilhete?
*possoo apanyahr oong bahrkoo
myish saidoo kohm ayste beelyait?*

P
O
R
T
U
G
U
E
S
E

55
↕
67

235

Notices and Signs

68 **Carruagem-Restaurante**
karrooahzhayng rishtowrahnt
Buffet (Dining) Car

69 **Autocarro**
owtokahrroo
Bus

70 **Água potável /não potável**
ahgwa pootahvel/nown pootahvel
Drinking/Non-drinking water

71 **Entrada**
entrahda
Entrance

72 **Saída**
saihda
Exit

73 **Informações**
eemfoormasoyesh
Information

74 **Recolha de Bagagem**
rrecohliya do bagahzhayng
Left Luggage (Baggage Claim)

75 **Cacifos de bagagem**
kaseefoosh di bagahzhayng
Luggage Lockers

76 **Correio**
koorrayoo
Post Office

77 **Linha**
leenya
Platform

78 **Estação de Caminho de Ferro**
ishtasowng di kamihnyo di fehrroo
Railway (Railroad) tation

79 **Aeroporto**
aehrohportoo
Airport

80 **Porto**
porto
Port

81 **Restaurante**
ristowrangt
Restaurant

82 **Fumadores/Não fumadores**
foomadohrsh/nown-foomadohrsh
Smoking/Non-Smoking

83 **Telefone**
tilifohne
Telephone

84 **Bilheteira**
beelyaytayra
Ticket Office

85 **Balcão de check-in**
bahlkowng di check-een
Check-in Desk

86 **Horário**
orahreo
Timetable (Schedule)

87 **Lavabos**
lavahboosh
Toilets (Restrooms)

88 **Homens/Cavalheiros**
omayngsh/kavalyayroosh
Gentlemen

89 **Senhoras**
sinyohrash
Ladies'

90 **Carro eléctrico**
kahrroo elehtreekoo

Tram (Streetcar)

91 **Metropolitano**
metropooleetahnoo
Underground (Subway)

92 **Sala de espera**
sahla di ishpehra
Waiting-Room

Buying a Ticket

93 I would like a first-class/
second-class single (one-
way)/return (round-trip)
ticket to . . .
Queria um bilhete de primeira
classe/segunda classe/simples/
ida e volta para . . .
*kireea oong beelyayt di preemayra/
sigoonda klahs/seemplish/eeda ee
vohlta para . . .*

94 Is my rail pass valid on this
train/ferry/bus?
A minha assinatura é válida para
este combóio/barco/autocarro?
*a meenya aseenatoora eh vahleeda
para eshte lohmboyoo/bahrkoo/
owtohkahrroo?*

95 I would like an aisle/window
seat.
Queria um lugar no corredor/na
janela.
*kireea oong loogahr noo korridohr/
na zhanehla*

96 No smoking/smoking, please.
Por favor, fumador/não
fumador
*poor favohr, foomadohr/nown
foomadohr*

97 We would like to sit
together.
Queríamos lugares juntos
*kireeamoosh loogahrsh
zhoongtoosh*

98 I would like to make a seat
reservation.
Queria marcar um lugar
kireea marcahr oong loogahr

99 I would like to reserve a
couchette/sleeper for one
person/two people/for my
family.
Queria marcar uma couchette/
cama para uma pessoa/duas
pessoas/para a minha família.
*kireea marcahr ooma koooshet/
kama para ooma pesoha/dooash
pesohash/para a meenya
fameehleea*

100 I would like to reserve a
cabin.
Queria marcar uma cabina.
kireea markahr ooma kahbeena

Timetables (Schedules)

101 **Chegada**
shigahda
Arrive

102 **Com paragem em . . .**
kohng parahzhayng ayng
Calls (Stops) at

103 **Serviço de Restaurante**
serveehsoo di rishtowrangt
Catering Service

237

104 Mudar em . . .
Moodahr ayng . . .
Change at . . .

105 Ligação
leegasowng
Connection

106 Todos os dias
tohdoosh oosh deeash
Daily

107 De 40 em 40 minutos
di kwarayngta ayng kwarayngta meenootoosh
Every 40 Minutes

108 Primeira Classe
preemayra klahs
First-Class

109 De hora a hora
di ora a ora
Hourly

110 Recomenda-se marcação de lugares
rrikoomaynda-si markasowng si loogahrsh
Seat reservations are recommended

111 Segunda classe
sigoonda klahs
Second-class

112 Suplemento Pagável
sooplimayngtoo pagahvel
Supplement Payable

113 Via
veeah
Via

Luggage

114 How much will it cost to send (ship) my luggage in advance?
Quánto custa mandar a minha bagagem primeiro?
kwantoo kooshta mandahr a meenya bagahzhayng preemayuroo?

115 Where is the left luggage (baggage claim) office?
Onde é o escritório de recolha de bagagem?
ohngdee eh oo ishkreetohreeoo di rricohliyadi bagahzhayng

116 What time do you open/close?
A que horas abre/fecha?
a ke orash ahbre/fesha

117 Where are the luggage trolleys (carts)?
Onde estão os carrinhos (trolleys)
ohngdee ishtowng oos karreenyoosh (trolleysh)

118 Where are the lockers?
Onde são os cacifos?
ohngd sowng oos kaseefoosh?

119 I have lost my locker key.
Perdi a chave do meu cacifo.
Perdee a shahve doo mayo kaseefoo

On Board

120 Is this seat taken?
Este lugar está ocupado?
aysht loogahr istah ohkoopahdoo?

121 Excuse me, you are sitting in my reserved seat.
Desculpe, está sentado no meu lugar marcado.
dishkoolp, istah sayntahdoo noo mayo loogahr markahdoo

122 Which station is this?
Que estação é esta?
ki ishtasowng eh ehshta?

123 What time is this train/bus/ferry/flight due to arrive/depart?
A que horas deve chegar/partir este combóio/autocarro/barco/voo?
a ke orash dehv shigahr/parteer aysht kohngboyoo/owtohkahrro/bahrkoo/vo'oo

124 Will you wake me just before we arrive?
Acorda-me antes de chegarmos?
akohrda-mi antishdi shegahrmoosh?

Customs and Passports

125 Os passaportes, por favor!
oosh pahsaportsh poor favohr!
Passports, please!

126 I have nothing to declare.I have wine/spirits (alcohol)/tobacco to declare.
Não tenho nada a declarar.
Tenho/vinho/bebidas alcoólicas/tabaco a declarar.
nown taynyoo nahda a deklarahr.
Taynyoo nahda/veenyo/bibeedash ahlcohleecash/tabahkoo a deklarahr

127 I shall be staying for . . . days/weeks/months.
Vou ficar durante . . . dias/semanas/meses.
voh feecahr doorangt . . . deeash/simahnash/mehzesh

AT THE TOURIST OFFICE

128 Do you have a map of the town/area?
Tem um mapa da cidade/zona?
tayng oong mahpa da seedahde/zohna?

129 Can I reserve accommodation here?
Posso fazer marcação de alojamento aqui?
possoo fazayr markasowng de aloozhamayntoo akee?

130 Do you have a list of accommodation?
Tem uma lista de alojamentos?
tayng ooma leeshta di aloozhamayntoosh?

ACCOMMODATION

Hotels

131 I have a reservation in the name of . . .
Tenho uma marcação em nome de . . .
taynyo ooma markasowng ayng nohmi di . . .

132 I wrote to/faxed/telephoned you last month/last week in . . .
Escrevi/mandei um fax/telefonei no mês passado/na semana passada . . .
ishkrevee/manday oong fahks/tilifoonay noo mays pasahdoo/na simahna pasahda . . .

133 Do you have any rooms free?
Tem quartos vagos?
tayng kwahrtoosh vahgoosh?

134 I would like to reserve a single/double room with/without bath/shower.
Queria marcar um quarto para uma pessoa/para duas pessoas com/sem banho/chuveiro
kireea marcahr oong kwahrtoo para ooma pesoha/ para dooash pesoash

135 I would like bed and breakfast/(room and) half board/(room and) full board.
Queria cama e pequeno almoço/meia pensão/pensão completa
kireea kam ee pikayno ahlmohso/ maya pengsowng/pengsowng komplehta

136 How much is it per night?
Quanto custa por noite?
kwantoo koosta poor noyt?

137 Is breakfast included?
O pequeno almoço está incluído?
oo pikaynoo ahlmohsoo istah eenklooeedoo?

138 May I see the room?
Posso ver o quarto?
possoo vayr oo kwartoo?

139 Do you have any cheaper rooms?
Tem quartos mais baratos?
tayng kwartoosh myish barahtoosh?

140 I would like to take the room.
Queria ficar com o quarto.
kireea feecahr kohm oo kwartoo

141 I would like to stay for . . . nights.
Queria ficar por . . . noites.
kireea ficahr poor . . . noytish

142 The shower/light/tap doesn't work.
O chuveiro/a luz/a torneira não funciona.
oo shoovayroo/er loosh/er toornayra nown foongsyona.

143 At what time/where is breakfast served?
A que horas/onde é servido o pequeno almoço?
er ke orash eh sirveedo oo pikaynoo ahlmossoo?

144 What time do I have to check-out?
A que horas tenho de deixar o quarto?
a ke orash taynyo di dayshahr oo kwahrto?

145 Can I have the key to room no . . ?
Pode-me dar a chave do quarto número . . ?

pohdi-mi dahr er shahv doo kwahrtoo noomiroo . . ?

146 My room number is . . .

O número do meu quarto é . . .
oo noomiroo doo mayo kwahrto eh . . .

147 Do you accept travellers' cheques/Eurocheques/credit cards?

Aceita cheques de viagem/ Eurocheques/cartões de crédito?
asayta shehkiesh di veeahzhayng/ ayoorosheksh/kartoyesh di kredeetoo

148 May I have the bill please?

Pode-me dar a conta, por favor?
pohd-mi dahr er kohngta, poor favohr?

149 Excuse me, I think there is a mistake in this bill.

Desculpe, acho que há um erro nesta conta.
dishkoolp, ahshoo ke ah oong ayrroo na kohngta

Youth Hostels

150 How much is a dormitory bed per night?

Quanto é uma cama num dormitório por noite?
kwantoo eh ooma kama noong dormeetohreeoo poor noyt?

151 I am/am not an HI member.

Sou/não sou membro do HI
soh/nown soh mayngbroo doo agah ee

152 May I use my own sleeping bag?

Posso usar o meu saco de dormir?
possoo oozahr oo mayu sahkoo di dormeer?

153 What time do you lock the doors at night?

A que horas fecham as portas à noite?
er ki orash fayshowm as pportash ah noyt?

Camping

154 May I camp here for the night/two nights?

Posso acampar aqui esta noite/ por duas noites?
posso akampahr akee eshta noyt/ poor dooash noytsh?

155 Where can I pitch my tent?

Onde posso armar a minha tenda?
ohngd possoo ahrmahr er meenya tayngda?

156 How much does it cost for one night/week?

Quanto custa por uma noite/ uma semana?
kwantoo kooshta poor ooma noyt/ ooma simana?

157 Where can we park our caravan?

Onde podemos estacionar a nossa roulotte?
ohngd podaymosh ishtaseeoonahr er nossa roolohte?

158 Where are the washing facilities?
Onde são as casas de banho?
ohngd sowng ash kahzash di banyoo?

159 Is there a restaurant/ supermarket/swimming pool on site/nearby?
Há aqui/perto um restaurante/ supermercado/uma piscina?
ah akee pehrtoo oong ristowrangt/ soopermercahdoo/ooma peeshseena?

160 Do you have a safety deposit box?
Tem cofre para guardar valores?
tayng kohfr para gwardahr valohrsh?

EATING AND DRINKING

Cafés and Bars

161 I would like a cup of/two cups of/another coffee/tea.
Queria uma chávena de/duas chávenas de/outro café/chá.
kireea ooma shahvna di/dooash shahvnash di ohtroo kafeh/shah

162 With/without milk/sugar.
Com/sem leite/açúcar
kohng/sayng layt/asookar

163 I would like a bottle/glass/ two glasses of mineral water/ red wine/white wine, please.
Queria uma garrafa/um copo/ dois copos/ de água mineral/ vinho tinto/vinho branco, por favor

kireea ooma garrahfa/oong kohpoo/doysh kopoosh/ di ahgwa meenirahl/veenyo teengto/ veenyo brahngkoo poor favohr

164 I would like a beer/two beers, please.
Queria uma cerveja/duas cervejas, por favor.
kireea ooma servayzha/dooash servaizhash, poor favohr.

165 May I have some ice?
Pode-me dar gelo?
pohd-mi dahr zhayloo?

166 Do you have any matches/ cigarettes/cigars?
Tem fósforos/cigarros/ charutos?
tayng fohshfooroosh/seegahrroosh/ sharootoosh?

Restaurants

167 Can you recommend a good/ inexpensive restaurant in this area?
Pode recomendar um restaurante bom/económico nesta área?
pohd rrikoomayndahr oong ristowrangt bohm/eekinohmeekoo nehshta ahreea?

168 I would like a table for . . . people.
Queria uma mesa para . . . pessoas.
kireea ooma mehza para . . . pesoash.

169 Do you have a non-smoking area?
Tem uma área de não fumadores?
tayng ooma ahreea di nown foomadohrsh?

170 Waiter/Waitress!
Faz favor!
fash favohr!

171 Do you have a set menu/ children's menu/wine list?
Tem uma ementa turística/ ementa para crianças/carta de vinhos?
tayng oom eemaynta tooreehshteeka para kreeangsash/ kahrta di veenyoosh?

172 Do you have any vegetarian dishes, please?
Tem pratos vegetarianos, por favor?
tayng prahtoosh vezhetareeahnoosh, poor favohr?

173 Are there any local specialities?
Há algumas especialidades locais?
ah ahlgoomash ishpiseeealeedahdsh lookeyish?

174 Are vegetables included?
Os legumes estão incluídos?
oosh ligoomish ishtowng eenklooihdoosh?

175 Could I have it well-cooked/ medium/rare please?
Posso escolher bem passado/ médio/mal passado, por favor?

possoo ishkoolyer bayng pasahdoo/mahl pasahdoo, poor favohr?

176 What does this dish consist of?
De que consiste este prato?
di ki konseesht aysht prahtoo?

177 I would like the set menu, please.
Queria a ementa turística, por favor
kireea er eemengta toorihshteeca, poor favohr

178 We have not been served yet.
Ainda não fomos servidos.
aeehnda nown fohmoosh serveedosh.

179 Excuse me, this is not what I ordered.
Desculpe, não foi isto que encomendei.
dishkoolp, nown fohee eeshtoo ki inkoomaynday

180 May I have some/some more bread/water/coffee/tea?
Pode-me dar pão/mais pão/ água/café/chá?
pohde-mi dahr myish powng/ ahgwa/cafeh/shah

181 May I have the bill, please?
Pode-me dar a conta, por favor?
pohd-mi dahr er kohngta, poor favohr?

182 Does this bill include service?
A conta inclui serviço?
er kohngta eengklooee sirveesso?

P
O
R
T
U
G
U
E
S
E

169
↑
182

243

¹⁸³ **Do you accept travellers'
cheques (travelers' checks)/
Eurocheques/MasterCard/US
dollars?**
Aceita cheques de viagem/
Eurocheques/MasterCard/
Dólares americanos?
*asayta shehkish di veeahzhayng/
ayoorohsheksh/mahshtehrkahrd/
dohlarsh amireekahnoosh*

¹⁸⁴ **Can I have a receipt, please?**
Pode-me dar um recibo, por
favor?
*pohd-mi dahr oong rriseeboo, poor
favohr?*

¹⁸⁵ **Where is the toilet
(restroom), please?**
Por favor, onde são os lavabos?
*poor favohr, ohngdee sowng oos
lavahboosh?*

On the Menu

¹⁸⁶ **First courses**
Entradas
intrahdash

¹⁸⁷ **Soups**
Sopas
sohpash

¹⁸⁸ **Main courses**
Pratos principais
prahtoosh preengseepaheesh

¹⁸⁹ **Fish dishes**
Pratos de peixe
prahtoosh di paysh

¹⁹⁰ **Meat dishes**
Pratos de carne
prahtoosh di kahrni

¹⁹¹ **Vegetarian dishes**
Pratos vegetarianos
prahtoosh vizhitareeanoosh

¹⁹² **Cheese**
Queijo
kayzhoo

¹⁹³ **Desserts**
Sobremesas
sohbrimehzash

¹⁹⁴ **Specialities**
Especialidades
ishpiseealeedahdsh

GETTING AROUND

Public Transport

¹⁹⁵ **Where is the bus stop/coach
station/nearest metro
(subway) station?**
Onde é a paragem do autocarro/
garagem das camionetas/a
estação de metro mais próxima?
*âgdee eh er parahzhayng doo
owtohkahrroo/garahzhayng das
kameeonehtash/er ishtasowng di
mehtroo myish prohseema?*

¹⁹⁶ **When is the next/last bus
to . . ?**
Quando sai o próximo/último
autocarro para . . ?
*kwandoo sahee oo prohseemoo
owtohkahrroo para . . ?*

¹⁹⁷ **How much is the fare to the
city centre (downtown)/
railway (railroad) station/
airport?**

Quanto é o bilhete para o
centro da cidade/estação de
caminho de ferro/ aeroporto?
*ântoo eh oo beelyayte para oo
sengtroo da seedahdi/ishtasowng
di kaminyoo di fehrroo/
aehrohportoo*

198 Will you tell me when to get
off?
Diz-me quando devo sair?
deesh-mi kwandoo dehvoo saeehr?

199 Does this bus go to . . ?
Este autocarro vai para . . ?
aysht owtohkahrroo va'ee para . . ?

200 Which number bus goes to . . ?
Qual é o número do autocarro
que vai para . . ?
*kwal eh oo noomiroo doo
owtohkahrroo ki va'ee para . . ?*

201 May I have a single (one-
way)/return (round-trip)/day
ticket/book of tickets?
Pode-me dar um bilhete
simples/ida e volta/diário/
caderneta de bilhetes?
*Pohd-mi dahr oong beelyayt
seemplish/eeda ee vohlta/
deeahreeoo/kadirnayta di
beelyaytsh?*

Taxis

202 I would like to go to . . .
How much will it cost?
Queria ir para . . .
Quanto custa?
*kireea eer para . . . kwngtoo
kooshta?*

203 Please stop here.
Pare aqui, por favor.
pahr akee, poor favohr

204 I would like to order a taxi
today/tomorrow/at 2pm to
go from . . . to . . .
Queria um táxi para hoje/
amanhã/ às duas da tarde para ir
de . . . para . . .
*kireea oong tahksee para ohzhay/
ahmanyang/ahsh dooash da tahrd
para eer de . . . para . . .*

Asking the Way

205 Excuse me, do you speak
English?
Desculpe, fala Inglês?
dishkoolp, fahla eenglays?

206 Excuse me, is this the right
way to . . ?
Desculpe é este o caminho certo
para . . ?
*dishkoolp, eh aysht oo kameenyo
sehrtoo para . . ?*

207 . . . the cathedral/the tourist
information office/the castle/
the old town
. . . a catedral/os serviços de
informações turísticas (o
turismo)/o castelo/a cidade
velha
*. . . er katidrahl/ oos sirveessoos de
eemfoormasoyesh tooreehshteekash
(oo tooreesmoo)/ oo kastehloo/ er
seedahd vehlya.*

208 **Can you tell me the way to the railway (railroad) station/bus station/taxi rank (stand)/city centre (downtown)/beach?**
Pode-me indicar o caminho para a estação de caminho de ferro/a estação de autocarros/a paragem de táxis/o centro da cidade/a praia?
podd-mi eendeecahr oo kameenyoo para er ishtasowng de kameenyo do fehrro/er ishtasowng de owtohkahrrosh/er parahzhayng de tahkseesh/oo sayntroo da seedahd/er prahya?

209 **First/second left/right/straight ahead.**
Primeira/segunda à esquerda/à direita/sempre em frente
premayra/sigoonda ah ishkehrda/ah deerayta/sayngpri ayng frayNti

210 **Where is the nearest police station/post office?**
Onde é o posto da polícia/o correio mais próximo?
ohngdee eh oo pohshtoo da pooleesseea/ oo koorrayoo myish prohseemoo?

211 **Is it far?**
É longe?
eh lohnzhi?

212 **Do I need to take a taxi/catch a bus?**
Preciso de apanhar um táxi/um autocarro?

preseezoo di apanyahr oong tahksee/oong owtohkahrroo

213 **Can you point to it on my map?**
Pode indicá-lo no meu mapa?
pohd eendeecahloo noo mayo mahpa?

214 **Thank you for your help.**
Obrigado pela sua ajuda.
ohbreegahdoo pehla sooa azhooda

SIGHTSEEING

215 **Where is the Tourist Information office?**
Onde é o Turismo?
ohngdee eh oo tooreeshmoo?

216 **Where is the cathedral/church/museum?**
Onde é a catedral/igreja/museu?
ohngdee eh er katidrahl/ eegrayzha/moosayo?

217 **How much is the entrance (admission) charge?**
Qual é o preço da entrada?
kwal eh oo preso do ayntrahda?

218 **Is there a discount for children/students/senior citizens?**
Há desconto para crianças/estudantes/pessoas da terceira idade?
ah dishkohngtoo para kreeangsash/ishtoodangtish/ pisoahsh da tersayra eedahd?

219 **What time does the next guided tour start?**

A que horas começa a próxima
visita guiada?
*er ki orash koomehsa er prohseema
veezeeta gueeahda?*

220 **One/two adults/children,
please.**
Um/dois adultos, uma/duas
cria ças, por favor.
*oong/doysh adooltoosh, ooma/
dooash kreeangsash poor favohr.*

221 **May I take photographs
here?**
Posso tirar fotografias aqui?
*posso teerahr footoografeeash
akee?*

ENTERTAINMENT

222 **Can you recommend a good
bar/nightclub?**
Pode recomendar um bom bar/
clube nocturno?
*pohd rrikoomayngdahr oong bohm
bahre/kloob nohtoornoo*

223 **Do you know what is on at
the cinema (playing at the
movies)/theatre at the
moment?**
Sabe o que vai no cinema/teatro
de momento?
*sahb oo ke va'ee noo seenayma/
teeahtroo do momayngtoo?*

224 **I would like to book
(purchase) . . . tickets for the
matinee/evening
performance on Monday.**

Queria comprar . . . bilhetes
para a sessão da tarde/noite,
segunda-feira.
*kireea komprahr . . . beelyaytsh
para er sessowngda tahrd/noyt,
sigoonda-fayra*

225 **What time does the film/
performance start?**
A que horas começa o filme/a
sessão?
*er ki orash koomehsa oo film/er
sesowng?*

MEETING PEOPLE

226 **Hello/Goodbye.**
Olá/Adeus
ohlah/adayoosh

227 **Good morning/good
afternoon/good evening/
goodnight.**
Bom dia/boa tarde/boa noite/
boa noite
bohm deea/boha tahrd/boha noyt

228 **Pleased to meet you.**
Muito prazer
muhingtoo prazayr

229 **How are you?**
Como está?
kohmoo istah?

230 **Fine, thank you. And you?**
Bem obrigado. E você?
bayng ohbreegahdoo. ee vohsay?

231 **My name is . . .**
Chamo-me . . .
shamoo-mi . . .

232 This is my friend/boyfriend/
girlfriend/husband/wife/
brother/sister.
Este é o meu/minha amigo/
amiga/namorado/namorada/
marido/mulher/irmão/irmã
*aysht e oo mayoo/meenya
amighoo/amigha/namoorahdoo/
namoorahda/mareedoo/moolyer/
eermowng/eermang*

233 Where are you travelling to?
Para onde vai viajar?
para ohngdee va'ee veeazhahr?

234 I am/we are going to . . .
Vou/vamos para . . .
voh/vamoosh para . . .

235 How long are you travelling
for?
Vai para muito longe?
va'ee para muhingtoo lohngzhe?

236 Where do you come from?
De onde vem?
di ohngd vayng?

237 I am/we are from . . .
Sou/somos de . . .
soh/sohmoosh di . . .

238 We're on holiday.
Estamos em férias.
ishtahmoos ayng fehreeas

239 This is our first visit here.
Esta é a nossa primeira visita
aqui
ehshta e er nossa

240 Would you like/May I have a
cigarette?
Quer um cigarro/posso fumar?

*ker oong seegahrro/possoo
foomahr*

241 I am sorry but I do not
understand.
Desculpe mas não entendo.
*dishkoolp maysh nown
ayngtayngdoo*

242 Please speak slowly.
Por favor, fale devagar.
poor favohr fahl divagahr

243 Do you mind if I smoke?
Importa-se se eu fumar?
eemporta-si see ayoo foomahr?

244 Do you have a light?
Tem lume?
tayng loome?

245 I am waiting for my husband/
wife/boyfriend/girlfriend.
Estou à espera do meu/minha
marido/mulher/namorado/
namorada.
*ishtoh ah ishpehra doo mayoo/
meenyia mareedoo/moolyer/
namoorahdoo/namoorahda*

TRAVELLING WITH CHILDREN

246 Do you have a high chair/
baby-sitting service/cot?
Tem uma cadeira alta/serviço
de baby-sitting/cama de bébé?
*tayng ooma kadayra ahlta/
sirveessoo di baby sitting/kama di
behbeh?*

247 Where is the nursery/
playroom?
Onde é a creche/infantário?

ohngd e er kresh/eengfantahreeoo

248 **Where can I warm the baby's bottle?**

Onde posso aquecer o biberon do bébé?

ohngd possoo akesayr oo beeberohng doo behbeh?

COMMUNICATIONS

Post

249 **How much will it cost to send a letter/postcard/this package to Britain/Ireland/America/Canada/Australia/New Zealand?**

Quanto custa mandar uma carta/postal/este pacote para Grã-Bretanha/Irlanda/América/Canadá/Austrália/Nova Zelândia?

kwantoo kooshta mandahr ooma kahrta/pooshtahl/esht pakoht para grang-britanya/ eerlangda/ amehreeka/kanadah/owstrahleea/ nohva zelangdeea?

250 **I would like one stamp/two stamps.**

Queria um selo/dois selos.

kireea oong saylo/doysh sayllosh

251 **I'd like . . . stamps for postcards to send abroad, please.**

Queria . . . selos para postais para o estrangeiro, por favor.

kireea . . . sayloosh para pooshtiysh para o ishtrangzhayroo, poor favohr.

Phones

252 **I would like to make a telephone call/reverse the charges to (make a collect call to) . . .**

Queria fazer uma chamada/a pagar por quem recebe

kireea fazayr ooma shamahda/er pagahr poor kayng ressebe

253 **Which coins do I need for the telephone?**

Que moedas preciso para telefonar?

ki mwedash preseezoo para tilifoonahr?

254 **The line is engaged (busy).**

A linha está impedida.

a leenya istah eempideeda

255 **The number is . . .**

O número é . . .

oo noomiroo e . . .

256 **Hello, this is . . .**

Está, aqui fala . . .

ishtah, akee fahla . . .

257 **May I speak to . . ?**

Posso falar com . . ?

possoo falahr kom . . .

258 **He/She is not in at the moment. Can you call back?**

Não está neste momento. Pode tornar a chamar?

nown ishtah nayshte moomayntoo. pohd toornahr a shamahr?

MONEY

259 I would like to change these travellers' cheques (travelers' checks)/this currency/this Eurocheque.
Queria trocar estes cheques de viagem/estas divisas/este Eurocheque.
kireea trookahr aystsh shehkish di veeazhayng/ehshtash deeveezash/ayst ayroshek

260 How much commission do you charge? (What is the service charge?)
Que comissão cobra?
ke coomeessowng kohbra?

261 Can I obtain money with my MasterCard?
Posso levantar dinheiro com o meu MasterCard?
possoo levangtahr deenyayroo kohm oo mayo mahstercahrd

SHOPPING

Names of Shops and Departments

262 Livraria/Papelaria
leevrareea/papilareea
Bookshop/Stationery

263 Joalharia/Presentes
zhooalyareea/prizayntsh
Jeweller's/Gifts

264 Sapatos
sapahtoosh
Shoes

265 Ferragens
ferrahzhayngsh
Hardware

266 Antiguidades
anteegweedadish
Antiques

267 Cabeleireiro (de homens)/(de senhoras)
kabilayrayroo (di ohmayns)/(di sinyorash)
Hairdressers (men's)/(women's)

268 Tabacaria
tabakareea
Tobacconist

269 Padaria
padareea
Baker's

270 Supermercado
soopermercahdoo
Supermarket

271 Fotografia
footoografeea
Photoshop

272 Brinquedos
breengkehdoosh
Toys

273 Agente de Viagens
azhayngt di veeahzhayngsh
Travel Agent

274 Perfumarias
pirfoomareeash
Toiletries

275 Discos
deeshkoosh
Records

In the Shop

276 What time do the shops open/close?

A que horas abrem/fecham as lojas?
a kee orah abrayng/fayshown ash lohzhash

277 Where is the nearest market?

Onde é o mercado mais próximo?
ohngdee eh oo mercahdoo myish prohseemoo?

278 Can you show me the one in the window/this one?

Pode mostrar-me aquele na janela/este
pohd mooshtrahr-mi akehle na zhanehla/aysht

279 Can I try this on?

Posso provar este?
possoo proovahr aysht?

280 What size is this?

Que tamanho (número) é este?
ki tamanyo (noomiroo) eh ayst?

281 This is too large/too small/ too expensive.

Este é muito grande/muito pequeno/muito caro.
aysht eh muingtoo grangdi/ muingtoo pikaynoo/muingtoo kahroo

282 Do you have any others?

Tem outros
tayng ohtroosh

283 My size is . . .

O meu tamanho (número) é . . .
oo mayo tamanyo (noomiroo) eh . . .

284 Where is the changing room/ childrens/cosmetic/ ladieswear/menswear/food department?

Onde é o gabinete de prova/ secção infantil/cosmética/roupa de senhora/roupa de homem/ secção de alimentos?
ohngdee eh oo gabeeneht di prohva/sehksowng eengfangteel/ koosmehteeca/rohpa di sinyora/ rohpa di omayng/seksowng di aleemayngtoosh

285 I would like . . .

Queria . . .
kireea . . .

286 I would like a quarter of a kilo/half a kilo/a kilo of bread/ butter/cheese/ham/ tomatoes.

Queria duzentos e cinquenta gramas/meio quilo/um quilo de pão/manteiga/queijo/ fiambre/ tomate.
kireea doozayntoosh ee seengkwayngta gramash/mayoo keeloo/ oong keeloo di powng/ mangtayga/kayzhoo/feeangbri/ toomaht

287 How much is this?

Quanto custa isto?
kwantoo kooshta eeshtoo?

288 I'll take this one, thank you.

Levo este, obrigado
lehvoo aysht, ohbreegahdoo

289 Do you have a carrier (shopping) bag?
Tem um saco de plástico com pegas?
tayng oong sahkoo di plahshteekoo kohng pehgash.

290 Do you have anything cheaper/larger/smaller/of better quality?
Tem alguma coisa mais barata/maior/mais pequena/de melhor qualidade?
tayngahlgooma kohyza myish barahta/mahyohr/myish peekayna/do melior kwaleedahd?

291 I would like a film for this camera.
Queria um rolo para esta máquina.
kireea oongrohloo para ehshta mahkeena

292 I would like some batteries, the same size as this old one.
Queria umas pilhas do mesmo tamanho que esta.
kireea oomash peelyash doo maysmoo tamahnyo ki ehshta.

293 Would you mind wrapping this for me, please?
Importa-se de me embrulhar isto, por favor?
eemporta-si di mi aymbroolyahr eeshtoo, poor favohr?

294 Sorry, but you seem to have given me the wrong change.
Desculpe mas parece que me deu o troco errado.
dishkoolp maysh parehse ki mi dayoo oo trohcoo eerrahdoo

MOTORING

Car Hire (Rental)

295 I have ordered (rented) a car in the name of . . .
Reservei um carro em nome de . . .
rrizervay oongkahrrooay nohmdi

296 How much does it cost to hire (rent) a car for one day/two days/one week?
Quanto custa alugar um carro por um dia/dois dias/uma semana?
kwantoo kooshta aloogahr oong kahrroo poor oong deea/doysh deeash/ooma simahna?

297 Is the tank already full of petrol (gas)?
O depósito já está cheio de gasolina?
oo depohzeetoo zhah ishtah shayoo di gazooleena?

298 Is insurance and tax included? How much is the deposit?
O seguro e o imposto estão incluídos? Quanto é o depósito?
oosigooro ee oo eempohshtoo ishtowng eenklooeehdoosh? kwantoo eh oo depohzeetoo?

299 By what time must I return the car?

A que horas devo devolver o carro?
a ki orash devoo divolvehr oo kahrroo?

300 I would like a small/family car with a radio/cassette player.
Queria um carro pequeno/familiar com rádio/leitor de cassettes.
kireea oong kahrroo pikayni/fameeleeahr kohng rahdeeoo/laytohr do casehtsh

Asking the Way

301 Excuse me, can you help me please?
Desculpe, pode dar-me uma ajuda?
dishkoolp, pohd dahr-mi ooma azhooda?

302 How do I reach the motorway/main road?
Como vou para a autoestrada/estrada principal?
kohngoo voh para a owtoishtrahda/ishtrahda preengseepahl?

303 I think I have taken the wrong turning.
Acho que virei no sítio errado.
ahshoo ki veeray noo seeteeoo irradoo

304 I am looking for this address.
Estou à procura desta morada.
ishtoh ah prohkoora deshta moorahda.

305 I am looking for the . . . hotel.
Estou à procura do hotel . . .
ishtou ah prokoora doo otel . . .

306 How far is it to . . . from here?
A que distância daqui fica . . .
a ki deeshtangseea dakee feeka . . .

307 Carry straight on for . . . kilometres.
Continui a direito por . . . quilómetros.
kongteenooee a deeraytoo poor . . . keelohmetrosh

308 Take the next turning on the right/left.
Vire na próxima à direita/esquerda
veer na prohseema ah deerayta/ishkayrda

309 Turn right/left at the next crossroads/traffic lights.
Vire à direita/esquerda no próximo cruzamento/semáforo
veer ah deerayta/ishkayrda noo prohseemoo kroozamengtoo/simahfooroo

310 You are going in the wrong direction.
Vai na direcção errada.
va'ee na deeresowng irrahda

Parking

311 How long can I park here?
Por quanto tempo posso estacionar aqui?
poor kwantoo taympoo possoo ishtaseeoonahr akee?

312 Is there a car park near here?
Há um parque de
estacionamento aqui perto?
*ah oong pahrki di
ishtaseeoonamayngtoo akee
pehrtoo?*

313 At what time does this car
park close?
A que horas fecha este parque
de estacionamento?
*a ki orash faysha aysht pahrk di
ishtaseeoonamayngtoo?*

Signs and Notices

314 Via única
veea oohneeka
One way.

315 Entrada proibida
ayntrahda proeebeeda
No entry.

316 Estacionamento proibido
ishtaseeoonamayngto proeebeedoo
No parking.

317 Desvio
dishveeoo
Detour (diversion).

318 Stop (paragem)
stop (parahzhayng)
Stop.

319 Dê passagem
deh passahzhayng
Give way (yield).

320 Estrada escorregadia
ishtrahda iskorregadeea
Slippery road.

321 Ultrapassagem proibida
ultrapassahzhayng proeebeeda
No overtaking.

At the Filling Station

322 Unleaded (lead-free)/
Standard/Premium
Sem chumbo/Normal/Super
sayng shoongboo/normahl/sooper

323 Fill the tank please.
Encha o depósito por favor.
*ayngsha oo depohzeetoo poor
favohr*

324 Do you have a road map of
this area?
Tem um mapa das estradas
desta zona?
*tayng oong mahpa dash ishtradash
dehshya zona?*

325 How much is the car-wash?
Quanto é a lavagem do carro?
*kwanto eh a lavazhayng doo
kahrroo*

Breakdowns

326 I've had a breakdown at . . .
Tive uma avaria em . . .
teev ooma avareea ayng . . .

327 I am on the road from . . .
to . . .
Estou na estrada de . . .
para . . .
*ishtoh na ishtrahda di . . .
para . . .*

328 I can't move the car. Can you
send a tow-truck?

Não posso mover o carro. Pode
mandar um reboque?
*nown possoo moovehr oo kahrroo.
pohd mandahr oong ribok*

329 I have a flat tyre.
Tenho um pneu furado.
tayngoo oong pnayoo foorahdoo

330 The windscreen (windshield) has smashed/cracked.
O pára-brisas estilhaçou-se/
rachou.
*oo pahra-breezash isteelyasoh-si/
rrashoh.*

331 There is something wrong with the engine/brakes/ lights/steering/gearbox/ clutch/exhaust.
Qualquer coisa está mal com o
motor/os travões/os faróis/o
volante/a caixa de velocidades/ a
embraiagem/ o tubo de escape.
*kwalkehr kohiza ishtah mahl
kohng oo mootohr/oosh
travoyesh/oosh faroysh/oo
voolangt/a kaisha dash
vilooseedahdish/a
aymbriyahzhayng*

332 It's overheating.
Está a aquecer demais.
istah a akehser demaish

333 It won't start.
Não arranca
nown arrangka

334 Where can I get it repaired?
Onde posso mandá-lo arranjar?
*ohngd possoo mandahloo
arrangzhahr?*

335 Can you take me there?
Pode-me levar lá?
pohdmi livahr lah?

336 Will it take long to fix?
Leva muito tempo a arranjar?
*lehva muingtoo tayngpoo a
arrangzhahr?*

337 How much will it cost?
Quanto vai custar?
kwantoo va'ee kooshtahr?

Accidents

338 Can you help me? There has been an accident.
Pode-me ajudar? Houve um
acidente.
*pohdmi azhoodahr? ohv oong
aseedayngt*

339 Please call the police/an ambulance.
Por favor chame a polícia/uma
ambulância.
*poor favohr, shahm a pooleesya/
ooma angboolansya*

340 Is anyone hurt?
Há alguém ferido?
ah ahlguayng fereedoo?

Traffic Offences

341 I'm sorry, I didn't see the sign.
Desculpe, não vi o sinal.
dishkoolp nown vee oo seenahl

³⁴² Must I pay a fine? How much?
Tenho de pagar uma multa? De quanto?
taynyoo di pagahr ooma moolta? di kwantoo?

³⁴³ Show me your documents.
Mostre-me os seus documentos.
mohshtrimi oosh sayosh dokoomayngtoosh

HEALTH

Pharmacy

³⁴⁴ Do you have anything for a stomachache/headache/sore throat/toothache?
Tem qualquer coisa para dores de estômago/dores de cabeça/ dores de garganta/ dores de dentes?
tayng kwalkehr kohiza para dohrish di ishtohmago/dohrish di kabehsa/ dorish do gargangta/ dorish di dengtish?

³⁴⁵ I need something for diarrhoea (diarrhea)/ constipation/a cold/a cough/ insect bites/sunburn/travel (motion) sickness.
Preciso de alguma coisa contra diarreia/prisão de ventre/ uma constipação/ tosse/picadas de insectos/queimaduras do sol/ enzhoo.
preseezoo di ahlgooma kohiza kongtra deearraya/preezowng di ventre/ooma konshteepasowng/

tohs/peekahdash do eensetoosh/ kaymadoorash doo sohl/ingzho'oo

³⁴⁶ How much/how many do I take?
Quanto/quantos devo tomar?
kwantoo/kwantoosh dayvoo toomahr?

³⁴⁷ How often do I take it/them?
Quantas vezes devo tomar isto?
kwantash vehzesh dayvoo toomahr ishto?

³⁴⁸ How much does it cost?
Quanto custa?
kwantoo kooshta?

³⁴⁹ Can you recommend a good doctor/dentist?
Pode recomendar um bom médico/dentista?
pohd rrikoomayngdahr oong bohm mehdeekoo/dayngteeshta?

³⁵⁰ Is it suitable for children?
É bom para crianças?
eh bohm para kreeansash?

Doctor

³⁵¹ I have a pain here/in my arm/ leg/chest/stomach.
Tenho uma dor aqui/no braço/ na perna/no peito/no estômago.
taynyoo ooma dohr akee noo brahsoo/na perna/noo ishtohmagoo.

³⁵² Please call a doctor, this is an emergency.

Por favor, chame um médico.
É uma emergência.
*poor favohr sahmi oong
mehdeekoo. eh ooma
imerzhayngseea.*

353 **I would like to make an
appointment to see a doctor.**
Queria marcar uma consulta
para um médico.
*kireea markahr ooma kongsoolta
para oong mehdeekoo.*

354 **I am diabetic/pregnant.**
Sou diabético(a)/estou grávida.
*soh deeabehteekoo (a)/ishtoh
grahveeda*

355 **I need a prescription for . . .**
Preciso de uma receita para . . .
priseezoo di ooma rresayta para . . .

356 **Can you give me something
to ease the pain?**
Pode-me dar alguma coisa para
as dores?
*pod-mi dahr ahlgwma kohiza para
as dohrish?*

357 **I am/he is/she is allergic to
penicillin.**
Sou/ele é/ela é/ alérgico/
alérgica à penicilina.
*soh/ili eh/ ehla eh/alehrzheekoo/
alehrzheeka ah peneeseeleena*

358 **Does this hurt?**
Isso faz doer?
eesso fahsh dooayr?

359 **You must/he must/she must
go to hospital.**
Você deve/ele deve/ele deve ir
para o hospital.

*dev/dev/dev eer para oo
ohspeetahl*

360 **Take these once/twice /three
times a day.**
Tome isto uma vez/duas vezes/
três vezes ao dia.
*tohmi ishtoo ooma vays/dooash
vayzish/traysh vayzish ow deea*

361 **I am/he is/she is taking this
medication.**
Estou/ele está/ela está a tomar
este medicamento.
*ishtoh/ishtah a toomahr aysht
medeekamayngtoo*

362 **I have medical insurance.**
Tenho seguro médico.
taynyo sigooroo mehdeekoo

Dentist

363 **I have toothache.**
Tenho uma dor de dente.
taynyo ooma dohr do daynteesh

364 **My filling has come out.**
O meu chumbo caiu.
oo mayo shoongboo kaeehoo

365 **I do/do not want to have an
injection first.**
Quero/não quero levar uma
injecç#ao primeiro.
*kehroo/nown kehroo levahr ooma
eenzhehsowng preemayroo.*

EMERGENCIES

366 **Help!**
Socorro!
sookohrroo!

367 Call an ambulance/a doctor/
the police!
Chame uma ambulância/um
médico/a polícia!
*shami ooma angboolangsya/oong
medeekoo/ a pooleesseeya*

368 I have had my travellers'
cheques (travelers' checks)/
credit cards/purse/handbag/
rucksack (knapsack)/
luggage/wallet stolen.
Roubaram-me os meus cheques
de viagem/cartões de crédito/a
minha bolsa/ mala de mão/a
minha mochila/bagagem/
carteira.
*rrohbahrowm˜-mi oosh mayos
shehkish di veeahzhayng/
kartoyesh di kredeetoo/ a meenya
bohlsa/mahla di mowng/a
meenya moosheela/bagahzhayng/
kartayra*

369 Can you help me, I have lost
my daughter/son?
Pode ajudar-me? Perdi a minha
filha/o meu filho.

*pohdee azhoodahr-mi? perdee a
meenya feelya/oo mayo feelyoo*

370 Please go away/leave me
alone.
Por favor, vá-se embora/deixe-
me em paz.
*poor favohr, vah-see ayngbohra/
daysh-mi ayng pahsh*

371 Fire!
Fogo!
fohgoo!

372 I want to contact the British/
American/Canadian/Irish/
Australian/New Zealand/
South African consulate.
Quero contactar o consulado
Britânico/Americano/
Canadiano/Irlandês/
Australiano/da Nova Zelândia/
Sul Africano.
*keroo kohntaktahr oo
konsoolahdoo breetahngeekoo/
amireekanoo/kanadeeanoo/
eerlahngdays/ owshtraleeanoo/da
nohva zeelangdeea/sool afreekanoo*

367
↑
372

Introduction

Alone among the languages of Eastern Europe, Romanian is a Romance tongue, descended from Latin and therefore a distant cousin of French, Italian, Spanish and Portuguese. This is of more than academic interest, since many words in written Romanian can easily be understood, at least in basic meaning, by someone with a knowledge of one of these other languages. Spoken Romanian is reminiscent of French, which is the most likely second language you will encounter, at least among older and better-educated Romanians. In some regions of the country Hungarian or German will be understood; English is spoken to a limited degree, in the most tourist-oriented parts of the country.

ROMANIAN

Addresses for travel and tourist information

UK: *Romanian National Tourist Office*, 83A Marylebone High St, London W1M 3DE; tel: (0171) 224 3692.
USA: *Romanian National Tourist Office*, 573 Third Ave, New York, NY 10016; tel: (212 697-6971.

ESSENTIALS

ESSENTIALS

Alphabet

A	B
Ah	*Beh*
C	D
Cheh	*Deh*
E	F
Eh	*Eff*
G	H
Djeh	*Hash*
I	J
Ee	*Zheu*
K	L
Kah	*Ell*
M	N
Em	*En*
O	P
Oh	*Peh*
Q	R
Kew	*Airr*
S	T
Ess	*Teh*
U	V
Oo	*Veh*
W	X
Doobloveh	*Ecks*
Y	Z
Ee-grek	*Zed*

R O M A N I A N

01 ↕ 12

Basic Words and Phrases

1 Yes — **No**
Da — Nu
Dah — *Noo*

2 Please — **Thank you**
Te rog — Mulţumesc
Teh rohg — *Multzumesc*

3 That's O.K. — **Perhaps**
E în regulă — Poate
Eh an rehgoolah — *Pwahteh*

4 To — **From**
La — De la
Lah — *Deh lah*

5 Here — **There**
Aici — Acolo
Aich — *Acohlo*

6 None — **Also**
Nici unul/una — De asemenea
Neech oonool/oona — *Deh asehmehneya*

7 How — **When**
Cum? — Când?
Coom — *Cund*

8 What — **Why**
Ce? — De ce?
Cheh — *Deh cheh*

9 I don't understand.
Nu înţeleg.
Noo antzehleg

10 I don't speak Romanian.
Nu vorbesc româneşte.
Noo vorbesc romaneshteh

11 Do you speak English?
Vorbiţi englezeşte?
Vorbeetz englezeshteh?

12 Can you please write it down?
Scrieţi vă rog.
Screeyetz vah rohg

260

13 **Can you please speak more
slowly?**
Vorbiți mai rar vă rog.
Vorbeetz my rar vah rohg.

14 **How much does it/this cost?**
Cît costa?
Kewt costa?

Days

15 **Monday**   **Tuesday**
Luni   Marți
Loony   *Martz*

16 **Wednesday**   **Thursday**
Miercuri   Joi
Me-aircooree   *Zhoy*

17 **Friday**   **Saturday**
Vineri.   Sâmbătă.
Vinairee   *Sumbahtah*

18 **Sunday**   **Morning**
Duminică.   Dimineața.
Doomeeneeka   *Deemeeneyatza*

19 **Afternoon**   **Evening**
După amiază.   Seară
Dupah amiazah.   *Sara*

20 **Night**   **Week**
Noapte   Săptămână.
Nwapteh   *Saptamerna.*

21 **Yesterday**   **Tomorrow**
Ieri   Mâine
Eeyairee   *Meu-eeneh*

Numbers

22 **Zero**   **One**
Zero   Unu.
Zehro   *Oonoo*

23 **Two**   **Three**
Doi   Trei.
Doy   *Tray*

24 **Four**   **Five**
Patru.   Cinci.
Patroo   *Chinch*

25 **Six**   **Seven**
Șase.   Șapte.
Shaseh   *Shapteh*

26 **Eight**   **Nine**
Opt.   Nouă.
Opt   *Nower*

27 **Ten**   **Eleven**
Zece   Unsprezece.
Zecheh   *Oonsprezecheh*

28 **Twelve**   **Thirteen**
Doisprezece   Treisprezece
Doysprezecheh   *Traysprezecheh*

29 **Fourteen**   **Fifteen**
Paisprezece.   Cincisprezece.
Pie-sprezecheh   *Cheenchsprezecheh*

30 **Sixteen**   **Seventeen**
Șaisprezece   Șaptesprezece
Shy-sprezecheh   *Shaptesprezecheh*

31 **Eighteen**   **Nineteen**
Optsprezece   Nouăsprezece
Optsprezecheh   *Nowahsprezecheh.*

32 **Twenty**   **Twenty-one**
Douăzeci.   Douăzeci și unu.
Douahzech.   *Duoahzech she oonoo.*

33 **Twenty-two**   **Thirty**
Douăzeci și doi.   Treizeci.
Douahzech she doy *Trayzech*

**R
O
M
A
N
I
A
N**

13
↑
33

261

34 **Forty** **Fifty**
Patruzeci. Cincizeci.
Patroozech. *Cheench-zech*

35 **Sixty** **Seventy**
Șaizeci Șaptezeci
Shy-zech *Shaptezech*

36 **Eighty** **Ninety**
Optzeci Nouăzeci
Optzech *Nowahzech*

37 **One hundred** **Five hundred**
O sută Cinci sute
Oh sooter *Chinch sooteh*

38 **One thousand** **One million**
O mie Un milion
Oh meeyeh *Oon milion*

Time

39 **9.00**
Nouă.
Nowa

40 **9.05**
Nouă și cinci.
Nowa she chinch

41 **9.10**
Nouă și zece.
Nowa she zecheh

42 **9.15**
Nouă și un sfert.
Nowa she oon sfehrt

43 **9.20**
Nouă și douăzeci.
Nowa she dowazech

44 **9.25**
Nouă și douăzeci și cinci.
Nowa she dowazech she chinch

45 **9.30**
Nouă și jumătate.
Nowa she zhoomahtateh

46 **9.35**
Zece fără douăzeci și cinci.
Zecheh fahrah dowazech she chinch

47 **9.40**
Zece fără douăzeci.
Zecheh fahrah dowazech

48 **9.45**
Zece fără un sfert.
Zecheh fahrah oon sfehrt

49 **9.50**
Zece fără zece.
Zecheh fahrah zecheh

50 **9.55**
Zece fără cinci.
Zecheh fahrah chinch

51 **12.00/Midday/Midnight**
Douăsprezece/Amiază/Miezul nopții.
Dowasprezecheh/Amiazah/Meeyehzool noptz

52 **What time is it?**
Cât este ceasul?
Cut esteh cheyasool?

53 **It is . . .**
Este ora . . .
Esteh ora . . .

ARRIVING AND DEPARTING

Airport

54 **Excuse me, where is the check-in desk for . . . airline?**

Scuzați-mă, unde este ghișeul
liniei aeriene . . ?
*Scoozatz-mah, oondeh esteh gisherl
leeneeyeh aereeyehneh . . ?*

55 hat is the boarding gate/
time for my flight?
Care este poarta/ora de
îmbarcare pentru zborul meu?
*Cahreh esteh pwarta/ora deh
umbarcareh pentroo zborool meu?*

56 How long is the delay likely
to be?
Cît de lungă poate fi
întârzierea?
*Cut deh loongah pwateh fee
unterzeeyaireya?*

57 Where is the duty-free shop?
Unde este magazinul duty-free?
*Oondeh esteh magazinool duty-
free?*

58 Which way is the baggage
reclaim?
De unde se colectează bagajele?
*Deh oondeh seh colectayah-zah
bagazhehleh?*

59 Where can I get the bus to
the city centre?
De unde pot lua autobuzul spre
centru?
*Deh oondeh pot lwah autoboozul
spreh chentroo?*

Train Station

60 Where is the ticket office/
information desk?
Unde este ghișeul de bilete/
ghișeul de informații?

*Oondeh esteh gisherl deh bileteh/
gisherl deh informatzi?*

61 Which platform does the
train to . . . depart from?
De la ce peron pleacă trenul
spre . . ?
*Deh la cheh pehron pleyacah
trehnool spreh . . ?*

62 Where is platform . . ?
Unde este peronul . . ?
Oondeh esteh peronool . . ?

63 When is the next train to . . ?
La ce ora pleacă următorul tren
spre . . ?
*La cheh orah pleyacah
oormahtorool tren spreh . . ?*

64 Is there a later train to . . ?
Mai este un alt tren spre . . ?
My esteh oon alt tren spreh . . ?

Port

65 How do I get to the port?
Cum ajung în port?
Coom azhung un port?

66 When is the next sailing
to . . ?
Când este viitoarea cursa
spre . . ?
*Cund esteh veetwareya coorsa
spreh . . ?*

67 Can I catch an earlier ferry
with this ticket?
Pot ua cu acest bilet un vas care
pleacă mai devreme?
*Pot ooah coo achest bilet oon vas
cahreh pleyacah my devrehmeh?*

**R
O
M
A
N
I
A
N**

55
↑
67

263

Notices and Signs

68 **Bufet/Vagon restaurant.**
Buffet/Vagon restaurant
Buffet (Dining) Car

69 **Autobuz.**
Autobooz
Bus

70 **Apă potabilă/Apă ne potabilă.**
Apah potabilah/Apah neh potabilah
Drinking/Non-drinking water

71 **Intrare**
Intrareh
Entrance

72 **Ieşire**
Yesheereh
Exit

73 **Informaţii**
Informatzee
Information

74 **Birou de bagaje**
Beero deh bagazheh
Left Luggage (Baggage Claim)

75 **Dulăpioare pentru bagaje**
Doolapeeyowahreh pentroo bagazheh
Luggage Lockers

76 **Oficiul poştal**
Ofeecheeyool poshtal
Post Office

77 **Peron**
Pehron
Platform

78 **Gară**
Garah
Railway (Railroad) Station

79 **Aeroport**
Aeroport
Airport

80 **Port**
Port
Port

81 **Restaurant**
Restaurant
Restaurant

82 **Zona pentru fumători/ nefumători**
Zonah pentroo foomahtoree/ nehfoomahtoree
Smoking/Non-Smoking

83 **Telefon**
Telefon
Telephone

84 **Ghişeu de bilete**
Geesheeyoo deh bileteh
Ticket Office

85 **Ghişeu de înregistrare**
Geesheeyoo deh unredjeestrareh
Check-in Desk

86 **Orar**
Orar
Timetable (Schedule)

87 **Toalete**
Twaleht
Toilets (Restrooms)

88 **Bărbaţi**
Bahrbatz
Gentlemen

R
O
M
A
N
I
A
N

68
↕
88

89 **Femei**
Femay
Ladies'

90 **Tramvai**
Tramvye
Tram (Streetcar)

91 **Metrou**
Metro
Underground (Subway)

92 **Sală de aşteptare**
Salah deh ashteptareh
Waiting-Room

Buying a Ticket

93 I would like a first-class/
second-class single (one-
way)/return (round-trip)
ticket to . . .
Un bilet de clasa întâi/a doua
dus/dus-întors până la . . . vă
rog.
*Oon bilett deh classa unteuy/ah
dowa dooss/dooss-untors peunah
la . . . vah rohg.*

94 Is my rail pass valid on this
train/ferry/bus?
Este permisul meu valabil pe
acest tren/vapor/autobuz?
*Esteh permeesool meh-oo valabil
peh achest tren/vapor/autobooz?*

95 I would like an aisle/window
seat.
Un loc pe coridor/lângă
fereastră, vă rog.
*Oon lock peh coridor/lungah
fehreyastra, vah rohg.*

96 No smoking/smoking, please.
Pentru nefumători/fumători, vă
rog.
*Pentroo neh foomahtoree/
foomahtoree, vah rohg.*

97 We would like to sit
together.
Dorim să stăm împreună.
Doreem sa stahm umpreyunah.

98 I would like to make a seat
reservation.
Doresc să rezerv un loc.
Doresc sa rezerv oon lock

99 I would like to reserve a
couchette/sleeper for one
person/two people/for my
family.
Doresc să rezerv o cuşetă/un
pat pentru o persoană/două
persoane/familia mea, la vagonu
de dormit.
*Doresc sah rezerv oh cooshetta/oon
pat pentroo oh persowahnah/
douah persowahneh/familia meya,
la vagonool deh dormeet.*

100 I would like to reserve a
cabin.
Doresc să rezerv o cabină.
Doresc sa rezerv oh cabinah.

Timetables (Schedules)

101 Sosiri
Soseeree
Arrive

102 Opriri la
Opreeree la
Calls (Stops) at

103 **Bufet-Restaurant**
Boofet-Restaurant
Catering Service

104 **Schimbați la . . .**
Skeembatz la
Change at . . .

105 **Legătură**
Legahtoora
Connection

106 **Zilnic**
Zilnic
Daily

107 **La fiecare patruzeci de minute**
La fiehcareh patroozech deh minuteh
Every 40 Minutes

108 **Clasa întâi**
Classa untuy
First-Class

109 **La fiecare oră**
La fiehcareh orah
Hourly

110 **Sânt recomandate rezervările**
Sunt rehcomandateh rezervoahrileh
Seat reservations are recommended

111 **Clasa a doua**
Classa a doua
Second-class

112 **De plătit supliment**
Deh plahtit soopleement
Supplement Payable

113 **Via/Prin**
Veeya/Preen
Via

Luggage

114 **How much will it cost to send (ship) my luggage in advance?**
Cît mă costă dacă expediez bagajele în avans?
Cut mah costah dacah expediez bagazhehleh un avans?

115 **Where is the left luggage (baggage claim) office?**
Unde este biroul de bagaje?
Oondeh esteh beerol deh bagazheh?

116 **What time do you open/close?**
La ce ora deschideți/închideți?
La cheh ora deskidetz/unkidetz?

117 **Where are the luggage trolleys (carts)?**
Unde sânt cărucioarele de bagaje?
Oondeh sunt cahroochioahrehleh deh bagazheh?

118 **Where are the lockers?**
Unde sânt dulăpioarele?
Oondeh sunt doolapeeyowahreleh?

119 **I have lost my locker key.**
Am pierdut cheia de la dulăpior
Am piehrdoot kaya deh la doolapior

**R
O
M
A
N
I
A
N**

103
↑
119

ARRIVING/TOURIST OFFICE/ACCOMMODATION

On Board

120 **Is this seat taken?**
Este locul acesta ocupat?
Esteh locool achesta ocoopat?

121 **Excuse me, you are sitting in my reserved seat.**
Scuzaţi-mă, dar staţi pe locul meu rezervat.
Scoozatz-mah, dar statz peh locool meyoo rezervat.

122 **Which station is this?**
La ce gară ne aflăm?
La cheh garah neh aflahm?

123 **What time is this train/bus/ ferry/flight due to arrive/ depart?**
La ce oră urmează să sosească/ să plece/trenul/autobuzul/ avionul/acesta?
La cheh orah oormeyazah sah soseyascah/sah plecheh/trenool/ owtoboozool/avionool/achesta?

124 **Will you wake me just before we arrive?**
Sculaţi-mă vă rog înainte de sosire.
Sculatz-mah vah rohg unainteh deh soseereh.

Customs and Passports

125 Paşapoartele, vă rog!
Pashapoarteleh, vah rohg!
Passports, please!

126 **I have nothing/wine/spirits (alcohol)/tobacco to declare.**
Nu am nimic/vin/alcool/ţigări/ de declarat.
Noo am neemeek/veen/alcol/ tzigahree/deh declarat.

127 **I shall be staying for . . . days/weeks/months.**
Voi sta . . . zile/săptămâni/luni.
Voy sta . . . zeeleh/sahptahmuni/ loony.

AT THE TOURIST OFFICE

128 **Do you have a map of the town/area?**
Aveţi o hartă a oraşului/ regiunii?
Avetz oh hartah a orashoolui/ redjeeyoonee?

129 **Can I reserve accommodation here?**
Pot rezerva aici şederea?
Pot rezerva aich shehdehreya?

130 **Do you have a list of accommodation?**
Aveţi o listă cu locuri disponibile?
Avetz oh listah coo locooree deesponeebeeleh?

ACCOMMODATION

Hotels

131 **I have a reservation in the name of . . .**
Am făcut o rezervare pe numele . . .
Am fahcoot oh rezervareh peh numehleh . . .

120
↑
131

267

132 I wrote to/faxed/telephoned
you last month/last week in . . .
V-am scris/faxat/telefonat/
luna/săptămâna trecută . . .
*Vam screece/faxat/telefonat/loona/
sahptahmurna trehcootah . . .*

133 Do you have any rooms free?
Aveţi vreo cameră li eră?
Avetz vrehoh camerah leebehrah?

134 I would like to reserve a
single/double room with/
without bath/shower.
Doresc să rezerv o cameră cu
pat simplu/dublu cu/fără baie/
duş.
*Doresc sah rezerv oh camerah coo
pat seemploo/doobloo coo/fahrah
baieh/doosh.*

135 I would like bed and
breakfast/(room and) half
board/(room and) full board.
Doresc o cameră cu micul
dejun/semi pensiune/pensiune
*Doresc oh camerah coo meecool
dehzhoon/semi pensiuneh/
pensiuneh*

136 How much is it per night?
Cât costă pe noapte?
Cut costah peh nowapteh?

137 Is breakfast included?
Este micul dejun inclus în preţ?
*Esteh meecool dehzhoon incloose
un pretz?*

138 May I see the room?
Pot să văo camera?
Pot sah vahd camehra?

139 Do you have any cheaper
rooms?
Aveţi camere mai ieftine?
Avetz camehreh my yefteeneh?

140 I would like to take the
room.
Doresc să închiriez o camera.
*Doresc sah uncheeryez o
camehrah.*

141 I would like to stay for . . .
nights.
Aş dori să stau . . . nopţi.
Ash doree sah stau . . . noptz.

142 The shower/light/tap doesn't
work.
Duşul/lumina/robinetul/este
defect.
*Dooshool/loomeenah/robinetool/
esteh dehfect.*

143 At what time/where is
breakfast served?
La ce ora/unde se serveşte micul
dejun?
*La cheh orah/oondeh seh
serveshteh meecool dehzhoon?*

144 What time do I have to
check-out?
La ce oră trebuie să părăsesc
camera?
*La cheh orah trebooyeh sah
parhsesc camehra?*

145 Can I have the key to room
no . . ?
Daţi-mi vă rog cheia de la
camera numărul . . .
*Datz-mee vah rohg kaya deh la
camehra noomahrool . . .*

146 My room number is . . .
Numărul camerei mele este . . .
Noomahrool camehrey mehleh esteh . . .

147 Do you accept travellers' cheques/Eurocheques/credit cards?
Acceptați cecuri de călătorie/Eurocheques/cărți de credit?
Akcheptatz checooree deh cahlahtoreeyah/Eurocheques/cahrtz deh credit?

148 May I have the bill please?
Nota de plată vă rog!
Nohta deh platah vah rohg!

149 Excuse me, I think there is a mistake in this bill.
Mă tem că s-a strecurat o eroare în nota de plată.
Mah tem cah sa strecoorat oh ero-arreh un nota deh platah.

Youth Hostels

150 How much is a dormitory bed per night?
Cât este un pat pe noapte în dormitor?
Cut esteh oon pat peh nowapteh un dormeetor?

151 I am/am not an HI member.
Nu sânt membru HI
Noo sunt membroo hash ee

152 May I use my own sleeping bag?
Pot folosi sacul meu de dormit?
Pot folosee sacool meyoo deh dormeet?

153 What time do you lock the doors at night?
La ce oră se închid porțile?
La cheh orah seh unkhid portzeeleh?

Camping

154 May I camp here for the night/two nights?
Pot campa aici pentru o noapte/două nopți?
Pot campa aich pentroo oh nwapteh/douah noptz?

155 Where can I pitch my tent?
Unde pot instala cortul?
Oondeh pot instahla cortool?

156 How much does it cost for one night/week?
Cît costă pe noapte/pe săptămână?
Cut costah peh nwapteh/peh sahptahmurnah?

157 Where can we park our caravan?
Unde putem parca caravana?
Oondeh pootem parca caravahna?

158 Where are the washing facilities?
Unde sânt lavabourile?
Oondeh sunt lavaboureeleh?

R
O
M
A
N
I
A
N

146
↑
158

159 Is there a restaurant/
supermarket/swimming pool
on site/nearby?
Există un restaurant/
supermarket/piscină la faţa
locului/în apropiere?
*Existah oon restaurant/
supermarket/pischeenah la fatza
locoolui/eun apropiereh?*

160 Do you have a safety deposit
box?
Unde pot fi păstrate lucrurile de
valoare?
*Oondeh pot fee pahstrateh
loocroorileh deh valwareh?*

EATING AND DRINKING

Cafés and Bars

161 I would like a cup of/two
cups of/another coffee.
I would like a cup of/two
cups of/another tea.
O cafea/două cafele/altă cafea,
vă rog.
Uh ceai/două ceaiuri/alt ceai,
vă rog.
*Oh cafeya/douah cafehleh/altah
cafeya, vah rohg.
Oon cheai/douah cheaiooree/alt
cheai, vah rohg.*

162 With/without milk/sugar.
Cu/fără lapte/zahăr.
Coo/fahrah lapteh/zahahr.

163 I would like a bottle/glass/
two glasses of mineral water/
red wine/white wine, please.

O sticlă/un pahar/două pahare
cu apă minerală/vin roşu/vin
alb, vă rog.
*O steeclah/oon pahar/dowah
pahareh coo apah minehralah/
veen roshoo/veen alb, vah rohg.*

164 I would like a beer/two
beers, please.
O bere/două beri, vă rog.
O bereh/dowah beree, vah rohg.

165 May I have some ice?
Gheaţă, vă rog
Gheyatzah, vah rohg

166 Do you have any matches/
cigarettes/cigars?
Aveţi chibrituri/ţigări/ţigări de
foi?
*Avetz keebreetooree/tzigahree/
tzigahree deh foy?*

Restaurants

167 Can you recommend a good/
inexpensive restaurant in this
area?
Îmi puteţi recomanda un
restaurant bun/ieftin în această
zonă?
*Eumi pootetz rehcomanda oon
restaurant boon/yefteen eun
acheyasta zona?*

168 I would like a table for . . .
people.
Doresc să rezerv o masă pentru
. . . persoane.
*Doresc sah rezerv oh masah
pentroo . . . perswaneh.*

169 Do you have a non-smoking area?
Există un loc pentru nefumători?
Existah oon loc pentroo nehfumahtoree?

170 Waiter/Waitress!
Chelner/chelneriță.
Kelner/Kelnehreetza.

171 Do you have a set menu/children's menu/wine list?
Aveți un menu fix/un menu pentru copii/o listă cu vinuri?
Avetz oon mehnoo fix/oon mehnoo pentroo copii/oh leestah coo veenooree?

172 Do you have any vegetarian dishes, please?
Aveți mîncăruri pentru vegetarieni?
Avetz muncahrooree pentroo vegetaryehnee?

173 Are there any local specialities?
Există specialități locale?
Existah spechialitahtz localeh?

174 Are vegetables included?
Sânt legumele incluse în nota de plată?
Sunt legoomehleh inclooseh eun nota deh platah?

175 Could I have it well-cooked/medium/rare please?
Doresc carnea bine prajită/nu foarte prajită/în sânge.
Doresc carneya beeneh prazheetah/noo fwarteh prazheetah/un sundjeh.

176 What does this dish consist of?
Ce fel de mîncare este asta?
Cheh fell deh muncahreh esteh asta?

177 I would like the set menu, please.
Aș dori un menu fix, vă rog.
Ash doree oon mehnoo fix, vah rohg.

178 We have not been served yet.
N-am fost serviți încă.
Nam fost serveetz uncah.

179 Excuse me, this is not what I ordered.
Scuzați-mă, n-am comandat așa ceva.
Scoozatz-mah, nam comandat asha chehva.

180 May I have some/some more bread/water/coffee/tea?
Pot avea mai multă pâine/apă/cafea/mai mult ceai?
Pot aveya my mooltah peu-eeneh/apah/cafeya/my moolt cheyai?

181 May I have the bill, please?
Nota de plată, vă rog.
Nota deh platah, vah rohg.

182 Does this bill include service?
E bacșișul inclus în nota de plată?
Eh bacshishool incloose un nota deh platah?

R
O
M
A
N
I
A
N

169
↕
182

271

183 Do you accept travellers'
cheques (travelers' checks)/
Eurocheques/MasterCard/US
dollars?
Acceptați ceguri de călătorie/
Eurocheques/MasterCard/
Dolari americani?
*Akcheptatz checooree deh
cahlahtoreeyeh/Eurocheque/
MasterCard/Dolaree
americahnee?*

184 Can I have a receipt, please?
Pot avea o chitanță vă rog?
*Pot aveya oh keetantzah va
rohg?*

185 Where is the toilet
(restroom), please?
Unde este toaleta, vă rog?
Oondeh esteh twalehta, vah rog?

On the Menu

186 First courses
Primul fel
Preemool fel

187 Soups
Supe
Soopeh

188 Main courses
Felul principal
Feloool princheepal

189 Fish dishes
Pescărie
Pescahrieh

190 Meat dishes
Mâncăruri cu carne
Muncahrooree coo carneh

191 Vegetarian dishes
Mâncăruri cu legume
Muncahrooree coo legoomeh

192 Cheese
Brânză
Brunzah

193 Desserts
Deserturi
Dehsertooree

194 Specialities
Specialități culinare
Spechialitahtz coolinareh

GETTING AROUND

Public Transport

195 Where is the bus stop/coach
station/nearest metro
(subway) station?
Unde este stația de autobuz/
autocar/metrou, cea mai
apropiată?
*Oondeh esteh statzia deh
owtobooz/owtocar/metro, cheya
my apropiatah?*

196 When is the next/last bus
to . . ?
La ce oră vine următorul/
ultimul autobuz spre . . ?
*La cheh orah veeneh
oormahtorool/ooolteemool
owtobooz spreh . . ?*

197 How much is the fare to the
city centre (downtown)/
railway (railroad) station/
airport?

Cât costă biletul până-n centru/
până la gară/aeroport?
*Cut costah biletool peunahn
chentroo/peunah la garah/
aeroport?*

198 Will you tell me when to get
off?
Vreţi să-mi spuneţi când să
cobor?
*Vretz sah-mee spoonetz cund sah
cobor?*

199 Does this bus go to . . ?
Merge autobuzul ăsta la . . ?
Mehrdjeh owtoboozool ahsta la . . ?

200 Which number bus goes to . . ?
Care autobuz merge la . . ?
Careh owtobooz mehrdjeh la . . ?

201 May I have a single (one-
way)/return (roun -trip)/day
ticket/book of tickets?
Un bilet dus/dus-întors/valabil
24 de ore/un abonament, vă
rog.
*Oon bilet doos/doos-untors/
valabil dwahzech deh oreh/oon
abonament, vah rohg.*

Taxis

202 I would like to go to . . . How
much will it cost?
Vreau să merg la . . ? Cât costă
până la . . ?
*Vreyow sah mairg la . . ? Cut
costah pernah la . . ?*

203 Please stop here.
Opriţi aici, vă rog.
Opreetz ayeechee, vah rohg.

204 I would like to order a taxi
today/tomorrow/at 2pm to
go from . . . to . . .
Doresc să comand un taxi azi/
mâine/la ora două după amiază,
care să mă ducă de la . . .
la . . .
*Doresc sah comand oon taxi
ahzee/meu-eeneh/la ora dowa
doopah ameeyazah, careh sah mah
ducah deh la . . . la . . .*

Asking the Way

205 Excuse me, do you speak
English?
Scuzaţi-mă. Vorbiţi englezeşte?
*Scoozatz-mah. Vorbeetz
englehzeshteh?*

206 Excuse me, is this the right
way to . . ?
Scuzaţi-mă. Ăsta este drumul
spre . . ?
*Scoozatz-mah. Asta esteh
droomool spreh . . ?*

207 . . . the cathedral/the tourist
information office/the castle/
the old town
. . . catedrala/oficiul de
informaţii turistice/castelul/
oraşul vechi
*. . . catedralah/ofeechiool deh
informatzee tooristicheh/castelool/
orashool vehk?*

273

208 Can you tell me the way to the railway (railroad) station/ bus station/taxi rank (stand)/ city centre (downtown)/ beach?

Vreți vă rog să-mi spuneți cum ajung la gară/stația de autobuz/ stația de taxiuri/în centru/la plajă?

Vretz vah rohg sah-mee spoonetz koom azhoong la garah/statzia deh owtobooz/statzia deh taxiooree/un chentroo/la plazhah?

209 First/second left/right/ straight ahead.

Prima/a doua la stînga/dreapta/ drept înainte.

Preema/a dowa la stunga/ dreyapta/drept unainteh.

210 Where is the nearest police station/post office?

Unde este postul de poliție/ oficiul poștal cel mai apropiat?

Oondeh esteh postool deh politzieh/ofeechiool pshtal chel my apropiat?

211 Is it far?

Este departe?

Esteh dehparteh?

212 Do I need to take a taxi/ catch a bus?

Trebuie să iau un taxi/un autobuz?

Trebooyeh sah eeyow oon taxi/oon owtobooz?

213 Can you point to it on my map?

Puteți să-mi arătați pe hartă?

Pootetz sa-mee arahtatz peh hartah?

214 Thank you for your help.

Mulțumesc pentru ajutor.

Mooltzoomesc pentroo azhootor.

SIGHTSEEING

215 Where is the Tourist Information office?

Unde este Oficiul de Informații Turistice?

Oondeh esteh ofeechiool dee eenformatzee tooristicheh?

216 Where is the cathedral/ church/museum?

Unde este catedrala/biserica/ muzeul?

Oondeh esteh catedrahla/ bisehrica/moozeul?

217 How much is the entrance (admission) charge?

Cît costă intrarea?

Cut costah intrareya?

218 Is there a reduction for children/students/senior citizens?

Au copiii/studenții/bătrânii reducere?

Ow copeeyee/studentzee/ bahtreuneu redoochehreh?

219 What time does the next guided tour start?

La ce oră începe următorul tur cu ghizi?

*La cheh orah unchehpeh
oormahtorool toor coo gheeze*

**220 One/two adults/children,
please.**
Un adult/doi adulţi/copii, vă
rog
*Oon adoolt/doy adooltz/copeeyee,
vah rohg*

**221 May I take photographs
here?**
Am voie să fotografiez aici?
Am voyeh sah fotografiez aich?

ENTERTAINMENT

**222 Can you recommend a good
bar/nightclub?**
Puteţi recomanda un bar/club
de noapte bun?
*Pootetz rehcomanda oon bar/club
deh nwapteh boon?*

**223 Do you know what is on at
the cinema (playing at the
movies)/theatre at the
moment?**
Ştiţi cumva ce filme rulează/ce
piese se joacă în momentul de
faţă?
*Shtitz coomva cheh feelmeh
rooleyahza/cheh peeyeseh seh
zhowacah un momentool deh
fatzah?*

**224 I would like to book
(purchase) . . . tickets for the
matinée/evening
performance on Monday.**
. . . bilete pentru matineul/seara
de luni, vă rog.

. . . bileteh pentroo mateeneyool/
seyara deh loony, vah rohg.

**225 What time does the film/
performance start?**
La ce oră începe filmul/
spectacolul?
*La cheh orah unchehpeh feelmool/
spectacolool?*

MEETING PEOPLE

226 Hello/Goodbye.
Salut/La revedere.
Saloot/La revehdereh.

**227 Good morning/good
afternoon/good evening/
goodnight.**
Bună dimineaţa/Bună ziua/bună
seara/noapte bună.
*Boonah deemeenayatz/Boonah
zeeyua/boonah seyara/nwapteh
boonah.*

228 Pleased to meet you.
Încântat de cunoştinţă.
Uncuntat deh coonoshteentzah.

229 How are you?
Ce mai faceţi?
Cheh my fachetz?

230 Fine, thank you. And you?
Bine, mulţumesc. Dar
dumneavoastră?
*Beeneh, mooltzoomesc. Dar
doomneyavowastrah?*

231 My name is . . .
Mă numesc . . .
Mah noomesc . . .

232 This is my friend/boyfriend/
girlfriend/husband/wife/
brother/sister.
Vă prezint prietenul/prietena/
soţul/soţia/fratele/sora.
*Vah prezint preeyetenool/
preeyetehna/sotzool/sotzia/
fratehleh/sora.*

233 Where are you travelling to?
Unde călătoriţi?
Oondeh cahlatoritz?

234 I am/we are going to . . .
Călătoresc/călătorim la . . .
Cahlatoresc/cahlahtoreem la . . .

235 How long are you travelling
for?
Cît timp călătoriţi?
Cut teemp cahlahtoritz?

236 Where do you come from?
De unde veniţi?
Deh oondeh veneetz?

237 I am/we are from . . .
Sânt/sântem din . . .
Sunt/suntem deen . . .

238 We're on holiday.
Sântem în vacanţă.
Suntem un vacantzah.

239 This is our first visit here.
Aceasta este prima noastră
vizită aici.
*Acheyasta esteh preema nwastrah
veezeetah aich*

240 Would you like/May I have a
cigarette?
Doriţi/pot sa iau o ţigară?
Doritz/pot sa iau oh tzigarah?

241 I am sorry but I do not
understand.
Mă scuzaţi dar nu înţeleg.
Ma scoozatz dar noo untzehleg.

242 Please speak slowly.
Vorbiţi mai rar vă rog.
Vorbeetz my rar vah rohg.

243 Do you mind if I smoke?
Pot aprinde o ţigară?
Pot apreendeh oh tzigarah?

244 Do you have a light?
Aveţi un foc?
Avetz oon fok?

245 I am waiting for my husband/
wife/boyfriend/girlfriend.
Îmi aştept soţul/soţia/prietenul/
prietena.
*Eumi ashtept sotzool/sotza/
prietenool/prietehna.*

TRAVELLING WITH CHILDREN

246 Do you have a high chair/
baby-sitting service/cot?
Aveţi un scaun pentru copii/un
serviciu baby-sitting/un pătuţ
pentru copii?
*Avetz oon scaun pentroo copee/oon
serveechioo baby-sitting/oon
pahtootz pentroo kopee?*

247 Where is the nursery/
playroom?
Unde este creşa/camera
copiilor?
*Oondeh esteh cresha/camehra
copeelor?*

248 Where can I warm the baby's bottle?

Unde pot încălzi biberonul?

Oondeh pot uncahlzi beebehronool?

COMMUNICATIONS

Post

249 How much will it cost to send a letter/postcard/this package to Britain/Ireland/America/Canada/Australia/New Zealand?

Cât costă timbrul pentru a expedia o scrisoare/carte poştală/pachetul acesta în Marea Britanie/Irlanda/America/Canada/Australia/Noua Zeelandă?

Cut costa timbrool pentroo ah expehdia oh scriswareh/karteh poshtala/paketool achesta un Mareya Britanyeh/Irlanda/Amehrica/Canada/Owstralia/Noua Zehlanda?

250 I would like one stamp/two stamps.

Un timbru/două timbre, vă rog.

Oon timbroo/douah timbreh, vah rohg.

251 I'd like . . . stamps for postcards to send abroad, please.

. . . timbre pentru cărţi poştale de expediat în străinătate, vă rog.

. . . timbreh pentroo cartz poshtaleh deh expediat un straheenahtateh, vah rohg.

Phones

252 I would like to make a telephone call/reverse the charges to (make a collect call to) . . .

Doresc să telefonez/cu taxă inversă la . . .

Doresc sah telefonez/coo taxah inversah la . . .

253 Which coins do I need for the telephone?

Cu ce monede funcţionează telefonul?

Koo cheh monehdeh functzioneyazah telefonool?

254 The line is engaged (busy).

Numărul este ocupat.

Noomahrool esteh ocupat.

255 The number is . . .

Numărul este . . .

Noomahrool esteh . . .

256 Hello, this is . . .

Alo, . . . sânt.

Alo, . . . sunt.

257 May I speak to . . ?

Pot vorbi vă rog cu . . ?

Pot vorbee vah rohg coo . . ?

258 He/She is not in at the moment. Can you call back?

El/ea nu este aici pentru moment. Sunaţi vă rog mai târziu.

Yel/ya noo esteh aich pentroo moment. Soonatz vah rohg my turzioo

MONEY

259 I would like to change these travellers' cheques (travelers' checks)/this currency/this Eurocheque.
Vreau să schimb aceste cecuri de călătorie/aceşti bani/acest Eurocheque.
Vreyau sa skeemb acheshteh cecooree deh cahlahtoreeyeh/achesht bahnee/achest Eurocheque.

260 How much commission do you charge? (What is the service charge?)
Cît este comisionul dumneavoastră?
Cut esteh comissionool doomneyavwastrah?

261 Can I obtain money with my MasterCard?
Pot încasa bani cu MasterCard?
Pot uncasa bahnee coo MasterCard?

SHOPPING

Names of Shops and Departments

262 Librărie/Papetărie
Leebrahrieh/Papetahrieh
Bookshop/Stationery

263 Bijuterii/Cadouri
Beezhootehrie/Kadoree
Jeweller's/Gifts

264 Încălţăminte
Euncahltzahmeenteh
Shoes

265 Ferometal
Feromehtahl
Hardware

266 Antichităţi
Antikitahtz
Antiques

267 Frizer/Coafor
Freezer/Cwafor
Hairdressers (men's)/(women's)

268 Tutungerie
Tootoondjerie
Tobacconist

269 Brutărie
Brootahrie
Baker's

270 Supermarket
Supermarket
Supermarket

271 Magazin fotografic
Magazeen fotografic
Photoshop

272 Jucării
Zhoocahree
Toys

273 Agenţie de voiaj
Agentzieh de voyazh
Travel Agent

274 Drogherie
Drogherie
Toiletries

275 Magazin de discuri
Magazeen deh deescooree
Records

In the Shop

276 What time do the shops open/close?
La ce oră deschid/închid magazinele?
La cheh ora deskyd/unkyd magazeenehleh?

277 Where is the nearest market?
Unde este piaţa cea mai apropiată?
Oondeh esteh piatza cheya my apropiatah?

278 Can you show me the one in the window/this one?
Puteţi să mi-l/mi-o arătaţi pe cel/cea din vitrină/acesta/aceasta?
Pootetz sa mee-l/mee-o arahtatz peh chel/cheya deen veetreena/achesta/acheyasta?

279 Can I try this on?
Pot să-l/s-o încerc?
Pot sa-l/s-o unchairk?

280 What size is this?
Ce măsură are?
Cheh mahsoora areh?

281 This is too large/too small/too expensive.
E prea mare/prea mic/prea scump.
Eh preya mareh/preya meek/preya scoomp.

282 Do you have any others?
Aveţi alţii/altele?
Avetz altzee/altehleh?

283 My size is . . .
Măsura mea este . . .
Mahsoora meya esteh . . .

284 Where is the changing room/childrens/cosmetic/ladieswear/menswear/food department?
Unde este cabina de probă/raionul de confecţii pentru copii/cosmetice/confecţii pentru femei/bărbaţi/alimentara?
Oondeh esteh cabina deh prohbah/raionool deh confectzee pentroo copee/cosmeticheh/confectzee pentroo femay/bahrbatz/alimentahra?

285 I would like . . .
Daţi-mi . . .
Datz-mee . . .

286 I would like a quarter of a kilo/half a kilo/a kilo of bread/ butter/cheese/ham/tomatoes.
Daţi-mi un sfert/o jumătate/un kilogram de pâine/unt/brînză/şuncă/roşii.
Datz-mee oon sfert/oh zhoomahtateh/oon keelogram deh peuineh/oont/breunzah/shooncah/roshee.

287 How much is this?
Cît costă?
Cut costah?

288 I'll take this one, thank you.
Îl iau pe acesta, mulţumesc.
Eul iau peh achesta, mooltzoomesc.

289 Do you have a carrier (shopping) bag?

Aveți o pungă de plastic?

Avetz oh pungah deh plastic?

290 Do you have anything cheaper/larger/smaller/of better quality?

Nu aveți nimic mai ieftin/mai mare/mai mic/de mai bună calitate?

Noo avetz neemeek my yefteen/my mareh/my meek/deh my boonah calitahteh?

291 I would like a film for this camera.

Dați-mi vă rog un film pentru acest aparat.

Datz-mee vah rohg oon feelm pentroo achest aparat.

292 I would like some batteries, the same size as this old one.

Dați-mi vă rog nişte baterii, de acceeaşi mărime cu aceasta.

Datz-mee vah rohg neeshteh bateree, deh acheeyashi mahrimeh coo acheyasta.

293 Would you mind wrapping this for me, please?

Vreți vă rog s-o/să-l ambalați?

Vretz vah rohg so/sahl ambalatz?

294 Sorry, but you seem to have given me the wrong change.

Mă scuzați dar am impresia că nu mi-ați dat restul corect.

Mah scoozatz dar am impresia cah noo mee-atz dat restool correct.

MOTORING

Car Hire (Rental)

295 I have ordered (rented) a car in the name of . . .

Am comandat/închiriat un automobil pe numele . . .

Am comandat/unkyriat oon automobeel peh noomehleh . . .

296 How much does it cost to hire (rent) a car for one day/two days/one week?

Cît costă închirierea unui automobil pe o zi/două zile/o săptămână?

Cut costah unkyriereya oonui automobeel peh oh zee/dowah zeeleh/oh saptahmunah?

297 Is the tank already full of petrol (gas)?

I-ați făcut plinul?

Ee-atz fahcoot pleenool?

298 Is insurance and tax included? How much is the deposit?

Sânt asigurarea şi taxa incluse? Cât este depozitul?

Sunt aseegurareya shee taxa incluseh? Cut esteh dehpositool?

299 By what time must I return the car?

Când trebuie să înapoiez maşina?

Cund trebooyeh sah unapoyez mashina?

289
↕
299

300 I would like a small/family car with a radio/cassette player.

Vreau o maşină mică/limuzină cu radio/casetofoh.

Vreyau oh mashinah meecah/ leemoozeenah coo rahdio/ cassetofon.

Asking the Way

301 Excuse me, can you help me please?

Vă rog frumos, puteţi să mă ajutaţi?

Vah rohg froomos, pootetz sah mah azhootatz?

302 How do I reach the motorway/main road?

În ce direcţie este autostrada/ şoseaua naţională?

Eun cheh directzieh esteh owtostrahda/shoseh-awua natzionalah?

303 I think I have taken the wrong turning.

Mă tem că am luat cotitura greşită.

Mah tem cah am lwat coteetoora greshitah.

304 I am looking for this address.

Caut această adresă.

Caut acheyastah adresah.

305 I am looking for the . . . hotel.

Caut hotelul . . .

Caut hotelool . . .

306 How far is it to . . . from here?

Cât de departe de aici se afla . . ?

Cut deh dehparteh deh aich seh afla . . ?

307 Carry straight on for . . . kilometres.

Continuaţi drept înainte vreo . . . kilometri.

Continooatz drept unainteh vreh- oh . . . kilometree.

308 Take the next turning on the right/left.

Cotiţi prima la dreapta/la stânga.

Cotitz preema la dreyapta/la stunga.

309 Turn right/left at the next crossroads/traffic lights.

Luaţi-o la dreapta/la stânga la prima intersecţie/la primul semafor.

Lowatz-oh la dreyapta/la stunga la preema eentersectzieh/la preemool sehmafor.

310 You are going in the wrong direction.

Circulaţi în direcţie greşită.

Cheercoolatz un directzieh gresheetah.

Parking

311 How long can I park here?

Cât timp pot parca aici?

Cut teemp pot parca aich?

312 Is there a car park near here?

Este vreun garaj prin apropiere?

Esteh vreh-oon garahzh preen apropeeyereh?

313 At what time does this car
park close?
La ce oră se închide garajul?
*La cheh orah seh unkeedeh
garazhool?*

Signs and Notices

314 Sens unic
Sens ooneek
One way.

315 Intrarea interzisă
Eentrareya eenterzeesah
No entry.

316 Staţionarea interzisă
Statzionareya eenterzeesah
No parking.

317 Deviaţie
Deviatzieh
Detour (diversion)

318 Stop
Stop
Stop.

319 Daţi prioritate
Datz prioritahteh
Give way (yield).

320 Pericol de derapaj
Pereecol deh dehrapazh
Slippery road.

321 Depăşirea interzisă
Dehpahsheereya eenterzeesah
No overtaking.

At the Filling Station

322 Unleaded (lead-free)/
Standard/Premium
Benzină neetilată/Standard/

Supercarburant
*Benzeena neeteelahtah/Standard/
Supercarboorant*

323 Fill the tank please.
Faceţi plinul vă rog.
Fachetz pleenool vah rohg.

324 Do you have a road map of
this area?
Aveţi o hartă a regiunii?
Avetz oh hartah ah redjeeyoonee?

325 How much is the car-wash?
Cât costă spălatul maşinii?
Cut costah spahlatool mashineei?

Breakdowns

326 I've had a breakdown at . . .
Sânt în pană la . . .
Sunt un panah la . . .

327 I am on the road from . . .
to . . .
Sânt pe şoseaua de la . . .
la . . .
*Sunt pey shosehowua deh la
. . . la . . .*

328 I can't move the car. Can
you send a tow-truck?
Nu pot porni automobilul.
Puteţi trimite o maşină care să
mă remorcheze?
*Noo pot pornee owtomobeelool.
Pootetz treemeeteh oh mashinah
careh sah mah rehmorchezeh?*

329 I have a flat tyre.
Am un cauciuc pe geantă.
*Am oon cowoochiook peh
djeyantah.*

ROMANIAN

330 The windscreen (windshield) has smashed/cracked.
Parbrizul este spart/crăpat.
Parbreezool esteh spart/crahpat.

331 There is something wrong with the engine/brakes/lights/steering/gearbox/clutch/exhaust.
Motorul/frânele/farurile/direcţia/cutia de viteze/ambreiajul/eşapamentul nu funcţionează.
Motorool/fruneleh/farooreeleh/deerectzia/cootia deh veetehzeh/ambreyazhool/eshapamentool noo foonctzioneyazah.

332 It's overheating.
Supraîncălzeşte.
Sooprauncahlzeshteh.

333 It won't start.
Nu porneşte.
Noo porneshteh.

334 Where can I get it repaired?
Unde o pot repara?
Oondeh oh pot rehpara?

335 Can you take me there?
Mă puteţi transporta acolo?
Mah pootetz transporta acolo?

336 Will it take long to fix?
Cât timp va dura reparaţia?
Cut teemp va doora rehparatzia?

337 How much will it cost?
Cît costă?
Cut costah?

Accidents

338 Can you help me? There has been an accident.
Vreţi să mă ajutaţi vă rog? Am avut un accident.
Vretz sah mah azhootatz vah rohg? Am avoot oon akcheedent.

339 Please call the police/an ambulance.
Chemaţi vă rog poliţia/salvarea.
Kehmatz vah rohg poleetzia/salvareya.

340 Is anyone hurt?
Sânt răniţi?
Sunt rahneetz?

Traffic Offences

341 I'm sorry, I didn't see the sign.
Îmi cer scuze dar n-am văzut semnul.
Eumi chair scoozeh dar nam vahzoot semnool.

342 Must I pay a fine? How much?
Trebuie să plătesc amendă? Cât costă?
Trebooyeh sah plahtesc amendah? Cut costah?

343 Show me your documents.
Arătaţi-mi hărtiile de identitate.
Arahtatz-mee hahrteeleh deh eedenteetahteh.

330
↑
343

HEALTH

Pharmacy

344 **Do you have anything for a stomachache/headache/sore throat/toothache?**
Puteți să-mi dați ceva pentru dureri de stomac/dureri de cap/dureri în gât/dureri de dinți?
Pootetz sah-mee datz chehva pentroo doorehree deh stomac/doorehree deh cap/doorehree un gut/doorehree deh deentz?

345 **I need something for diarrhoea (diarrhea)/constipation/a cold/a cough/insect bites/sunburn/travel (motion) sickness.**
Am nevoie de un medicament contra diareei/constipației/răcelii/tusei/mușcăturilor de insecte/arsurilor de soare/răului de călătorie.
Am nevowyeh deh oon medicament contra deeyareh-ee/consteepatzee-ay/rachehlee/toosay/mooshcatooreelor deh insecteh/arsooreelor deh swahreh/rahvlui deh cahlahtorieh.

346 **How much/how many do I take?**
Ce cantitate/câte iau?
Cheh cantitahteh/cuteh yow?

347 **How often do I take it/them?**
Cât de des iau medicamentul?
Cut deh des yow medeecamentool?

348 **How much does it cost?**
Cât costă
Cut costah

349 **Can you recommend a good doctor/dentist?**
Puteți să-mi recomandați un doctor/dentist bun?
Pootetz sah-mee rehcomandatz oon doctor/denteest boon?

350 **Is it suitable for children?**
Este indicat pentru copii?
Esteh eendeecat pentroo copee?

Doctor

351 **I have a pain here/in my arm/leg/chest/stomach.**
Am o durere aici/în braț/picior/piept/stomac.
Am oh doorehreh aich/un bratz/peechior/pee-ept/stomac.

352 **Please call a doctor, this is an emergency.**
Chemați vă rog un doctor de urgență.
Kehmatz vah rohg oon doctor deh oordjentzah.

353 **I would like to make an appointment to see a doctor.**
Vreau să văd un doctor.
Vreh-ow sah vahd oon doctor.

354 **I am diabetic/pregnant.**
Sânt diabetic/însărcinată.
Sunt deeyabetic/unsahrcheenatah.

355 I need a prescription for . . .
Dați-mi vă rog o rețetă pentru . . .
Datz-mee vah rohg oh retzehtah pentroo . . .

356 Can you give me something to ease the pain?
Puteți să-mi dați ceva contra durerilor?
Pootetz sa-mee datz chehva contra doorehreelor?

357 I am/he is/she is allergic to penicillin.
Sânt alergic/el este alergic/ea este alergică la penicilină
Sunt alehrzheek/el esteh alerzheek/ eya esteh alerzheekah la peneecheeleenah

358 Does this hurt?
Doare?
Dwareh?

359 You must/he must/she must go to hospital.
Trebuie să mergeți/el/ea trebuie să meargă la spital.
Trebweh sah mehrdjetz/el/eya trebooyeh sah meyargah la spital.

360 Take these once/twice /three times a day.
Luați medicamentul o dată/de două ori/de trei ori pe zi.
Lowatz medeecamentool oh datah/ deh dowah oree/deh tray oree peh zee.

361 I am/he is/she is taking this medication.
Iau/el ia/ea ia acest medicament.
Yow/el ya/eya ya achest medeecament.

362 I have medical insurance.
Am asigurare medicală.
Am aseegoorareh medeecalah.

Dentist

363 I have toothache.
Am o durere de dinți.
Am oh doorehreh deh deentz.

364 My filling has come out.
Am pierdut o plombă.
Am peeyerdoot oh plombah.

365 I do/do not want to have an injection first.
Vreau/nu vreau un anestetic.
Vreh-aoo/noo vreh-aoo oon anestetik.

EMERGENCIES

366 Help!
Ajutor!
Azhootor!

367 Call an ambulance/a doctor/ the police!
Chemați salvarea/doctorul/ poliția.
Kehmatz salvareya/doctorool/ politzia.

368 I have had my travellers' cheques (travelers' checks)/ credit cards/purse/handbag/ rucksack (knapsack)/ luggage/wallet stolen.

Mi s-au furat cecurile de călătorie/cărţile de credit/ portmoneul/geanta/rucsacul/ valiza/portofelul.

Mee saow foorat cecooreeleh deh calatoreeyeh/cartzeeleh deh credit/ portmoneyool/djeyanta/ rooksacool/valeeza/portofelool.

369 Can you help me, I have lost my daughter/son?

Vreţi să mă ajutaţi vă rog? Mi-am pierdut fetiţa/băiatul.

Vretz sah mah azhootatz vah rohg? Mee-am peeyerdoot fetitza/ bye-atool.

370 Please go away/leave me alone.

Vă rog plecaţi de aici. Lăsaţi-mă în pace.

Vah rohg plecatz deh aich. Lasatz-mah un pacheh.

371 Fire!

Foc!

Foc!

372 I want to contact the British/ American/Canadian/Irish/ Australian/New Zealand/ South African consulate.

Vreau să contactez consulatul britanic/american/canadian/ irlandez/australian/neo zeelandez/sud african.

Vreyau sah contactez consoolatool britaneek/americahn/canadiahn/ eerlandez/owstraliahn/neyo zehlandez/sood africahn.

ROMANIAN

368
↕
372

Introduction

Castilian Spanish, the official form of the language, is spoken all over Spain. Although some regions have their own official languages (Catalan in Catalonia and the Balearic Islands, Galego in Galicia and Basque in parts of the north-east, all of which are separate languages and not dialects of Spanish), Spanish will be understood everywhere. In the popular tourist areas English is also widely understood by people working in tourist-related trades..

If using a Spanish dictionary, phone directory or other alphabetical listing, remember that words beginning with 'ch' come after all the other 'c's, and words starting with 'll' after all the other 'l's.

S P A N I S H

Addresses for travel and tourist information

UK: *Spanish National Tourist Office*, 57 St James's St, London SW1A 1LD; tel: (0171) 499 0901.

USA: *Spanish National Tourist Office*, 665 Fifth Ave, New York, NY 10022; tel: (212) 759-8822.

ESSENTIALS

ALPHABET

A	B
a	*be*
C	CH
ce	*che*
D	E
de	*e*
F	G
efey	*ge*
H	I
atchey	*ee latina*
J	K
hota	*ka*
L	LL
eley	*elyey*
M	N
emey	*eney*
Ñ	O
enyey	*o*
P	Q
pe	*cu*
R	RR
ere	*erre*
S	T
eseh	*te*
U	V
oo	*ubey*
W	X
ubey doble	*ekees*
Y	Z
ee greeayga	*theta*

Basic Words and Phrases

1. **Yes**   **No**
   Si   No
   Si   *noh*

2. **Please**   **Thank you**
   Por favor   Gracias
   Por fabor   *Gratheeas*

3. **That's O.K.**   **Perhaps**
   De acuerdo   Quizá
   Dey acwerdo   *Keetha*

4. **To**   **From**
   a   desde/de
   a   *desdey/dey*

5. **Here**   **There**
   Aquí   Allí
   akee   *ayee*

6. **None**   **Also**
   Ninguno/a   También
   Ningoono/a   *Tambeeyen*

7. **How?**   **When?**
   ¿Cómo?   ¿Cuándo?
   como   *cwandoe*

8. **What?**   **Why?**
   ¿Qué?   ¿Por qué?
   kay   *porkay*

9. **I don't understand.**
   No entiendo.
   Noh enteeyendo.

10. **I don't speak Spanish.**
    No hablo español.
    Noh ahblo espanyol.

11. **Do you speak English?**
    ¿Habla usted inglés?
    Ahbla oosteth eengless?

288

12 **Can you please write it down?**
Lo puede escribir, por favor?
Lo pwedeh escreebeer, porr abor?

13 **Can you please speak more slowly?**
Quiere usted hablar más despacio?
Keyerehh oosteth ablar mas despathio?

14 **How much does it/this cost?**
Cuánto cuesta?
Kwanto kwesta?

Days

15 **Monday** **Tuesday**
Lunes Martes
Loones *Martes*

16 **Wednesday** **Thursday**
Miércoles Jueves
Meeyercoles *Hooebes*

17 **Friday** **Saturday**
Viernes Sábado
Beeyernes *Sabadoe*

18 **Sunday** **Morning**
Domingo Mañana
Domeengo *Manyana*

19 **Afternoon** **Evening**
Tarde Noche
Tardey *Nochey*

20 **Night** **Week**
Noche Semana
Nochey *Semanna*

21 **Yesterday** **Tomorrow**
Ayer Mañana
Ayer *Manyana*

Numbers

22 **Zero** **One**
Cero Uno
Theroe *Oono*

23 **Two** **Three**
Dos Tres
Dos *Tres*

24 **Four** **Five**
Cuatro Cinco
Cwatro *Thinco*

25 **Six** **Seven**
Seis Siete
Seys *Seeyetey*

26 **Eight** **Nine**
Ocho Nueve
Ocho *Nwebey*

27 **Ten** **Eleven**
Diez Once
Deeyeth *Onthey*

28 **Twelve** **Thirteen**
Doce Trece
Dothey *Trethey*

29 **Fourteen** **Fifteen**
Catorce Quince
Catorthey *Keeyenthe*

30 **Sixteen** **Seventeen**
Dieciséis Diecisiete
Deeyetheeseys *Deeyetheeseeyetey*

31 **Eighteen** **Nineteen**
Dieciocho Diecinueve
Deeyetheoocho *Deeyetheenwebey*

32 **Twenty** **Twenty-one**
Veinte Veintiuno
Beintey *Beinteoono*

S
P
A
N
I
S
H

12
↑
32

33 **Twenty-two** **Thirty**
Veintidós Treinta
Beintedos *Treinta*

34 **Forty** **Fifty**
Cuarenta Cincuenta
Cwarenta *Thincwenta*

35 **Sixty** **Seventy**
Sesenta Setenta
Sesenta *Setenta*

36 **Eighty** **Ninety**
Ochenta Noventa
Ochenta *Nobenta*

37 **One hundred** **Five hundred**
Cien Quinientos
Thien *Keyneeyentos*

38 **One thousand** **One million**
Mil Un millón
Mil *Oon mellion*

Time

39 **9.00**
Las nueve
Nwebey

40 **9.05**
Las nueve y cinco
Nwebey ee thinco

41 **9.10**
Las nueve y diez
Nwebey ee deeyeth

42 **9.15**
Las nueve y cuarto
Nwebey ee quarto

43 **9.20**
Las nueve y veinte
Nwebey ee beinte

44 **9.25**
Las nueve y veinticinco
Nwebey ee beintethinco

45 **9.30**
Las nueve y media
Nwebey ee medeea

46 **9.35**
Las diez menos veinticinco
Deeyeth menos beinteethinco

47 **9.40**
Las diez menos veinte
Deeyeth menos beinte

48 **9.45**
Las diez menos cuarto
Deeyeth menos quarto

49 **9.50**
Las diez menos diez
Deeyeth menos deeyeth

50 **9.55**
Las diez menos cinco
Deeyeth menos thinco

51 **12.00/Midday/**
Midnight
Las doce/Mediodía/
Medianoche
Las dothe/medeeodeea/
medeeanoche

52 **What time is it?**
¿Qué hora es?
¿Kay ora es

53 **It is . . .**
Son las . . .
Son las . . .

Airport

54 **Excuse me, where is the check-in desk for . . . airline?**
¿Perdone, dónde está la facturación de la línea . . ?
Perdoneh, dondeh estah el mostrador deh faktoorathion deh la leenya . . ?

55 **What is the boarding gate/ time for my flight?**
¿Por qué puerta/a qué hora sale mi vuelo?
Porr keh pwerta/ah keh ora saleh mee bwehlo?

56 **How long is the delay likely to be?**
¿Cuánto lleva de retraso, aproximadamente?
Kwanto llieba deh rehtraso, aproksimadamenteh?

57 **Where is the duty-free shop?**
¿Dónde está el duty free?
Dondeh esta el duty free?

58 **Which way is the baggage reclaim?**
¿Por dónde se va a la recogida de equipajes?
Porr dondeh seh ba ah rekoheeda deh ekeypahess?

59 **Where can I get the bus to the city centre?**
¿De dónde sale el autobús al centro?
Deh dondeh saleh el outoboos al thentro?

Train Station

60 **Where is the ticket office/ information desk?**
¿Dónde está la taquilla de billetes/la ventanilla de información?
¿Donde estaa la taakeellia dey beellietes/la bentaaneellia dey informatheeon?

61 **Which platform does the train to . . . depart from?**
¿De qué andén sale el tren para . . ?
¿Deke anden sale el tren para . . ?

62 **Where is platform . . ?**
¿Dónde está el andén . . ?
¿Donde esta el anden . . ?

63 **When is the next train to . . ?**
¿A qué hora sale el próximo tren para . . ?
¿A key ora sale el proxseemo tren para . . ?

64 **Is there a later train to . . ?**
¿Hay un tren más tarde para . . ?
¿Eye oon tren mass tarde para . . ?

Port

65 **How do I get to the port?**
¿Cómo se va al puerto?
¿Como se ba al pooerto?

66 **When is the next sailing to . . ?**
¿A qué hora zarpa el próximo transbordador para . . ?
¿A kay ora tharpa el proxeemo transbordador para?

S
P
A
N
I
S
H

54
↑
66

291

⁶⁷ **Can I catch an earlier ferry with this ticket?**
¿Puedo coger un ferry más temprano con este billete?
Pwedo coherr oon ferry mas temprano kon esteh billieteh?

Notices and Signs

⁶⁸ **Coche restaurante**
Koche restaorante
Buffet (Dining) Car

⁶⁹ **Autobús**
Awtoeboos
Bus

⁷⁰ **Agua potable/Agua no potable**
Agwa potable/agwa no potable
Drinking/Non-drinking water

⁷¹ **Entrada**
Entrada
Entrance

⁷² **Salida**
Saleeda
Exit

⁷³ **Información**
Informatheeon
Information

⁷⁴ **Consigna**
Consigna
Left Luggage (Baggage Claim)

⁷⁵ **Consigna automática**
Consigna awtomateeka
Luggage Lockers

⁷⁶ **Oficina de Correos**
Ofeetheena de korreos
Post Office

⁷⁷ **Vía**
Veea
Platform

⁷⁸ **Estación de trenes**
Estatheeon de tren
Railway (Railroad) Station

⁷⁹ **Aeropuerto**
Aehropwerto
Airport

⁸⁰ **Puerto**
Pwerto
Port

⁸¹ **Restaurante**
Restaoorante
Restaurant

⁸² **Fumadores/No fumadores**
Foomadoores/no foomadoores
Smoking/Non-smoking

⁸³ **Teléfono**
Telephono
Telephone

⁸⁴ **Taquilla de billetes**
Takeellia de beellietes
Ticket Office

⁸⁵ **Facturación**
Faktoorathion
Check-in Desk

⁸⁶ **Horario**
Orareeo
Timetable (Schedule)

⁸⁷ **Servicios**
Serbeetheeos
Toilets (Restrooms)

⁸⁸ **Caballeros**
Kaballieros

S
P
A
N
I
S
H

67
↕
88

292

Gentlemen

89 Señoras
Senyoras
Ladies'

90 Tranvía
Tranbeea
Tram (Streetcar)

91 Metro
Metro
Underground (Subway)

92 Sala de espera
Sala de espera
Waiting Room

Buying a Ticket

**93 I would like a first-class/
second-class single (one-
way)/return (round-trip)
ticket to . . .**
Quisiera un billete de primera
clase/de segunda clase/de ida/
de ida y vuelta a . . .
*Keyseeyera oon beelliete de premera
clase/dey segoonda clase/dey eeda/
dey eeda ee bwelta a . . .*

**94 Is my rail pass valid on this
train?**
Puedo usar mi pase en este
tren/ferry/autobús?
*Pwedo usar mee pasey en esteh
tren/ferry/outoboos?*

**95 I would like an aisle/window
seat.**
Me gustaría un asiento junto al
pasillo/de ventanilla.

*Me goosetareea oon aseeyento
hoontee al paseellio/de
bentaneellya.*

**96 No smoking/smoking,
please.**
No fumadores/fumadores, por
favor.
*No foomadoores/foomadoores, por
farbor*

**97 We would like to sit
together.**
Nos gustaría sentarnos juntos.
*Nos goosetareea sentarnos
hoontos.*

**98 I would like to make a seat
reservation?**
Quisiera reservar una plaza.
Keyseeyera rehzerbar oona platha.

**99 I would like to reserve a
couchette/sleeper for one
person/two people/for my
family.**
Quisiera hacer una reserva en el
coche-literas/coche-camas para
una persona/dos personas/mi
familia.
*Keyseeyera ather oona resserba en
el koche-literas/koche-kama para
oona persawna/dos persawnas/
mee fameleeya.*

**100 I would like to reserve a
cabin.**
Quisiera reservar un
camarote.
*Keyseeyera rehzerbar oon
kamarote.*

S
P
A
N
I
S
H

89
↑
100

293

Timetables (Schedules)

101 **Llegada**
Yeygada
Arrival

102 **Para en**
Para en
Calls (stops) at

103 **Servicio de restauración**
Serbeetheeo dey restawratheeon
Catering Service

104 **Transbordo en**
Transbordoe en
Change at

105 **Correspondencia**
Correespondenthia
Connection

106 **Diario**
Deeareeo
Daily

107 **Cada 40 minutos**
Kada cwarenta menootos
Every 40 Minutes

108 **Primera clase**
Preemera clase
First-class

109 **Cada hora**
Kada ora
Hourly

110 **Se recomienda reservar plaza**
Se rekomeenda reserbar platha
Seat reservations are recommended

111 **Segunda clase**
Segoonda clase
Second-class

112 **Hay que pagar suplemento**
Eye ke pagar sueplemento
Supplement Payable

113 **Por**
Beea
Por

Luggage

114 **How much will it cost to send (ship) my luggage in advance?**
¿Cuánto costaría enviar mi equipaje por adelantado?
¿Cwantoe costareea enbeear mee ekeypahe por adelantado?

115 **here is the left luggage (baggage claim) office?**
¿Dónde está la consigna?
¿Donde esta la consinya?

116 **What time do you open/close?**
¿A qué hora abren/cierran?
¿a kay ora abren/theeyeran?

117 **Where are the luggage trolleys (carts)?**
¿Dónde están los carretillas para el equipaje?
¿Donde estan las karretillias para el ekeypahe?

118 **Where are the lockers?**
Dónde está la consigna automática?
Dondeh esta la konseegna awtoematika?

119 I have lost my locker key.
He perdido la llave de la consigna automática.
Ey perdeedo la lliabe de la consigna awtoematecar.

On Board

120 Is this seat taken?
¿Está libre este asiento?
¿Esta leebre este aseeyento?

121 Excuse me, you are sitting in my reserved seat.
Perdone, pero se ha sentado en mi asiento reservado.
Perdone pero sey a sentado en mee aseeyento resserbado.

122 Which station is this?
¿Qué estación es esta?
¿Kay estatheeon es esta?

123 What time is this train/bus/ferry/flight due to arrive/depart?
A qué hora sale/llega este tren/autobús/vuelo?
Ah keh ora saleh/lliega esteh tren/outoboos/bwelo?

124 Will you wake me just before we arrive?
¿Le importaría despertarme un poco antes de llegar?
¿Ley inportareea despertarme oon poco antes de lliegar?

Customs and Passports

125 Los pasaportes, por favor!
¡Los pasaportes por farbor!
Passports, please!

126 I have nothing to declare. I have wine/spirits (alcohol)/tobacco to declare.
No tengo nada que declarar.
Tengo vino/licores/tabaco que declarar.
No tengo nada kay declarar.
Tengo beeno/leekores/tabaco kay declarar.

127 I shall be staying for . . . days/weeks/months.
Me quedaré por . . . días/semanas/meses.
Mey keydarey por . . . deeas/semanas/messes.

AT THE TOURIST OFFICE

128 Do you have a map of the town/area?
¿Tiene un mapa de la ciudad/de la zona?
¿Teeyene oon mapa de la theeoodath/de la thona?

129 Can I reserve accommodation here?
¿Puedo reservar alojamiento aquí?
¿Pwedo reserbar alohameeyento akee?

130 Do you have a list of accommodation?
¿Tiene una lista de hoteles?
Teeyene oona leesta deh oteles?

295

ACCOMMODATION

Hotels

131 I have a reservation in the name of . . .
Tengo una reserva a nombre de . . .
Tengo oona resserba a nonbre dey . . .

132 I wrote to/faxed/telephoned you last month/last week in . . .
El mes pasado/la semana pasada les escribí/envié un fax/llamé por teléfono
El mes passado/la sehmanna passada les eskreebee/embeeyeh oon faks/lliameh porr tehlehfono.

133 Do you have any rooms free?
¿Tienen habitaciones?
Teeyenen abeetathiones?

134 I would like to reserve a single/double room with/without bath/shower.
Quisiera reservar una habitación individual/doble con/sin baño/ducha.
keyseeyera resserbar oona abeetatheeon indeebeedooal/doeble con/sin banyo/doocha.

135 I would like bed and breakfast/(room and) half board/(room and) full board.
Me gustaría cama y desayuno/media pensión/pensión completa.
Mey goosetareea kama ee desayuno/medeea penseeon/penseeon conpleta.

136 How much is it per night?
¿Cuánto cuesta por noche?
¿Cwantoe cwesta por noche?

137 Is breakfast included?
¿Está el desayuno incluido?
¿Esta el desayoonoh inclueedo?

138 May I see the room?
¿Puedo ver la habitación?
¿Pwedo ber la abeetatheeon?

139 Do you have any cheaper rooms?
¿Tienen habitaciones más baratas?
¿Teeyenen abeetatheeones mass baratas?

140 I would like to take the room.
Me gustaría ocupar la habitación.
Mey goosetareea ocoopar la abeetatheeon.

141 I would like to stay for . . . nights.
Quisiera quedarme por . . . noches.
Keyseeyera keydarme por . . . noches.

142 The shower/light/tap doesn't work.
La ducha/luz/el grifo no funciona.
La dootcha/looth/el greefoh noh foonthiona.

SPANISH

131
↕
142

296

143 At what time/where is breakfast served?

¿A qué hora/dónde se sirve el desayuno?

¿A kay ora/donde sey seervey el desayoono?

144 What time do I have to check-out?

¿A qué hora debo desalojar la habitación?

¿A kay ora debo desalohar la abeetatheeon?

145 Can I have the key to room number?

¿Me quiere dar la llave de la habitación número . . ?

Meh keyereh dahrr la lliabeh deh la abeetathion noomero . . ?

146 My room number is . . .

Mi habitación es el número . . .

me abeetatheeon es el noomero . . .

147 Do you accept travellers' cheques/Eurocheques/credit cards?

¿Aceptan cheques de viaje/ Eurocheques/tarjetas de crédito?

Atheptan tchekes deh biaheh/ ehwrotchekes/tarhetas deh credeeto?

148 May I have the bill please?

¿Por favor me da la cuenta?

¿Por farbor meh da la cwenta?

149 Excuse me, I think there is a mistake in this bill.

Oiga, me parece que la cuenta está mal.

Oyga, meh parethe keh la kwenta esta mal.

Youth Hostels

150 How much is a dormitory bed per night?

¿Cuánto cuesta una cama por noche?

¿Cwantoe cwesta oona kama por noche?

151 I am/am not an HI member.

Soy/no soy miembro de HI.

Soy/no soy meeyembro dey hachey ee.

152 May I use my own sleeping bag?

¿Puedo utilizar mi propio saco de dormir?

¿Pwedo ooteeleethar mee propeeo saco de dormeer?

153 What time do you lock the doors at night?

¿A qué hora cierran por la noche?

¿A kay ora theeyerran por la noche?

Camping

154 May I camp here for the night/two nights?

¿Puedo acampar aquí por esta noche/dos noches?

¿Pwedo acanpar akee por esta noche/dos noches?

S
P
A
N
I
S
H

143
↑
154

¹⁵⁵ Where can I pitch my tent?
¿Dónde puedo montar la tienda?
¿Donde pwedo montar la teeyenda?

¹⁵⁶ How much does it cost for one night/week?
¿Cuánto cuesta por noche/semana?
¿Cwantoee cwesta por noche/semana?

¹⁵⁷ Where can we park our caravan?
¿Dónde podemos aparcar la caravana?
Dondeh pohdemos aparkahrr la carabana?

¹⁵⁸ Where are the washing facilities?
¿Dónde están los aseos?
¿Donde estan los aseos?

¹⁵⁹ Is there a restaurant/supermarket/swimming pool on site/nearby?
¿Hay algún restaurante/supermercado/alguna piscina por aquí/cerca?
¿Eye algoon restawrante/suepermerkadoe/algoona pistheena por akee/therca?

¹⁶⁰ Do you have a safety deposit box?
¿Tienen cajafuerte?
¿Teeyenen kahafwerte?

EATING AND DRINKING

Cafés and Bars

¹⁶¹ I would like a cup of/two cups of/another coffee/tea.
Quisiera una taza de/dos tazas de/otra taza de café/té.
Keyseeyera oona tatha dey/dos tathas/otra tatha dey kafey/te.

¹⁶² With/without milk/sugar.
Con/sin leche/azucar.
Con/seen leche/athoocar.

¹⁶³ I would like a bottle/glass/two glasses of mineral water/red wine/white wine, please.
Quisiera una botella/un vaso/dos vasos de agua mineral/de vino tinto/de vino blanco, por favor.
Keyseeyera oona botellia/oon baso/dos basos dey agwa meneral/dey beeno tintoe/dey beeno blanco, por farbor.

¹⁶⁴ I would like a beer/two beers, please.
Quisiera una cerveza/dos cervezas, por favor.
Keyseeyera oona therbeytha/dos therbeythas, por farbor.

¹⁶⁵ May I have some ice?
¿Pueden ponerme hielo?
¿Pweden ponerme eeyelloe?

¹⁶⁶ Do you have any matches/cigarettes/cigars?
¿Tienen cerillas/cigarrillos/puros?

*¿Teeyenen thereellias/
theegarrellios/pooros?*

Restaurants

**167 Can you recommend a good/
inexpensive restaurant in this
area?**
¿Puede recomendarme un buen/
restaurante barato en la zona?
*¿Pwede recomendarme oon bwen/
restaurante barato en la thona?*

**168 I would like a table for . . .
people.**
Quisiera una mesa para . . .
personas.
*Keyseeyera oona mesa para . . .
personas.*

**169 Do you have a non-smoking
area?**
¿Tiene una zona reservada para
no fumadores?
*Teeyene oona thona rehzerbada
para noh foomadores?*

170 Waiter/Waitress!
¡Camarero/Camarera!
¡Camareroe/camarera!

**171 Do you have a set menu/
children's menu/wine list?**
¿Tienen menú del Día/menú
para niños/ la carta de vinos?
*¿Teeyenen menoo del deea/menoo
para neenios/la carta dey beenos?*

**172 Do you have any vegetarian
dishes, please?**
¿Dan comidas vegetarianas, por
favor?

*¿Dan comeedas behetareanas, por
farbor?*

**173 Are there any local
specialities?**
¿Tienen especialidades del
lugar?
*¿Teeyenen espethialeedades del
loogar?*

174 Are vegetables included?
¿Están incluidas las verduras?
¿Estan eenclooeedas las berdooras?

**175 Could I have it well-cooked/
medium/rare please?**
Por favor, la carne bien cocida/
al punto/roja.
*Porr fabor, la kahrrne beeyen
kotheeda/al poontoh/roha.*

**176 What does this dish consist
of?**
¿Qué contiene este plato?
¿Kay conteeyene este platoe?

**177 I would like the set menu,
please.**
Quisiera el menú del día, por
favor.
*Keyseeyera el menoo del deea, por
farbor.*

178 We have not been served yet.
Todavía no nos han servido.
Toedabeea no nos an serbeedoe.

**179 Excuse me, this is not what I
ordered.**
Perdone, no he pedido esto.
Perdoneh, noh eh pedeedo esto.

S
P
A
N
I
S
H

167
↑
179

18 **May I have some/some more bread/water/coffee/tea?**
¿Podría traerme/más pan/agua/café/té?
¿Pordreea trayerme/mass pan/agwa/kafey/te?

181 **May I have the bill, please?**
¿Podría traerme la cuenta por favor?
¿Pordreea trayerme la cwenta por farbor?

182 **Does this bill include service?**
¿Está incluido el servicio en la cuenta?
¿Esta inclueedoe el serbeetheeo en la cwenta?

183 **Do you accept travellers' cheques (travelers' checks)/Eurocheques/MasterCard/US dollars?**
¿Aceptan cheques de viaje/Eurocheques/MasterCard/dólares americanos?
¿Atheptan chekes de beeahe/eurochekes/MasterCard/doelares amereecarnos?

184 **Can I have a receipt, please?**
¿Me quiere dar un recibo, por favor?
¿Meh keyereh dahrr oon resgwardo, porr fabor?

185 **Where is the toilet (restroom), please?**
¿Dónde están los servicios, por favor?
¿Donde estan los serbeetheeos, por farbor?

On the Menu

186 **First courses**
Entradas
Entradas

187 **Soups**
Sopas
Sohpas

188 **Main courses**
Platos principales
Platos preentheepales

189 **Fish dishes**
Pescados
Peskados

190 **Meat dishes**
Carnes
Kahrrnes

191 **Vegetarian dishes**
Platos vegetarianos
Platos behetaryanos

192 **Cheese**
Queso
Kehso

193 **Desserts**
Postres
Postres

194 **Specialities**
Especialidades
Espetheealeedades

GETTING AROUND

Public Transport

195 **Where is the bus stop/coach station/nearest metro (subway) station?**

¿Dónde está la parada de
autobuses/la estación de
autobuses/la estación de metro
más cercana?
*¿Donde esta la parrada dey
awtoebooses/la estatheeon dey
awtoebooses/la estatheeon dey
metro mass thercana?*

196 When is the next/last bus
to . . ?
¿A qué hora sale el próximo
autobús/el último autobús
para . . ?
*¿A kay ora sale el proxseemo
awtoeboos/el ultimo awtoeboos
para . . ?*

197 How much is the fare to the
city centre (downtown)/
railway (railroad) station/
airport?
¿Cuánto cuesta el billete hasta el
centro/la estación de trenes/el
aeropuerto?
*¿Cwantoe cwesta el beelliete asta el
thentro/la estatheeon de trenes/el
aeropwerto?*

198 Will you tell me when to get
off?
¿Podría decirme cuando tendré
que bajar?
*¿Poordreea detheerme cwandoe
tendray kay bahar?*

199 Does this bus go to . . ?
¿Es este el autobús de . . ?
¿Es este el awtoeboos de . . ?

200 Which number bus goes
to . . ?
¿Cuál es el número del autobús
que va a . . ?
*¿Cwal es el noomero del awtoeboos
kay ba a . . ?*

201 May I have a single (one-
way)/return (round-trip)/day
ticket/multi-journey ticket?
¿Quisiera un billete de ida/de
ida y vuelta/de día/tarjeta
*¿Keyseeyera oon beelliete dey eeda/
dey eda ee bwelta/dey dea/
tarheyta?*

Taxis

202 I would like to go to . . .
How much will it cost?
Quisiera ir a . . . ¿Cuánto me
costaría?
*Keyseeyera eer a . . . ¿cwantoe
me costarea?*

203 Please stop here.
Por favor pare aquí.
Por farbor parey akee.

204 I would like to order a taxi
today/tomorrow/at 2pm to
go from . . . to . . .
Quisiera reservar un taxi para
hoy/mañana/a las dos de la
tarde para ir de . . . a . . .
*Keyseeyera resserbar oon taxsee
para oy/manyana/a las dos de la
tarde para eer dey . . . a . . .*

**S
P
A
N
I
S
H**

**196
↑
204**

Asking the Way

205 Excuse me, do you speak English?
Perdone, ¿habla usted inglés?
Perdoene, ¿abla oosteth ingles?

206 Excuse me, is this the right way to . . ?
Perdone, ¿por aquí se va a . . ?
Perdoneh, ¿porr akee seh bah ah . . ?

207 . . . the cathedral/the tourist information office/the castle/the old town.
. . . la catedral/oficina de turismo/el castillo/el casco antiguo.
. . . la katehdral/offeetheena deh toorismoe/el kasteellio/el kasko antiguo.

208 Can you tell me the way to the railway (railroad) station/bus station/taxi rank (stand)/city centre (downtown)/beach?
¿Puede decirme cómo se va a la estación de trenes/estación de autobuses/parada de taxis/al centro de la ciudad/a la playa?
¿Pwede detheerme como sey ba a la estatheeon de trenes/estatheeon dey awtoebooses/parada de taxsis/al thentroe de la theeoodath/a la playa?

209 First/second left/right/straight ahead.
Primera/segunda a la izquierda/derecha/todo seguido.

Preemera/segoonda a la eethkeyerda/derecha/toedoe segeedoe.

210 Where is the nearest police station/post office?
¿Dónde está la comisaría de policía/la oficina de correos más cercana?
¿Donde esta la comeesarea dey poleetheea/la ofeetheena dey coreos mass thercarna?

211 Is it far?
¿Está lejos?
¿Esta lehos?

212 Do I need to take a taxi/catch a bus?
¿Necesito coger un taxi/un autobús?
¿Netheeseeto coher oon taxsee/oon aootoeboos?

213 Can you point to it on my map?
¿Puede señalármelo en el mapa?
¿Pwede senyarlarmeloe en el mapa?

214 Thank you for your help.
Muchas gracias por su ayuda.
Moochas gratheeas poor soo ayuda.

SIGHTSEEING

215 Where is the Tourist Information office?
¿Dónde está la oficina de información y turismo?
¿Donde esta la ofeetheena de informatheeon ee toorismo?

216 Where is the cathedral/
church/museum?
¿Dónde está la catedral/la
iglesia/el museo?
*¿Donde esta la catedral/la
igleeseea/el mooseo?*

217 How much is the entrance
(admission) charge?
¿Cuánto cuesta la entrada?
¿Cwantoe cwesta la entrada?

218 Is there a discount for
children/students/senior
citizens?
¿Tienen descuento los niños/los
estudiantes/los jubilados?
*¿Teeyenen descwento los neenyos/
los estoodeeantes/los hubeelados?*

219 What time does the next
guided tour start?
¿A qué hora empieza la
siguiente guía?
*¿A kay ora enpeeyetha la
seegeeyente geea?*

220 One/two adults/children,
please.
Uno/dos adultos/niños, por
favor.
*Oonoh/dos adooltos/neenios
porfarbor.*

221 May I take photographs
here?
Puedo sacar fotos?
Pwedo sakar fotos?

ENTERTAINMENT

222 Can you recommend a good
bar/nightclub?
¿Puede recomendarme un bar
bueno/una discoteca buena?
*¿Pwede recomendarme oon bar
bweno/oona discoteca bwena?*

223 Do you know what is on at
the cinema (playing at the
movies)/theatre at the
moment?
¿Sabe lo que están dando en el
cine/en el teatro en estos
momentos?
*¿Sabe lo key estan dando en el
theenne/en el tayatro en estos
momentos?*

224 I would like to book
(purchase) . . . tickets for the
matinee/evening
performance on Monday.
Quisiera reservar . . . entradas
para la sesión de tarde/de noche
del lunes.
*Keyseeyera resserbar . . . entradas
para la seseeon dey tarde dey noche
del loones.*

225 What time does the film/
performance start?
¿A qué hora empieza la sesión/
la función?
*¿A key ora enpeeyetha la seseeon/
la foontheeon?*

S
P
A
N
I
S
H

216
↑
225

303

MEETING PEOPLE

226 Hello/Goodbye.
Hola/adiós.
Ola/adeeos.

227 Good morning/good afternoon/good evening/goodnight.
Buenos días/buenas tardes/buenas noches.
Bwenos dee-ahs/bwenas tarrdess/bwenas notchess.

228 Pleased to meet you.
Encantado de conocerle.
Encantadoe dey conotherle.

229 How are you?
¿Cómo está usted?
¿Como esta oosteth?

230 Fine, thank you. And you?
Bien, gracias. Y usted?
Beeyen, grathias. Ee oosteth?

231 My name is . . .
Me llamo . . .
Meh lliamo . . .

232 This is my friend/boyfriend/girlfriend/husband/wife/brother/sister.
Este es mi amigo/novio/novia/marido/esposa/hermano/hermana.
Este es mee ameego/nobeeo/nobeea/mareedo/esposa/ermano/ermana.

233 Where are you travelling to?
¿A dónde viaja?
¿A donde beeaha?

234 I am/we are going to . . .

voy/vamos a . . .
Boy/bamos a . . .

235 How long are you travelling for?
¿Cuánto tiempo van a viajar?
¿Cwantoe teaempo ban a beahar?

236 Where do you come from?
¿De dónde es usted?
¿Dey donde es oosteth?

237 I am/we are from . . .
Soy/somos de . . .
Soy/somos . . .

238 We're on holiday.
Estamos de vacación.
Estamos deh bakathion.

239 This is our first visit here.
Es la primera vez que venimos aquí.
Es la preemera beth keh benimos akee.

240 Would you like/May I have a cigarette?
¿Quiere un cigarrillo/Me da un cigarillo?
¿Keyerey oon theegarrellio/Mey da oon theegarrellio?

241 I am sorry but I do not understand.
Lo siento pero no entiendo.
Loh siento pero no entiendo.

242 Please speak slowly.
Por favor hable despacio.
Por farbor abley despathio.

243 Do you mind if I smoke?
¿Le molesta si fumo?
¿Ley molesta see foomo?

S
P
A
N
I
S
H

226
↕
243

304

244 **Do you have a light?**
¿Tiene fuego?
¿Teeyene fwego?

245 **I am waiting for my husband/
wife/boyfriend/girlfriend.**
Estoy esperando a mi marido/
mujer/novio/novia.
*Estoy esperando a mee mareedo/
mooher/nobyoh/nobya.*

TRAVELLING WITH CHILDREN

246 **Do you have a high chair/
babysitting service/cot?**
¿Tienen sillas para bebés/
servicio de kanguro/cuna?
*¿Teeyenen seellias para bebes/
serbeetheeo de cangooro/coona?*

247 **Where is the nursery/
playroom?**
¿Dónde está la guardería/el
cuarto de niños?
*¿Donde esta la gwardereea/el
kwarto de neenyos?*

248 **Where can I warm the baby's
bottle?**
¿Dónde puedo calentar el
biberón?
¿Donde pwedo calentar el beeberron?

COMMUNICATIONS

Post

249 **How much will it cost to
send a letter/postcard/this
package to Britain/Ireland/
America/Canada/Australia/
New Zealand?**

¿Cuánto cuesta enviar esta
carta/postal/paquete a Gran
Bretaña/Irlanda/América/
Canadá/Australia/Nueva
Zelanda?
*¿Cwantoe cwesta enbeear esta
carta/pohstal/pakete a gran
bretannia/eerlandda/amereeca/
canada/awstralea/nweyba
theylanda?*

250 **I would like one stamp/two
stamps.**
Quisiera un sello/dos sellos.
Keyseeyera oon sellio/dos sellios.

251 **I'd like . . . stamps for
postcards to send abroad,
please.**
Quisiera . . . sellos para postales
al extranjero, por favor.
*Keysyera . . . sellios para postales
al estranhero, porr fabor.*

Phones

252 **I would like to make a
telephone call/reverse the
charges to (make a collect
call to) . . .**
Quisiera llamar por teléfono/
llamar a cobro revertido a . . .
*Keyseeyera lliamar por telephono/
lliamar a cobro rebertedo a . . .*

253 **Which coins do I need for
the telephone?**
¿Qué monedas necesito para el
teléfono?
*¿Kay monehdas netheseeto para el
telephono?*

254 The line is engaged (busy).
La línea está comunicando.
La leeneea esta comooneecando.

255 The number is . . .
El número es el . . .
El noomero es el . . .

256 Hello, this is . . .
Hola, habla . . .
Ola, abla . . .

257 May I speak to . . ?
Puedo hablar con . . ?
Pwedo ablar kon . . ?

258 He/She is not in at the
moment. Can you call back?
No está. ¿Quiere volver a llamar
más tarde?
*Noh esta. Keyereh bolber a lliamar
mas tarrdeh?*

MONEY

259 I would like to change these
travellers' cheques (travelers'
checks)/this currency/this
Eurocheque.
Quisiera cambiar estos cheques
de viaje/dinero/este
Eurocheque.
*Keyseeeyera canbeear estos chekes
de beeahe/denero/este eoorocheke.*

260 How much commission do
you charge (What is the
service charge)?
¿Qué comisión recargan?
¿Kay comeeseeon recargan?

261 Can I obtain money with my
MasterCard?

¿Puedo sacar dinero con la
tarjeta MasterCard?
*¿Pwedo sacar deenero con la
tarheta MasterCard?*

SHOPPING

Names of Shops and
Departments

262 Librería/Papelería
Leebreree-ah/paplehree-ah
Bookshop/Stationery

263 Joyería/Regalos
Hoyeree-ah/regalos
Jeweller's/Gifts

264 Zapatería
Thapatos
Shoe Shop

265 Ferretería
Ferretehree-ah
Hardware

266 Anticuario
Antikwaryo
Antiques

267 Peluquería (caballeros)/
(damas)
*Pelookeree-ah (kaballieros)/
(damas)*
Hairdressers (men's)/(women's

268 Estanco/Tabaquería
Estanko/Tabakeree-ah
Tobacconist

269 Panadería
Panaderee-ah
Baker's

²⁷⁰ **Supermercado**
Soopermerkado
Supermarket

²⁷¹ **Tienda de fotos**
Teeyenda deh fotos
Photoshop

²⁷² **Juguetería**
Hoogetehree-ah
Toys

²⁷³ **Agencia de viajes**
Ahenthya deh byahes
Travel Agent

²⁷⁴ **Artículos de tocador**
Arteekoolos deh tokador
Toiletries

²⁷⁵ **Discos**
Deeskos
Records

In the Shop

²⁷⁶ **What time do the shops open/close?**
¿A qué hora abren/cierran las tiendas?
¿A kay ora abren/theeyerran las teeyendas?

²⁷⁷ **Where is the nearest market?**
Dónde está el mercado más próximo?
Dondeh kayda el merkado mas proksimo?

²⁷⁸ **Can you show me the one in the window/this one?**
Quiere enseñarme el del escaparate/este?

Keyereh ensehniarmeh el del eskaparateh/esteh?

²⁷⁹ **Can I try this on?**
¿Puedo probarme esto?
¿Pwedo probarme esto?

²⁸⁰ **What size is this?**
¿Qué talla es esta?
¿Kay tallia es esta?

²⁸¹ **This is too large/too small/ too expensive.**
Es muy grande/muy pequeño/ muy caro.
Es mooy grandeh/mooy pekenio/ mooy karo.

²⁸² **Do you have any others?**
¿Tienen más?
¿Teeyenen mas?

²⁸³ **My size is . . .**
Ni número es el . . .
Mee noomero es el . . .

²⁸⁴ **Where is the changing room/ childrens/cosmetic/ ladieswear/menswear/food department?**
¿Dónde están los probadores/ niños/perfumería/señoras/ caballeros/sección de alimentos?
¿Donde estan los probadores/ neenyos/perfoomereea/senyoras/ caballieros/sectheeon dey alimentos?

²⁸⁵ **I would like . . .**
Me gustaría . . .
Meh goostaree-ah . . .

²⁸⁶ I would like a quarter of a kilo/half a kilo/a kilo of bread/ butter/cheese/ham/ tomatoes.
Quisiera un cuarto de kilo/ medio kilo/un kilo de pan/ mantequilla/queso/jamón/ tomates.
Keyseeyera oon cwarto dey kilo/ medio kilo/oon kilo dey pan/ mantekillia/keso/hamon/tomates.

²⁸⁷ How much is this?
¿Cuánto es?
¿Cwantoe es?

²⁸⁸ I'll take this one, thank you.
Me llevo éste.
Meh llievo esteh.

²⁸⁹ Do you have a carrier (shopping) bag?
¿Me da una bolsa por favor?
¿Meh da oona bolsa por farbor?

²⁹⁰ Do you have anything cheaper/larger/smaller/of better quality?
¿Tiene algo más barato/grande/ pequeño/de mejor calidad?
¿Teeyene algo mass baratto/ grande/pekenio/de mehor caleedath?

²⁹¹ I would like a film for this camera.
Quisiera un rollo para esta cámara.
Keyseeyera oon rollio para esta camara.

²⁹² I would like some batteries, the same size as this old one.
Quisiera pilas, del mismo tamaño que esta vieja.
Keyseeyera peelas, del mismo tamanio kay esta beeha.

²⁹³ Would you mind wrapping this for me, please?
¿Le importaría envolvermelo?
¿Le inportareea enbolbermelo?

²⁹⁴ Sorry, but you seem to have given me the wrong change.
Lo siento, pero no me ha dado la vuelta correcta.
Lo seeyento, pero no meh a dado la vwelta correcta.

MOTORING

Car Hire (Rental)

²⁹⁵ I have ordered (rented) a car in the name of . . .
Tengo un coche alquilado a nombre de . . .
Tengo oon koche alkeyladoe a nombre de . . .

²⁹⁶ How much does it cost to hire (rent) a car for one day/ two days/one week?
¿Cuánto cuesta alquilar un coche por un día/dos días/una semana?
¿Cwantoe cwesta alkeylar oon koche por oon deea/dos deeas/oona semanna?

²⁹⁷ Is the tank already full of petrol (gas)?

¿Está el depósito de gasolina lleno?

¿Esta el deposeytoe de gasoleena llieno?

298 Is insurance and tax included? ¿How much is the deposit?

¿Está incluido en el precio los impuestos y el seguro? ¿Cuánto hay que poner de señal?

¿Esta inclooeedoe en el pretheeo los inpwestoes ee el segooro, cwantoee eye kay poner de senial?

299 By what time must I return the car?

¿A qué hora debo entregar el coche?

¿A kay ora debo entregar el koche?

300 I would like a small/family car with a radio/cassette player.

Quisiera un coche pequeño/familiar con radio/casete.

Keyseeyera oon koche pekenio/familiar con radeeo/caset.

Asking the Way

301 Excuse me, can you help me please?

¿Perdone, me puede ayudar?

¿Perdoneh, meh pwedeh aiyoodahrr?

302 How do I reach the motorway/main road?

¿Por dónde se va a la autopista/carretera principal?

¿Porr dondeh seh ba a la outopeesta/karretehrra printhipal?

303 I think I have taken the wrong turning.

Creo que me he equivocado de camino.

Kreoh keh meh eh ekeebokado deh kameeno.

304 I am looking for this address.

Busco esta dirección.

Boosko esta deerekthion.

305 I am looking for the . . . hotel.

Busco el hotel . . .

Boosko el ohtel . . .

306 How far is it to . . . from here?

¿ . . queda muy lejos de aquí?

¿ . . kayda mooy lehos deh akee?

307 Carry straight on for . . . kilometres.

Siga derecho unos . . . kilómetros.

Seega deretcho oonos . . . keelometros.

308 Take the next turning on the right/left.

La próxima a la derecha/izquierda.

La proksima a la deretcha/eethkyerda.

309 Turn right/left at the next crossroads/traffic lights.

Tire a la derecha/izquierda en el próximo cruce/semáforo.

Teereh a la deretcha/eethkyerda en el proksimo crootheh/sehmaforo.

MOTORING

³¹⁰ You are going in the wrong
direction.
No se va por ahí.
Noh seh ba porr ah-ee.

Parking

³¹¹ How long can I park here?
¿Cuanto tiempo puedo aparcar
aquí?
*¿Kwanto teeyempo pwedo aparkar
akee?*

³¹² Is there a car park near here?
¿Hay un aparcamiento cerca de
aquí?
*¿Eye oon aparkameeyento therka
deh akee?*

³¹³ At what time does this car
park close?
¿ qué hora cierra este
aparcamiento?
*¿A keh ora thierra esteh
aparkameeyento?*

Signs and Notices

³¹⁴ One way.
Sentido único.
Senteedo ooneeko.

³¹⁵ No entry.
Prohibido el paso.
Proeebeedoh el passoh.

³¹⁶ No parking.
Prohibido aparcar
Proeebeedo aparcar.

³¹⁷ Detour (diversion)
Desvío
Desbeeyathion.

³¹⁸ Stop.
Alto
Alto

³¹⁹ Give way (yield).
Ceda el paso
Theda el paso

³²⁰ Slippery road.
Camino resbaladizo.
Kameeno resbaladeetho.

³²¹ No overtaking.
Prohibido adelantar
Proybeedo adelantar

At the Filling Station

³²² Unleaded (lead-free)/
Standard/Premium
Sin plomo/normal/extra
Seen plohmoh/normall/ekstra

³²³ Fill the tank please.
¿Me llena el tanque, por favor?
¿Meh lliena el tankeh porr fabor?

³²⁴ Do you have a road map of
this area?
¿Tiene un mapa de carreteras de
la zona?
*¿Teeyene oon mapa deh
karretehrras deh la thona?*

³²⁵ How much is the car-wash?
¿Cuánto cuesta el lavado?
¿Kwanto kwesta el labahdo?

Breakdowns

³²⁶ I've had a breakdown at . . .
El coche se ha averiado en . . .
*El cotcheh seh ah aberyado
en . . .*

327 I am on the road from . . .
to . . .
Estoy en la carretera de . . .
a . . .
Estoy en la karretehrra deh . . .
a . . .

328 I can't move the car. Can you
send a tow-truck?
El coche no se mueve. ¿Puede
enviar una grúa?
El cotcheh noh seh mwehbeh.
¿Pwedeh embeeyar oona groo-ah?

329 I have a flat tyre.
He tenido un pinchazo.
Eh tehneedo oom pintchatho.

330 The windscreen (windshield)
has smashed/cracked.
El parabrisas se ha hecho trizas/
se ha rajado.
El parabreesas seh ah etcho
treethas/seh ah rahado.

331 There is something wrong
with the engine/brakes/
lights/steering/gearbox/
clutch/exhaust.
El motor/los frenos/las luces/la
dirección/la caja de cambios/el
embrague/el escape no funciona
bien.
El motor/los frenos/las loothes/la
deerekthion/la caha deh cambyos/
el embrahge/el escape noh
foonthiona bien.

332 It's overheating.
Se sobrecalienta
Seh sobrekalienta.

333 It won't start.
No arranca.
Noh arranka

334 Where can I get it
repaired?
¿Dónde lo pueden arreglar?
¿Dondeh lo pweden arreglar?

335 Can you take me there?
¿Me puede llevar allí?
¿Meh pwedeh lliebar allyee?

336 Will it take long to fix?
¿Va a tardar mucho en
arreglarlo?
¿Ba a tardahrr mootcho en
arreglarlo?

337 How much will it cost?
¿Cuanto me va a cobrar?
¿Kwanto meh ba a kobrar?

Accidents

338 Can you help me? There has
been an accident.
¿Me puede ayudar? Ha habido
un accidente.
¿Meh pwedeh aiyoodahrr? Ah
ahbeedo oon akthidenteh.

339 Please call the police/an
ambulance.
Llame a la policía/ambulancia.
Lliameh a la poleethee-ah/
amboolanthia

340 Is anyone hurt?
¿Se ha lastimado alguién?
¿Seh ah lasteemado algyen?

S
P
A
N
I
S
H

327
↑
340

311

Traffic Offences

341 **I'm sorry, I didn't see the sign.**
Lo siento, no me fijé en la señal.
Lo seeyento, noh meh feeheh en el lehtrero.

342 **Must I pay a fine? How much?**
¿Tengo que pagar una multa? ¿Cuánto?
¿Tengo keh pagar oona moolta? ¿Kwanto?

343 **Show me your documents.**
Enséñeme sus documentos.
Ensehniemeh soos dokoomentos.

HEALTH

Pharmacy

344 **Do you have anything for a stomachache/headache/sore throat/toothache?**
¿Tienen algo para el dolor de estómago/cabeza/garganta/dientes?
¿Teeyenen algo para el doelor de estoemago/cabeetha/garganta deeyentes?

345 **I need something for diarrhoea (diarrhea)/constipation/a cold/a cough/insect bites/sunburn/travel (motion) sickness.**
Necesito algo contra la diarrea/el estreñimiento/el catarro/la tos/las picaduras de insectos/la quemadura del sol/el mareo.
Netheseeto algo contra la deeareea/el estrenyiemeeyento/el catarro/la tos/las peecadooras de insectos/la khemadoora del sol/el mareo.

346 **How much/how many do I take?**
¿Cuánto/cuántas tengo que tomar?
¿Cwantoe/cwantas tengo kay toemar?

347 **How often do I take it/them?**
¿Cada cuánto tiempo tengo que tomarlo/tomarlas?
¿Cada cwantoe teaenpo tengo kay toemarlo/toemarlas?

348 **How much does it cost?**
¿Cuánto cuesta?
¿Cwantoe cwesta?

349 **Can you recommend a good doctor/dentist?**
¿Puede recomendarme un buen médico/dentista?
¿Pwede recomendarmeh oon bwen meddeeco/denteesta?

350 **Is it suitable for children?**
¿Es adecuado para niños?
¿Es adecwado para neenios?

Doctor

351 **I have a pain here/in my arm/leg/chest/stomach.**
Tengo dolor aquí/en el brazo/la pierna/el pecho/el estómago.
Tengo oon doelor akee/en el bratho/la peeyerna/el pecho/el estomago.

352 Please call a doctor, this is an emergency.
Por favor, llamen a un médico, es una emergencia.
Por farbor lliamen a oon meddeeco, es oona emerhentheea.

353 I would like to make an appointment to see a doctor.
Quisiera una cita para una consulta.
Keyseeyera oona thita para oona consoolta.

354 I am diabetic/pregnant.
Soy diabético(a)/estoy embarazada.
Soy deeabetteeko/estoy enbarathada.

355 I need a prescription for . . .
Necesito una receta para . . .
Netheseeto oona rethetta para . . .

356 Can you give me something to ease the pain?
¿Puede darme algo para aliviar el dolor?
¿Pwede darme algo para aleebear el doelor?

357 I am/he is/she is allergic to penicillin.
I am/he is/she is allergic to penicillin.
Soy/es alérgico/alérgica a la penicilina.
Soy alerheeko/alerheeka a la peneetheeleena.

358 Does this hurt?
¿Le duele esto?
¿Leh dweleh esto?

359 You must/he must/she must go to hospital.
Usted/él/ella tiene que ir al hospital.
Oosteth/el/ellia teeyene keh eer al ospeetal.

360 Take these once/twice/three times a day.
Tome esto una vez/dos/tres veces al día.
Tomeh esto oonah beth/dos/tres bethess al dee-ah.

361 I am/he is/she is taking this medication.
Estoy/está tomando este medicamento.
Estoy/esta tomando esteh medeekamento.

362 I have medical insurance.
Tengo seguro médico.
Tengo sehgooro mehdeeko.

Dentist

363 I have toothache.
Tengo dolor de muelas/me duelen las muelas.
Tengo dolor de mwelas/mey dwelen las mooeylas.

364 My filling has come out.
Se me ha caído un empaste.
Se meh a cayeedo oon enpaste.

365 I do/do not want to have an injection first.
Quiero/no quiero que me den una inyección.
Kiero/no kiero kay meh den oona inyecthion.

S
P
A
N
I
S
H

352
↑
365

EMERGENCIES

366 **Help!**
¡Socorro!
¡Sawkoro!

367 **Call an ambulance/a doctor/ the police!**
¡Llame a una ambulancia/un médico/la policía!
¡Lliame a oona anboolanthea/oon meydico/la poletheea!

368 **I have had my travellers cheques (traveler's checks)/ credit cards/purse/handbag/ rucksack (knapsack)/ luggage/wallet stolen.**
Me han robado los cheques de viaje/las tarjetas de crédito/el bolso/la mochila/el equipaje/el billetero.
Meh an robadoe los chekes dey beahe/las tarhetas dey credeeto/el bolso/la mocheela/el ekeypahe/el bellietero.

369 **Can you help me, I have lost my daughter/son.**
¿Puede ayudarme, se ha extraviado mi hija/mi hijo.
¿Pwede ajudarme, sey a extrabeeado mee eekha/mee eekho?

370 **Please go away/leave me alone.**
Por favor váyase/déjeme en paz.
Por farbor bayase/deheme en path.

371 **Fire!**
¡Fuego!
¡Fwegoh!

372 **I want to contact the British/ American/Canadian/Irish/ Australian/New Zealand/ South African consulate.**
Quisiera llamar al consulado británico/americano/ candadiense/irlandés/de Nueva Zelanda/surafricano.
Keyseeyera lliamar al konsoolado britaneeko/amehreekano/ kanadeyenseh/eerlandess/deh nweba theylanda/surafrikano.

Introduction

Turkish, brought to the shores of Europe from central-eastern Asia by the invading Ottomans, is unrelated to other European languages; although it contains modern words borrowed from English, the main linguistic influence over the centuries has been Arabic. Turkish uses a roman alphabet, albeit with a large number of accented characters, which was introduced this century as part of the modernising reforms which followed on the fall of the Ottoman Empire.

English, German and French are widely spoken in the cosmopolitan and tourist-frequented areas of Istanbul and the Aegean coast, but elsewhere you will need Turkish phrases.

Addresses for travel and tourist information

UK: *Turkish Tourist Office*, First Floor, 170/173 Piccadilly, London W1V 9DD; tel: (0171) 734 8681/2.
USA: *Turkish Tourist Office*, 821 UN Plaza, New York, NY 10017; tel: (212) 687 2194/6.

T
U
R
K
I
S
H

ESSENTIALS

Alphabet

The letters Q, W and X are only used in describing foreign words.

A	B
ah	*beh*
C	D
jeh	*deh*
E	F
eh	*feh*
G	H
geh	*heh*
I	J
ee	*zheh*
K	L
keh	*leh*
M	N
meh	*neh*
O	P
o	*peh*
Q	R
qu	*reh*
S	T
seh	*teh*
U	V
u	*veh*
W	X
dueblueveh	*iks*
Y	Z
yeh	*zeh*

T
U
R
K
I
S
H

01
↕
11

Basic Words and Phrases

1 **Yes** **No**
Evet Hayır
Evet *Hayer*

2 **Please** **Thank you**
Lütfen Teşekkür ederim
Luetphen *Teshekkuer ederim*

3 **That's O.K.** **Perhaps**
Bir şey değil Belki
Bir shey de'el *Belki*

4 **To** **From**
e/a den/dan
e/a *dan/den*

5 **Here** **There**
Burada Orada
Burada *Orada*

6 **None** **Also**
Hiç de/da
Hich *de/da*

7 **How** **When**
Nasıl Ne zaman
Nasel *Ne zaman*

8 **What** **Why**
Ne Neden
Ne *Neden*

9 **I don't understand.**
Anlamıyorum.
Anlameyourum.

10 **I don't speak Turkish.**
Türkçe bilmiyorum.
Tuerkche bilmiyourum.

11 **Do you speak English?**
İngilizce biliyor musunuz?
İnghilizh'dje biliyour musunuz?

12 Can you please write it down?
Lütfen şuraya yazar mısınız?
Luetfen shuraya yazar me'se'nez?

13 Can you please speak more slowly?
Lütfen biraz daha yavaş konuşur musunuz?
Luetfen biraz daha yavash konushur musunuz?

14 How much does it/this cost?
O/Bu kaç para?
O/Bu kach para?

Days

15 Monday	Tuesday
Pazartesi	Salı
Pazartesi	*Salae*
16 Wednesday	Thursday
Çarşamba	Perşembe
Charshamba	*Pershembe*
17 Friday	Saturday
Cuma	Cumartesi
Djuma	*Djumartesi*
18 Sunday	Morning
Pazar	Sabah
Pazar	*Sabah*
19 Afternoon	Evening
öğleden sonra	Akşam
Oe'leden sonra	*Aksham*
20 Night	Week
Gece	Hafta
Ghedje	*Haphta*

21 Yesterday	Tomorrow
Dün	Yarın
Duen	*Yaren*

Numbers

22 Zero	One
Sıfır	Bir
Saephaer	*Beer*
23 Two	Three
İki	Üç
Eki	*Uech*
24 Four	Five
Dört	Beş
Doert	*Besh*
25 Six	Seven
Altı	Yedi
Alte	*Yedi*
26 Eight	Nine
Sekiz	Dokuz
Sekiz	*Dokuz*
27 Ten	Eleven
On	On bir
On	*On beer*
28 Twelve	Thirteen
On iki	On üç
On eki	*On uech*
29 Fourteen	Fifteen
On dört	On beş
On doert	*On besh*
30 Sixteen	Seventeen
On altı	On yedi
On alte	*On yedi*
31 Eighteen	Nineteen
On sekiz	On dokuz
On sekiz	*On dokuz*

T
U
R
K
I
S
H

12
↑
31

ESSENTIALS

32 **Twenty** **Twenty-one**
Yirmi Yirmi bir
Yirmi *Yirmi beer*

33 **Twenty-two** **Thirty**
Yirmi iki Otuz
Yirmi eki *Otuz*

34 **Forty** **Fifty**
Kırk Elli
Kaerk *Elli*

35 **Sixty** **Seventy**
Altmış Yetmiş
Altmaesh *Yetmish*

36 **Eighty** **Ninety**
Seksen Doksan
Seksen *Doksan*

37 **One hundred** **Five hundred**
Yüz Beş yüz
Yuez *Besh yuez*

38 **One thousand** **One million**
Bin Bir milyon
Been *Beer million*

Time

39 **9.00**
Dokuz
Dokuz

40 **9.05**
Dokuzu beş geçiyor
Dokuzu besh gechiyour

41 **9.10**
Dokuzu on geçiyor
Dokuzu on gechiyour

42 **9.15**
Dokuzu onbeş geçiyor
Dokuzu onbesh gechiyour

43 **9.20**
Dokuzu yirmi geçiyor
Dokuzu yirmi gechiyour

44 **9.25**
Dokuzu yirmibeş geçiyor
Dokuzu yirmibesh gechiyour

45 **9.30**
Dokuz buçuk
Dokuz buchuk

46 **9.35**
Ona yirmibeş var
Ona yirmibesh var

47 **9.40**
Ona yirmi var
Ona yirmi var

48 **9.45**
Ona çeyrek var
Ona cheyrek var

49 **9.50**
Ona on var
Ona on var

50 **9.55**
Ona beş var
Ona besh var

51 **12.00/Midday/Midnight**
On iki/öğle üzeri/Gece yarısı
Oneki/Oe'le uezeri/ghedje yarese

52 **What time is it?**
Saat kaç?
Saat kach?

53 **It is . . .**
Saat . . .
Saat . . .

ARRIVING AND DEPARTING

Airport

54 Excuse me, where is the
check-in desk for . . . airline?
Afedersiniz, . . . havayollarının
çekin bürosu neresi acaba?
*Afedersiniz, . . . havayollarenen
checkin buerosu ne'resi adjaba?*

55 What is the boarding gate/
time for my flight?
Benim uçağımın biniş kapısı
neresi/biniş saati kaç acaba?
*Benim ucha'emen binish kapese
neresi/binish saati kach adjaba?*

56 How long is the delay likely
to be?
Uçağın gecikme süresi ne kadar
acaba?
*Ucha'en gedjikme sueresi ne kadar
adjaba?*

57 Where is the duty-free shop?
Gümrüksüz mal satış yeri neresi
acaba?
*Guemrueksuez mal satesh yeri
ne'resi adjaba?*

58 Which way is the baggage
reclaim?
Bavulları alma yeri neresi acaba?
Bavullare alma yeri neresi adjaba?

59 Where can I get the bus to
the city centre?
Kentin merkezine otobüs
nereden kalkıyor acaba?
*Kentin merkezine otobues nereden
kalkeyor adjaba?*

Train Station

60 Where is the ticket office/
information desk?
Bilet gişesi nerede?/
Enformasyon masası nerede?
*Bilet gishesi nerede?/Enformasyon
masase nerede?*

61 Which platform does the
train to . . . depart from?
. . . treni hangi perondan hareket
ediyor?
*. . . treni hangi perondan hareket
ediyor?*

62 Where is platform . . ?
. . . peronu nerede?
. . . peronu nerede?

63 When is the next train
to . . ?
. . . treni ne zaman?
. . . treni ne zaman?

64 Is there a later train to . . ?
. . . a/e başka tren var mı?
. . . a/e bashka tren var mae?

Port

65 How do I get to the port?
Limana nasıl gidebilirim?
Leemana nasael gedebilirim?

66 When is the next sailing
to . . ?
Bundan sonraki sefer kaçta?
Bundan sonraki sepher kachta?

67 Can I catch an earlier ferry with this ticket?
Bu biletle daha erken kalkan feribota binebilir miyim?
Bu biletle daha erken kalkan feribota binebilir miyim?

Notices and Signs

68 Büfe vagonu
Beufe vagonu
Buffet (Dining) Car

69 Otobüs
Otobeus
Bus

70 İçilir/içilmez su
Echilir/echilmez su
Drinking/ on-drinking water

71 Giriş
Girish
Entrance

72 Çıkış
Chekesh
Exit

73 Enformasyon
Enformasyon
Information

74 Emanet
Emanet
Left Luggage (Baggage Claim)

75 Bagaj dolapları
Bagadj dolaplare
Luggage Lockers

76 Postane
Postane
Post Office

77 Peron
Peron
Platform

78 Estasion
Istasyon
Railway (Railroad) Station

79 Havaalanı
Hava a'lane
Airport

80 Liman
Liman
Port

81 Restoran
Restoran
Restaurant

82 Sigara içilir/içilmez
Sigara echilir/echilmez
Smoking/Non-Smoking

83 Telefon
Telephon
Telephone

84 Bilet gişesi
Beelet ghishese
Ticket Office

85 Çekin bürosu
Checkin buerosu
Check-in Desk

86 Tarife
Tarife
Timetable (Schedule)

87 Tuvaletler
Tuvaletler
Toilets (Restrooms)

88 **Erkekler**
Erkekler
Gentlemen

89 **Bayanlar**
Baianlar
Ladies'

90 **Tramvay**
Trumvai
Tram (Streetcar)

91 **Metro**
Metro
Underground (Subway)

92 **Bekleme Odası**
Bekleme Odase
Waiting Room

Buying a Ticket

93 **I would like a first-class/
second-class single (one-
way)/return (round-trip)
ticket to . . .**
. . . e/a birinci/ikinci mevki
sadece gidiş/gidiş geliş bileti
istiyorum.
*. . . e/a beerindji/ekindji mevki
sadedje ghedish/ghedish ghelis
beelete estiyourum.*

94 **Is my rail pass valid on this
train?**
Benim tren pasom bu trende/
feribotta/otobüste geçer mi?
*Benim teren pasom bu terende/
feribotta/otobueste gecher mi?*

95 **I would like an aisle/window
seat.**

Pencere kenarında/koridor
tarafında bir yer istiyorum.
*Pendjere koridoor/kenaraenda
tarafaenda beer yer estiyourum.*

96 **No smoking/smoking, please.**
Sigara içilmez/sigara içilir,
lütfen
*Sigara icheler/sigara echelmez,
leutphen*

97 **We would like to sit together**
Yan yana oturmak istiyoruz.
Yan yana otoormak estiyouruz

98 **I would like to make a seat
reservation.**
Bir yer ayırtmak istiyorum.
Bir yer ayertmak istiyourum.

99 **I would like to reserve a
couchette/sleeper for one
person/two people/for my
family.**
Kuşetlide/yataklıda bir kişilik/
iki kişilik/ailem için yer
ayırtmak istiyorum.
*Coushetleede/yataklaeda beer
kishelik/eki kishelik yer
ayeaertmak estiyourum.*

100 **I would like to reserve a
cabin.**
Bir kabin ayırtmak istiyorum.
Bir kabin ayertmak istiyourum.

Timetables (Schedules)

101 Varış
Vareash
Arrive

102 **. . . da durur**
. . . da durur
Calls (Stops) at

103 **Lokanta**
Lokanta
Catering Service

104 **. . . da değiştirin**
. . . da de'shtirin
Change at

105 **Bağlantı**
Ba'lantae
Connection

106 **Günlük**
Geunleuk
Daily

107 **Her kırk dakikada bir**
Haer kerk dakekada beer
Every 40 Minutes

108 **Birinci mevki**
Beerindji mevke
First-class

109 **Saatte bir**
Sa'atte beer
Hourly

110 **Yer ayırtılması tavsiye edilir**
Yer ayertelmase tavsiye edilir
Seat reservations are recommended

111 **Ikinci mevki**
Ekinci mevki
Second-class

112 **Ek ücret ödenir**
Ek eudjret eadenir
Supplement Payable

113 **Üzerinden**
euzerinden
Via

Luggage

114 **How much will it cost to send (ship) my luggage in advance?**
Bagajımı önceden göndermek kaça mal olur?
Baghadjaemae eandjeden geandermek kacha mal oleur?

115 **Where is the left luggage (baggage claim) office?**
Emanet nerede?
Emanet nerede?

116 **What time do you open/close?**
Ne zaman açıyorsunuz/kapatıyorsunuz?
Ne zaman achaeyoursunuz/kapataeyoursunuz?

117 **Where are the luggage trolleys (carts)?**
Bagaj troleyleri nerede?
Badghadj troleylere nerede?

118 **Where are the lockers?**
Kilitli dolaplar nerede acaba?
Kilitli dolaplar neresi adjaba?

119 **I have lost my locker key.**
Dolap anahtarımı kaybettim.
Dolap anahtaraeme kaibettim.

On Board

120 **Is this seat taken?**
Bu yer boş mu?
Bu yer bosh mu?

121 Excuse me, you are sitting in my reserved seat.
Pardon, bana ayrılmış yerde oturuyorsunuz.
Pardon, bana airaelmaesh yerde oturuyoursunuz.

122 Which station is this?
Bu hangi istasyon?
Bu hange istasion?

123 What time is this train/bus/ferry/flight due to arrive/depart?
Bu tren/feribot/uçak saat kaçta gelecek/kalkacak?
Bu teren/feribot/uchak sa't kachta gelecek/kalkadjak?

124 Will you wake me just before we arrive?
Varmadan önce beni uyandırır mısınız?
Varmadan oendje beni uyandaeraer maesaeniz?

Customs and Passports

125 Pasaportlar, lütfen!
Pasaportlar luetphen!
Passports, please!

126 I have nothing/wine/spirits (alcohol)/tobacco to declare.
Gümrüğe tabi (hiçbir eşyam yok)/şarap/içki/tütün var.
Geumreu'e tabe (hichbir eshiam yok)/sharap/eachki/tuetuen var.

127 I shall be staying for . . . days/weeks/months.
. . . gün/hafta/ay kalacağım.
. . . guen/hafta/ai kaladja'em.

AT THE TOURIST OFFICE

128 Do you have a map of the town/area?
Bu kentin/bölgenin haritası var mı?
Bu kentin/boelgenin haritasae var mae?

129 Can I reserve accommodation here?
Burada kalacak yer ayırtabilir miyim?
Beurada kaladjak yer ayaertabeler meyem?

130 Do you have a list of accommodation?
Kalacak yerlerin bir listesi var mı?
Kaladjak yerlerin bir listesi var me?

ACCOMMODATION

Hotels

131 I have a reservation in the name of . . .
. . . adına rezervasyon yaptırmıştım.
. . . adaena rezervasyon yaptaermaeshtaem.

T
U
R
K
I
S
H

121
↑
131

132 I wrote to/faxed/telephoned you last month/last week in . . .

Geçen ay/geçen hafta size yazmıştım/faks çekmiştim/telefon etmiştim.

Gechen ay/gechen hafta size yazmeshtem/fax chekmishtim/telephon etmishtim.

133 Do you have any rooms free?

Hiç boş odanız var mı?

Hich bosh odanez var me?

134 I would like to reserve a single/double room with/without bath/shower.

Bir/iki kişilik banyolu/banyosuz duşlu/duşsuz oda ayırtmak istiyorum.

Bir/iki kieshielik banyolu/dushlu banyosuz/dushsuz oda ayaertmak istiyourum.

135 I would like bed and breakfast/(room and) half board/(room and) full board.

Sadece kahvaltılı/kahvaltı ve bir öğün yemekli/üç öğün yemekli bir oda istiyorum.

Sadedje kahvaltaelae/kahvaltae ve beer oe'oen yemekli/euch oe'oen yemekli oda istiyourum.

136 How much is it per night?

Gecesi kaça?

Ghedjesi kacha?

137 Is breakfast included?

Kahvaltı dahil mi?

Kahvaltae dahil me?

138 May I see the room?

Odayı görebilir miyim?

Odayae goerebilir miim?

139 Do you have any cheaper rooms?

Daha ucuz odalarınız var mı?

Daha oodjuz odalaraenaez var me?

140 I would like to take the room

Odayı tutuyorum.

Odayae tootooyorum.

141 I would like to stay for . . . nights.

. . . gece kalmak istiyorum.

. . . gedje kalmak istiyourum

142 The shower/light/tap doesn't work.

Duş/elektrik/musluk bozuk galiba.

Dush/electric/musluk bozuk ga'liba.

143 At what time/where is breakfast served?

Kahvaltı servisi nerede/ne zaman?

Kahvaltee servisi nerede/ne zaman?

144 What time do I have to check-out?

Saat kaçta ayrılmam lazım?

Sa'at kachta ayraelmam lazaem?

145 Can I have the key to room no . . ?

. . . numaralı odanın anahtarını rica ediyorum.

. . . numarale odanen anakhtarene ridja ediyourum.

146 My room number is . . .
Oda numaram . . .
Oda numaram . . .

147 Do you accept travellers'
cheques/Eurocheques/credit
cards?
Seyahat çeki/Euroçek/kredi
kartı kabul ediyor musunuz?
*Seyahat cheki/Eurocheck/kredi
karte kabul ediyor musunu ?*

148 May I have the bill please?
Hesabı, lütfen
Hesabee, luetphen.

149 Excuse me, I think there is a
mistake in this bill.
Afedersiniz, bu hesapta bir
yanlışlık var galiba.
*Afedersiniz, bu hesapta bir
yanleshlek var ga'liba.*

Youth Hostels

150 How much is a dormitory
bed per night?
Bir gecelik yatakhane ücreti ne
kadar?
*Beer ghedjelik yatakhane uedjreti
ne kadar?*

151 I am/am not an HI member.
Uluslararası Gençlik Hostelleri
Birliği üyesiyim/üyesi değilim.
*Euluslararasae Ghenchlik Hostelleri
Beerli'e ueyesiim/ueyesi deelim.*

152 May I use my own sleeping
bag?
Kendi uyku tulumumu
kullanabilir miyim?

*Kendi uyku tulumumu kullanabilir
miyim?*

153 What time do you lock the
doors at night?
Gece kapıları kaçta
kilitliyorsunuz?
*Ghedje kapaelarae kachta
kilitliyoursunuz?*

Camping

154 May I camp here for the
night/two nights?
Burada bu gece/iki gece kamp
yapabilir miyim?
*Burada bu ghedje/eki ghedje kamp
yapabilir miyim?*

155 Where can I pitch my tent?
Çadırımı nereye kurabilirim?
*Chadaeraemae nereye
kurabilirim?*

156 How much does it cost for
one night/week?
Bir geceliği/bir haftalığı kaça?
*Beer ghedjeli'e/beer haftalae'e
kacha?*

157 Where can we park our
caravan?
Karavanımızı nereye park
edebiliriz?
*Karava'nemezhe nereye park
edebiliriz?*

158 Where are the washing
facilities?
Yıkanma yerleri nerede?
Yaekanma yerleri nerede?

T
U
R
K
I
S
H

146
↕
158

159 Is there a restaurant/
supermarket/swimming pool
on site/nearby?
Burada/yakında bir restoran/
çarşı/yüzme havuzu var mı?
*Burada/yakaenda bir restoran,
charshae/yuezme havuzu var
mae?*

160 Do you have a safety deposit
box?
Kıymetli eşya için kasanız var
mı?
*Kaeymetli eshia eachin kasanaez
var mae?*

EATING AND DRINKING

Cafés and Bars

161 I would like a cup of/two
cups of/another coffee/tea.
Bir fincan/iki fincan/bir fincan
daha kahve/çay istiyorum.
*Beer findjan/eki findjan/beer
findjan daha kahve/chai
istiyourum.*

162 With/without milk/sugar.
Sütlü/şekerli (with), sütsüz/
şekersiz (without)
*Suetlue/shekerli, suetsuez/
shekersiz.*

163 I would like a bottle/glass/
two glasses of mineral water/
red wine/white wine, please.
Bir şişe/bardak/iki şişe maden
suyu/kırmızı şarap/beyaz şarap
lütfen.

*Beer shishe/bardak/eki shishe
maden suyu/kaermaezae sharap/
beyaz sharap luetphen.*

164 I would like a beer/two
beers, please.
Bir bira/iki bira lütfen.
Beer beera/eki beera luetphen.

165 May I have some ice?
Biraz buz alabilir miyim?
Biraz buz alabilir miyim?

166 Do you have any matches/
cigarettes/cigars?
Kibritiniz/sigaranız/puronuz
var mı?
*Kibritiniz/sigaranaez/pueronuz
var m?*

Restaurants

167 Can you recommend a good/
inexpensive restaurant in this
area?
Bu bölgede iyi/ucuz bir restoran
tavsiye eder misiniz?
*Bu boelgede eyi/udjuz beer
restoran tavsiye eder misiniz?*

168 I would like a table for . . .
people.
. . . lik bir masa istiyorum.
. . . lik beer masa istiyourum.

169 Do you have a non-smoking
area?
Sigara içilmeyen bir yeriniz var
mı?
*Sighara ichilmeyen bir yeriniz var
me?*

170 Waiter/Waitress!
Garson
Garson

**171 Do you have a set menu/
children's menu/wine list?**
Yemek listesi/çocuklar için
yemek listesi/şarap listesi var
mı?
*Yemek listesi/chodjuklar ichin
yemek listesi/sharap listesi var
mae?*

**172 Do you have any vegetarian
dishes, please?**
Etsiz yemekleriniz var mı?
Etsiz yemekleriniz var mae?

**173 Are there any local
specialities?**
Bu bölgeye has yemekler var
mı?
Bu boelgheye has yemekler var me?

174 Are vegetables included?
Garnitür de dahil mi?
Garnituer de dahil mi?

**175 Could I have it well-cooked/
medium/rare please?**
İyice kızartılmış/Normal/Az
pişmiş olsun lütfen.
*Iyidje kezartelmesh/Normal/Az
pishmish olsun luetfen.*

**176 What does this dish consist
of?**
Bu yemeğin içinde neler var?
Bu yeme'en ichinde neler var?

**177 I would like the set menu,
please.**
Tabldot lütfen.

Tabldot luetphen.

178 We have not been served yet.
Bize hala servis yapılmadı.
Bize hala servis yapaelmadae.

**179 Excuse me, this is not what I
ordered.**
Afedersiniz, benim ısmarladığım
bu değildi.
*Afedersiniz, benim esmarlade'em
bu de'ildi.*

**180 May I have some/some more
bread/water/coffee/tea?**
Biraz/biraz daha ekmek/su/
kahve/çay verir misiniz?
*Beeraz/beeraz daha ekmek/su/
kahve/chai verir misiniz?*

181 May I have the bill, please?
Hesap, lütfen?
Hesap, luetphen?

182 Does this bill include service?
Servis bu hesaba dahil mi?
Servis bu hesaba dahil mi?

**183 Do you accept travellers'
cheques (travelers' checks)/
Eurocheques/MasterCard/US
dollars?**
Seyahat çeki/Mastır kart/
Amerikan doları alıyor
musunuz?
*Seyahat cheki/master cart/
american dolarae alaeyour
musunuz?*

184 Can I have a receipt, please?
Bir makbuz rica etsem?
Bir makbuz ridja etsem?

T
U
R
K
I
S
H

170
↑
184

185 Where is the toilet
(restroom), please?
Tuvalet nerede acaba?
Tuvalet nerede adjaba?

On the Menu

186 First courses
Aperitifler
Aperitifler

187 Soups
Çorbalar
Chorbalar

188 Main courses
Ana yemekler
An'a yemekler

189 Fish dishes
Balık yemekleri
Balek yemekleri

190 Meat dishes
Et yemekleri
Et yemekleri

191 Vegetarian dishes
Sebze yemekleri
Sebze yemekleri

192 Cheese
Peynir
Peynir

193 Desserts
Tatlılar
Tatlelar

194 Specialities
Buraya özgü yemekler
Buraya oezgue yemekler

GETTING AROUND

Public Transport

195 Where is the bus stop/coach
station/nearest metro
(subway) station?
Otobüs durağı/otobüs
terminali/en yakın metro
istasyonu nerede?
*Otobues dura'ae/otobues
terminali/en yakaen metro
istasionu nerede?*

196 When is the next/last bus
to . . ?
. . . e/a bundan sonraki otobüs
ne zaman?
*. . . e/a bundan sonrakee otobues
ne zaman?*

197 How much is the fare to the
city centre (downtown)/
railway (railroad) station/
airport?
Şehir merkezine/tren
istasyonuna/hava alanına bilet
kaça?
*Shehir merkezine/tren istasionuna/
hava alanaena bilet kacha?*

198 Will you tell me when to get
off?
Ne zaman ineceğimi söyler
misiniz?
*Ne zaman enedje'emi soeyler
misiniz?*

199 Does this bus go to . . ?
Bu otobüs . . . a/e gidiyor mu?
Bu otobues . . . a/e gidiyour mu?

200 Which number bus goes
to . . ?
. . . ya/ye kaç numaralı
otobüs gidiyor?
*. . . ye/ya kach numaralae
otobues gidiyour?*

201 May I have a single (one-
way)/return (round-trip)/day
ticket/book of tickets?
Gidiş/gidiş-geliş/günlük/koçan
halinde bilet istiyorum?
*Gidish/gidish-gelish/guenleuk/
kochan halinde bilet istiyourum?*

Taxis

202 I would like to go to . . . , how
much will it cost?
. . . a/e gitmek istiyorum, kaç
para tutar?
*. . . a/e ghitmek istiyourum, kach
para tutar?*

203 Please stop here.
Burada durur musunuz.
Burada durur musunuz.

204 I would like to order a taxi
today/tomorrow/at 2pm to
go from . . . to . . .
Bugün/yarın öğleden sonra saat
2'ye . . . den/dan . . . e/a taksi
ısmarlamak istiyorum.
*Buguen/yaraen oe'leden sonra
sa'at ikiye . . . den/dan . . . e/a taxi
aesmarlamak istiyourum.*

Asking the Way

205 Excuse me, do you speak
English?
Afedersiniz, Ingilizce biliyor
musunuz?
*Afedersiniz, engilizdje biliyor
musunuz?*

206 Excuse me, is this the right
way to . . ?
Afedersiniz, . . .'e/a/ye/ya
buradan mı gidilir?
*Afedersiniz, . . .'e/a/ye/ya
buradan me gidilir?*

207 . . . the cathedral/the tourist
information office/the castle/
the old town
. . . Katedral/turist
enformasyon bürosu/şato/eski
şehir
*. . . Cathedral/tourist
enformasyon buerosu/shato/eski
shehir*

208 Can you tell me the way to
the railway station/bus
station/taxi rank (stand)/city
centre (downtown)/beach?
Istasyona/otobüs terminaline/
taksi durağına/şehir merkezine/
plaja nasıl gidilir, söyler misiniz?
*Estasyona/otobues terminaline/
taxi dura'aena/shehir merkezine/
paeladja nasael ghidilir, soeyler
misiniz?*

T U R K I S H

200
↑
208

329

209 First/second left/right/
straight ahead.
Birinci/soldan ikinci/sağda/
dosdoğru.
*Beerindji/soldan ekindji/sa'da/
dosdo'ru.*

210 Where is the nearest police
station/post office?
En yakın polis karakolu/postane
nerede?
*En yakaen polis karakolu/postaine
nerede?*

211 Is it far?
Uzak mı?
Uzak mae?

212 Do I need to take a taxi/
catch a bus?
Taksiye mi/otobüse mi binmem
gerekli?
*Taxiye me/otobuese me binmem
gherekle?*

213 Can yo point to it on my map?
Haritamın üzerinde gösterebilir
misiniz?
*Haritamaen uezerinde goesterebilir
misiniz?*

214 Thank you for your help.
Yardımınız için teşekkür ederim.
*Yardaemaenaez ichin teshekkuer
ederim.*

SIGHTSEEING

215 Where is the Tourist
Information office?
Turist enformasyon bürosu
nerede?

*Tourist enformasion buerosu
nerede?*

216 Where is the cathedral/
church/museum?
Katedral/Kilise/Müze nerede?
Catedral/Kilise/Mueze nerede?

217 How much is the admission
charge?
Giriş ücreti ne kadar?
Gherish eudjreti ne kadar?

218 Is there a reduction for
children/students/senior
citizens?
Çocuklara/ögrencilere/yaşlılara
indirim var mı?
*Chodjuklara/eurendjilere/
yashlaelara endirim var mae?*

219 What time does the next
guided tour start?
Bundan sonraki kılavuzlu tur ne
zaman başlıyor?
*Bundan sonraki khaelavuzlu tour
ne zaman bashlaeyour?*

220 One/two adults/children,
please.
Bir/iki büyük/çocuk, lütfen.
*Beer/eki bueyuek/chodjuk,
luetphen.*

221 May I take photographs
here?
Burada resim çekebilir miyim?
Burada resim chekebilir miyim?

ENTERTAINMENT

222 Can you recommend a good
bar/nightclub?

TURKISH

209 ↕ 222

330

Iyi bir bar/gece kulübü tavsiye edebilir misiniz?
Eyi bir bar/gedje kuluebue tavsiye edebilir misiniz?

²²³ **Do you know what is on at the cinema (playing at the movies)/theatre at the moment?**
Şu anda sinemada/tiyatroda ne oynuyor?
Shu anda sinemada/teyatroda ne oynuyor?

²²⁴ **I would like to book (purchase) . . . tickets for the matinee/evening performance on Monday.**
Pazartesi günü öğle seansı/akşam için . . . bilet ayırtmak istiyorum.
Pazartesi guenue oe'le seansae/aksham ichin . . . bilet ayaertmak istiyourum.

²²⁵ **What time does the film/performance start?**
Film/gösteri kaçta başlıyor?
Film/goesteri kachta bashleyour?

MEETING PEOPLE

²²⁶ **Hello/Goodbye.**
Merhaba/Hoşça kal
Merhaba/hoshcha kal

²²⁷ **Good morning/good afternoon/good evening/goodnight.**
Günaydın/merhaba/iyi akşamlar/iyi geceler
Guenayden/merhaba/iyi akshamlar/iyi gedjeler

²²⁸ **Pleased to meet you.**
Tanıştığımıza memnun oldum.
Tanaeshtae'maeza memnun oldum.

²²⁹ **How are you?**
Nasılsınız?
Nasaelsaenaez?

²³⁰ **Fine, thank you. And you?**
Teşekkür ederim, iyiyim. Siz nasılsınız?
Teshekkuer ederim, iyiyim. Siz naselsenez?

²³¹ **My name is . . .**
Adım . . .
Adaem . . .

²³² **This is my friend/boyfriend/girlfriend/husband/wife/brother/sister.**
Bu benim arkadaşım/erkek arkadaşım/kız arkadaşım/kocam/karım/erkek kardeşim/kız kardeşim
Bu benim arkadashaem/erkek arkadashaem/kaez arkadashaem/kodjam/karaem/erkek kardeshaem/kaez kardeshaem

²³³ **Where are you travelling to?**
Nereye gidiyorsunuz?
Nereye ghidiyoursunuz?

²³⁴ **I am/we are going to . . .**
Ben/biz . . . e/a gidiyoruz.
Ben/beez . . . e/a ghidiyouruz.

T U R K I S H

223
↑
234

331

235 How long are you travelling for?
Kaç günlük bir geziye çıkıyorsunuz?
Kach guenluek beer gheziye chekeyoursunuz?

236 Where do you come from?
Neredensiniz?
Neredensiniz?

237 I am/we are from . . .
. . . den/dan
. . . den/dan

238 We're on holiday.
Tatildeyiz.
Tatildeyiz.

239 This is our first visit here.
İlk defa buraya geliyoruz.
Ilk def'a buraya geliyouruz.

240 Would you like/May I have a cigarette?
Sigara alır mısınız?/Sigara alabilir miyim?
Sigara aler mesenez?/Sigara alabilir miyim?

241 I am sorry, but I do not understand.
Kusura bakmayın, anlamıyourum.
Kusura bakmayaen, anlameyourum.

242 Please speak slowly.
Lütfen ağır ağır (tane tane/tek tek) söyleyin.
Luetphen a'ar a'ar (tane tane/tek tek) soeyleyin.

243 Do you mind if I smoke?
Sigara içmem sizi rahatsız eder mi?
Sigara ichmem sizi rahatsaez eder mi?

244 Do you have a light?
Kibritiniz/çakmağınız var mı?
Kibritiniz/chakma'anaez var mae?

245 I am waiting for my husband/wife/boyfriend/girlfriend.
Kocamı/eşimi/erkek arkadaşımı/kız arkadaşımı bekliyorum.
Kodjame/eshimi/erkek arkadasheme/kez arkadasheme bekliyorum.

TRAVELLING WITH CHILDREN

246 Do you have a high chair/baby-sitting service/cot?
Bebek için sandalye/çocuk bakım servisi/karyola var mı?
Bebek ichin sandalie/chodjuk bakem servisi/kariola var mae?

247 Where is the nursery/playroom?
Çocuk yuvası/oyun odası nerede?
Chodjuk yuvase/oyun odase nerede?

248 Where can I warm the baby's bottle?
Biberonu nerede ısıtabilirim?
Beeberonu nerede aesetabilirim?

COMMUNICATIONS

Post

249 How much will it cost to send a letter/postcard/this package to Britain/Ireland/America/Canada/Australia/New Zealand?
Ingiltere'ye/Irlanda'ya/Amerika'ya/Kanada'ya/Avustralya'ya/Yeni Zelanda'ya mektup/kartpostal/bu paket kaça gider?
Inghiltere'ye/Erlanda'ya/Amerika'ya/Kanada'ya/Avustralia'ya/Yeni Zelanda'ya mektup/cartpostal/bu paket kacha geder?

250 I would like one stamp/two stamps.
Bir pul/iki pul istiyorum.
Bir pul/eki pul istiyourum.

251 I'd like . . . stamps for postcards to send abroad, please.
Yurt dışına kartpostal göndermek için . . . pul rica ediyorum.
Yurt deshena kartpostal goendermek ichin . . . pul ridja ediyourum.

Phones

252 I would like to make a telephone call/reverse the charges to (make a collect call to) . . .
Telefon etmek/ telefon etmek istiyorum.
Telephon etmek/telephon etmek istiyourum.

253 Which coins do I need for the telephone?
Telefon için hangi parayı kullanmam lazım?
Telephon ichin hangi parayae kullanmam lazaem?

254 The line is engaged (busy).
Hat meşgul.
Hat meshgul.

255 The number is . . .
Numara . . .
Numara . . .

256 Hello, this is . . .
Alo, ben . . .
Alo, ben . . .

257 May I speak to . . ?
. . .'i/ı/yi/yı rica edecektim.
. . .'i/e/yi/ye ridja ededjektim.

258 He/She is not in at the moment. Can you call back?
Kendisi şimdi burada değil. Daha sonra arar mısınız?
Kendisi shimdi burada de'il. Daha sonra arar mesenez?

T
U
R
K
I
S
H

249
↕
258

MONEY

259 I would like to change these travellers' cheques (travelers' checks)/this currency/this Eurocheque.
Bu seyahat çeklerini/bu parayı/bu Euro çeki bozdurmak istiyorum.
Bu sey'ahat cheklerini/bu paray/bu Euro cheki bozdurmak istiyourum.

260 How much commission do you charge (what is the service charge)?
Ne kadar komisyon alıyorsunuz?
Ne kadar komision alaeyorsunuz?

261 Can I obtain money with my MasterCard?
Master Kartla para alabilir miyim?
Mastaer Cartla para alabilir miyim?

SHOPPING

Names of Shops and Departments

262 Kitapçı/kırtasiyeci
Kitapche/kertasiyedji
Bookshop/Stationery

263 Mücevheratçı/Hediyelik eşya
Muedjevheratche/Hediyelik eshya
Jeweller's/Gifts

264 Ayakkabılar/ayakkabı
Ayakka'belar/ayakka'be
Shoes

265 Hırdavat
Herdavat
Hardware

266 Antika eşya
Antika eshya
Antiques

267 Erkek berberi/Kadın berberi
Erkek berberi/Kaden berberi
Hairdressers (men's)/(women's)

268 Sigara bayii/tütüncü
Sighara bayee/tuetuendjue
Tobacconist

269 Hamur işleri/Fırın
Hamur ishleri/Feren
Baker's

270 Süpermarket
Suepermarket
Supermarket

271 Fotoğrafçı
Photo'rafche
Photoshop

272 Oyuncaklar
Oyundjaklar
Toys

273 Seyahat Acentası
Seyahat Adjenta'se
Travel Agent

274 Makyaj malzemeleri
Makiazh maldzemeleri
Toiletries

275 Plaklar
Pilaklar
Records

In the Shop

276 What time do the shops open/close?
Dükkanlar ne zaman açılır/kapanır?
Duekkanlar ne zaman a heler/kapanaer?

277 Where is the nearest market?
En yakın alışveriş merkezi/pazar neresi?
En yaken aleshverish merkedzi/padzar neresi?

278 Can you show me the one in the window/this one?
Vitrindekini/bunu görmek istiyorum.
Vitrindekini/bunu goermek istiyourum.

279 Can I try this on?
Bunu prova edebilir miyim?
Bunu prova edebilir miim?

280 What size is this?
Bunun numarası kaç?
Bunun numarase kach?

281 This is too large/too small/too expensive.
Bu çok büyük/çok küçük/çok pahalı
Bu chok bueyuek/chok kuechuek/chok paha'le

282 Do you have any others?
Başka çeşitleriniz de var mı?
Bashka cheshitleriniz de var me?

283 My size is . . .
Benim ölçüm . . .
Benim oelchuem . . .

284 Where is the changing room/childrens/cosmetic/ladieswear/menswear/food department?
Giyinme odaları/çocuk/kozmetik eşya/bayan giysileri/erkek giysileri/yiyecek bölümü nerede?
Giyinme odalarae/chodjuk/kozmetik eshia/bayan giysileri/erkek giysileri/yiyedjek boeluemue nerede?

285 I would like . . .
. . . istiyorum/rica edecektim.
. . . istiyourum/ridja ededjektim.

286 I would like a quarter of/half a kilo/a kilo of bread/ butter/cheese/ham/tomatoes.
İkiyüzelli gram/yarım kilo/bir kilo ekmek/tereyağ/peynir/jambon/domates istiyorum.
Ekiyuezelli gram/yarem kilo/bir kilo ekmek/tereya' peinir/djambon/domates estiyourum.

287 How much is this?
Kaça?
Kacha?

288 I'll take this one, thank you.
Bunu alacağım, teşekkür ederim.
Bunu aladja'em, teshekkuer ederim.

289 Do you have a carrier
(shopping) bag?
Plastik torbanız var mı?
Plastic torbanez var me?

290 Do you have anything
cheaper/larger/smaller/of
better quality?
Daha ucuz/büyük/küçük/iyi
kalite bir şeyiniz var mı?
*Daha eudjuz/bueyuek/kuechuek/
eyi kalite bir sheyiniz var mi?*

291 I would like a film for this
camera.
Bu makineye bir film
istiyorum.
*Bu makineye bir film
istiyourum.*

292 I would like some batteries,
the same size as this old
one.
Bunlarla aynı büyüklükte yeni
pil istiyorum.
*Bunlarla ayne bueyuekluekte peel
istiyourum.*

293 Would you mind wrapping
this for me, please?
Lütfen bunu sarar mısınız?
Luetphen bunu sarar mesenez?

294 Sorry, but you seem to have
given me the wrong change.
Kusura bakmayın ama paranın
üstünü yanlış verdiniz.
*Kusura baknayen ama paranen
uestuenue yanlesh verdiniz.*

MOTORING

Car Hire (Rental)

295 I have ordered (rented) a car
in the name of . . .
. . . adına araba ısmarladım.
. . . adaena araba aesmarladaem.

296 How much does it cost to
hire (rent) a car for one day/
two days/one week?
Bir günlük/iki günlük/bir
haftalık araba kiralama ücreti ne
kadar?
*Beer guenluek/eki guenluek/beer
haftalaek araba kiralama eudjreti
ne kadar?*

297 Is the tank already full of
petrol (gas)?
Benzin deposu dolu mu?
Benzin deposu dolu mu?

298 Is insurance and tax
included? How much is the
deposit?
Sigorta ve vergi dahil mi?
Depozit ne kadar?
*Sigorta ve verghi dahil me?
Depozit ne kadar?*

299 By what time must I return
the car?
Arabayı ne zamana kadar geri
getirmem lazım?
*arabayae ne zamana kadar geri
ghetirmem lazaem?*

300 I would like a small/family
car with a radio/cassette
player.

Radyolu/teypli küçük bir araba/
aile arabası istiyorum.
*Radiolu/teipli kuechuk beer araba/
aile arabasae istiyourum.*

Asking the Way

301 Excuse me, can you help me
please?
Afedersiniz, sizden bir ricada
bulunacaktım.
*Afedersiniz, sizden bir ridjada
bulunadjaktem.*

302 How do I reach the
motorway/main road?
Otobana/ana yola nasıl
çıkabilirim?
*Autoba'na/ana yola nasel
chekabilirim?*

303 I think I have taken the
wrong turning.
Galiba yanlış yerden/kavşaktan
dönüş yaptım.
*Ga'liba yanlesh yerden/
kavshaktan doenuesh yaptem.*

304 I am looking for this address.
Şu adresi arıyorum.
Shu adresi a'reyourum.

305 I am looking for the . . . hotel.
. . . oteli/otelini arıyorum.
. . . oteli/otelini a'reyourum.

306 How far is it to . . . from
here?
Buradan . . .'e/a/ye/ya mesafe/
uzaklık ne kadar?
*Buradan . . .'e/a/ye/ya mesa'fe/
uzhaklek ne kadar?*

307 Carry straight on for . . .
kilometres.
Dosdoğru . . . kilometre daha
gidin/sürün.
*Dosdo'ru . . . kilometre daha
ghidin/sueruen.*

308 Take the next turning on the
right/left.
Bundan sonraki sapaktan/
dönemeçten sağa/sola dönün/
sapın.
*Bundan sonra'ki sapaktan/
doenemechten sa'a/sola doenuen/
sa'pen.*

309 Turn right/left at the next
crossroads/traffic lights.
Bundan sonraki kavşaktan/trafik
ışıklarından sağa/sola sapın.
*Bundan sonra'ki kavshaktan/
traffic eshekla'rendan sa'a/sola
sapen.*

310 You are going in the wrong
direction.
Ters yönde gidiyorsunuz.
Ters yoende ghidiyoursunuz.

Parking

311 How long can I park here?
Burada ne kadar süreyle/kaç
saat park edebilirim.
*Burada ne kadar suereyle/kach sa't
park edebilirim?*

312 Is there a car park near here?
Yakınlarda bir otopark var mı?
Yakenlarda bir autopark var me?

301
↑
312

³¹³ At what time does this car park close?
Bu otopark saat kaçta kapanıyor?
Bu autopark sa't kachta kapa'neyor?

Signs and Notices

³¹⁴ Tek yön
Tek yoen
One way

³¹⁵ Girilmez/Girmek yasaktır
Ghirilmez/Girmek yasakter
No entry

³¹⁶ Park yapılmaz/Park etmek yasaktır
Park yapelmaz/Park etmek yasakter
No parking

³¹⁷ Zorunlu sapış
Zhorunlu sapesh
Detour (diversion)

³¹⁸ Dur!
Dur!
Stop!

³¹⁹ Yol ver
Yol ver
Give way (yield)

³²⁰ Kaygan yol
Kayghan yol
Slippery road

³²¹ Sollama yapılmaz.
Sol'lama yapelmez
No overtaking

At the Filling Station

³²² Unleaded (lead-free)/ Standard/Premium
Kurşunsuz/Normal/Süper
Kurshunsuz/Normal/Sueper

³²³ Fill the tank please.
Depoyu doldurun lütfen.
Depoyu doldurun luetfen.

³²⁴ Do you have a road map of this area?
Sizde bu yörenin yol haritası var mı?
Sizde bu yoerenin yol harita'se var me?

³²⁵ How much is the car-wash?
Araba kaça yıkanıyor?
Araba kacha yeka'neyor?

Breakdowns

³²⁶ I've had a breakdown at . . .
. . .'de/da arabam bozuldu.
. . .'de/da arabam bozhuldu.

³²⁷ I am on the road from
. . . to . . .
. . .'den/dan . . .'e/a/ye/ya giden yol üzerindeyim.
. . .'den/dan . . .'e/a/ye/ya ghiden yol uezerindeyim.

³²⁸ I can't move the car.
Can you send a tow-truck?
Arabayı çekemiyorum. Bir çekme aracı gönderebilir misiniz?

T
U
R
K
I
S
H

313
↕
328

338

Arabaye che'kemiyourum. Bir chekme aradje goenderebilir misiniz?

329 I have a flat tyre.
Lastiğim patladı.
Lasti'im patla'de.

330 The windscreen (windshield) has smashed/cracked.
Ön cam kırıldı/çatladı.
Oen djam ke'relde/chatla'de.

331 There is something wrong with the engine/brakes/lights/steering/gearbox/clutch/exhaust.
Motorda/frenlerde/ışıklarda/direksiyonda/vites kutusunda/debriyajda/egzosta bir arıza var galiba.
Motorda/frenlerde/esheklerde/direxiyonda/vites kutusunda/debriyazhda/eghzosta bir areza var ga'liba.

332 It's overheating.
Motor fazla ısınmış/su kaynatıyor.
Motor fazla esenmesh/su kayna'teyor.

333 It won't start.
Araba çalışmıyor/Marş basmıyor.
Araba chaleshmeyor/Marsh basmeyor.

334 Where can I get it repaired?
Nerede tamir ettirebilirim?
Ne're'de tamir etti'rebilirim?

335 Can you take me there?
Beni oraya götürebilir misiniz?
Beni oraya goetuerebilir misiniz?

336 Will it take long to fix?
Tamiri/takması uzun sürer mi?
Tamiri/takma'se uzhun suerer mi?

337 How much will it cost?
Kaça çıkar/malolur?
Kacha chekar/malolur?

Accidents

338 Can you help me? There has been an accident.
Bir kaza oldu. Bana yardım edebilir misiniz?
Bir kazha oldu. Bana yardem e'debilir misiniz?

339 Please call the police/an ambulance.
Lütfen polisi/bir ambulans çağırın.
Luetfen polisi/bir ambulans cha'eren.

340 Is anyone hurt?
Yaralı var mı?
Yara'le var me?

Traffic Offences

341 I'm sorry, I didn't see the sign.
Özür dilerim, işareti görmedim.
Oezuer dilerim, isha'reti goermedim.

329
↑
341

342 Must I pay a fine? How much?
Para cezası mı ödemem gerekiyor? Kaç para?
Para djeza'se me oedemem ghe'rekiyor? Kach para?

343 Show me your documents.
Ehliyetinizi/belgelerinizi gösterin.
Ehliyetinizhi/belghe'lerinizhi goesterin.

HEALTH

Pharmacy

344 Do you have anything for a stomachache/headache/sore throat/toothache?
Mide/baş ağrısı/boğaz ağrısı/diş ağrısı için bir ilacınız var mı?
Mee'de/bash a'raesae/bo'az a'raesae/dish a'raesae ichin bir eladjaenaez var mae?

345 I need something for diarrhoea (diarrhea)/constipation/a cold/a cough/insect bites/sunburn/travel (motion) sickness.
Ishal/kabız/soğuk algınlığı/öksürük/böcek ısırması/güneş yanığı/otobüs tutması için bir şey istiyorum.
Eshaal/kabaez/so'uk algaenlae'ae/oeksueruek/boedjek aesaermasae/guenesh yanae'ae/otobues tutmasae ichin bir shei estiyourum.

346 How much/how many do I take?
Ne kadar/kaç tane alayım?
Ne kadar/kach tane alayeem?

347 How often do I take it/them?
Ne kadar aralıklarla alayım?
Ne kadar aralaeklarla alayeem?

348 How much does it cost?
Kaç para?
Kach para?

349 Can you recommend a good doctor/dentist?
Iyi bir doktor/dişçi tavsiye edebilir misiniz?
Eyi bir doktor/dishchi tavsiye edebilir misiniz?

350 Is it suitable for children?
Çocuklara uygun mu?
Chodjuklara uygun mu?

Doctor

351 I have a pain here/in my arm/leg/chest/stomach.
Şuram/kolum/ayağım/göğsüm/karnım ağrıyor.
Shuram/kolum/aya'aem/goe'suem/karnaem a'raeyour.

352 Please call a doctor, this is an emergency!
Lütfen doktor çağırın, acil bir vak'a!
uetphen doktor cha'raen, adjil beer vak'a!

353 I would like to make an appointment to see a doctor.
Doktoru görmek için randevu almak istiyorum.
Doctoru goermek ichin randevu almak estiyourum.

354 I am diabetic/pregnant.
Şeker hastasıyım/hamileyim.
Sheker hastasaeyaem/hamileyim.

355 I need a prescription for . . .
. . . için reçete istiyorum.
. . . ichin rechete estiyourum.

356 Can you give me something to ease the pain?
Ağrıyı azaltacak bir şey verebilir misiniz?
A'raeyae azaltadjak bershey verebilir misiniz?

357 I am/he is/she is allergic to penicillin.
Benim/onun/onun penisiline karşı alerjim/alerjisi var.
Benim/onun/onun penicillin'e karshe allergim/allergisi var.

358 Does this hurt?
Acıtıyor mu?
Adje'teyor mu?

359 You must/he must/she must go to hospital.
Hastaneye gitmelisiniz/gitmeli.
Hasta'neye ghitmelisiniz/ghitmeli.

360 Take these once/twice /three times a day.
Bundan günde bir/iki/üç kere alın.

Bundan guende bir/iki/uech ke're a'len.

361 I am/he is/she is taking this medication.
Ben/o/o bu ilaçları alıyorum/alıyor.
Ben/o/o bu ilachla're a'leyourum.

362 I have medical insurance.
Sağlık sigortam var.
Sa'lek sighortam var.

Dentist

363 I have toothache.
Dişim ağrıyor.
Dishim a'raeyour.

364 My filling has come out.
Dolgum düştü.
Dolgum dueshtue.

365 I do/do not want to have an injection first.
önceden iğne istiyorum/istemiyorum.
Oendjeden e'ne estiyourum/estemiyourum.

EMERGENCIES

366 Help!
Imdat!/Yardım!
Imdat/Yardaem!

367 Call an ambulance/a doctor/the police!
Ambulans/doktor/polis çağırın!
Ambulance/doctor/police cha'ren!

³⁶⁸ **I have had my travellers' cheques (travelers' checks)/ credit cards/purse/handbag/ rucksack (knapsack)/ luggage/wallet stolen.**
Seyahat çeklerim/kredi kartlarım/çantam/el çantam/sırt çantam/bagajım/cüzdanım çalındı.
Sey'ahat cheklerim/credi cartlarem/chantam/el chantam/ saert chantam/bagadjem/ djuezdanem chalendae.

³⁶⁹ **Can you help me, I have lost my daughter/son?**
Bana yardım eder misiniz, kızımı/oğlumu kaybettim.
Bana yardem eder misiniz, kezeme/o'lumu kaybettim.

³⁷⁰ **Please go away/leave me alone.**

Lütfen gidin/beni yalnız bırakın.
Luetphen ghidin/beni yalnaez baeraken.

³⁷¹ **Fire!**
Yangın!
Yanghen!

³⁷² **I want to contact the British/ American/Canadian/Irish/ Australian/New Zealand/ South African consulate.**
İngiliz/Amerikan/Kanada/ İrlanda/Avustralya/Yeni Zelanda/Güney Afrika konsolosluğuyla görüşmek istiyorum.
Inghilizh/Amerikan/Kanada/ Irlanda/Yeni Zhelanda/Gueney Afrika konsoloslu'yla goerueshmek istiyourum.

International Time

Winter time: last weekend in September–last weekend in March.
Summer time: last weekend in March–last weekend in September.

WINTER:	GMT	GMT + 1	GMT + 2	GMT + 3
SUMMER:	GMT + 1	GMT + 2	GMT + 3	GMT + 4
	Canary Isles Faroes Iceland * Ireland ** UK **	Albania Croatia France Hungary Poland Spain Austria Czech Republic Germany Italy Netherlands Portugal Sweden Yugoslavia Belgium Denmark Gibraltar Luxembourg Norway Slovakia Slovenia Switzerland	Belarus Cyprus Finland Latvia Moldova Turkey Bulgaria Estonia Greece Lithuania Romania Ukraine	Georgia Russia (European)

* Summer time ends in October   **GMT all year

Midnight depart	=	0000
1 am	=	0100
5 am	=	0500
5.30 am	=	0530
11 am	=	1100
12 noon	=	1200
1 pm	=	1300
3.45 pm	=	1545
Midnight arrive	=	2400

Weather

The weather in Europe is generally mild and pleasant although it varies greatly between the north and the south and between the east and the west. Temperature is also affected by altitude.

Highest = Average highest daily temperature in °C.
Lowest = Average lowest daily temperature in °C.

	London	Rome	Stockholm	Budapest
JANUARY				
Highest	6	12	2	0
Lowest	1	4	-4	-5
Rain days	15	8	7	8
APRIL				
Highest	13	20	17	7
Lowest	4	8	6	0
Rain days	13	6	8	6
JULY				
Highest	22	31	28	21
Lowest	12	18	16	13
Rain days	13	3	7	9
OCTOBER				
Highest	14	23	16	9
Lowest	6	11	7	4
Rain days	16	9	8	9

TEMPERATURE

°C	°F		°C	°F
-20	-4		10	50
-15	5		15	59
-10	14		20	68
-5	23		25	77
0	32		30	86
5	41		35	95
			40	104

Conversion formulae

°C x 9 ÷ 5 + 32 = °F
1 Deg. °C = 1.8 Deg. °F
1 Deg. °F = 0.55 Deg. °C

DISTANCE

km	miles	km	miles	km	miles
1	0.62	40	24.85	500	310.69
2	1.24	50	31.07	600	372.82
3	1.86	60	37.28	700	434.96
4	2.49	70	43.50	800	497.10
5	3.11	80	49.71	900	559.23
6	3.73	90	55.92	1000	621.37
7	4.35	100	62.14	1100	683.54
8	4.97	125	77.67	1200	745.68
9	5.59	150	93.21	1300	807.82
10	6.21	175	108.74	1400	869.96
15	9.32	200	124.27	1500	932.10
20	12.43	300	186.41	2000	1242.74
30	18.64	400	248.45	3000	1864.11

1 Kilometre = 0.6214 Miles
1 Mile = 1.609 Kilometres

WEIGHT

Unit	Kilograms	Pounds
1	0.45	2.205
2	0.90	4.405
3	1.35	6.614
4	1.80	8.818
5	2.25	11.023
6	2.70	13.227
7	3.15	15.432
8	3.60	17.636
9	4.05	19.840
10	4.50	22.045
15	6.75	33.068
20	9.00	44.889
50	22.50	110.225
100	45.00	220.450

1 kilogram (kg) = 1000 grammes (g)
100g = 3.5 oz.
1 oz. = 28.35 g.
1 lb = 453.60 g.

FLUID MEASURES

Litres	Imp. gal.	US gal.
5	1.1	1.3
10	2.2	2.6
15	3.3	3.9
20	4.4	5.2
25	5.5	6.5
30	6.6	7.8
35	7.7	9.1
40	8.8	10.4
45	9.9	11.7
50	11.0	13.0

1 litre (l) = 0.88 imp. quarts
1 litre (l) = 1.06 US quarts
1 imp. quart = 1.14 l
1 imp. gallon = 4.55 l
1 US quart = 0.95 l
1 US gallon = 3.81 l

REFERENCE SECTION

METRES AND FEET

Unit	Metres	Feet
1	0.30	3.281
2	0.61	6.563
3	0.91	9.843
4	1.22	13.124
5	1.52	16.403
6	1.83	19.686
7	2.13	22.967
8	2.44	26.248
9	2.74	29.529
10	3.05	32.810
12	3.66	39.372
18	5.49	59.058
20	6.10	65.520
50	15.24	164.046
75	22.86	246.069
100	30.48	328.092

LADIES' CLOTHES SIZES

UK	France, Italy, Rest of Europe	USA
10	36, 38, 34	8
12	38, 40, 36	10
14	40, 42, 38	12
16	42, 44, 40	14
18	44, 46, 42	16
20	46, 48, 44	18

MEN'S SUIT SIZES

UK	Europe	USA
36	46	36
38	48	38
40	50	40
42	52	42
44	54	44
46	56	46

LADIES' SHOE SIZES

UK	Europe	USA
3	36	4.5
4	37	5.5
5	38	6.5
6	39	7.5
7	40	8.5

MEN'S SHOE SIZES

UK	Europe	USA
6	40	7
7	41	8
8	42	9
9	43	10
10	44	11
11	45	12

MEN'S SHIRT SIZES

UK	Europe	USA
14	36	14
15	38	15
15.5	39	15.5
16	41	16
16.5	42	16.5

INCHES AND CENTIMETRES

Unit	Inches	Feet	Yards
1mm	0.039	0.003	0.001
1cm	0.39	0.03	0.01
1metre	39.40	3.28	1.09

Unit	mm	cm	metres
1 inch	25.4	2.54	0.025
1 foot	304.8	30.48	0.304
1 yard	914.4	91.44	0.914

To convert cms into inches, multiply by 0.3937
To convert inches into cms, multiply by 2.54